**Alan Sked** is Reader in International History at the London School of Economics, where he has taught all his professional life. His books on Habsburg history include: *The Survival of the Habsburg Empire. Radetzky, the Imperial Army and the Class War 1848*; *The Decline and Fall of the Habsburg Empire 1815–1918*, and *Metternich and Austria: An Evaluation*.

# Also by the Author

*The Decline and Fall of the Habsburg Empire 1815–1918.*

*The Survival of the Habsburg Empire. Radetzky, the Imperial Army and the Class War 1848.*

*Metternich and Austria: An Evaluation.*

*Europe's Balance of Power, 1815–1848* (editor).

*Crisis and Controversy: Essays in Honour of A. J. P. Taylor* (co-editor).

*Postwar Britain: A Political History, 1945–1992* (principal author).

*Britain's Decline: Problems and Perspectives.*

*An Intelligent Person's Guide to Postwar Britain.*

# RADETZKY

## IMPERIAL VICTOR
## AND MILITARY GENIUS

ALAN SKED

I.B. TAURIS

LONDON · NEW YORK

Published in 2011 by I.B.Tauris & Co Ltd
6 Salem Road, London W2 4BU
175 Fifth Avenue, New York NY 10010
www.ibtauris.com

Distributed in the United States and Canada Exclusively by Palgrave Macmillan
175 Fifth Avenue, New York NY 10010

ISBN: 978 1 84885 677 6

A full CIP record for this book is available from the British Library
A full CIP record is available from the Library of Congress

Library of Congress Catalog Card Number: available

Printed and bound in Great Britain by
CPI Antony Rowe, Chippenham

FSC
www.fsc.org
MIX
Paper from
responsible sources
FSC® C013604

I dedicate this book with affection and respect to
István Deák, doyen of Habsburg studies in the
United States, whose work on Central European
military history has long been an inspiration to me.

# CONTENTS

# ILLUSTRATIONS

(following page 104)

# MAPS

(following page xiv)

# CHRONOLOGY

| | |
|---|---|
| 1766 | Count Johann Josef Wenzel Anton Franz Karl Radetzky von Radetz born on 2 November at the castle of Třebnic in Bohemia, son of Count Peter Eusebius Radetzky von Radetz and Maria Venantia Bechyně Countess von Lažau. His mother dies in childbirth. |
| 1776 | Death of Radetzky's father. Radetzky goes to live with his grandfather in Prague. |
| 1781 | Death of grandfather. Radetzky goes to school at the Collegium Nobilium in Brünn before it is merged with the Theresianum Military Academy in Vienna. |
| 1784 | Radetzky enters the Austrian army as a cadet. |
| 1788–91 | He participates in the Turkish Wars. |
| 1789 | Outbreak of French Revolution. |
| 1790 | Death of Joseph II. |
| 1791 | Peace of Sistowa with Turkey. |
| 1792–1815 | French Revolutionary and Napoleonic Wars. |
| 1792 | Radetzky fights on the Rhine. |
| 1796 | Radetzky transferred to Italian theatre. |
| 1797 | Napoleon takes Mantua. Peace of Camo Formio. |
| 1798 | Radetzky marries Franziska Romana, Countess Strassoldo-Graffemberg. |
| 1799–1802 | Second Coalition against France. |
| 1799 | Radetzky distinguishes himself in fighting in Italy at battles on the Trebbia and at Novi. |
| 1800 | Radetzky experiences defeats at Marengo (by Napoleon) and at Hohenlinden (by Moreau). |
| 1801 | Peace of Lunéville. |
| 1801–5 | Garrison duty at Ödenburg. |
| 1802 | Peace of Amiens. |
| 1805–7 | War of Third Coalition against France. |

| | |
|---|---|
| 1805 | Radetzky becomes major-general. |
| | Nelson's victory at Trafalgar. |
| | Battle of Austerlitz. |
| | Radetzky fights in Italian theatre. |
| | Peace of Pressburg. |
| 1806–9 | Radetzky commands brigade in Vienna. |
| 1809 | Austria declares war on Napoleon. |
| | Battles of Aspern and Wagram. |
| | Peace of Schönbrunn. |
| 1809–17 | Radetzky, with one short interruption (in 1813 to inspect the army in Bohemia) serves as chief-of-staff of the Austrian army. |
| 1813–15 | Wars of Liberation. Radetzky is made chief-of-staff to the allied supreme commander, Prince Schwarzenberg. |
| 1813 | Battle of Leipzig. |
| 1816–18 | Radetzky serves as division commander in Ödenburg. |
| 1818–29 | Radetzky serves as division commander in Buda. |
| 1829–31 | Radetzky serves as fort commander at Olmütz. |
| 1831–57 | Radetzky serves as commander-in-chief of the Austrian army in Italy. |
| 1848 | War between Austria and Sardinia. |
| | Radetzky defeats Charles Albert at Custoza. |
| 1849 | Second war against Sardinia. |
| | Radetzky defeats Charles Albert again at Mortara and Novara. |
| 1849 | Radetzky made Civil and Military Governor General of Lombardy-Venetia. |
| 1853 | Mazzini organises uprising in Milan which fails. |
| 1858 | Radetzky is pensioned off after 72 years' service. |
| 1859 | Radetzky dies on 6 January in Milan. |

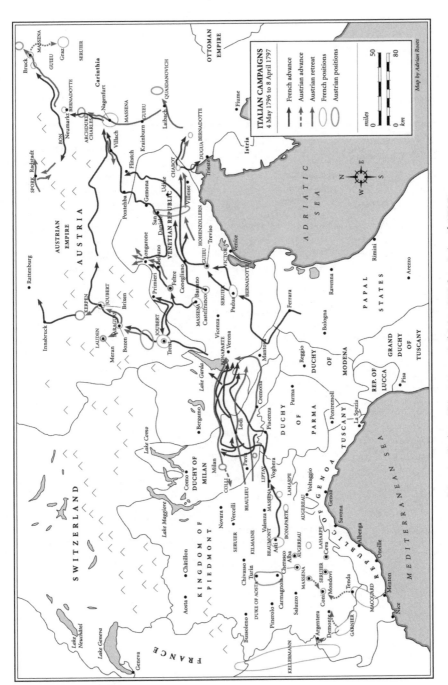

*Map 1* Italian Campaigns – 4 May 1796 to 8 April 1797

*Map 2*   Crossing the Alps – 15 May to 14 June 1800

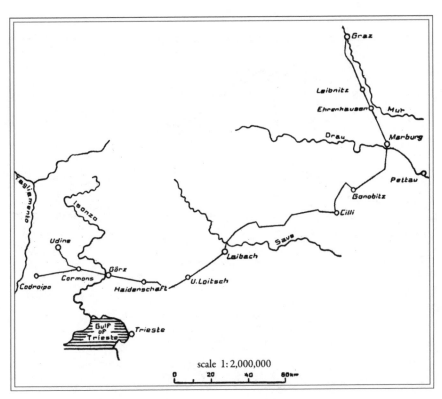

*Map 3* Radetzky's 'Dash to the Drau' in 1805

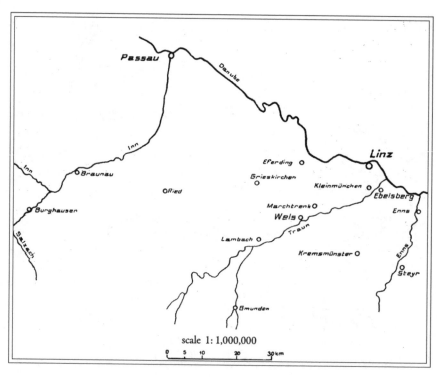

*Map 4*  Radetzky's retreat towards the Danube in 1809

Russ-Bach

Deutsch-Wagram

Aderklaa O

Süssenbrunn O

Markgrafneusiedl
O

Grosshofen O

Nussdorf
O

O Floridsdorf

Danube

O Kagran

Raasdorf O

Glinzendorf
O

Russ-Bach

O Aspern

O Esslingen

O Gr.Enzersdorf

VIENNA

Danube Canal

Lobau

Danube

scale 1: 300,000

0          5          10 km

*Map 5*  Radetzky's area of activity during the battle of Wagram, 1809

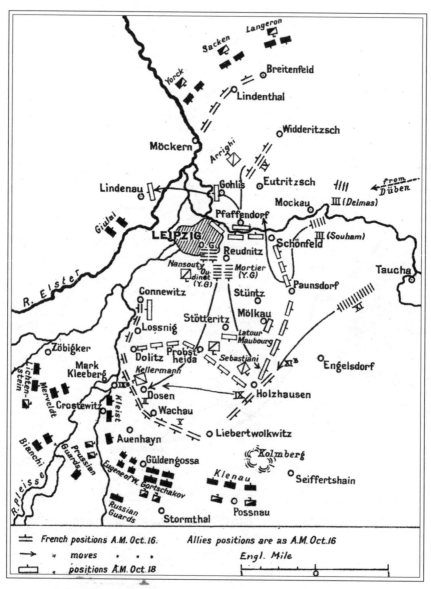

*Map 6*   The Battle of Leipzig – 16 October to 19 October 1813

*Map 7* The Campaign in Germany 1813

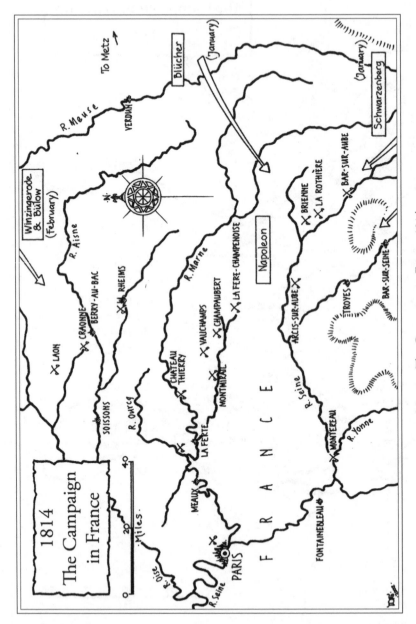

*Map 8*   The Campaign in France 1814

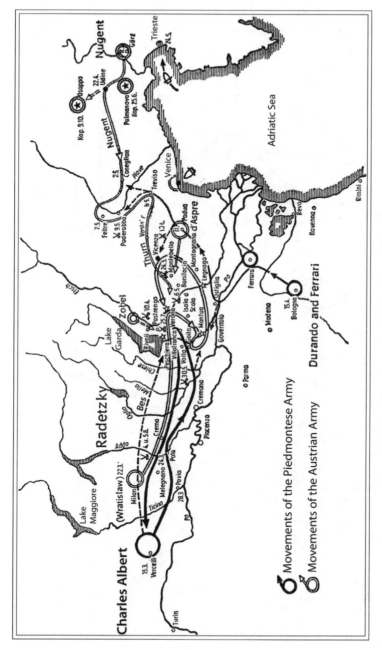

*Map 9*  The Campaign in Northern Italy 1848

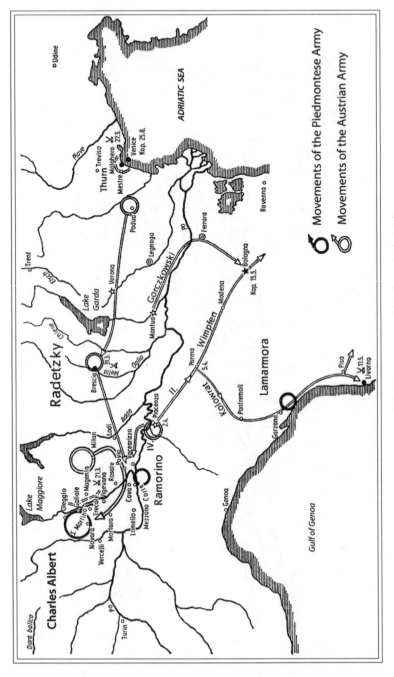

Map 10  The Campaign in Northern Italy 1849

# INTRODUCTION

What is a military genius? And is it possible to discover a new one? Apparently yes. Very few people are aware of Radetzky. The elder Strauss's stirring and exciting *Radetzky March* is known to music lovers; those of a literary disposition may even know of Joseph Roth's novel *Radetzkymarsch*. Yet the Field Marshal himself remains an obscure figure, although he was a military commander of world-historical significance.

It was Radetzky, who, as chief of staff to the allied army under its Austrian commander, Prince Schwarzenberg, determined the nature of the most decisive campaigns of the Napoleonic wars and who thought up the strategy that in a matter of months defeated Napoleon, one of the greatest commanders of all time, in 1813–14. After his defeat in Russia, Napoleon still occupied and controlled the whole of Europe. Neither Russia nor Prussia had been able to defeat him in battle and the forces these powers controlled between them in 1813 were in no position to challenge him in Europe. It took the diplomacy of Metternich and the military genius of Radetzky to ensure that he lost. In short, the Austrian contribution decisively tipped the balance against him – something which today is always overlooked by historians.

In 1848 and again in 1849 it was Radetzky who defeated a much superior army not merely to maintain the political and geographical integrity of the Habsburg Monarchy but thereby almost certainly preventing a whole continent from dissolving once again into war and revolution as in 1792–1815. He was far from being a minor military leader in minor theatres of war. The wars he fought – and always won – were of the greatest possible significance. Had Napoleon been able to defeat the allies in 1813 and unite the whole of Europe under his dominion, the consequences for America, the Caribbean, the Middle East and India, would probably have been far-reaching. Had the Habsburg Monarchy disappeared in 1848, the future of the whole of Europe and perhaps the world would have been different.

As a result of his decisive military record, Radetzky should rank on the same level as Napoleon (although he went down to defeat), Ulysses

S. Grant (a winner like Radetzky, although not such a quick or decisive one), the elder Moltke (who, like Radetzky, won two European wars, although, unlike Radetzky, was never tested in European coalition warfare), or even Eisenhower (who was involved in coalition warfare against a tyrant, but never won campaigns on his own). Radetzky was a greater general than Marlborough and at least the equal of Wellington and Frederick the Great (who was defeated more than once in battle and was only saved from destruction by the death of the Empress of Russia). He was certainly the best soldier the Habsburgs ever produced. If winning battles, planning successful military campaigns and thinking out new strategies and tactics are the marks of a military genius – a supreme military commander – and what else can be said? – then Radetzky was indeed in that category.

Yet he was not simply a commander. He was a military thinker, who examined all the key issues of his day – not merely strategy and tactics but fortifications, the role of a general staff, the role of horses in warfare, the need for technical corps among others. He was also basically progressive politically: he believed in moving with the times, in constitutionalism and in popular defence. Only the excesses of the revolutionaries in 1830 and 1848 changed his mind. But his was an active mind, which remained active right up until he retired in 1857 at the age of ninety. By that stage he had become the Habsburg Monarchy's version of El Cid, a magnetic military force, despite all his physical infirmities.

With the disappearance of the Habsburg Monarchy in the twentieth century those who prolonged its existence in the nineteenth might no longer seem relevant. If Radetzky postponed the breakup of an empire, why should anyone care? The answer is straightforward: because all history has to be taken on its own terms, examined from the viewpoint of those alive at the time, who had no idea what the future would hold. If we take a different viewpoint, then all history becomes irrelevant, save that of the last few years. Radetzky, therefore, must be seen within the context of his times. To contemporaries he was without doubt a great and imposing figure, indeed, the major military figure of his age. Apart from Napoleon, whom he defeated, Radetzky was the greatest military commander of the nineteenth century. It behoves us, therefore, to take his glorious military career seriously, to analyse and think about it, and to restore him to his rightful place in our historical consciousness.

# 1

## Early Career

In 1778 a doctor delivered his medical opinion on a twelve-year-old boy wishing to enter Vienna's prestigious Theresianum Military Academy:[1]

> I regret infinitely to have to report that the medical examination unfortunately has not produced the result that ... the young Count Radetzky might perhaps have wanted ... The young count is much too weak to be able to bear the burdens of military service even for a few years. As a doctor and a man of conscience might I suggest that Your Excellency [Radetzky's grandfather – author] should not expose the young nobleman either now or later to the exertions of a soldier's life.

Needless to say, this seemingly unlikely candidate entered the army in 1784 at the age of 18 and served in it for no less than 72 years. The army he served was that of the the Habsburgs, Europe's greatest dynasty, which between the thirteenth and twentieth centuries provided rulers for empires, kingdoms, duchies and principalities in lands stretching across most of modern-day Europe.

In Radetzky's day imperial possessions were still vast. In 1815 they included the Austrian lands (the Archduchies of Upper and Lower Austria; the Duchies of Styria, Carniola, and Carinthia; the counties of Tyrol and Vorarlberg, Gorizia and Gradisca, plus the Margraviate of Istria and the city of Trieste), the lands of the Hungarian Crown (the Kingdoms of Hungary, Croatia and Slavonia, with the city of Fiume; the Grand Duchy of Transylvania; plus the Croatian-Slavonian and Servian-Hungarian military frontiers), the lands of the Bohemian Crown (the Kingdom of Bohemia; the Margraviate of Moravia; the Duchy of Upper and Lower Silesia), the Kingdom of Lombardy-Venetia, the Kingdom of Galicia and the Grand Duchy of Cracow, the Duchy of the Bukovina, the Kingdom of Dalmatia and the Duchy of Salzburg. Taken together and known either as the Habsburg Monarchy or the Austrian Empire (after 1804) with a population of 37.5 million people by 1848 of numerous nationalities, religions and creeds, these territories made up the largest state in Europe outside Russia. If this were not enough, Habsburg emperors also claimed to rule territories no longer in their possession – for example, Upper and Lower Lusatia, Lorraine, Kyburg and Habsburg, not to mention the Kingdom of Jerusalem, which had ceased to exist in 1291.[2] These lands ensured that the Monarchy was at the centre of Europe's affairs, not just geographically, but diplomatically and militarily. The Habsburg Monarchy was seen as an essential part of the European balance of power, a European necessity, a state without which the European state system simply could not function.

Radetzky's family stemmed from the ancient Bohemian nobility and had been raised to the *Grafenstand* – in other words became counts – in 1764, two years before Radetzky's birth. His father and grandfather had been soldiers and the family had been rewarded for its services to imperial arms. Radetzky himself was born on All Souls Day, 2 November 1766, at his father's estate at Trebnitz near Selčan in Bohemia, his mother dying in childbirth. He was christened Johann Joseph Wenzel Anton, Count Radetzky von Radetz. His father died when he was ten and afterwards he was sent to live with his grandfather who, in turn, died five years later. The family was rich in glory rather than in wealth, although in the course of the centuries it had owned about 22 estates in Bohemia. Radetzky was to purchase one in Carinthia in 1807 from his mother-in-law, which he attempted, without great success, to develop for a decade or so as an industrial centre producing specialised steel and steel implements.[3]

Having failed to enter Vienna's prestigious Theresianum military academy, the young Radetzky was sent in 1781 to the Collegium Nobilium in Brünn in Moravia, which, as it happened, was merged with the Theresianum in Vienna in 1782, before the emperor, Joseph II, dissolved the institution in 1784. Radetzky, now eighteen, was able to join the army as a paying cadet (an *ex-propriis*) at his third attempt and was assigned to the Caramelli cuirassier regiment then billeted in Hungary. 'I was without parents, without a homeland. I chose the profession of a soldier and I have never regretted it,' he wrote, adding: 'The army became my home.'[4]

The army, however, had acquired a highly critical cadet. As a boy Radetzky had already read up everything he could on wars and soldiers and their commanders[5] and had been dismayed at the low intellectual standards he found at the Theresianum.[6] The teaching was 'pedantic' and 'superficial' and the professors' main objective had been simply 'to pass the time'. Life in the army was not much better at first. In his outpost in Hungary he 'remained remote from any educated company' and, 'left more or less to [himself]', he learned little more than 'the usual forms of exercises and internal squadron duties'. As he wrote bitterly: 'The real aim of our profession, training for war, remained foreign to us subalterns and perhaps also to the colonel.' The situation of young officers was lamentable: 'The regimental commanders and the other staff officers had acquired the ranks they possessed laboriously. They now wanted to have peace and, after surviving physical fatigue, to cultivate their leisure. They had long since grown accustomed to intellectual idleness.'

Given his great thirst to learn everything, circumstances compelled Radetzky to become an 'autodidact'. He always carried books around with him, eventually acquired a considerable library, and later would always establish regimental reading rooms for his officers. Indeed, his disgust at military education would never leave him, so that 'whenever he had a free hand, he acted as a schoolteacher'.[7] Given the physician's report on him as a child, it might be thought that physical weakness encouraged his scholarly interests, but his later exploits on horseback and in swimming, not to mention the barrel chest he developed, seem to suggest otherwise. He was always noted for his over-active mind, which bubbled over with ideas and new techniques to try out in drill, riding, engineering or cartography. Sharp and fiercely inquisitive, Radetzky always asked questions and sought for answers, qualities displayed in both his writings and actions.

Radetzky's first real experience of soldiering came with the Turkish wars of 1787–90 in which he served as a cavalry officer. Austria, as the ally of Russia, had declared war on the Ottoman Empire. Joseph II, the Habsburg emperor, had concluded the alliance both to curb the Balkan ambitions of Catherine the Great of Russia and to use her as a shield against the ambitions of Austria's rival and neighbour, Prussia; he had no interest in a war with Turkey. When one broke out, however, Catherine gave him no immediate assistance and although he had an army of 200,000 to employ under the command of Field Marshal Lacy, the latter proved indecisive and was unable to stop the Turks invading Austrian territory (the Banat). Joseph then took over the command himself, but instead of military glory (and perhaps the epithet 'the Great' like Catherine or Frederick II of Prussia) he acquired only tuberculosis for his trouble and had to return to Vienna where he died in 1790. Meanwhile, command of the army had been given to Field Marshal Laudon, a sickly seventy-two year old of whom Frederick the Great had said:[8] 'If the Austrians lose Laudon, they will have no general of significance who can command an army.' Laudon died a few months after Joseph, but before then he retrieved Austrian honour in the Balkans by conquering both Bosnia and Serbia (including Belgrade), while another army captured most of Moldavia. Given that the Russian Marshal Suvarov now also took Wallachia (including Bucharest), Laudon proposed that the two powers should partition the Balkans between them.

Alas, the Prussians now allied themselves with the Turks, stirred up the Hungarians within the Habsburg Monarchy, and threatened to invade Bohemia. The Austrian Netherlands also rose in revolt so that by the time Joseph died he could pronounce his own epitaph on his deathbed:[9] 'Here lies Joseph II who failed in everything he undertook.' His brother and successor, Leopold II, was left to reach agreement with Prussia and the Turks. Austria's gains in the Balkans were surrendered and Prussia was told that Austria would seek no more territory there.

Radetzky during these Turkish wars had served in the cavalry, which in 1787 was still a decisive weapon on the battlefield although its importance was diminishing. Its relative size fell from about one third of the army's manpower in 1716 to about 16 per cent at most in 1848. The nobility was well represented in it, since ownership of an estate and the financial resources attached to one, meant that good riders were produced.[10] Radetzky had served long enough to have been promoted lieutenant on 3 February 1786 and *Oberleutnant* on 11 November 1787. These promotions gave him direct access to the commanding generals – Lacy and Laudon, to the latter of whom he was assigned as 'permanent staff (*Ordonnanz*) officer' – and provided him with valuable experience of military life: the use of the cordon system (the quasi-immigration or military control system to keep out undesirables and those suspected of having been in contact with the plague); raids against the Turks; the epidemics that exhausted the army; the conquest of Belgrade with 10,700 infantry and 2,500 cavalry; the taking of bridges; and the use of the Danube flotilla. Most importantly, it allowed Radetzky to demonstrate his own personal courage and wisdom, since he was mentioned in despatches for the role he played in calming and leading his panicking troops at Illova while holding off pursuing Janisseries (elite Turkish troops originally recruited from Christian slaves).[11]

Yet Radetzky was predictably highly critical of Austria's military record against the Turks. He conceded that the men had been well looked after ('and this was all the more praiseworthy since many campaigns against the Turks failed on account of sickness, which developed in the army which was unused to the climate.'[12]) Yet, despite the fine condition of the army, the campaign achieved little and Radetzky's analysis of why this occurred would determine his thinking for ever afterwards:[13] 'The defensive was chosen.' This, according to Radetzky undermined morale. He would always look to enthuse his troops by attacking the enemy.

According to Radetzky, it was only after Marshal Laudon took command in 1788 that matters improved in the Balkans. Self-confidence returned. Yet even Laudon's tactics left much to be desired, since they lacked speed and imagination.[14] The problem was a familiar one: the use of the line (spreading the troops along a thin front) bound the infantry to the defensive. It formed itself into large unhelpful squares with the cavalry positioned in between in reserve. Other cavalry was placed in front, which meant there was little room for movement or manoeuvrability. The artillery was given a three-pound gun per battalion, while heavier six- and twelve-pounders were kept in reserve. Marching in column was very difficult since columns had to be ready to quickly form squares and endless practice was needed for this in open ground.

Clearly, therefore, even the very young Radetzky wanted an educated and trained army that was led by commanders who would lift its spirits by taking the offensive and fighting large battles. He also wanted to end dependence on the line to enhance mobility and room for manoeuvre on the battlefield, while using heavier artillery. Soon Radetzky would be advocating the need for a plan of operations. In short, his instincts were truly Napoleonic, even before the advent of Napoleon himself.

Between the end of the Turkish wars in 1790 and the start of the French revolutionary ones in 1792 Radetzky and his regiment spent their time in Bohemia, where he studied horses, horsemanship and cavalry exercises. He also continued his private studies in geography, military history and fortifications.[15] With the wars of the French Revolution, he was sent first to Luxemburg and the Rhine and then to Northern Italy. His regular displays of unusual courage particularly in cavalry charges and close quarter fighting again won him fame, but his analysis of events would strike by now familiar chords.

The reason why Austria and Prussia had been able to agree to end the Turkish wars so quickly was that they had a new, but mutual, problem to confront: the outbreak of the French Revolution in 1789[16] and, with it, the prospect of war with France in an attempt to save the French royal family. Leopold had no great opinion of Louis XVI and Marie Antoinette (his own sister) but he had to try to do something once the French monarchy was threatened. However, the warning given to France in the Declaration of Pillnitz (August 1791) and the invasion of the country under the Prussian commander, the Duke of Brunswick, after France declared war in April 1792, backfired. Brunswick was humiliated at Valmy on 20 September 1792 and in October Savoy was captured, followed by the Austrian Netherlands (Belgium) in November.

The French now offered help to all peoples struggling to be free, told their generals to abolish feudalism everywhere and proclaimed a doctrine of national frontiers (the Rhine, the Pyrenees and the Alps). In 1793 they declared war on other powers and found themselves facing the First Coalition of Holland, Prussia, Austria, Sardinia, Britain and Spain. In March 1793, however, the Austrians defeated the French at Neerwinden and captured Brussels. Two leading figures in France, General Dumouriez and Louis Philippe, Duke of Chartres, then defected to them. France fell under the grip of the Committee of Public Safety and the Reign of Terror. But terror worked. New armies were raised and young generals promoted.

During 1794 the allies were driven back across the Rhine and Spain, Holland and Prussia all withdrew from the coalition. In June 1794 the Austrians had to evacuate the Austrian Netherlands after defeat at Fleurus. By the Treaty of Basle in April 1795 Prussia promised France a free hand on the left bank of the Rhine in return for her neutrality in North Germany, which Prussia meant to dominate. In May 1795 some south-western German states withdrew from the war, fearful of Austrian ambitions regarding Bavaria and hoping to receive favours from France. Russian designs on Poland now led both Austria and Prussia to protect their interests there. In 1795 Poland was wiped off the map by the Third Partition of the country. By 1796 Europe was war-weary, but France still wanted to put Austria in her place and attacked her.

The Archduke Charles, the brother of the new Habsburg emperor, Francis II (Leopold died in 1792), managed to defeat the French generals Jourdan and Moreau in southern Germany, although Austria was defeated at Rivoli in Italy by a brilliant new young general, Napoleon Bonaparte (not yet launched on his political career), who forced Sardinia to cede Nice and Savoy to France and the Pope to agree to the creation of a Cisalpine Republic including Bologna, Ferrara and the Romagna. His Holiness had also to cede Avignon to France. Given these diplomatic setbacks and military defeats, Austria now also came to terms with France. By the Treaty of Campo Formio of 17 October 1797 she agreed to recognise the French conquest of the Austrian Netherlands and her newly won Rhine frontier, to cede Lombardy to the French-controlled Cisalpine republic, and to take the much despoiled Republic of Venice (including Dalmatia) in return.

Ironically, the Monarchy was now greater in size than ever before, given its gains from the last Polish Partition and, in view of some observers, more powerful than before given the loss of the far-flung Austrian Netherlands. Yet this was an illusion. Austria had lost her dominating position in Italy and was about to lose the same in Germany, since those princes who had lost territory on the left bank were now, according to Campo Formio, to be compensated with territory from within the Holy Roman Empire.

The Austrian army had viewed the outbreak of war with France in 1792 as an event that would provide opportunities for promotion by acts of daring. The spirit of the troops had been excellent. Yet, once again, little had been achieved. According to Radetzky,[17] this was because 'the defensive, and an inactive one at that, was almost always the guiding principle adopted'. And this despite the fact that there were countless examples to prove that Austrian troops always won in small engagements (*Detailgefechten*) when they 'went for the enemy bodily with cold steel (*mit blanker Waffe*)'.

Radetzky's second complaint was the lack of a fixed plan of operations. In the course of the war too many people interfered, who were neither qualified intellectually or emotionally to do so. If people did not know clearly what was needed, nothing ever succeeded, least of all military actions. With knowledge, he thought, came energy and unity in the whole body of the fighting force, if also a certain degree of risk. Yet fortune usually favoured the brave. Radetzky's preference was for taking the offensive in accordance with an operational plan to meet the enemy with full force at the most appropriate place. Like Napoleon himself, he also believed in leadership: 'A clearly defined task in the hands of an experienced, mentally strong leader, placed at the head of an army prepared for war, constitutes a guarantee for success, which seldom fails.' There was little in either Radetzky's ideas or actions, therefore, from his youngest years on, to suggest that he would ever fail to pursue his enemy with determination or courage.

Radetzky, rather remarkably for someone so young (at least in the Austrian army – the French revolutionary one was by now making young bloods generals in their thirties), also had criticisms of the way that whole armies went about their operations. Large advanced guards, posted in front of the main armies and placed under the orders of one or more commanders, and usually extended over at least three (often many more) German miles, had the task of keeping the enemy in view and reporting on what territory it held. Yet despite the fact that their reports were often wrong and insufficient, these reports determined the army's movements, often involving the calling up of the nearest troops to support endangered positions ahead.

The result was almost daily fighting with such high losses that advanced guards could barely justify their name. From the main army itself, reinforcements were often sent in small numbers – often by battalions. Often it happened that a general would find himself with a battalion without knowing where the rest of his troops had been sent by adjutants or staff officers. In this way a whole army could be drawn into battle without any clarity of organisation or prospect of success. If it did meet with success, this was usually due either to the bravery of the troops or the enemy having exhausted its supply of men. In any case, the successes were discrete because they had not resulted from a superior force having held together. Thus, at the end of each campaign, there was often no great result to show.

The main armies, meanwhile, often failed to take proper security measures because they felt protected by the advanced guard. If the enemy showed some enterprise then they were attacked, often when the main army was on the march; no wonder, when strong but indolent columns could be set upon unexpectedly by lesser numbers of men. One general in Northern Italy in 1796, for example, lost three grenadier battalions and one fusilier battalion. Astonishingly, they were taken prisoner by the French while the army ahead of them continued its march. Similar losses occurred during the winter of 1797.

It was against this diplomatic and military background that Radetzky himself was to gain his reputation as a fighting soldier. In 1793 the First Coalition of Austria, Prussia, Holland, Sardinia, Britain and Spain fielded 270,000 men against Carnot's levee of 300,000 French. In March 1793 the Austrians defeated the French at Neerwinden and captured Brussels. Radetzky's regiment first joined battle in the Low Countries in July having covered more than 1,000 kilometres in 66 days. It formed part of General Beaulieu's corps on the left flank of the army of the Prince of Coburg. Radetzky was responsible for repulsing an attack from Montmédy and was promoted 'permanent staff officer' to Beaulieu (albeit unofficially, since Beaulieu's son-in-law officially occupied the post.) 'Still mine was a pleasant position,' Radetzky recalled,[18] 'since through it I had the chance to view the events of the war and it itself in a true light.' Beaulieu's corps managed to force the French over their border but in 1794 was caught up in the three battles of Fleurus, after the first of which Radetzky was promoted *Rittmeister* (cavalry captain) on account of his actions ('for proven excellence' ran the citation[19]), although as the oldest *Oberleutnant*, he pointed out that he was due this promotion in any case (promotion in the Austrian army usually being by seniority).

He had suffered two slight head wounds and had swum the Sambre to bring news of the capitulation of the enemy to the town of Charleroi. However, with defeat at Fleurus, the end result of the campaign was retreat over the Rhine and the loss of the Low Countries, leaving the French in occupation of the Left Bank in overwhelming strength (700,000 men). In 1795 Prussia made peace with France, and Austria, deprived also of the Spanish, Portuguese, Tuscans and some of the German states as allies, faced the French alone, holding on to the Rhine frontier only with difficulty.

Radetzky remained with Beaulieu till 1795 and in 1796 accompanied him to Italy, where he had become commander-in-chief. However, Beaulieu, who was 70 years old, was not popular there and gave the impression of being unwell and physically not up to the job, the latter compounded by the incompetent staff chief he was given.

As Heller's 'biography' (dictated, it should be remembered by Radetzky and based also on his correspondence) suggests:[20] 'General Beaulieu found himself in a country that was completely unknown to him opposite a Bonaparte, used to energetic and independent action.' Napoleon had now taken over command of the French forces about to attack Italy. According to Radetzky, he could have been beaten by quick action on the part of Austria, given the state of the French army:[21]

> But there was no one in headquarters or in the entire general staff with the faintest idea of what an offensive operation in the [Alpine] mountains required, still less anyone who understood the ways and means to organise supplies for mountain warfare or the necessities for conducting such a war. The army lacked all draught animals, without which in mountain warfare nothing can be accomplished.

The Austrians, moreover, numbered only 23,000 men out of an army of 57,000, 20,000 of whom were Piedmontese. Yet no plan of operations or any preparations for war had been made with Piedmont:[22] 'In the first days of April when hostilities began, no What? or How? had been established.' From the very start, therefore, by Radetzky's reckoning, the most vital requirements of the campaign were missing.

Still, along with the Piedmontese, Beaulieu attacked the French at Voltri on 10 April and won, stating in his report that he 'could not thank [Radetzky] enough' for rousing the troops to victory.[23] Almost immediately, however, an opportunist Piedmont deserted to the French and Beaulieu ordered a retreat behind the Po. The French were supposed to be stopped at Lodi, but the Austrians neglected to occupy an island next to the bridge which was due to be destroyed there, and Napoleon used it to fire on his enemy and force the bridge. The Austrians then retreated to Mantua to defend the Mincio. Some 10,000 of Beaulieu's troops were left in the town while the rest of the army extended itself in a line 22 Italian miles in length along the river. Beaulieu fell ill. Peschiera was taken from the Venetian Republic and left occupied with only two companies of troops. Most Austrians now lost faith in the campaign and wanted merely to retreat to the Tyrol, which was deemed unconquerable. No one in the army had local knowledge of the terrain and Beaulieu had chosen to defend the wrong part of the river. In any case, hearing of Napoleon's advance, the key Austrian defender immediately retreated. The rest of the Austrians then fled before the French attack. Radetzky managed to restore order among many of them, but in any case Napoleon surprisingly left the retreating Austrians in peace, turning instead to besiege Mantua in preparation for an offensive against Papal territories.

Beaulieu was replaced by Melas, a cold Dutchman, who was the oldest general available. Colonel Zach was chief of staff and Radetzky acted as adjutant. Almost immediately, however, Field Marshal Wurmser arrived to take overall command. With Melas taking command of his former division, General Baron Duka became chief of staff, Colonel Zach was made head of the general staff chancellery, and Radetzky was given charge of the so-called 'detail chancellery'. Instead, he requested that he take up an active post and was made head of the Pioneer Corps, responsible for road- and bridge-building and maintenance. However, he was not discharged from staff duty since both his local knowledge and military record were too good to spare.

The Pioneer Corps, which dated from 1758, became under Radetzky's leadership not merely a respectable corps but an elite unit – and Radetzky himself the greatest name in its history. By 1797 it had ten companies and 1,723 men. Its practical operations building roads and bridges would prove indispensable and Radetzky himself, ever eager to learn, took great interest in its technical operations and potential. Yet, for now, the main task at hand for him and the army in Italy was the relief of Mantua.

Napoleon had decided to take the town in preparation for his bid to control the whole of Italy. The siege lasted from 7 June 1796 till 12 February 1797, taking the lives of 16,333 men and 4,893 horses. The Austrians attempted to relieve it four times, without success. Inside, the lack of food, medical supplies and sanitation was appalling. Eventually a capitulation agreement was made whereby 500 infantrymen, 200 cavalry, and six guns were given a free exit – including Radetzky with 214 pioneers, since during the second relief effort – much to the consternation of the fort commander, General Canto d'Yrles, who had only three days' worth of supplies of food left – Radetzky, Wurmser and their relief column had been forced to move inside the fort.

In his four and a half months besieged in Mantua, Radetzky impressed everyone with his bravery and defensive tactics. At San Giorgio and in front of the Tore Ceresa, for example, he erected defence works. He also led expeditions out of the fort to plunder and forage for food and established links with the outside world and the other relief armies. One official report on events of 23 November 1796 ran:[24]

> Radetzky, head of the pioneers left without delay over both moats under the protection of the guns, without regard for the heavy gunfire of the enemy, constructed temporary bridges, and crossed these with his pioneers followed by the infantry. The enemy was repulsed. General Heister having been wounded in this action, Major Radetzky assumed command, occupied San Giovanni, Bono, Conino and Prada with great determination and skill and took 300 prisoners.

The Austrian troops then returned to the fort.

The military situation inside the fort gave Radetzky his first object of study on a grand scale. He soon realised the need to have a correct knowledge of fortifications and provisions as well as local geography in order to organise resistance. He saw the need for a fixed, if flexible, plan. And 'in a dramatic way he experienced all the pressures on those besieged – the slaughtering of cavalry horses, the incredible price to be paid for a portion of cat – in emergency currency rather than in ready cash. He also learned how hunger and disease (Mantua fever) and badly organised, hence useless sorties, could undermine even the best soldiers' will to hang on.'[25] Indeed, despite his own bravery, Radetzky himself recognised[26] that thoughtless expeditions merely increased the number of wounded and depressed morale. But there were also positive lessons to be learned. He became aware, for example, of the key importance of Mantua for the Mincio-Etsch region and its relationship with the other fortresses of the area, without ever suspecting, of course, what would happen in 1848–9. That he never ever forgot his experience of Mantua is clear in his vain but persistent efforts, once he took command of Austrian forces in Italy in 1831, to upgrade the fortifications of all north Italian fortresses.

The Austrians handled the siege as best they could. Official reports praised the fact that Mantua had held out as long as it did and Field Marshal Wurmser, the army commander himself, wrote that history provided no other example of a garrison surviving for so long on the flesh of 3,828 horses and maize bread.[27] Radetzky in his memoirs was, predictably, much more critical. The planning of the first relief efforts had shown no local knowledge, while the army, once trapped inside the fort, had at first neglected to secure its fortifications, supplies or medical requirements. By the time of the last (fourth) relief expedition, Austrian troops did manage to reach the doors of San Giorgio; yet, as there was no means of feeding these troops, the doors remained closed. They were all taken prisoner. Radetzky recognised[28] this demoralising blow to 'the now scarcely breathing garrison of Mantua', describing it as 'an open confession of impotence and resignation to becoming prisoners; in fact the demand to surrender came at the same time'. Radetzky believed that had there been proper planning, faster movement and less reliance on the defensive by Wurmser and Duka, during the first relief efforts, Mantua could have been saved. As it was,[29] 'in a period of not quite ten months the House of Austria lost the whole of Lombardy, three armies and Mantua, the last bulwark in Italy'. Military education in the Austrian army was often the result of painful experience.

After Mantua, Radetzky was ordered to rebuild the Pioneer Corps from the men of the baggage-train, a task he accomplished as the army retreated, eventually reaching Carinthia in the eastern Alps. The Italian army was now under the command of the Archduke Charles, but was greatly inferior in numbers and equipment to the French. Radetzky was still complaining:[30] 'Since the army always chose only the main roads for its defence, the enemy pursued [it] through the mountain heights at the side, so that all encounters ended disadvantageously with significant numbers taken prisoner.' Soon, however, an armistice was negotiated at Leoben, which was followed by the Peace of Campo Formio (17 October 1797).

The winter of 1797–8 was spent by Radetzky and his pioneers in Northern Italy constructing fortifications in the Isonzo region. Radetzky's reports from this period show what an intense interest he now took in the technical aspects of this work. Since 1798 was a year of peace, his pioneers were employed building roads from Villanuova through Padua, Monselice, Este, and Montagna to Legnano.

A Second Coalition was formed of Russia, Britain, Austria, Portugal, Naples and Turkey between 1799 and 1801, while Bonaparte was in Egypt.

The Archduke Charles again defeated the French, this time near Lake Constance (March 1799), while the Russian Field Marshal, Suvarov, supported by the Austrians, defeated the French at the battles of the Trebbia (June) and Novi (August) 1799 and drove them out of Italy. However, things went wrong when Suvarov was defeated in Switzerland and Russia, having quarrelled with Austria over strategy, withdrew from the war in 1800. By 1800, too, Napoleon had returned from Egypt and defeated the Austrians at Marengo (June) and reconquered Northern Italy; in Germany, they were defeated by Moreau at Hohenlinden (December). Hence by the Treaty of Lunéville of 1801 Austria was forced to recognise the republics set up by France in Holland, Switzerland and Italy as well as the cession of all territory on the left bank of the Rhine to France. Austria retained Venice and received the bishoprics of Passau, Brixen and Trent, but the displaced Habsburg rulers of Tuscany and Modena were awarded Salzburg and part of Austrian Swabia in compensation. Bonaparte also forced Francis to make the rulers of Baden, Württemberg and Hesse-Kassel electors within the Holy Roman Empire and although Salzburg became an electorate as well, there were now only four Catholic electors out of nine. Not that Vienna was too worried by this Protestant majority. When Napoleon made himself hereditary Emperor of the French in 1804 raising the possibility of next having himself elected Holy Roman Emperor (and together with the Tsar of Russia outranking a non-imperial Francis I) Francis simply declared himself 'hereditary Emperor of Austria' on 11 August 1804.

In 1799 with the War of the Second Coalition Radetzky's pioneers had been expanded to eight companies and almost 2,000 men and on 11 April he was promoted to lieutenant-colonel and general adjutant to the Austrian commander General Melas. The Russian Field Marshal Suvarov was now in charge of the coalition forces in Northern Italy and in an outstanding campaign pushed the French back to Genoa.

Suvarov himself (supposedly adored by his own troops, though Radetzky doubted it) was seen as peculiar by the Austrians who also grew to hate his Austrian chief of staff, the intelligent General Chasteler, for what was seen as his pro-Russian bias.[31] Radetzky himself maintained that Suvarov, on account of his ugliness, could not bear to look at himself in a mirror and smashed any he encountered upon entering a room. His campaign plan, according to Radetzky, was no less brash, consisting of one order only: 'Attack! Break through the ranks and rows of the enemy! Turn round and kill your opponents!' This stridency, held by the Austrians to be the result of Suvarov's previous experience of fighting only Turks, did not make him popular with his coalition ally. Nor did his unkempt appearance and mistrust of rank help. Instead of finding Suvarov imposing, most Austrian troops found him laughable. Their morale became depressed, trust in the army's leadership vanished, and 'an open split between the allied troops was the result'.[32] Austrians at headquarters were also split, but Melas did everything possible to carry out Suvarov's orders.

Suvarov may have lacked finesse, but his coalition army managed to take all the major towns of Northern Italy. His Cossacks were able to enter Milan, however, only because Radetzky's pioneers (commanded by Count Hardegg) proved capable of seizing the bridge over the Adda. The Citadel in Milan had to be besieged, but the city itself received the allied troops with unprecedented rejoicing.

After taking Turin, Alessandria and Milan, Suvarov then turned south against Marshal Macdonald and met him on the Trebbia in a three-day battle from 17 to 19 June 1799 with 32,000 men against his 34,000. The Russian Field Marshal was unable to force the river, until Radetzky, who had scouted the land, directed the troops of Prince Liechtenstein to approach. They used used the cover of trees and brushwood to win the day. Melas, who had covered 80 kilometres in 36 hours to join the battle, officially reported to Vienna that Radetzky in every respect deserved the Maria Theresa Order for his outstanding valour. He wrote:[33]

> On the battlefield itself, through presence of mind, zeal, and a speedy understanding of the situation, he performed the key service. I cannot praise sufficiently the enthusiasm with which he brought the advancing troops, always at their head, to the most dangerous points and must bear witness for him that he, through his famous action, conducted completely by himself, contributed fundamentally to achieving victory.

Radetzky, however, had to give yet more outstanding proof of his military intelligence and bravery before the honour was awarded.

Not that he needed much time to do so. The battle of Novi, on 15 August, provided the occasion. There Suvarov's aim was to challenge the French general Joubert with a frontal attack, while Melas and his troops were kept in reserve. However, when Suvarov's initial attacks failed, Melas was ordered to attack the French centre and right wing. Radetzky, however, aware of both the position of the French army and local geography, advised the Austrian commander to ignore orders and to allow him (Radetzky) to attack the weak French left wing and rear. After initial protests Melas agreed and the battle, after being in doubt for 15 hours, was won, Joubert was killed, and the enemy retreated in disorder.

Radetzky was once again recommended for the Maria Theresa Order, Melas praising his valour and unique contribution, and noting how he had taken command of the attack and achieved victory. But there was still no decoration. However, to Melas's persistent recommendations the Emperor replied in September 1799:[34] 'I will pay due attention to the services of Lt. Colonel Count Radetzky and his reward.' Radetzky was promoted colonel on 5 November at the age of 33, though this did little to appease his disgust with allied leadership. Recalling the battle of Genola on 4 November 1799, the final major French defeat in Italy that year, he wrote:[35] 'People generally expected that the enemy would be pursued with energy, Genoa would be bombed, the enemy would be chased out of the Genoese territories, and all Italy would be cleansed of the French.'

However, the lack of draught animals, the difficulties with supplies, and most of all the fear of a mountain war, determined Suvarov to retreat to Alessandria the next morning, without even sending a detachment to observe the enemy. Soon worse happened: the discord between the Russians and Austrians led the Russians to withdraw their troops and thus under-mined the whole position of the Austrian army in Northern Italy.

Radetzky eventually received the Knight's Cross of the Maria Theresa Order on 18 August 1801 for his valour at the battles of Trebbia, Genola and Novi after a series of highly favourable reports from Melas. And despite his condemnation of the outcome of the 1799 campaign, there were at least a couple of factors he could take comfort in: his reformed Pioneers were now exemplary in road- and bridge-building, crossing rivers, besieg-ing forts and crossing mountains; and he himself had learned valuable les-sons regarding the limits and peculiarities of coalition warfare, particularly those involved in cooperating with the Russians – 'a rare practical prepara-tion for his future leadership position in the wars of liberation'.[36]

The siege of Cuneo – which by early December 1799 saw the Austrians capture the last French stronghold in the northern Italian plains – and the departure of the Russians, caused Austrian forces to become depleted with a severe lack of money and supplies, particularly of uniforms, coats, food and horses, not to mention the need for reinforcements after suffering tens of thousands of casualties. Melas decided to retreat for the winter and to allow his army to recuperate and reinforce itself in the rich Lombard plain. His chief of staff, General Zach, on the other hand, pressed him to con-tinue the campaign in France and produced a letter of support from the

Austrian foreign minister, Thugut. Melas declared that he, not Zach, was in command and that he took his orders from the Emperor, not Thugut. Zach had been in constant correspondence with the foreign minister behind the back of his commander. The trust that Melas had once placed in Zach he now vested in Radetzky.

The decision was taken to move headquarters to Turin and to keep the army ready to return to the mountains if needed. Prince Liechtenstein was sent to Vienna, meanwhile, to stress the need for reinforcements and supplies. Yet despite all efforts neither men nor mules were sent. And the cold winter made it impossible to start any new campaign before April 1800,[37] when the Austrian army then indeed pushed the French back to Nice. They then heard news that Napoleon had returned from Egypt and was gathering an army at Dijon. The Austrians were instructed, should that prove true, to retreat and unite at Alessandria, but in the event significantly fewer troops than foreseen were assembled there. None the less with 50,000 men there was still a chance of defeating Napoleon and this nearly came about.

The Austrians under Melas took the offensive – something which Radetzky believed was 'to his special credit'[38] – and engaged Napoleon's forces at the battle of Marengo on 14 June. Radetzky changed the battle plan and his pioneers created gangways over the swampy Fontanone trenches which surrounded the village, allowing Austrian troops to invest it. The battle seemed to be won and indeed Melas withdrew his troops and ordered them to pursue the apparently defeated enemy. However, General Desaix, who was later killed, appeared with French reinforcements and General Kellermann rounded on the Austrians pursuing the French to win the day. Although Radetzky was himself again singled out for praise in the official report, he recalled in his memoirs how at the dénouement the Austrians panicked and the cavalry fled.[39] Yet Napoleon himself was so impressed by the Austrian performance (Radetzky was again singled out in the official report) that he wrote to Melas telling him that he regretted they could not meet and offering him, as a sign of respect for 'the courage of your army on the field of Marengo', the sword he had used against the barbarians in Egypt. Given Melas's own view of Radetzky's contribution to the battle, perhaps he should have been the recipient of such an extraordinary gift.[40]

Austria chose to surrender all forts in Genoa, Piedmont, and Lombardy up to the Adda, while her army retreated to the Oglio by the Convention of Alessandria of 15 June 1800. The territory between the Adda and Oglio was designated neutral and the ceasefire was to last for six weeks, during which time peace negotiations were to take place. This surrender was perhaps an easy one. Melas might have chosen to retreat to Genoa and to have used the British fleet to transport his troops to Tuscany. He might also have chosen to fight his way through the relatively weak and scattered French divisions on the north side of the Po, although Radetzky, who owed much to him, does not examine these possibilities. In any case, Melas was recalled to a Bohemian command. The Archduke Charles arranged for Radetzky to be transferred to the army in Germany as commander of the Albert Cuirassier regiment, thus ending his career as head of the Pioneers. On Italy he recorded sarcastically:[41] 'So ended the successful and for Austrian arms glorious campaign of 1799 with the loss of all forts in Genoa, Piedmont and Lombardy.' That said, in an 1854 review of Radetzky's career *Coburn's United Services Magazine* stated:[42] 'These campaigns in Italy proved of good service to him afterwards when as Field Marshal, he had to fight over the same ground in 1848.'

On taking up his regimental command, Radetzky was informed by a Major Bodi that the officers in the regiment, and himself in particular, had no confidence in either their staff officers, who were assigned to individual regiments to inform them of their operational tasks, write up reports and do the general paperwork, or the general staff, the brains of the army, in charge of planning wars, battles and campaigns and organising its intelligence, cartography and military history. Radetzky merely replied that he hoped he would win their confidence in time and the battle of Hohenlinden on 3 December 1800 enabled him to do so.

The battle itself was an utter disaster for the Austrians. No proper precautions had been taken to secure the simultaneous cooperation of the various columns, no men patrolled the flanks, no reserve was in place, and the artillery and baggage were allowed to take the main road (between Muhldorf and Munich) before it had been properly secured. In a final insult, the Archduke John, in command of the army, along with his staff, were reported to have been sound asleep as the troops began their moves. The retreating Austrians left behind them 17,000 men who had either been killed or taken prisoner. The commander of the allied Bavarian army wrote sadly to his master:[43] 'Your Highness's troops have been sacrificed to ignorance and ineptitude.'

Radetzky's part in the battle, however, had again been a distinguished one. As usual he had reconnoitred the battlefield himself but when he reported that the wood surrounding Hohenlinden had already been occupied by the French, 'people laughed at [him]'. When he told the same to General Kolowrat who was about to enter the wood, 'people laughed at me again'. When the truth became clear, Radetzky was eventually ordered by Prince Liechtenstein to clear the wood with cavalry but told only to take half a squadron. In the fray he lost three officers and half his men and had his own horse shot from under him.[44] In fact, Radetzky was involved in various actions between 9am and 3pm. At one point, having no bullets left in his pistol, he threw it at the head of a French officer and incapacitated him. He also got shot in the left foot by a ricochet bullet. At the end of the day he helped coordinate the Austrian retreat, but more to the point, had proved to his regiment that he was not part of the staff who had caused the debacle. Rather, he had taken an active and decisive part in the action. Indeed, Prince Liechtenstein felt obliged in his official report to emphasise the 'outstanding' part Radetzky had played.[45]

After Hohenlinden came the armistice of Speyer (Christmas 1800). Humiliating as the terms were, they were better than the alternative, which, as the Archduke Charles told the Emperor, was defeat and prostration before the enemy.[46] Soon afterwards came the Peace of Lunéville, in the negotiation of which Bonaparte was in a position to name his conditions.

During the years of peace, Radetzky at the head of his cuirassiers (heavy cavalry) was able to spend some time at Ödenburg (Sopron) in Hungary, exercising them and winning fame within the army. He also collaborated in reforming it under the Archduke Charles, under whom he took command in 1805, when a Third Coalition came into being.

In April of that year the Russians and British combined forces to drive the French out of Switzerland and Holland. Austria, upset by Napoleon making himself King of Italy in May and also by the annexation of Genoa, joined the coalition in August. Sweden also joined. Napoleon had intended to invade Britain at this time but even before Nelson defeated the French and Spanish fleets at Trafalgar on 21 October, Napoleon had abandoned his plan in favour of a rapid march across Europe to fight Austria and Russia. An Austrian army was captured at Ulm on 20 October, despite a promise by its commander, General Mack, 'to triumph or die'.[47] Napoleon subsequently entered Vienna, the first foreign foe to do this since the Hungarian Matthias Corvinus 320 years previously. Then, when against the advice of his military commander Kutusev, Alexander I of Russia refused to await reinforcements, the combined Austrian and Russian armies were completely routed at Austerlitz on 2 December, after which the headstrong young Tsar left the battlefield and fled to Russia.

Austria was now punished at the peace table. By the Treaty of Pressburg (26 December 1805) she was forced to give Venice to Napoleon's Kingdom of Italy, the Tyrol, Vorarlberg and the recently acquired archbishoprics of Passau, Brixen and Trent to Bavaria (although she acquired Salzburg), and the rest of her Swabian lands to Württemberg. The rulers of Bavaria and Württemberg were made kings with no legal obligations in future to Francis as Holy Roman Emperor (instead they were to support Napoleon in future wars), while Austria was saddled with a war indemnity of 40 million francs, intended, without a doubt, to make her military recovery impossible. Napoleon even toyed with the idea of replacing Francis as Austrian Emperor with the Archduke Charles, but abandoned the idea when the latter displayed no interest. His challenge to Francis came instead when on 12 July 1806 he bound his German allies into a newly-created Confederation of the Rhine with himself as Protector. Francis formally abolished the Holy Roman Empire a month later, 1,006 years after it had been created by Charlemagne. But it was Prussia who would fare worst.

Prussia had been neutral since 1795 and was still neutral in 1805. She wanted to be paid for her neutrality by acquiring Hanover, and this was done by the Treaty of Schönbrunn of 15 December. But then Britain opened peace negotiations and France offered to return Hanover to her. A furious Prussia now demanded that France withdraw her troops from that state. Napoleon, furious in turn, attacked and defeated the Prussian army at Jena and Auerstädt on 14 October 1806 before occupying Berlin. The Russians were then defeated at Friedland on 14 June 1807 and forced to come to terms. Napoleon and Alexander met on a raft in the middle of the River Niemen and by 9 July had agreed in a treaty of peace and alliance that Prussian territory should be reduced by a third; that Jerome Bonaparte would be recognised as king of a new state, Westphalia, to the west of Prussia; that Prussia's former Polish territories were to be formed into the Grand Duchy of Warsaw and ruled by the King of Saxony; that almost all Prussia's fortresses were to be occupied by French troops; and that the country was to be saddled with a huge indemnity, the exact total of which was not yet decided. Her army would be limited to 40,000 men. Napoleon made it clear that Prussia had only been allowed to survive by the grace of the Tsar and would now be tolerated by France merely as a sort of buffer between the French and Russian Empires.

As far as Russia was concerned, the Tsar agreed to join Napoleon's Continental System (an economic blockade of Britain) and to force it on Sweden; the Tsar promised to mediate between France and Britain, Napoleon between Russia and the Ottoman Empire. Russia and Prussia both agreed to recognise Joseph Bonaparte as King of Naples and Louis Bonaparte as King of Holland, as well as recognising the Confederation of the Rhine.

Prussia was absolutely humiliated, her neutrality and servility towards Napoleon bringing her only misery and contempt. Austria on the other hand never gave up her desire to defeat the Corsican. And whereas Britain as a financial and naval superpower could sustain her opposition to the tyrant relatively easily, Austria, as a financially struggling land power, had a much more difficult task of conducting her wars. She needed British subsidies and allies, although allies were often difficult to find. Prussia, in particular, preferred neutrality, although a lot of good that did her. Russia had joined in several coalitions but could (and did) withdraw into her vast interior whenever it suited her.

Austria, by 1809, having joined all coalitions and having suffered financially and territorially in successive peace settlements, now feared that she would be next on Napoleon's list of states to be destroyed. He had after all grabbed Spain and Portugal and put his relatives on a large number of European thrones. What was to stop him from destroying the Austrian Empire, dividing it up into a number of kingdoms for his family (Hungary? Bohemia? Austria? Illyria?) or from taking one for himself? He was already King of Italy, Emperor of the French and Protector of Germany. Austria's survival seemed rather improbable. Hence in 1809, encouraged by Napoleon's difficulties in Spain (where the population had risen in revolt against the French) Austria decided to declare war on France.

During the previous year public opinion had been stirred up, a *Landwehr* or national militia of conscripted troops had been created to form a sort of reserve for the professional army, and exiled German publicists were now used to create propaganda. The Emperor toured the provinces to raise patriotic feeling, the Archduke John helped organise revolt against Bavaria in the Tyrol, while promises of support from Prussia were received. Britain promised a diversion in the Low Countries, but Russia, on the other hand, now an ally of Napoleon, warned that she would have to declare war on Austria. The Archduke Charles, weighing up the diplomatic, military and financial risks, came out strongly against a war, but when the Emperor Francis declared one anyway, Charles agreed to lead the army as Austrian commander-in-chief, albeit very defensively and with no enthusiasm. Vienna was soon occupied again (13 May) and although the Archduke defeated Napoleon at the battle of Aspern (21 May) – the French Emperor's first defeat in Europe – Napoleon struck back and defeated

Charles at Wagram on 6 July. The Archduke then signed an armistice even though his army had withdrawn in good order and was ready to fight on.

When Britain's 'diversion' (at Flushing) failed, Francis had once again to sue for peace. After having lost four wars in a row, he himself now thought of relinquishing his throne, while the French considered carving up his empire. Talleyrand, Napoleon's foreign minister, however, thought that Austria was necessary for any European balance of power and so Napoleon refrained. Still, the Peace of Schönbrunn was harsh. Austria lost access to the sea and 3.5 million people. She had to cede her Illyrian provinces to France (including Croatia, Dalmatia and Slovenia); her Polish provinces also disappeared, West Galicia with Cracow going to the Grand Duchy of Warsaw, East Galicia to Russia (who had declared war but had avoided clashing with any Austrian army, in effect remaining neutral, along with Prussia, whose promised assistance failed to materialise). Bavaria received some extra territory (the *Innviertel* plus Salzburg); the Austrian army was reduced to a maximum size of 150,000 men; while an indemnity of 85 million francs was levied (which could not be paid in Austrian paper currency). It seemed that both Austria and Prussia had been reduced to the status of Napoleonic client states. Even Russia was Napoleon's ally.

Prussia's reaction to this situation was to introduce a series of reforms, most importantly military ones under Scharnhorst, that provided for the rapid training of troops by transferring them after three years into a national militia known as the *Landwehr*.[48] Better-off young men were allowed to join Jaeger (sharp-shooter) regiments for a year and pay for their own uniforms and weapons. Later they could serve as *Landwehr* officers. The serfs were freed, towns given self-government and guilds abolished. Austria, which had introduced a *Landwehr* during the war of 1809, had to structure her army as a 'cadre' force, given its limit of 150,000 men, retaining as many officers and NCOs as possible so as to be able to quickly train new conscripts if and when any war broke out.[49] Her financial liablilities meant that not much money could be spent on equipment or armaments.

During these years of Napoleonic warfare, Radetzky's record continued to impress. With the formation of the Third Coalition and the resumption of war in 1805, he had received news en route to the German theatre that he had been promoted to major-general with the rank backdated to 1802. He had also been appointed head of a 'light brigade' in the army of Upper Italy. He met his brigade at Legnano and his first act in command was to swim the River Etsch with his men to attack an enemy outpost, returning with fifty prisoners.[50] Already beloved by his brigade, however, such was Radetzky's fame and standing by this point that he was appointed chief of staff to the English general, Sir John Moore, who was planning a raid behind French lines at Quiberon Bay. After the catastrophe of Ulm, however, when General Mack's Austrian forces were surrounded and surrendered, Radetzky persuaded the Emperor to abandon this plan. Francis chose him instead to go as imperial commissioner to the headquarters of the Russian army. However, Radetzky managed to persuade the *Hofkriegsrat* (War Office) President, Count Latour, to send General Schmidt instead and to arrange his own return to his brigade at the Tagliamento.[51]

It was at this point in his career that Radetzky undertook a task that marked him out not merely as brave and battle-wise, but destined for higher leadership. The Archduke Charles had to decide what to do about the threat from the French General Marmont who was approaching Styria and threatening to prevent the armies of Archduke Charles and Archduke John from joining up. The latter was retreating from the Tyrol and heading for the valley of the Drau (Drave) and was due to unite with his brother's army in Inner Austria. Hence Radetzky was ordered to advance with the Archduke Charles's Uhlan regiment by way of Görz, Laibach and Cilli to cover Charles's approach. Radetzky aimed to arrive at the Drau Valley before Marmont and to cross the river and head him off. He accomplished this by proceeding with astonishing speed, leaving the Tagliamento on 11 November and reaching Marburg by the 15th, covering c.270 kilometres in five days. The journey was made in difficult country and in bad weather. Still, Radetzky covered c.40–45 kilometres per day during the first two days and about 60 kilometres a day for the next three. Such speed was almost unknown of at that time, so that when Radetzky arrived at the Drau Valley, no French forces were to be seen. He found time, therefore, to organise a local civil defence (*Landsturm*) with optic telegraphs, small ceremonial cannon (instead of artillery) and watch-fires in the mountains overlooking the river, before advancing to Ehrenhausen to meet Marmont's advance troops, repulse them and drive them back to Leibnitz, where he defeated them again. Marmont himself withdrew to Graz, leaving Radetzky's troops free to secure the bridge and passes across the Drau with the aid of newly arrived troops under Archduke John. As a result, the two Austrian armies could combine along the Drau between Marburg and Pettau. Soon, however, came news of Napoleon's stunning victory at Austerlitz which effectively terminated the Third Coalition. After the Peace of Pressburg, Radetzky once again found himself back in Vienna carrying out reforms with the Archduke Charles. However, the speed and success of his personal exploit became legendary inside the army.

Lack of speed and decisiveness were the factors which would undo the Austrian campaigns during Radetzky's formative years, allowing his own star to shine ever brighter. It continued to shine in the campaign of 1809 when, save for the Spanish peasantry and the British fleet, Austria stood alone against Napoleon, unsupported by the Prussians or Russians and even attacked by Napoleon's German allies. The Archduke Charles, whose active military career would be ended by the events of 1809, himself had voted against Austria's declaration of war on 8 February 1809, although there was much enthusiasm in the Habsburg lands for the cause. Even the Hungarians in 1808 voted for extra troops and a reserve, and had given their monarch permission to summon the noble *insurrectio* at any time within the next six years. In the eyes of one commentator:[52] 'Everything seemed to promise a successful campaign.' Radetzky was more blunt in his assessment, saying:[53] 'The campaign of 1809 was already doomed from the start ("*schon im Entstehen verunglückt*").' He meant that the Archduke's reforms had not had time to work, although he might have added the declaration of war had come too late, that the best moment to have declared war would have been when Napoleon was in Spain. Austria had not been ready then and was too committed to war to draw back later. Thereafter it was the Archduke's poor military leadership – despite defeating Napoleon at Aspern in May – that really brought failure.[54] Charles altered his original plan, which had been to launch his offensive from Bohemia to the Main in an attempt to rouse North Germany. Then he changed his mind and ordered his forces to concentrate in Bavaria. This may have been a better plan in theory – theoretically it saved Vienna from the prospect of being cut off from its main army – but it wasted ten valuable days moving the army from Bohemia to Bavaria, threw supply and administrative arrangements into disorder, and gave the French time to concentrate their own forces. Thereafter, the Austrians continued to move slowly, failed to crush Napoleon's Bavarian allies, divided themselves unnecessarily and were pushed back towards Vienna by Napoleon himself.

Once again, however, Radetzky's own role was outstanding. Having reached Wels as part of the rearguard of Hiller's corps, he received the order on 2 May to cross the bridge over the Traun and then to destroy it. However, he risked his own brigade to allow time for General Schusteckh's division to cross first. This entailed involvement in a fierce battle with the French but in spite of serious losses the saving of Schusteckh's division was worth it. Radetzky then conducted a masterly retreat towards Vienna which allowed the main army to defend the capital. For his own part in these events, Radetzky was awarded the Commander's Cross of the Maria Theresa Order in January 1810. Numerous citations lauded his bravery. Baron Schusteckh felt that:[55]

> What he (Radetzky) did was to be expected from him as a widely known and admired general. I am in no position to list specifically all his famous deeds, deeds which have also been so advantageous for the army. He unexpectedly made a determined and daring attack and thereby created for me the opportunity to continue my retreat.

After this Radetzky's brigade was put in charge of the defence of the Danube between Nussdorf and Tulln. Unable to remain in a passive role, however, he crossed the river and attacked the French on the south bank on 30 May and took 50 prisoners. News then arrived that the Archduke Charles had defeated Napoleon at Aspern, allowing Radetzky to issue a rousing proclamation to the people:[56] '...Make speed brave Austrians! Join your brave warriors like the Tyrolese and help destroy the enemy, the robbers and plunderers of your fatherland!' A few days later Radetzky was promoted FML (*Feldmarschalleutnant* or general) and given a division in the fourth corps of General Prince Orsini-Rosenburg. Four weeks after that came the battle of Wagram (5 and 6 July).

Seeking to avenge his defeat at Aspern, Napoleon once again prepared to cross the Danube. The Austrians had planned to attack him before his crossing was completed but on the night of 4 July, the French with their German allies used ten bridges to reach the other side. By 5 July Napoleon's whole army was skirmishing with the Austrian outposts. The Archduke Charles in response to these changed circumstances ordered his army to start a huge outflanking movement for the following day. The eastern part – the far left wing – was to regroup in preparation behind the Rußbach stream between Deutsch-Wagram and Markgrafneusiedl. The army of the Archduke John was supposed to join them but it was too far off at Pressburg. This was precisely the position that Napoleon chose to attack. Markgrafneusiedl was defended by Rosenburg's fourth corps, including Radetzky's division. On 5 July Napoleon began his attack and destroyed the Austrian resistance. At four o'clock the following morning Radetzky counter-attacked and drove the French out of Grosshofen and Glinzensdorf, before the rather astonished fourth corps was ordered to withdraw to the heights of Markgrafneusiedl and hold them. Napoleon now tried to outflank the Austrian left flank. His first attempt failed miserably but his second succeeded. Since there was still no sign of the Archduke John, however, the Archduke Charles broke off fighting in the early afternoon. Radetzky collected remnants of the Austrian left flank and led them in lively rearguard actions as the Austrians retreated to Bohemia.

The Battle of Wagram has proved enormously controversial. The sides were equally matched. At Wagram 128,000 Austrians with 410 guns fought 181,700 French with 450 guns. The Austrians lost 15 generals, 772 officers, 37,608 men, 20 guns and 10 flags. The French lost 40 generals, 1,782 officers, 35,000 men, 21 guns, and 12 flags and eagles.[57] The fact that Austria submitted to a vicious peace and that the Archduke Charles lost the will to fight has perhaps obscured the fact that in military terms the battle was really a draw. Indeed, the Austrian army left the field unbroken and ready to fight on.

The roles of the Archduke John and of the Archduke Charles's adjutant, Count Grünne, have also given rise to debate. In his memoirs, however, Radetzky said that he had been precisely informed of events and that Grünne could be cleared of any blame.[58] Likewise Radetzky was of the view that '... the appearance of the Archduke John on 6 July would have made no difference at all ...',[59] a view which subsequent historical research appears to have vindicated.[60] Napoleon still had four divisions in reserve – he, too, had heard reports that the Archduke might turn up. Besides, the Archduke was too far away.

After the battle, on account of his again excellent performance, Radetzky was made second proprietor (*Inhaber*) of the fourth cuirassier regiment, although the Emperor very soon made him the first proprietor of the fifth hussars, a position he kept for life.[61] After the ceasefire at Znaim on 12 July, he was given the command of a division at Pistyan and it was there, at the age of 42, that he heard the news of his appointment as Chief of the General Staff. The Emperor jocularly dismissed Radetzky's reservations about taking up the post:[62] 'That you will make no deliberate blunders, your character guarantees; if you make the usual ones, well I have long become used to them.' Habsburg monarchs were indeed unaccustomed to great military successes. When Count Neipperg in 1741 lost Silesia to Frederick the Great of Prussia after the battle of Mollwitz, the Empress Maria Theresa had consoled him thus:[63] 'Regarding your own position there is no need to worry. You are not the first officer to have met with such an accident ...' Radetzky, however, would rarely blunder and as a commander would never lose a war.

# 2

# SAVING AUSTRIA AND EUROPE

Radetzky had been recommended for his new post by the new Austrian supreme commander, Prince Johannes Liechtenstein, with whom he had served in Northern Italy. His hesitation to accept the position, however, had caused Francis I to consult one of his court cronies, who, despite a positive report, suggested that Radetzky liked to gamble and had considerable debts.[1] This did not trouble the Emperor, who needed the best soldier available and Radetzky fitted the bill. He had served in all Austria's campaigns since 1788, fought with the infantry, cavalry and the pioneers, had built roads and constructed fortifications. He had been wounded seven times, had nine horses shot from under him, had swum the Sambre, the Po and the Etsch fully equipped without a horse, and had dodged hundreds of bullets. He had proved an outstanding leader as a general adjutant and as an independent general had proved more reliable and responsible than any of his comrades. Year upon year he had reaped success and glory. No one did anything for him; he was first with ideas, first to execute them and last to hold out against the enemy. He was known not only to be fearless but to be a tireless organiser, thinker and reformer, who had created the cavalry school, the veterinary institute and service corps (*Trainwesen*), and who had transformed the pioneers into an elite body. He also enjoyed a fine reputation in England and Russia.

However, Radetzky was not immediately enamoured of his new post since he had little actual authority. Instead, the job involved 'communicating every report first of all to Field Marshal Bellegarde, General Duka and General Count Bubna' – all on the board of the Court War Council or *Hofkriegsrat*, where Radetzky was also *ex-officio* a departmental head – 'to solicit their opinions, then to report to the Commanding General Prince Liechtenstein to reach a conclusion, before reporting the outcome to the Emperor'.[2] Offical life was highly frustrating.

His first task in Vienna had been to prepare the Empire's widely distributed forces along a defensive line before the ceasefire agreed at Znaim came to an end. Radetzky himself believed that the war could not continue and when this was reluctantly accepted by the Emperor, the Peace of Schönbrunn was concluded on 14 October 1809. Bureaucracy, in fact, was only the start of his problems. Austria lost valuable provinces (110,000 square kilometres and 3.5 million subjects) and was cut off from the sea. She had to pay a war indemnity of 75 million Gulden (and to ensure the ruin of her finances, Napoleon had flooded the Monarchy with 300 million Gulden in counterfeit notes) and had an upper limit of 150,000 men placed on her armed forces. Prussia, which had not resisted so ably had been limited to 40,000 after Tilsit and subjected to a military occupation. Militarily, Austria had lost six regimental recruiting areas and the six regiments of the Croatian military border. This necessitated a complete reorganisation of her recruiting system. Financially, the state faced something akin to meltdown and the new Finance Minister, Count Michael Wallis, believed that no war could be undertaken by Austria for at least ten, perhaps another thirty years.[3] Fortunately, the suave, charming and extremely able Count Metternich – now in charge of the Monarchy's foreign policy – had a much greater regard for military considerations.[4]

On 15 December 1809, the Emperor decreed a reorganisation of the *Hofkriegsrat*, which placed the 'head of the general staff in charge of all military affairs' with his own staff responsible for carrying out his orders. However, the Emperor's old cronies opposed Radetzky's new powers and soon persuaded Francis I to create a special 'military department' within the *Hofkriegsrat* that sidelined the chief of staff completely.[5] Radetzky, therefore, concentrated on ensuring that his staff officers were as well-trained and educated as possible and that they were chosen from men who had experienced war and had learned from it. He made them study the lessons of recent military history and he increased their knowledge of cartography and surveying, although he lacked the funds to organise training exercises or manoeuvres.

The immediate prospects looked bleak: with the army limited to 150,000, the complement of an infantry company (Hungarian regiments excepted) was down to 50 men. Regiments consisted of only two battalions with six such companies each, the third battalion having only officers for four companies, but no men. This was the so-called cadre system that would allow rapid expansion later. Jäger battalions were cut to two companies, heavy cavalry regiments cut from six squadrons to four, light cavalry regiments cut from eight to six squadrons, while all *Landwehr* militias, many of which had served well, were dissolved. Arsenals were full of unusable rifles and guns, which all needed upgrading; other armament depots stood empty. Given Count Wallis's views, Radetzky's rearmament proposals got nowhere, although events would soon, quite unforeseeably, come to his rescue.[6]

After being rejected by the Russian court as a suitable marriage partner for a Grand Duchess, Napoleon surprised the Austrians by suggesting he marry the eighteen-year-old daughter of Francis I (of Austria, rather than Francis II of the Holy Roman Empire, as he had been up to 1806). Agreement was secured by Austria's new foreign minister, Metternich, a Rhinelander, whose father had been in imperial service, and who as ambassador to France between 1806 and 1809 had grown close to Talleyrand, who had betrayed all Napoleon's war plans to the Austrians for large sums of money in 1809.[7] (They still lost!)

Metternich had never been an enthusiast for the war, rejected the German nationalism of the Prussian reformers around Scharnhorst, and wanted to create a European balance of power between enlightened, absolute monarchies. He admired the way in which Napoleon had created order out of chaos in France and had tamed the revolution; on the other hand, he believed that Austria would never be safe so long as Napoleon was master of Italy, Germany, Poland and Illyria and believed that an Austrian alliance with Russia was the only way to break his military hold on Europe. Still, he did not want Russia to dominate Europe either, so that she too must be subject to a European balance.

At first Metternich had no idea how matters would develop but he stuck to one basic fact: Napoleon's rule was unnatural; it depended on the charisma and talents of one man and that man was mortal. No successor would be able to win battles in the same way. In fact, Napoleon himself could not win every battle he fought. At some point he would either lose or be killed and when that happened his empire would collapse.[8] Everyone in Europe knew this: the only exception was Napoleon himself, who believed it was his destiny to rule and to defy mortal odds. He would always bet, therefore, on winning his next battle.

By 1812 Napoleon and Alexander had quarrelled. Alexander had relaxed the Continental System which was damaging Russian trade and Napoleon had occupied Oldenburg, the territory of the Tsar's brother-in-law. Moreover, Alexander resented France's treatment of Prussia and worried that Napoleon's policy of building up the Grand Duchy of Warsaw would lead to it – or even worse – a resurrected Poland, being used as a launch-pad for an invasion of Russia. By 1810, Alexander and his military chief, General Barclay de Tolly, were planning a defensive strategy in case the worst happened.[9] Indeed, for the next year or so, the French and the Russians both began making military preparations.

Napoleon did invade in 1812 (23–25 June) with an army of 600,000 men which the smaller Russian army could not defeat. Instead, the Russian forces retreated to stretch Napoleon's supply lines before giving battle. And Tolly's strategy proved very wise. There was eventually a huge and very bloody battle at the Borodino outside Moscow on 7 September, which Napoleon might have won had he committed his Guards, but the stand-off still allowed him to occupy Moscow a week later, although the Russians, under unknown orders, then set part of the city on fire. Seduced by the possibility of peace negotiations, Napoleon remained there till 18 October, which was too late to escape the Russian winter. That, plus the lack of supplies of food and clothing, the death of perhaps hundreds of thousands of horses, and the constant pressure from skirmishing Cossacks and Russian light cavalry, meant that only about 20,000–30,000 of Napoleon's army recrossed the Niemen in December 1812. With his humiliating retreat, first the Prussian auxiliary corps under General Yorck went over to the Russians at Tauroggen in December 1812 – seen by some as an act of treason against Frederick William III,[10] but soon legitimised when the king himself signed an alliance with Russia (the Treaty of Kalisch) in February 1813. This was designed to clear Germany of the French, restore Prussia's territorial extent of 1806 and to compensate Prussia for her Polish territories which would go to Russia.

Meanwhile the Austrian auxiliary corps under Prince Schwarzenberg had signed an agreement with the Russians and Poles making itself neutral and had withdrawn to Galicia. It had had a good record in Russia, although it had lost over half its strength – 6,300 casualties and 11,000 invalids. It had fought five large and 50 small battles and had marched 2,800 kilometres; twice Napoleon had offered to make its commander, Prince Schwarzenberg, a French marshal and on 9 April 1813 he had told him at St. Cloud: 'You led a good campaign.'[11] Schwarzenberg, however, obeyed the instructions of Francis and Metternich not to follow the example of the Prussian corps and to refuse to make an alliance with Russia. The latter now discovered that Napoleon, having re-assembled a new army from France, Italy and the German states, all of which he was still allied to, was again facing her, despite the Prussian alliance, with a numerically superior army.

By August 1813 he had assembled no fewer than 400,000 men including 88,000 in foreign contingents (Danes, Poles, Germans and Italians).

The Russians and Prussians, meanwhile, had only around 110,000 men between them, although Bernadotte, the former French marshal who was now Crown Prince and effective ruler of Sweden, brought another 35,000 men to Pomerania in May. On 2 May, however, Napoleon had been able to defeat the Russians and Prussians at Lützen and did so again, albeit less conclusively, on 22 May at Bautzen.[12] Only his lack of cavalry saved the allies from a rout. The allied forces then retreated to positions south-west of Berlin to protect the Prussian capital and Silesia, while Napoleon entered Dresden and Marshal Davout, Hamburg. Since both sides now required time to recuperate Napoleon (probably unwisely, since the allies had a greater need of rest and reinforcements than he did) agreed to a ceasefire on 4 June, which was eventually extended to 17 August. Napoleon was later to describe the agreement as 'the dumbest decision of [his] life'.[13]

It was during this period that Metternich, with Napoleon's consent – the Emperor of the French still hoped that Austria would end up on his side – shifted Austrian policy from mediation to armed mediation, and thence to armed intervention and military opposition. Napoleon had refused all Metternich's offers of territorial compromise and peace, preferring to risk everything on winning battles: 'I shall know how to die, but I shall not yield a handbreadth of soil,' he told Metternich at Dresden on 26 June.[14]

Meanwhile, his invasion of Russia, his spring campaign of 1813 against the Russians and Prussians, plus Metternich's time-consuming diplomacy during the armistice period, all allowed Radetzky to revive Austria's military base. Indeed, as a result of both his bravery and ingenuity during the earlier Napoleonic campaigns and of his activities during his period in office as chief of the Austrian general staff, Radetzky, in the words of Rudolf von Friederich, head of the historical section of the Great Prussian General Staff, rose to become by 1813 '... a decisive leader, who possessed a military experience like perhaps no other generals of his time, including the French ...', an accolade that made him almost the equal of Napoleon[15]. How then did he establish such a reputation?

Radetzky's hopes after 1809 had risen with every rumour that Napoleon was planning a great attack on Russia. Napoleon's allies across the whole of Europe had had to start readying and moving their troops long before the actual invasion – the Swiss division in Southern Italy began doing so in January 1811 – and Radetzky began to get restless. Napoleon demanded from Austria an offensive and defensive alliance against Russia. When this was refused, by a treaty signed in Paris on 14 March 1812,

Napoleon arranged for the Austrian auxiliary corps under his direct command to accompany him on his campaign. Although it was to remain separate its upkeep would be met by the French and it could retain any booty or trophies it acquired. It was to consist of 24,000 infantry, 6,000 cavalry and 60 guns. To secure Austria's own borders a reserve corps of 30,000 was also to be formed, although both France and Russia in fact agreed to respect Austria's neutrality. Napoleon agreed that the 60,000 troops now required would not be counted as part of the 150,000 maximum he had already imposed on Austria.

Radetzky foresaw that the two corps could only be mobilised and made battle-ready by depriving the standing army. Still, that would be no great harm, since it forced the army to take on more recruits and resources. Yet, even after Napoleon's defeat in Russia, Radetzky still encountered opposition from the bureaucrats. His memorandums encouraging speedier rearmament met with comments such as 'it's not going much better for the Emperor of the French' or Napoleon would be defeated 'if people seriously intended it'.[16] But how?

Under these circumstances Radetzky had to resort to some highly unusual stratagems. As he himself recorded in his memoirs,[17] and his notes on the campaigns of 1813 and 1814,[18] while on an inspection tour in Bohemia in 1813, he arranged with Count Kolowrat, the Governor there, to hold back 2 million Gulden owed to Vienna under the guarantee of the local Diet and spend it on the army then being organised in Bohemia. The money was used to set up accounts with factories and merchants to supply uniforms, boots, undergarments, horses, carts, repaired rifles and stores. Within two months it proved possible to supply uniforms, shoes and underclothing for 60,000 troops and just as many recruits and to provide 60,000 horses and 15,000 country carts.

Radetzky then managed to persuade Archduke Ferdinand, the commanding general in Moravia, and the Governor there, Count Lažansky, to do the same, so that three weeks later an army of 120,000 men had assembled at Prague. They were all untrained, but none the less under arms. Bohemia also supplied 20,000 draught horses and 15,000 country carts to the Prussians, as well as providing sufficient munitions to Austria, Moravia and Bohemia to last an army of 300,000 men and 100,000 horses six weeks. In spite of all this, Radetzky still had to record:[19]

In the army display held on 12 September 1813 in the valley between Töplitz and Arbesau, which the artillery put on, its teams of men were clothed in linen smocks and underpants and performed to cries of 'gee-up!' and wailing from artillery officers...

– and by then Austria was at war!

Radetzky, however, would not have been overly shocked by this state of affairs. In a memorandum dated 1 December 1809 which he had sent to his new supreme commander, Prince Liechtenstein, from Pressburg (Bratislava) he had already examined Austria's failings in wartime.[20] In it he had sought to answer three questions: '1. How has Austria reached its present position? 2. What more is to be done to deal with it? 3. What decisions need now to be made?' He complained that Austria always made the same mistakes. Wars followed one after another in increasingly quick succession but Austria was never prepared. Her failings made each outcome worse. In essence, Austria based her policies on the assumption that peace was the norm; thus war always came as a surprise and shattered her domestic administration. Not even her military recruiting system was adapted to the new era. Nor did the whole of society bear the burden of war equally. Thus when war broke out, the first campaign was usually over before the army was ready for battle. In past times this did not matter – Austria could always raise new armies. But with the advent of Napoleon, Austria's armies were curtailed and the enemy raised new armies much more quickly. So wars had to be prepared for, all classes recruited, and intelligent men trained for officer duties. Generals and their staffs also had to be trained beforehand to know their individual army corps and responsibilities once war broke out. Finally, the decision had to be taken either to fall into line with Napoleon or (to avoid eternal shame) to oppose him ruthlessly.

By August 1813, on the other hand, Austria had raised no fewer than 470,000 officers and men of whom 298,000 were combat troops.[21] By the end of December, that had grown to around 568,000 of whom 389,000 were combat troops, to which could be added around a further 13,000 irregulars.[22] What, then, had happened? Not only had Radetzky's devious measures been a success but his system of organising regiments on the cadre system, which meant that they could be rapidly expanded once new manpower appeared, had paid quick dividends. Furthermore, on 13 April 1813, under pressure from Metternich, Radetzky and others, Count Wallis had finally released 43 million Gulden of *anticipation bonds* – surprisingly, the war was now seen to be a way of solving the financial crisis.[23] The time consumed by Metternich's mediation between the powers had also allowed

Austria to cover up the real state of her army and to give it much-needed extra training.

Austria suddenly became the largest military power in the alliance against Napoleon and Metternich recognised the value of having this be widely known:[24] 'The most important thing is to use the most precise language in military dispositions and against everyone to uphold the maxim that we for our part use to Tsar Alexander and which consists of this: that that power which puts 300,000 men in the field, is the leading one while all the rest are merely auxiliaries.' Indeed, neither Russia nor Prussia could now have fought Napoleon without Austria. Napoleon had already told Metternich at Dresden in June 1813:[25] 'Without your intervention I would have thrown them back beyond the Weichsel (Vistula) and peace would already have been signed.'

By the time the armistice ran out, Austria had joined the allies. When both sides squared up in the autumn of 1813, according to Gunther E. Rothenberg,[26] 'In round numbers the coalition had 800,000 against Napoleon's 600,000, which excluding minor theatres of operations, garrisons and rear echelons, came to 570,000 against 410,000.' With Austria on their side, the allies won.

Was it simply a matter of numbers then? One distinguished historian has argued that it seems so.[27] Napoleon was only defeated when the major powers coalesced and overwhelmed him with superior force.

The truth was far more complicated. First, it has to be remembered that the numbers are deceptive. It is in fact very difficult to know precisely how many men were available to any army at any given time.[28] Figures were often notional. Many experienced observers refused to believe the official figures. Secondly, the allies by 1813 were no longer fighting in the same way they had been in 1805–6; they now organised their forces into corps and field armies and used huge numbers of guns in artillery duels. Thirdly, given the marked lack of military intelligence – meaning that for much of the time fighting armies hardly knew where their comrades were, far less the enemy – there was a lot of luck involved. Fourthly, the armies were competing with Europe's leading diplomats. Most of the soldiers – including Radetzky and Schwarzenberg – simply wanted to march on Paris; most of the diplomats, on the other hand, wanted to negotiate a peace. Fifthly, there were the rivalries between the military men themselves, several of whom despised each other. Sixthly, there was the problem of how to run a campaign when every decision had to be approved by the three monarchs who travelled with Schwarzenberg's headquarters, sovereigns who were all absolute monarchs and who had their own private military advisers with them, sometimes whole teams of them. There were real problems here not merely for Schwarzenberg and Radetzky, but also for the Prussian military leaders who were distrusted by their king and clearly preferred the Tsar. Decision-making involved endless discussions with royal entourages; even Blücher's military headquarters had to set a dinner table for forty people and he himself complained that he feared going hungry.[29] Operations, seventhly, required a plan, which had to be a good one, since eighthly – last but not least – there was the factor almost everybody feared – Napoleon himself. The campaign, after all, was being directed against the greatest military genius of the age, perhaps of any age, who had not been beaten in Russia in battle nor in the spring campaign. Lützen and Bautzen may not have been decisive battles in the field, but they were decisive enough to make the Russian commander, Barclay de Tolly, threaten to quit Germany and take the Russian army back to Poland for six weeks' recuperation, thus leaving the Prussians in the lurch. Only two things stopped him (and thus stopped the coalition dissolving before the campaign really started): Napoleon's unexpected agreement to a ceasefire and the knowledge that Austria, on the brink of joining the allies, would never do so if Russia and Prussia went their separate ways at this key point.[30]

Austria, indeed, now became the key member of the Fourth Coalition. She was not only providing most troops but also the key figures: Schwarzenberg, the allied commander-in chief; Radetzky, the allied chief of staff who would produce the winning formula of how to beat Napoleon; and Metternich, the leading diplomat of the Coalition who would lay down the terms for the alliance and the terms to be presented to Napoleon. Metternich's influence operated wider still. It was he who secured Napoleon's consent to end the Austrian alliance with France and the prolongation of the armistice against the instincts of his allies. He negotiated the terms that proved crucial in procuring the defection of the Bavarians, followed by Napoleon's other allies in the Confederation of the Rhine; it was he who thus determined the fate of Germany as a confederation of independent sovereign states rather than a unified constitutional state; who arranged for moderate terms to be offered to Napoleon from Frankfurt; who arranged for the allied armies to invade Switzerland against the the views of Alexander; who prevented the latter from backing Bernadotte for the throne of France; and who insisted ultimately that the French should accept the Bourbons as their rulers and not some form of election as Alexander suggested. And it was he who consistently backed

Schwarzenberg against the 'madmen' at war councils who believed that Austria's heart was somehow not in the war effort.[31]

This view of Metternich may be contentious, but it is undoubtedly correct. As the young Lady Burghersh – the future Countess of Westmorland and niece of the Duke of Wellington, now wife of the British military commissioner to the Austrian army, a determined young woman who had arrived at the war zone in Germany by herself in mid-October 1813 – wrote to her sister from Bar-sur-Aube on 6 February 1814:[32]

> How can you ask who is Prince Metternich? I thought everybody knew the fame of so great a person who is, and has been for years, the mainspring of all that passes on the Continent. He is the Emperor of Austria's prime minister, and reckoned the best and deepest diplomatist going. He is wonderfully clever and manages all the emperors, kings and ministers, turning them around his little finger and they are all afraid of him…He is uncommonly agreeable and good looking…

No doubt Metternich exerted the same great charm on her as he did on everyone, but this young, intelligent and neutral observer, who dined and socialised daily with 'all the emperors, kings and ministers' at allied headquarters for most of the campaign, certainly did not miss much.

There is another, rather grubbier interpretation of Metternich and particularly of his position in the spring of 1813, namely that he brought Austria into the war simply because he had been bribed by the Russians. According to this account, when Napoleon refused to help Metternich out of his serious financial difficulties, Alexander I arranged for several chests of gold to be transferred to him via the Duchess of Sagan, one of Metternich's former lovers, whose castle in Silesia was being used by the allied leaders. This cannot be ruled out. Talleyrand always expected huge bribes (a habit he possibly picked up from Danton) and Metternich, along with Nesselrode (the *de facto* Russian foreign minister during these negotiations) and Coulaincourt (Napoleon's plenipotentiary to the Congress of Prague during the armistice where peace proposals were to be negotiated), had all been key members of Talleyrand's circle. Metternich's secretary, the publicist Gentz, was certainly in Alexander's pay (he claimed to be devoted to the Tsar 'body and soul' in one of his thank-you letters), and so, too, may have been his master. Yet the evidence is scant and circumstantial.[33]

With war came the considerable problem of military agreements and particularly a plan of campaign. Metternich had obtained from the allies an agreement that, in light of Austria's decisive contribution, the Austrian

Prince Schwarzenberg should become allied commander-in-chief and that Radetzky should be made allied chief of staff. The army and certainly the Tsar would have preferred to have had the Archduke Charles as allied commander, but he had quarrelled with his brother the Emperor Francis and was known to be in love with the Tsar's sister, the Grand Duchess Anna. Certainly the Tsar wrote to his sister stating:[34] 'Tell the Archduke Charles that I regret every day not seeing him at the head of our armies. I have tried on more than one occasion to arrange this but always without success.' Metternich, of course, suspected that the Archduke would be in the Russians' pocket:[35] 'We want a commander who makes war, not one who makes policy. The Archduke will want to be foreign minister at the same time which is not compatible with the functions of a commander.'

Schwarzenberg, on the other hand, had a fine military record, had led the Austrian auxiliary corps in Napoleon's army in 1812, was respected by Napoleon (who had wanted to make him a Marshal of France and had suggested that he be promoted Field Marshal in Austria), and had served as Austrian ambassador to Paris after Metternich. He also got on very well with Metternich, as he did with almost everyone (Frederick William III of Prussia, whom he loathed, was an exception.) Indeed, his talent for personal relationships, his charm and modesty, his ability to manage difficult personalities and to endure widespread stupidity, made him the ideal commander of the coalition army. In fact, he was probably indispensable, as concurred by a range of historians, whatever their views of his strategic sense (where they are usually more critical).[36] Many have seen him as the Eisenhower of the Fourth Coaltion. Certainly, it is impossible to imagine Blücher as commander-in-chief. He would have resigned within days in a fit of temper.

Interestingly, it is still not exactly clear how well Radetzky got on with Schwarzenberg. Perhaps, having cooperated with the Archduke Charles on military reforms he may have hoped for him to be commander. Radetzky had never met Schwarzenberg before he was appointed chief of staff (on Prince Liechtenstein's recommendation) and the two came from different social worlds, as Radetzky admitted in his memoirs. More important was the fact that Radetzky's military aptitude was recognised and celebrated by all his military contemporaries; for example Gneisenau, the Prussian chief of staff, in a famous letter of 15 January 1814 deferred to his better judgement:[37]

You, dear Excellency, know the art of war better than I do. ... To Your Excellency's more enlightened views and greater experience of war, therefore,

I submit these ideas of mine. If, however, a man such as yourself, general, should oppose my ideas on grounds arising from a higher view of things, I shall abandon mine.

Concerning the relationship between Schwarzenberg and Radetzky, there seems no doubt that it was Radetzky who did all the spade work as far as planning and strategy was concerned. His incessant memoranda prove this. And as Wilhelm Oncken, the historian who knew more about the politics of the 1813–14 campaign than any other, wrote: 'Apparently everything of any significance in the Austrian War Archives from this period is in his hand'; he concluded, therefore, that Radetzky was 'already the most significant strategist of the whole Austrian army'.[38]

Metternich's gifts to the Austrian army included not merely Schwarzenberg and Radetzky's appointments but his achievement in getting Russia and Prussia to accept the extension of the armistice. Napoleon wanted this but the allies were unconvinced (astoundingly the Prussians had not wanted one to start with) and the Austrians were desperate. They needed all the time they could get to rearm, re-equip and train their troops, who for the first part, if not the whole of the campaign were regularly disparaged on account of their clothes and equipment. Radetzky recorded:[39] 'The inferiority of our army compared to the allies had a deleterious affect on the Prince (Schwarzenberg), the officers and the troops; it gave the allies a sort of superiority that had a bad influence even on the high command.' Without the prolongation of the armistice, however, the position would have been even worse. According to the official Austrian history of the war written by the Austrian general staff, it was Metternich's 'masterstroke' that he managed to drag out negotiations, and therefore the armistice, until well into August.[40] And of course, the allies were so desperate for Austrian support they had to agree.

By this time, however, there was a general plan of operations. Usually it is referred to as the Trachenberg Plan and for a large part of the nineteenth and early twentieth centuries there was a long-running dispute as to who had authored it.[41] The passion behind the dispute is easily explained: the plan worked. This was immediately recognised at the time and in his exceptionally detailed three-volume work on the campaign published in 1817–18 in Berlin, the leading contemporary German military historian of the age, Carl von Plotho, wrote that it would for ever provide an example to coalition military leaders of how to plan a war. It had deprived Napoleon of all his traditional advantages, thrown him from the offensive to the defensive, and forced him into a number of choices, none of which was ideal.[42]

In fact, the plan was deceptively simple. In the past, Napoleon had usually destroyed his enemy with superior force by outflanking it and then punishing its centre. The Trachenberg Plan now divided the allied forces into three armies. Each would advance into Saxony but none would attack Napoleon if he offered battle, instead withdrawing before all superior forces. If, however, some of his corps commanders were found with inferior-sized forces, then they should be attacked. If any one of the three armies were to come under attack by a superior one, then the other two would come to its aid and attack the enemy in the flank and rear. The strategy was to force Napoleon onto the defensive, leaving him to decide whether to move in strength and leave his communication lines open to attack or whether to divide his forces and march back and forth against one allied army after another and exhaust his troops. Eventually, after encircling and wearing down Napoleon and pushing him back the three armies would come together with superior force and defeat him in a decisive encounter – exactly what happened at Leipzig.

In fact, this plan was not the one worked out by the Russian, Prussian and Swedish monarchs and staffs at Trachenberg on 12 July at all. That one only called for the Silesian Army (two-thirds Russian in composition), led by Blücher with Gneisenau as his chief of staff, to withdraw before superior force; it did not prescribe this rule for the Main or Bohemian Army (mainly Austrian and led by Schwarzenberg and Radetzky) or for the Northern Army (a mixture of Russian, Prussian, and Swedish troops led by the Crown Prince of Sweden, the former French Marshal Bernadotte). The true plan was drawn up by Radetzky at about the same time (although he had worked out his ideas as early as 10 May) at the request of Francis I (who was not present at Trachenberg) and sent to Alexander at Reichenbach a few days later, where he accepted it without demur. Perhaps Alexander was desperate to please the Austrians; perhaps the change did not seem to him to be as significant as it was.

The Radetzky Plan – even the Trachenberg Plan – was criticised by the Prussians at the time and by German historians since as being defensive and defeatist. Friederich, the head of the historical section of the Prussian General Staff, wrote in his history of the campaign that Radetzky's plan was a return to the warfare of the eighteenth century and that the lessons of Napoleonic warfare had been lost: 'any idea of a powerful, quick offensive had been abandoned' out of awe of Napoleon, abandoned for 'dilatory tactics' and 'small means' such as operating against the rear and flanks and lines of communicaton of the enemy, attacking single corps, and exhausting and wearing down the enemy. The real strategy should have been to exploit numerical superiority and fight a 'battle of annihilation', instead of exploiting 'weak spots' for only partial successes.[43] This was all very Clausewitzian and, of course, Clausewitz himself famously condemned the plan.[44] Yet at the end of his substantial chapter on war planning, Friederich found himself writing:[45] 'The question how it was possible that such a system of military leadership could lead to a stunning success against a master of the art of war, will therefore have to be the subject of a later thorough examination.'

Blücher, an old Prussian war-horse who had bombarded his king with letters urging him to fight in 1806, 1809 and again at the start of 1813 was also unlikely to accept such planning. In 1806 he had told the Prussian military commander in Westphalia:[46] 'Whenever possible never allow yourself to be attacked but always be the attacker ... you must never fear an enemy even twice your size and only give way to a greatly superior force,' adding: 'I know the French from experience. If the first action is bloody, decisive and successful, they are intimidated for the rest of the campaign.' When the Russian commanders Tolly and Diebitsch gave him his orders, therefore, he refused to accept them, claiming not to be a Fabius (the Roman general whose strategy was to avoid battle with Hannibal). He said he only knew how to attack. Tolly and Diebitsch then said his orders were for guidance only, and that he should merely feel obliged to follow the spirit of them. His request for this to be put in writing was never carried out, although he took silence to mean consent.[47] In fact, Blücher, for the most part, stuck with the Radetzky plan and when he did not, he paid a heavy price.

Friederich's interpretation of Radetzky's plan is clearly wrong. The whole of Radetzky's career was an ode to the offensive. He hated the defensive. His offensive attitude is manifest, for example, in Radetzky's discussions with Toll, the Russian general, who had been asked by Alexander to start Russian planning for a war. Clarification of certain matters to do with troop positions on the immediate outbreak of war had to be postponed until after Metternich's negotiations with the French in Dresden had been finalised, but in his *Notes on the Campaigns of 1813 and 1814*, a 200-page handwritten account, Radetzky recorded that 'other operations were then agreed for the main part' by both men.[48] These 'operations' included directives for the allied armies to enter the Saxon plain 'and after hopefully winning a battle', 'immediately to head for the Upper Rhine, cross over the same, so as to be able to pursue operations with the left-wing in front of Paris'. And almost *en passant* Radetzky added: 'General Toll, who initially intended a planned advance towards the Middle Rhine, agreed to Radetzky's proposal, as soon as the operations were more closely examined, which demonstrated the advantage of approaching Paris via Belfort and Langres.'[49]

In short, Radetzky not merely described an offensive operation, with a major battle being fought on the Saxon Plain, but an 'immediate' pursuit of Napoleon across the Rhine, via Langres, all the way to Paris. Which, of course, is more or less what happened. If the allies dithered about crossing the Rhine, this was largely because of the Prussian plan to cross the Middle Rhine and the doubts of Francis I but especially of Frederick William III about the need to cross the Rhine at all.

One final point about Radetzky's plan. When he had been in Prague during the spring and summer of 1813 attempting to find food and clothing for the army, he had visited the former Prussian chief of staff Scharnhorst, of whom he was a great admirer (so much so that the Austrian secret police worried lest he was a dangerous German nationalist, which, of course, he was not[50]). Scharnhorst, who was dying, having been wounded at Lützen, told him:[51] 'Austria must join forces with Prussia and Russia. Otherwise we are lost,' adding that the enemy must be sought out, immediately attacked and defeated. According to Radetzky:[52] 'I then told him my own views on the matter, which consisted of dividing the army as a whole into several parts, each of which was to take the first opportunity to damage the enemy but had to avoid any serious encounters. He told me: stick with them, you are right, don't allow yourself to go wrong.'

Radetzky and the other allied military leaders took it more or less for granted during the armistice that Napoleon would take the offensive and begin the fighting. That is why some 125,000 Russian and Prussian troops were ordered to Bohemia at the outset to join the Austrians in resisting the expected onslaught. All of them then became part of the Main or Bohemian Army. Blücher remained in Silesia (heading the Silesian Army) ready to move forward towards the Elbe. In North Germany Bernadotte led an assortment of corps plus his Swedish troops (together they formed the Northern Army) with the main task of defending Berlin, observing the French-occupied North German cities, forts and ports, and defending Brandenburg and its neighbouring territories.

At first it seemed as if the allies would not move. This was not merely because they assumed that Napoleon would move first but because many people at the allied courts harboured the 'illusion' (Radetzky's phrase) that lack of supplies and allied numerical superiority would force Napoleon to retreat without a battle. It soon became clear however that Napoleon's supply lines were secure and, ironically, that it was the Austrians who were running out of the supplies necessary to continue feeding an allied army as large as the one now existing in Bohemia. (Earlier Alexander had even proposed bringing 150,000 troops to Bohemia, a crisis only averted by Schwarzenberg and Kolowrat successfully prevailing on Francis I himself to come to Prague to deal with it. There were now continuous complaints that Russian troops were plundering the Bohemian countryside.[53]) Eventually the impending lack of supplies as well as Schwarzenberg and Radetzky putting pressure on the Prussians got things moving. Frederick William III's military adviser, General von dem Knesebeck, in an effort to remove French troops as far from Prussian territory as possible, agreed that Blücher should begin to advance towards the Elbe, while the Main Army would advance into Saxony to support him.[54] In fact, Blücher moved even before the ceasefire had properly expired.

When war broke out in August, Radetzky thought that Napoleon would outnumber the allies, perhaps because Blücher's quartermaster-general, Müffling, had written saying that the Russians were wildly exaggerating their troop numbers.[55] Radetzky awaited Napoleon's attack. When it did not arrive, there was at first some difficulty about what to do next, since Napoleon's whereabouts were still unknown. But Radetzky's plan was about to be tested and clearly vindicated. Napoleon, it turned out, was pursuing the Silesian army which had advanced all the way to the Bober. Napoleon had the advantage of interior lines and was attempting to defeat his opponents one by one. When confronted with the news that Napoleon was marching in his direction, however, Blücher sensibly withdrew – all the way back to where he had started – leaving Napoleon on 22 August to return to Dresden, his main base of operations, with its stores and fortifications. Marshal Macdonald was left behind to keep watch on Blücher. The latter now decided to implement the other part of Radetzky's plan and attack a weaker isolated corps, although Macdonald was actually looking for him, when, in extremely bad weather on 26 August, the two armies met at the Katzbach. It was Blücher, however, who won a convincing victory, destroying the French army as it was crossing the river. The French muskets did not work in the rain, there were no cavalry to protect them and the German *Landwehr* made good use of their bayonets. Macdonald lost almost 35,000 of his 75,000 troops. (Perhaps Macdonald should have been better prepared. According to one writer, the Saxon General von Gersdorff had already sold the Radetzky Plan to Napoleon for 250 golden Napoleon coins.[56])

Napoleon had also sent smaller forces under Ney and Oudinot against Berlin. Bernadotte lost his nerve at the news (fearing Napoleon himself was on the march against him) but his corps commanders Bülow and Tauntzien defeated Oudinot at Gross Beeren on 23 August. The French were again defeated two days later at Hagelberg with Ney next in turn at Dennewitz on 6 September. Bülow again was the key figure. He had surrendered to Bernadotte's corps at Jena in 1806 and had never forgotten the humiliation. Winning now, when his former enemy, now his commander, seemed to lack the will to do so, must have pleased him enormously. Bernadotte also failed to pursue the French after their defeat.

With Napoleon in pursuit of Blücher, the Main Army now entered Saxony. An initial plan to attack Leipzig was abandoned as too audacious and so the whole army headed for Dresden. The attack was postponed until 26 August to allow Klenau's corps to arrive. When it failed to do so, Schwarzenberg broke off the attack that same day. His orders were being ignored by the Russians in any case. The problem now was that Napoleon had returned and the town was much better fortified than had been thought. When the attack was resumed in driving rain on 27 August Napoleon bombarded the allied forces, killing Moreau, his former Marshal. Moreau had defected to the allies and like Bernadotte, was presumed to have special insight into Napoleon's mind. His advice, in fact, was almost a summary of Radetzky's plan:[57] 'Expect a defeat whenever the Emperor attacks in person. Attack and fight his lieutenants wherever you can. Once they are beaten, assemble all your forces against Napoleon and give him no respite.' Moreau had been just a few feet in front of Alexander I when he was hit, and Alexander himself was lucky to survive; meanwhile a whole series of generals – Gyulai, Frierenberger, Mariassy and Hessen-Homburg – were wounded. By midday, Schwarzenberg ordered the retreat to Teplitz in Bohemia in dreadful weather and difficult territory. Napoleon should have pursued the allies and attempted to destroy them in the Teplitz valley but left the job to General Vandamme, who did not lack energy but did lack troops. Napoleon, however, remained in Dresden (French apologists say he fell ill) and recalled St. Cyr from supporting Vandamme. The latter could have inflicted enormous damage if he had succeeded in turning the flank and rear of the allied forces during their retreat. However, he was held back by Prince Eugen of Württemberg and General Ostermann, both Russians, who were told by Radetzky:[58] 'The communications with Bohemia are sacred as far as you are concerned.' Vandamme still managed to reach Kulm, however, on the road to Teplitz. Radetzky and Schwarzenberg then arrived on the battlefield and arranged to surround Vandamme the next day (30 August) and defeat him. Vandamme tried to withdraw and battle recommenced. Schwarzenberg let Barclay lead the allies out of recognition of Russian gallantry (Ostermann had been wounded and had lost many men) and Vandamme was captured.

Radetzky also served well during the battle. Schwarzenberg reported:[59] 'The chief of the general staff, through his heroic courage, his eye for the battlefield, and his actions, gave the most important service at all opportunities, and particularly at the decisive moment in the battle of Kulm and has made new claims on the respect of the army.' Alexander I sent him the Order of St. Anne, first class.

After hearing the news of French defeats, on 2 September Napoleon set off for Bautzen, searching for Blücher, who once again withdrew. Meanwhile Ney advised Napoleon to quit the Elbe for the Saale. It would be five weeks until the decisive battle was fought at Leipzig, but until then Napoleon's fruitless advances hither and thither in ever-decreasing circles delivered the allies repeated successes in their efforts to help each other, both near and far, to attack Napoleon's armies in the flank and rear, to cut off reinforcements, to defeat his detachments (Pecheur at the Göhrde, Lefebvre-Desnouettes at Altenburg) and to raise their men's spirits. Radetzky's plan was certainly working. On 4 September he wrote:[60] 'The Emperor Napoleon has been prevented from using or totally developing his talents as a commander and his military forces against any of the three main armies. He has lost a whole army corps.... The excellence of the operations plan, despite several hard experiences, has been proved by its execution.' The aim in future would be the same – to inflict as many losses as possible on Napoleon, to stop him employing all his physical and moral force at once and to prevent him enlarging his army by attacking his communications with France. On 14 September Radetzky argued that the allied forces should not combine. They would simply form a 'helpless colossus' or 'an army of Xerxes.'[61] Operating separately, on the other hand, they could wear Napoleon down, never give him peace, and cut off his subsistence and reinforcements.

The quadrille continued. Twice Napoleon sought to attack Bohemia, albeit without any confidence of success and with daily growing recognition of his unfavourable position. On 10 September he stood on the

Gaersberg, looked down from the heights on Schwarzenberg's well-ordered army and gave up any thought of attack. In the following days – 11, 12 and 13 September – Macdonald had to retreat before Blücher to Bautzen. It was getting ever more urgent for Napoleon to take action. So on 15 September he once again headed for the Bohemian mountains. Meanwhile on 13 September an allied war council had decided that the Main Army should march to the left and approach the enemy lines of communication in Saxony. Barclay de Tolly, with Kleist's and Wittgenstein's corps, would remain back to protect the Bohemian mountain passes. Marshal Mouton's forces, observing the allies, would have to be rolled back, which indeed was done on the 14th, before Napoleon, with Mouton and St. Cyr, arrived the following day to attack the allied outposts. There was a hard battle here but the French failed to break through though the allies retreated as far as the narrow pass at Hillendorf. The next day Napoleon attacked again without success and on the day after that appeared on the Teplitz road. However, the allies counter-attacked on his flanks and rear and he withdrew to Dresden. The allies now postponed Schwarzenberg's sortie into Saxony until Benningsen's Army of Poland could arrive to defend the Bohemian base.

Napoleon, having scarcely arrived in Dresden, went looking for Blücher again on 22 September, pursuing him as far as Gödau before returning to Dresden. (The Silesian Army retreated again.) The Army of the North meanwhile harried Napoleon's fortresses in North Germany and even attacked Kassel.

It was time, however, for the allies to unite to encircle Napoleon and bring him to battle. This was to be done in Napoleon's rear, first, it was thought, at the Saale. The Bohemian Army therefore set out on 27 September and in early October reached Chemnitz and Zwicken. Blücher was to cross the Elbe, although since the battle of Dennowitz Ney had been protecting its bank between Torgau and Dessau. He forced a crossing with pontoon bridges on 26 August before defeating both Ney and Bertrand at Wartenburg. Bertrand then retreated behind the Mulde. On 4 and 5 October the Northern Army under Bernadotte also crossed the Elbe at Rosslau and Ackern. Ney withdrew to Delitsch, so there was nothing to stop the two armies joining up.

Napoleon now left Dresden, although astonishingly he left St. Cyr with 30,000 troops behind in this now strategically useless city. His army on 6 October had headed for Wurzen, where he joined them, although Murat was ordered to use some corps to attack the Bohemian Army. Napoleon himself was again looking for Blücher and moved his main army northwards either to fight the Silesian or Northern Army somewhere between the Mulde and the Elbe or to drive them over it in an apparent attack on Berlin. Once again, he was disappointed, since his opponents neither gave battle nor withdrew across the Elbe. Instead, they withdrew behind the Saale. In fact, when on 9 October the French withdrew from Wurzen on the Mulde, the Silesian Army was crossing that river around Eilenburg and Duben en route for the Saale. Uninformed of this move, Napoleon still clung to his aim of attacking the right bank of the Elbe and may indeed have been thinking of attacking Berlin as Bernadotte always feared. In any case he sent columns to Wartenburg, Wittenberg and Dassau and on 11 October was still moving towards the Elbe while the Silesian and Northern Armies were moving towards the Saale. The two sides therefore had their backs to each other.

Napoleon clearly had no idea what to do and was still dithering on 14 October when, according to French sources, he was informed by the King of Württemberg that Bavaria had deserted to the allies. (Metternich had achieved this by conceding Bavaria full sovereignty and making promises of territorial compensation in the negotiation of the Treaty of Ried of 8 October. Afterwards someone told him without exaggeration:[62] 'You have won twenty battles with the stroke of a pen and deserve more than anyone else the Great Cross of the Maria Theresa Order.' It was awarded to him after the battle of Leipzig, when he was also made a prince.) This news now made Napoleon retreat to Leipzig, no doubt to secure his line of retreat to the Rhine lest the Bavarians should close it. He was probably now also aware of Schwarzenberg's approach towards Leipzig and the Saale. Murat, meanwhile, was fighting daily as he retreated before the Main Army and on 14 October indulged in a splendid cavalry battle at Liebertwolkowitz. Since it was the anniversary of Jena, the Russians were aided by the Prussians and while all this was going on, the Emperor of the French arrived in Leipzig. Murat's battle ended in a stand-off.

The battle of Leipzig lasted three full days (16–19 October) and pitted 361,000 allied troops (with 166.5 batteries) against 202,000 French (with 114.5 batteries). The French lost 60,000 men, the allies, 54,000. The Russian reserve army arrived in time and on the final day Napoleon's Saxon and Baden troops went over to the enemy (or at least some of them did). The only bridge leading out of the city was prematurely destroyed so that 50,000 French troops could not escape. The allies also captured 325 guns. Napoleon was forced to evacuate Germany – defeating an attempt to stop his retreat by Austrian and Bavarian troops under Wrede at Hanau on 29–30 October. Still, only 70,000 French troops re-crossed the Rhine in proper formation, leaving another 40,000 to straggle back later and yet another 90,000 cut off in German fortresses, who would later have to surrender. The allies for their part now marched to the Rhine, unsure whether to cross it or not.

The battle of Leipzig itself has always been controversial with regard to the part played by Bernadotte. He was very slow to arrive for the battle at all and some critics believe if he had not been threatened with the loss of British subsidies he might have avoided it. Certainly the Prussians were sceptical that he would make it. On the other hand, he was very worried till the last moment that he might have to make a dash to save Berlin and his own line of retreat in the North. Napoleon's behaviour before the battle perhaps excuses him.

Still, Blücher had sent word that he and Bernadotte were ready for a major engagement on the 14 October. Schwarzenberg is also accused occasionally of wanting to avoid a battle, hoping perhaps that news of Bavaria's defection would push Napoleon into peace negotiations instead. There is no truth in this speculation. Schwarzenberg merely wanted to ensure that the Main Army was in the best position to fight. But was it? Here, too, there is controversy. Radetzky escapes blame here, since Schwarzenberg had left the troop dispositions for the start of the battle to Radetzky's ambitious and rather twisted deputy, the former Saxon chief of staff, General Count Langenau. (In late 1813, however, Langenau had a riding accident and so did not accompany the army across the Rhine.) Since Langenau was a Saxon, he was presumed to have superior local knowledge. However, the initial plan went wrong, and Radetzky, Alexander and others persuaded Schwarzenberg to make changes. The controversy centres around Schwarzenberg's desire to focus the initial attack (with Austrian troops) on the west of the city in a swampy area dominated by the Rivers Pleiss and Elster where the crucial point was a bridge over the Pleiss at Lindenau. Possession of this would have cut off Napoleon's line of retreat. Critics maintain that the area was always too swampy to make an attack here feasible and it was only when Schwarzenberg brought reinforcements into the centre at great cost and moved the focus of the battle to the east of the city that things went well.

Radetzky, in his *Notes on the Campaigns of 1813 and 1814*, gives an explanation of Schwarzenberg's thinking. According to these, the reconnaissance of the city before the battle suggested that the bridges over the Pleiss 'were temporarily guarded by only 8,000 men of Poniatowski's corps', although Napoleon's guards were assembled in Leipzig to give support if needed. Still, reconnoitering had found 'the weakest part' of the enemy position. Radetzky then writes:[63]

> To attack it with overwhelming force and overrun the bridges over the Pleiss seemed the most appropriate and most desirable aim of all at the start of the attack, because should we succeed we would find ourselves on the shortest way to Leipzig and establish contact with Blücher forcing Napoleon to direct his retreat not through Leipzig towards the Saale and his basis of operations but towards Magdeburg whereupon he would run into the Silesian army corps, [he clearly means the Northern Army, now perhaps combined with the Silesian one in Radetzky's mind] forcing the same *to drop its disguise*, since Bernadotte had until then given cause for mistrust through his movements by keeping as far as possible away from decisive actions (*Würden*).

So there was in fact a very audacious plan in place which took account not only of Napoleon's weakest spot but also that of the allies! Could Radetzky have recommended it? It would not have been out of character. Was it bound to fail on account of the terrain? Who knows? What we do know is that Gyulai and other troop commanders failed to seize Lindenau and its bridge and that one colonel actually got lost and went to the wrong bridge. Thereafter the plan had to be 'quickly changed'. Yet Radetzky's strategy had worked perfectly. Napoleon had been surrounded, the noose had been tightened and Germany saved by ultimately applying superior force as Radetzky's plan had laid down. The next part of it was to cross the Rhine and reach Paris.

There is one other controversy about the battle. Afterwards Schwarzenberg gave Blücher orders to pursue Napoleon and capture him. Blücher did indeed start his pursuit but then received orders to turn in another direction and take the main road to Frankfurt. Later he complained that he had been just on the point of capturing Napoleon when these orders arrived, so that, but for them, the war, and Napoleon's career, could have ended in Germany. Schwarzenberg usually gets the blame for this, which is not fair. According to Radetzky's *Notes*, it was the allied sovereigns who changed the orders fearing that Napoleon was still in a position to turn around and defeat Blücher. In any case, according to Müffling's memoirs, Blücher's men had little heart for the pursuit.[64] There was nothing more 'disagreeable and disgusting' than following the French;

it involved marching along a route covered in corpses and taking prisoners who already had the mark of death on them. The idea of sleeping in the same bivouacs, perhaps on the same straw, as these fever-stricken wretches had done the night before, caused sheer horror. So, wrote the baron, there were times when nothing seems to go right and 'a certain lukewarmness pervades the execution of orders. Such a time had now set in with the Silesian Army, but there is no accounting for the why or wherefore.'

The battle, of course, had been a dreadful affair. Lord Aberdeen, who rode out over the battlefield afterwards, reported:[65] 'For three or four miles the ground is covered with bodies of men and horses, many not dead. Wretches, wounded and unable to crawl crying for water amidst heaps of putrifying bodies. Their screams are heard at an immense distance and still ring in my ears.' And they always would. The young Lady Burghersh in similar vein reported from Weimar on 21 November on the French retreat from Germany:[66]

No language can describe the horrible devastation these French have left behind them and without seeing it no one can form an idea of the country through which such a retreat as theirs has been made. Every bridge blown up, every village burned or pulled down, fields completely devastated, orchards all turned up, and we traced their bivouacs all along by every horror you can conceive. None of the country people will bury them or their horses, so there they remain lying all over the fields and roads, with millions of crows feasting – we passed quantities, bones of all kinds, hats, shoes, epaulettes, a surprising quantity of rags and linen – every kind of horror.

War needs a strong stomach.

At a 'noisy' war council on 21 October the allies debated what to do next. According to Radetzky, Alexander's entourage was particularly loud and Schwarzenberg felt compelled to tell everyone 'to be realistic'.[67] Apparently he was thinking about bringing the Bavarians up to date and organising an observation corps around Strasbourg, but realism could have meant a number of things. For a start, it might have allowed people to reflect on how lucky they had been. During the battle of Leipzig, for example, the three monarchs had very nearly been captured or killed when the French had come within yards of their observation post. Schwarzenberg had had to cover their very hasty retreat personally by throwing himself at the French sword in hand. They may well have owed him their lives; they certainly owed him their freedom. Radetzky himself had been wounded at Leipzig as would Schwarzenberg be later in France. Alexander, of course, had only just eluded death at Dresden (Moreau was not so lucky) and, of course, Scharnhorst had been killed at Lützen. Luck played a great part due to the lamentable lack of intelligence in the campaign. In particular, thanks to Napoleon's lack of cavalry, he had remained ignorant of the whereabouts of his enemy; before Leipzig, therefore, he had been unable to take advantage of the interior lines, simply by being unable to track down either Blücher or Bernadotte. Müffling would later record:[68] 'It must be observed that however well Blücher's espionage was organised in Germany, here in France it could succeed but little in procuring intelligence by means of spies. The French, indeed liked well enough the money offered them, but they were too much afraid of Napoleon's severe measures, if after the close of the war, anything should be discovered.'

The immediate question after Leipzig was whether and when the allies should cross the Rhine. Radetzky and Schwarzenberg had assumed this in their planning and the Prussian military leaders were as usual only too happy to agree (although their plan meant crossing the Middle Rhine instead of going through Switzerland as the Austrians demanded). They now began to exaggerate the size of allied troop strength, as the Russians and Austrians had been accused regarding their own size earlier, with Müffling and Gneisenau talking of 'a million of disposable soldiers' ready to be deployed against the skeleton of a defeated French army plus a few conscripts.[69] They did not want to stop at the Rhine at all (although the six weeks spent there by the allied armies did in fact allow for much needed rest and vital reinforcements). At Frankfurt, however, it seems that Schwarzenberg and the Prussian military leaders conducted a 'confidential conference' in an attempt to coordinate military views.[70] Indeed, relations between Schwarzenberg and Blücher seem to have been much better during the whole campaign than Prussian historiography would later suggest. (According to Müffling, Schwarzenberg 'behaved to the Field Marshal with particular esteem and friendship'.[71])

The real problem regarding the crossing of the Rhine was the views of the sovereigns. These monarchs, who travelled with Schwarzenberg's headquarters for the whole of the campaign, were all absolute rulers whose views could not easily be overruled by the army leadership. Instead, Schwarzenberg and Radetzky had to submit all plans to them for their approval, which came only after they had consulted their various private military advisers, of whom there was a large number.

Alexander I of Russia was to prove the most irritating to the Austrians in this capacity. Although he had almost certainly been responsible for the disaster at Austerlitz in 1805 by insisting on starting the battle before reinforcements could arrive, and although his generals had conspired to bundle him off to St. Petersburg during the Moscow retreat, he still fancied himself for the post of allied commander-in-chief, an ambition which Frederick William of Prussia, for example, supported. (According to Hardenberg's diary, the King was even bold enough to ask the Tsar over lunch one day whether he would like the job, to the great consternation of the Austrians present.[72]) Considering all the allied armies were being led by non-Russians, the Russian generals believed that it would only be fair for the Tsar to lead the coalition as a whole.

There is some dispute, however, as to whether Alexander himself actually demanded the job. Radetzky wrote in his *Notes*: 'The Emperor Alexander pursued – through his voracious vanity – no greater aim than exercising the supreme command over all the allied armies, an aim which he took every opportunity to lay claim to, but which, out of modesty, he never demanded precisely, and which therefore was never given definite expression.' According to General Sir Robert Wilson, the British commissioner to the Austrian army, however, Alexander did indeed press his claim. Wilson had followed this dispute right from the start when in August 1813, the Tsar had originally lost his claim to the overall command to Schwarzenberg, noting:[73] 'The Emperor of Russia earnestly wishes it and I never saw a man more anxious than he was yesterday to obtain it, nor did I ever see disappointment more strongly expressed than when it was not offered to him.' Then on 22 October, after victory at Leipzig, Wilson wrote to Aberdeen, informing him:[74] '... the Emperor of Russia has had the indelicacy, not to say rashness, to propose taking from Schwarzenberg, *le baton de commandement*. This, Metternich peremptorily told him could never be.' He promised to tell him the details later, saying they did Metternich much honour. The details were:[75]

> He (Alexander I) indeed proposed himself as General-in-chief yesterday but professing not to understand the métier sufficiently he said he would have a council to direct him. Metternich frankly told him that he never would obtain the consent of Austria; that he had declared himself moreover unqualified; and that a council on the field of battle was a project that would never be productive of any other result than misfortune and disgrace.

None the less, Alexander continually acted as if he were supreme commander and surrounded himself with a veritable host of military experts – Russians such as Wolkonsky, Arakcheiev and Diebitsch, as well as the former French marshal, Moreau, and Napoleon's later great interpreter, Jomini – as a kind of council. Moreau, of course, was killed at Dresden at which time, too, according to Müffling, Jomini gave such impractical advice that he was never listened to again. More seriously, the Tsar managed to subvert Schwarzenberg's command structure, leading the true commander-in-chief to write to Francis, hinting at resignation:[76]

> General Barclay has no sense at all of obedience or of business and is therefore jealous to the highest degree. This leads to the great misfortune that no reliance can be placed on him or his troops with any precision at all, but also that generals Wittgenstein and Kleist receive my orders too late or often in such a contradictory fashion that already all the worst sorts of consequences ensue. All of this, combined with a thousand unavoidable troubles, make it quite impossible for me to take responsibility for the results of an undertaking in which the welfare and existence of the Monarchy are at stake.

In like fashion, as early as 5 September 1813, Schwarzenberg had written to his wife from Teplitz[77] complaining that he was 'surrounded by the feeble-minded, all sorts of fools, eccentric schemers, intriguers, asses, babblers, criticasters; in short, vermin in countless numbers gnaw at me and torment me to the marrow of my bones.' The only reason he had not resigned was that 'the objective is so solemn, so holy, and the position is such that I believe that anyone else in my place could only achieve less.'

During the campaign of 1813 Schwarzenberg was forced to hold 17 war councils and often to issue orders he did not really agree with. However, on the decisive issues he could rely on Metternich. Here, for example, is an extract from Metternich's private papers in Prague:[78]

> When in one of these war councils summoned by Prince Schwarzenberg, at which Tsar Alexander was present, it proved impossible to reach agreement between the different views of the commanders, the Emperor summoned me for my advice and explained that he and the generals would leave the verdict to me and would submit to the same. The Emperor Alexander himself took the trouble to explain the nature of the situation to me. I spoke on behalf of the plan of Prince Schwarzenberg as having the greater assurance of success.... My verdict was declared conclusive.

When it came to deciding whether the allies should cross the Rhine, however, the two main obstacles were Francis I of Austria and Frederick William III of Prussia. Francis was privately advised by his cautious generals Bubna and Duka, who would have preferred a peace settlement. However, it was Frederick William of Prussia – whose experience of defeat at Valmy in 1792 and of defeat and occupation after 1806, had made him extremely timid – who put up most resistance. Gneisenau complained in a letter to Clausewitz on 16 November that the king found it 'very vexatious' to hear people talking about crossing the Rhine and quoted him as follows:[79] 'That was never the aim. So why should people now have this crazy idea for the first time? ... What business is it of ours what happens on the other side? Why should we entertain the laughable idea of marching on Paris?' Frederick William's biographer quotes him as saying that the projected invasion of France made him shudder:[80] 'We risk spoiling everything and losing the best fruits that crowned the beautiful success of our previous efforts.' According to the same writer, he often left the Prussian Crown Prince in a state of depression.

Once the invasion took place at the new year, the king, who had not been in Frankfurt at the time, bitterly and repeatedly reproached Gneisenau and Müffling for ever having allowed it to happen. Indeed, his persistently cold treatment of Gneisenau, even at Leipzig but especially after the Rhine crossing and during the campaign in France, forced the latter to ask Hardenberg, the Prussian chancellor, to take steps as soon as the war ended, to allow him to leave the army and to take up the position of Postmaster General. He felt he could no longer work with the king, although he still needed funds to feed a growing family.[81] The Prussian military leadership, unsurprisingly, came to prefer Alexander of Russia, who in Müffling's words, became 'the rock around which everyone gathered, to which everyone clung, who comprehended the necessity of continuing the war and dethroning Bonaparte'.[82] Or as Radetzky put it: 'They felt obliged to follow the will of the Emperor Alexander.'[83] It was not just his own generals, however, who disliked Frederick William. Schwarzenberg said:[84] '... the King is a rough, course, unfeeling fellow who is to me as loathsome as the poor, brave Prussians are pleasant and estimable.' Radetzky's view was that in view of all the defeats Prussia had suffered in the past, Frederick William simply 'opposed everything' whenever a decision had to be taken.[85]

Eventually Radetzky was able to persuade Francis to agree with his plans, although it was not easy. They were first submitted to Francis on 5 December 1813 but failed to secure approval, largely because the Prussians (presumably Frederick William III) wanted to winter in Germany and remain on the defensive. In any case, General Duka 'had so determined our Emperor for the defensive that he threatened to remove me from the army and lock me up in a fortress if I did not change my mind'. However, the plan was re-submitted on 13 December and after Radetzky insisted that Francis should read it himself, a committee of Duka, Schwarzenberg, Metternich and Radetzky under the Emperor's chairmanship granted approval on the evening of 26 December. Schwarzenberg took the post-coach to inform the other leaders (including Alexander) and the army, which had already been made ready to start moving, of the good news.[86] The conquest of Holland by Bülow and its uprising against France had already given them great cause for cheer.

Radetzky's plan was much the same as that he had outlined to Toll in the summer of 1813. Unlike the proposals put forward by Gneisenau, it involved the Main Army advancing in a great loop through Switzerland (the Austrians had Italian concerns to think about and needed to maintain communication with their forces there; besides Switzerland could not be left unsecured behind allied lines) and the Franche Comté. It would then turn the lines of the Rhine and the Vosges and descend on Paris from the Plateau of Langres, an area previously spared the horrors of war and thus more able to support and supply an advancing army; an area, too, which enabled the allies to attack Napoleon's lines of communication. The Army of Silesia under Blücher plus part of the Northern Army, meanwhile, would cross the Rhine between Mannheim and Coblenz, advance through the Palatinate to Metz and eventually to the Marne, where it would link up with the Main Army. It would not be expected to attack the French Rhine forts, but merely to blockade and observe them. The rest of the Northern Army was either to help Bernadotte (who, predictably wanted no part in the invasion of France and who had opposed the Rhine crossing) to defeat Marshal Davout in Hamburg, blockade the forts still occupied by the French in North Germany, or help the British and Dutch in the Low Countries.

Predictably, the whole campaign was to be based on the same successful principles which had always animated Radetzky's plan. In the draft shown to Alexander I in November 1813, the principles laid down in the introduction ran:[87]

1. Not to stop at the forts encountered en route but simply leave forces to observe them.
2. To operate against the rear lines of operation of the enemy with the main forces.
3. To break his lines of communication and to thus force him either to make detachments or to speed with his entire force to the threatened points.

4. To undertake battle only when the enemy has divided his forces or superiority is decidedly on the part of the allies, but to avoid battle when the enemy forces are united and directed towards the points threatened by the allies.
5. In the case when the enemy turns en masse against one or other army, this is to retreat, the others, however, are to advance with great enthusiasm.
6. The rendez-vous of all armies is to be the enemy headquarters, all armies have the task of reaching it, as actually happened at Leipzig.

The question now was, would the strategic principles that had worked so well in Germany work equally well in France? And could Alexander be kept in his place with regard to military – or even diplomatic agreements?

It was not long before problems arose, for having assented to the Austrian plan to enter Switzerland, Alexander suddenly changed his mind, under the influence of both Jomini and La Harpe (his old tutor), both of whom were Swiss citizens. They now requested the Tsar to uphold Swiss sovereignty and neutrality. Since the Austrians were already on the march with troops inside Switzerland, the Tsar's new demand was absolutely infuriating. Radetzky wrote a long memorandum detailing how the Swiss were actively supporting the French (supplying materials to defend French forts, supplying volunteers to France, and returning Austrian troops who had escaped back to the French as prisoners of war) but Metternich once again intervened and through diplomacy managed to secure Swiss agreement to the invasion, allowing Alexander to back down.[88] It was a very poor start to the campaign. However, there was more trouble brewing over the so-called Frankfurt proposals, an extremely moderate deal that the allies had offered to Napoleon before crossing the Rhine, which would have allowed him to keep the throne of France and France's natural frontiers if he would relinquish his hold on the rest of Europe. The British representative on the Continent, Lord Aberdeen, had even agreed that Britain would make concessions over maritime rights and colonial gains – Metternich completely dominated him. Napoleon ignored the terms but did agree to hold a peace congress at Chatillon to discuss an end to the war.

By late January 1814, the main armies were on the point of joining up, having fulfilled their tasks without any serious resistance. The French under Marshals Victor and Mortier had retreated before Schwarzenberg, and Ney and Marmont did the same before Blücher. Superior force had won the day, allowing Gyulai to capture Langres on 18 January and Schwarzenberg to push on to the Aube, where he prepared to meet up with Blücher soon after 25 January. Blücher's army, however, had been reduced from 50,000 men to about only 25,000 by leaving troops behind to observe the main French forts on the Rhine frontier. Meanwhile, Generals Winzingerode and Bülow had crossed the lower Rhine at Düsburg and Düsseldorf forcing Marshal Macdonald to retreat before them to Lüttich and Nemur. Here Macdonald was ordered to hurry to Chalons, where Napoleon was assembling his main army, allowing Winzingerode and Bülow an open road to Belgium to fight Carnot and Maison. They were relieved by the forces of the Duke of Weimar and Generals Thielmann and Graham, leaving them free to swing left through Northern France to join up with Blücher. Everywhere the allies issued proclamations informing the French people that they were not fighting them, but only the tyrant Napoleon.

Napoleon himself had not bothered to leave Paris till 25 January – the main reason for the ease of the initial allied advance. Marie Louise was then left behind as regent, while Coulaincourt was sent to Chatillon as peace negotiator. His instructions, however, would depend upon military outcomes.

When Napoleon joined his army at Chalons on 26 January he found he had about 65,000 troops and immediately set out in pursuit of Blücher, hoping to prevent him joining up with Schwarzenberg. As it happened the Silesian Army had reached Brienne, where Napoleon had attended military school, and where Blücher intended to teach the Corsican some more lessons. Napoleon attacked Blücher there on 29 January and almost captured him and Gneisenau at their dinner in the local château. But although the castle was lost, the town remained in allied hands. Fortunately Blücher was close enough to Schwarzenberg to demand help which arrived in the shape of 2,000 cavalry under General Pahlen. Napoleon himself narrowly avoided capture before he withdrew. On 30 January Schwarzenberg then took Bar-sur-Aube. Both sides lost some 2,000–5,000 men at Brienne, but since the allies had expected a much more powerful showing from Napoleon the first time they encountered him in France, they regarded the stand-off as a victory.

They were even more amazed that Napoleon did not attack Blücher again on 30–31 January before he was properly reinforced by the Main Army. As it was, he was reinforced by so many allied troops – those of Wittgenstein, Gyulai, Barclay, Wrede and the Crown Prince of Württemberg – that these allies had to wear a white band around their left arm in order to be recognised.[89] Schwarzenberg himself even entered Trannes to discuss the battle of Brienne with Blücher. Napoleon had simply no information that the allies had met up until he heard a trumpeter announcing the arrival of Wrede, whereupon he intended to withdraw to Lesmont. Given the bad weather and the enthusiasm of his troops, he instead decided to give battle at La Rothière on 1 February after all, although in Radetzky's view, Napoleon showed that he expected to gain little from the battle. Allied headquarters was itself misled for two days on the position of the armies by the British General Stewart, until Radetzky himself reconnoitred the position.[90] The Main Army had given Blücher three to four army corps but during the battle 'people knew just as little of the position of the enemy as of the Silesian Army'.[91] The battle itself proved a fierce encounter and the village of La Rothière changed hands three times. Napoleon lost two generals and four allied ones were wounded. The French lost 6,000 dead and wounded and 3,000 prisoners. But the allies, too, lost 6,000 men. Yet Napoleon's army was demoralised and lost 6,000 men to desertion over the next few days; moreover, the local population received Napoleon very sullenly when he entered Troyes on 3 February. Meanwhile Radetzky's performance during the battle had won more praise. He was awarded the Knight's Cross of the Alexander Nevsky Order by Alexander, the Red Eagle, first class, by Frederick William, and the Great Cross of the Bavarian Max Joseph Order. The Austrian report lauded 'renewed proof of his correct grasp of perspective and military genius'.[92]

Between the battles of Brienne and La Rothière a curious incident took place, which demonstrated that the real tension in the allied camp was between the Prussian military leadership and their king rather than between them and the allied supreme command (Schwarzenberg and Radetzky) as Prussian historiography has suggested. Gneisenau reported to Hardenberg that Frederick William had considered Brienne a defeat and had sneered to Blücher:[93] 'So, the French Emperor made you a very unpleasant visit.' Gneisenau added: 'The Field Marshal did not rightly know what to say, since the "visitor" had been repulsed and he had lost eight cannon.'

At a war council after both battles, held at Brienne, it was agreed that Schwarzenberg and the Main Army (100,000 men) should proceed along the Seine, with Blücher and the Silesian Army proceeding along the Marne. It was 'laid down as a principle not to let Napoleon out of sight. If he attacked one army, the other should mount a quick operation against Paris and each should avoid an encounter with a larger army.'[94] Radetzky, however, seemed not to worry too much about Napoleon, writing that since the army was divided, 'the enemy was forced to send troops against both our armies, as a result of which, each of us was strong enough to give battle; should he break through in the middle he would lose his communications with Paris'.[95] Since the area between the two armies, roughly two–three days' march, seemed to be of little military use in winter, given its lack of roads and woods, it was to be secured only by nature plus some 4,000 cavalry. Yet it was to be here that Napoleon would use his interior lines to deliver a powerful surprise blow.

Scarcely had the the decision been made to split the two armies when Napoleon drew up plans to attack them separately – the Silesian first, marching with some 40,000 men against Blücher. The Main Army pressed on after some rest, crossing the Seine at Nogent, Bray and Montereau, capturing Sens on 11 February, with light skirmishes taking place all the way to Fontainebleau and Orleans. Platoff's Cossacks even reached Namours on the 16th, while the French withdrew, joining up at Yères. Blücher, for his part, had sent out 25,000 men in pursuit of Marshal Macdonald when Napoleon, now reinforced, unexpectedly attacked his three corps and defeated them one after another at Champaubert, Montmirail and Vauchamps between 10 and 15 February, with an allied loss of 15,000 men. Schwarzenberg could do nothing to help: just as Blücher had not known of Napleon's whereabouts, Schwarzenberg did not know of Blücher's. Allied headquarters, as Radetzky noted 'remained uninformed of the intentions and operations of the Silesian Army'.[96] Indeed, Gneisenau admitted in his 'secret history of the campaign' which he sketched out after its conclusion for Clausewitz in a long letter from Paris, that one of his mistakes had been deliberately severing communication with Schwarzenberg:[97] 'I was asked to abandon communications with the Grand Army. I gave in to this request.' Thus it was the French cannonade that first alerted Schwarzenberg that something was happening. He sent men under Prince Eugen of Württemberg to attack the French troops which had been left behind to observe the Main Army, took the bridges over the Seine at Nogent, Brey and Méry, and pushed on towards Fontainebleau and Paris, but 'bad weather, the lack of food supplies, and uprisings by the local population on all sides, meant that there was no more to be done'.[98] Lack of food supplies now became a very serious problem. In the meantime, to help Blücher, Schwarzenberg sent him the Russian guards and reserves.

Rather than Blücher being blamed for losing sight of Napoleon and failing to keep in touch with Schwarzenberg during this period, German historians have usually accused Schwarzenberg of dithering and moving too slowly, leaving the initiative to the Silesian Army. This accusation is unwarranted, however. Schwarzenberg had very good reasons to move slowly. As Radetzky pointed out, unlike the Silesian Army, the Main Army 'did not have another friendly one securing its left flank'.[99] And although an attack from the South from Marshal Augereau never materialised, Austrian intelligence was giving constant warnings that one would happen. Radetzky wrote of reports that Augerau was building up 'a strong army' to operate on the flank and rear of the Main Army drawing on French and other troops returning from Spain. (Napoleon would meanwhile rely on reinforcements from the Netherlands to attack it from the front.) So seriously was this threat taken at allied headquarters that the sovereigns agreed to form an allied Army of the South under the Prince of Hessen-Homburg with General Csollich as chief of staff and it was given almost half of Schwarzenberg's army to use for operations – Bianchi's division, Trauttenberg's grenadier division, a division of cuirassiers, and Moriz Liechtenstein's two light divisions. Bubna was told at the same time to suspend operations against Lyon and to concentrate on holding Geneva. These movements obviously restricted Schwarzenberg's ability to take the offensive.[100]

Again, Schwarzenberg had the three monarchs travelling with him, along with their entourages, all of whom 'had to be secured and could not be exposed to danger'. Alexander insisted upon moving along the main roads only. The guards and reserves meanwhile were also part of Schwarzenberg's responsibility, and they 'were to be used only in extreme necessity'. Other problems included the fact that food supplies had to be requisitioned and that the local peasants were now violently resisting this process – memories of Napoleon in Russia were reviving. Finally, there was little hope of any reinforcements arriving from Austria or Germany in the near future. If the Main Army was rather stretched out and was moving slowly, by the time Blücher was attacked, therefore, there were very good reasons for that. Moreover, it had been kept in ignorance of Blücher's movements.

Another reason for the delay was the parallel peace negotiations the monarchs and their diplomats were conducting with Napoleon. Schwarzenberg's troops were allowed to rest on 7, 8, and 9 February because in Radetzky's sarcastic phrase,[101] 'one did not wish to place obstacles in the way of progress with useless fighting.' Nessselrode had even entered into direct negotiations with Talleyrand to replace Napoleon with the Bourbons, although Alexander was not committed. Radetzky was convinced nothing would come of it – 'the struggle with Napoleon will be decided by the sword alone' – but the diplomats believed that peace by negotiation was worth a try.[102] True, they now offered only the historic frontiers of 1792 at Chatillon (allied victories demanded that) but Napoleon still hoped to divide them.

Metternich received a conciliatory letter from Coulaincourt agreeing to accept a ceasefire and to surrender some forts if French demands regarding borders were met, along with a request to show it to Francis. The latter, however, saw through this attempt to split him from his allies and politely rejected the move. Alexander and the Prussian generals demanded the occupation of Paris (Napoleon had occupied Berlin, Vienna and Moscow after all) and saw a ceasefire as helping only the French. As negotiations over a ceasefire continued, the whole position changed with Napoleon's victories over Blücher.[103]

Schwarzenberg's immediate thought was to concentrate his army and fight at Trainal. But Crown Prince Eugen of Württemberg, who had been ordered to destroy the bridge at Montereau, had given battle there instead and lost 4,000 men. Pahlen, leading Wittgenstein's advanced guard, was meanwhile defeated by Napoleon (resurgent with 70,000 troops) at Mormant. With the bridges still standing and the enemy approaching, Schwarzenberg decided instead to retreat.

Hearing of the three defeats of the Silesian Army, the allied monarchs had a single reaction: to demand an armistice. They sent Count Paar, Schwarzenberg's adjutant, to Napoleon on 17 February to demand one. Napoleon used the opportunity to send back a personal letter from Marie Louise to her father and one in his own hand to the monarchs demanding a compromise on lines much more indulgent to France than the Chatillon terms. Coulaincourt, however, who in the meantime had been told to accept these terms and save Paris, had his authority withdrawn. Given his victories, Napoleon would now only accept the Frankfurt terms – the natural borders plus concessions from Britain. He also boasted about how big and professional his army was, although the allies simply ignored him. Still, the outlook was not bright. News arrived that in the South, Augerau was attacking both Lyon and the approaches to Switzerland as well as advancing towards Macon, while pushing back the Austrians, who were everywhere being attacked by revolting French peasants. Schwarzenberg and his entourage were also almost captured by Napoleon's forces which were advancing from Nogent.

The Silesian army had meanwhile replenished its losses and arrived at Méry, 55,000 strong. Schwarzenberg wanted it to come across the Seine and join him immediately and give battle. However, the monarchs preferred defensive measures. Blücher sent Colonel Grollman to allied headquarters at Troyes, however, on 22 February, asking for permission to resume his movement towards Paris. Since it was felt that the division of the two armies would force Napoleon to divide his – the principle that had always lain behind Radetzky's thinking – this was agreed on 23 February. More to the point, it was agreed that the Silesian army would be reinforced – in fact almost doubled in size – by detaching Winzingerode's and Bülow's corps from Bernadotte's Northern Army and subordinating them to Blücher. This gave him a good chance of reaching Paris although Gneisenau's letters had been boasting for a month that victory would be easy and that a final battle would be 'neither bloody nor dangerous'.[104] The Silesian Army now again looked forward to destroying Napoleon. As Gneisenau put it:[105] 'I have no doubt that we can dethrone Napoleon ... We alone can put an end to this war.'

On 23 February Prince Alois Liechtenstein, another adjutant of Schwarzenberg's, was sent to Napoleon's headquarters at Chartres with Francis's reply to his letter. He was also asked to demand a temporary ceasefire. Napoleon now asked him if the allies favoured the Bourbons, to which the Prince replied that he did not know. In any case, Napoleon instructed his chief of staff to say that he would agree to a ceasefire and instructed commissioners to negotiate one at Lusigny. Meanwhile, Baron St. Aignan, who was foolish enough to express the opinion that all sacrifices should be made for peace, was insultingly dismissed by the Emperor, being told that he might soon have to make the greatest sacrifice himself. This, according to Radetzky, convinced everyone of Napoleon's true feelings. And indeed, General Flahaut at Lusigny ended ceasefire negotiations by saying that without being guaranteed Belgium as part of the natural frontiers, Napoleon was not prepared to negotiate.[106]

At this point (25 February) it was thought that Blücher should be recalled and that the armies should re-unite, given Napoleon's attitude. However, Blücher was already too far away and replied that instead he intended to cross the Marne on 27 February and march on Paris. Since he would be between Napoleon's army and those of Marshals Marmont and Mortier, Winzingerode and St. Priest and their corps were ordered to join up with him. The aim was that they should use Bernadotte's army at Lüttich as their base, but build up the Silesian Army to a strength of 100,000 men. The corps of the Duke of Weimar could remain in the Netherlands. The Main Army, meanwhile, decided on a strategic retreat to Langres, while the Prince of Hessen-Homburg was to advance on Lyon, supported by six corps which would be sent across the Rhine from the interior to join him. The threat in the South was still taken extremely seriously.

Alexander proposed that, instead of retreating, he would take his guards and join Blücher – indeed Gneisenau had put consistent pressure on him to do so.[107] When he asked Francis's permission, Francis replied:[108] 'While Your Majesty is on the march to Blücher, you will be of no use either there or here and will risk being met en route by the enemy and being destroyed by superior force.' Thus Alexander declared that he would remain with the Main Army. He had again given proof of unfitness for command.

The Tsar had already shown his petulance and lack of diplomatic sense in Troyes at the end of January and the beginning of February, threatening to break off diplomatic negotiations unilaterally at Chatillon and raising for the first time the possibility of taking his troops and heading for Paris by himself. He was also supposed to be behind an attempt to make Bernadotte (of all people) monarch of France. Metternich again slapped him down. 'It has never entered our mind,' he declared,[109] 'to sacrifice a single man to put Bernadotte on the throne of France. Do you think I am mad?' In any case, the Austrians were hardly likely to agree to swap Marie Louise for Madame Bernadotte.

In a special memorandum, Schwarzenberg pointed out the difficulties of any quick march on Paris – poor food supplies, local popular resistance, illness among the troops. The British agreed. So the coalition now 'came within an ace of dissolution'.[110] Metternich had threatened to halt the Austrian army and make a separate peace if Alexander did not see sense. The Tsar countered that he was not particularly in favour of Bernadotte but put forward the strange idea that once in Paris, he would summon an assembly to decide Napoleon's fate and choose a successor. He was simply against the Bourbons. Metternich ridiculed the whole idea – suppose they chose a Jacobin? – while Castlereagh, the British foreign secretary who had joined allied headquarters in mid-January, asked the Tsar incredulously exactly whose armies would support this new ruler in France against Napoleon if need be and for how long? Alexander retorted with bluster, accusing Castlereagh of not properly representing his king or government.[111]

The whole sad story ended, of course, when news arrived that Blücher had been defeated three times by Napoleon. The latter now insisted on the natural frontiers and the Tsar suddenly backed negotiations. Metternich at last got him to agree to Radetzky's and Schwarzenberg's military operations and to the policy that if Napoleon agreed to the 1792 frontiers he could still remain as Emperor, if the French agreed. If not, the allies would enter Paris to put Louis XVIII on the throne. By mid-March, however,

Metternich had almost had his fill of Alexander and his cronies, writing to Stadion:[112]

> You have absolutely no idea what we are made to suffer here at supreme headquarters. I cannot bear it any longer and the Emperor is already ill. They are all mad and belong in the madhouse. We are always being represented as wanting to sell out the Monarchy, as if we had no greater wish than to be defeated and dishonoured, as if Austria revered foreign slavery, in short as if we were idiots. I believe, however, that we alone are sane.

With the decision of 23 February to split the armies and allow Blücher to cross the Marne and meet up with Winzingerode, St. Priest and Bülow, the story by no means came to an end. Radetzky believed that Napoleon had about 100,000 men to use against the Main Army and that Mortier and Marmont had some 25,000–30,000 to use against the Silesian one. He also believed that Augerau had as many as 50,000–60,000 men in Lyon. By his reckoning the allies were by no means guaranteed a quick or certain victory.

The Silesian Army's leaders had a completely different outlook and believed that Napoleon's destruction was within their grasp. Napoleon, of course, had other ideas. He now planned to defeat Blücher before the latter could meet up with Winzingerode, Bülow and St. Priest at Meaux. Coulaincourt had also informed Napoleon that the allies had fixed a 10 March deadline for the negotiations now stalled at Chatillon.

Plans did not transpire as desired for the French. Soissons surrendered to Winzingerode without a fight, depriving Napoleon of men, stores and a key strategic point. Crucially, this also allowed the corps of the Northern Army to link up with Blücher, raising his forces above 100,000. He now expected to defeat Napoleon once and for all.

Napoleon, however, was still looking for a fight. He had left Macdonald and Oudinet to keep watch on Schwarzenberg's army, while he himself on 27 February went in pursuit, in dreadful weather, of Blücher. On 7 March he found him ready to fight at Craonne. Winzingerode, however, by moving his cavalry too slowly, frustrated Blücher's battle-plan to the disgust of the Silesian Army's Prussian leadership and although the army was able to withdraw without being defeated, the fact that Napoleon had also escaped defeat was a huge disappointment. 'Had Winzingerode done his duty,' wrote Gneisenau,[113] 'the fate of France would have been decided.' Blücher, however, retreated to Laon to a strong, prepared position, where Napoleon again attacked him on 9 March. The allies counter-attacked Marmont in Athis and the French lost 2,500 prisoners, 41 cannons and 150 powder wagons. On 13 March, Napoleon attacked again.

This time the Silesian leadership suffered some sort of collective breakdown. Blücher's nerves gave way and he had to retire to bed. He also acquired an eye infection which caused inflammation and sensitivity to light. Müffling had also been unwell, again probably from nervous pressure, and was in and out of bed during the battle. His critics at headquarters complained that his troop dispositions were all wrong since he was obviously in a state of nervous fever. In any case it was Gneisenau who replaced Blücher, and having been totally misled as to the size of Napoleon's army after interrogating a French prisoner, he lost his nerve and made the decision not to pursue the retreating French. He told an astonished Müffling:[114] 'The disposition you have planned is too bold and might bring us to destruction. All the four corps who have been sent out must be recalled immediately.' General Sacken complained:[115] 'Why have they altered the disposition which would have enabled us to give Napoleon his death blow?' General Yorck sent in his resignation and thanks to Gneisenau, Napoleon escaped the destruction that Gneisenau himself had boasted had been in store for him.The quarrel was hushed up to save the reputation of the Silesian army, which was out of action for about a week, although in his letters, Blücher still wrote of having achieved 'a decisive victory'.[116] The allies, however, were less than pleased. Napoleon went on to Rheims to defeat the former French émigré, General St. Priest, who was killed, the Emperor boasted, by exactly the same cannon which had killed that other traitor, Moreau, at Dresden.[117]

Hearing of Napoleon's attacks, the Main Army had also resumed the offensive. Having sent so many of its troops to the South, it only had about 45,000 men but still defeated Oudinot on 27 February at Bar-sur-Aube (where the enemy suffered about 2,000 casualties, the allies about 1,500) and then Macdonald at La Fère-Champenoise. Schwarzenberg himself was lightly wounded in this battle and there was some fear he would succumb to fever, but he was back on horseback within days. The allied attack then continued until Troyes. When news of Laon arrived, Schwarzenberg ordered his troops to cross the Seine and advance further. When news followed that Napoleon was now advancing against the Main Army, the commander-in-chief on 18 March retreated to a strong position at Arcis-sur-Aube, first ordering Francis, Metternich and all diplomats then at headquarters to travel to Dijon to ensure their safety. The decisive encounter with Napoleon would now be fought by the Main Army, not the Silesian one after all.

Napoleon believed that Schwarzenberg was still retreating and was astonished to find, after he had begun the attack, that he was being opposed by Bavarians, followed by the Austrians, and closely followed by the Russian reserves. He surely saw the significance of what was happening and fought in the middle of battle almost certainly seeking to be killed (as several of his household were). And, indeed, it almost happened. General Girardin deflected a fatal lance charge away from him. His horse fell under him. Napoleon then resorted to using his pistols. He later remembered:[118] 'I did all I could to meet with a glorious end. I continually exposed myself, bullets rained all around me, my clothes were full of them, yet not one touched me. I was condemned to live.' At the end of the day he and Ney left the battlefield with only 12,000 men.

Napoleon quickly regained his courage and still demonstrated a desire to pursue what he still took to be a retreating army. Only after a couple of days did he retreat behind the Aube. His only hope now was to attack the allies from the rear, get reinforcements from the eastern forts and start a war of popular resistance on the Rhine. But this depended on the population being armed and willing to support him and on the allies turning away from Paris to pursue him. In any case he ordered Marshals Marmont and Mortier to follow him in execution of this plan. The allies had in fact decided to disregard Napoleon and march on Paris, a strategy which was reconfirmed when Blücher's Russian scouts intercepted correspondence detailing the concern of the French Minister of Police that he could no longer hold Paris if the battlefield drew nearer. More important were letters outlining Napoleon's new plans. One of these, to his wife, Marie Louise, was particularly revealing:[119] 'I have decided to march on the Marne and their communications and to push them away from Paris.' This was sent to allied headquarters, where 'Prince Schwarzenberg, Radetzky and Diebitsch discussed the situation. Radetzky explained the grounds on which each operation against the capital should continue...'[120] The decision was taken therefore to head straight for Paris, although, in order to deceive Napoleon into thinking his plan was working, Winzingerode was given 8,000 men and told to shadow him and to pretend that he was the advanced guard of a large allied army.

On 19 March Schwarzenberg had been joined by Blücher. Some critics wondered why the Prussian should not have been offered more help before the battle of Laon, although this is extremely surprising given the strength of the Silesian Army after it joined up with Winzingerode and Bülow. Lord Burghersh in his account of the campaign refers to the controversy, but then publishes a memorandum from Schwarzenberg's headquarters, obviously written by Radetzky, which sets out Schwarzenberg's defence, namely that the Radetzky Plan was still at work. This should have been obvious, given Napoleon's endless dashes between the two allied armies and their occasional strategic retreats. But the memorandum of 7 March spells this out:[121] 'The two armies separated, so that while one army retired, the other could operate on the enemy's rear and upon his communications. Success has justified this principle.' Blücher would not give battle until strong enough to do so, while the Main Army having beaten the inferior numbers opposed to it, re-occupied its former positions. News of the Silesian Army's situation would soon arrive. If it won its battles, the Main Army would advance along the left bank of the Seine; if it had been defeated, 'the great army would then so far impose upon Buonaparte as to prevent his following up his victory. He would be forced to weary his troops with marches and countermarches and Marshal Blücher would thus be enabled to resume offensive movements against the forces of the enemy, which would be left to act against him.' The memorandum stated: 'Such were the only principles on which the allies ought to act; it would be easy to show the fallacy of any others.' It did, however, consider one other possibility. The Main Army might have marched to a point between the Aube and Marne on the enemy's flank. However, it could not have arrived there in time to save Blücher. If he had already been defeated, then the Main Army would have had to risk everything on a general battle, at a time when it would have lost its numerical superiority by having been forced to leave troops behind to defend its base on the Seine. If it had lost, the allies would have been both isolated and divided and forced to fight their way back to the Rhine through a line of imperfectly blockaded forts. If it had won, it would still have had to re-cross the Seine to operate against Paris 'the only true object of all its movements'. Altogether the memorandum was a comprehensive defence.

More good news poured into allied headquarters after the victory at Arcis-sur-Aube. The Prince of Hessen-Homburg and Bianchi captured Lyon, the second town of France. Marshal Maison was driven out of Belgium and Wellington beat Soult at Orthez. Meanwhile the Bourbon flag was flying over Bordeaux and in Paris Talleyrand was plotting the fall of Napoleon. However, Paris had still to be captured and before it fell, the Radetzky Plan paid one last dividend. Marshals Mortier and Marmont, who had been left behind to look after Blücher after Laon, but who were now on their way to join Napoleon, found themselves facing the approaching allied army at Fère-Champenoise on 25 March.[122] Generals Pachtod and Amey were defeated attempting to aid them but in the main battle, the French fought like lions. The allied sovereigns who watched the fighting looked on in amazement as the French squares held. When General Rapatel, formerly Moreau's adjutant, who was standing next to Alexander, called on them to surrender, he was killed by a bullet. His brother was fighting as an artillery captain in one of the same squares, along with many troops from La Vendée. After five allied assaults and all-night fighting, a sixth assault was launched on 26 March, proceeded by a three-hour cannonade from three sides. Allied troops then went into action with bayonets and sabres and the battle ended in a mighty bloodbath. The cavalry finished things off. Most of the French generals were killed, wounded or taken prisoner. All allied monarchs participated in the battle, along with Radetzky and Schwarzenberg. Amazingly Marmont and Mortier escaped with some of their troops and were pursued by allied troops, before, like all other French soldiers, they started to make their way again to Paris, where by 29 March the allies were formed into a long line outside the capital.

No enemy had appeared before its gates since 1419. For the first time in almost 400 years orders were given for battle on the morning of 30 March. During the fighting Schwarzenberg sent an emissary to try to take the city with the message that his quarrel was only with Napoleon, but, although the defences were weak and Joseph Bonaparte had given the marshals permission to surrender, fighting resumed led by Marmont. By 3pm his clothes were full of bullets and officers lay dead all around him. He then negotiated a ceasefire which was respected by Mortier who was still fighting Blücher. Schwarzenberg, meantime, had refused a final request to negotiate with Napoleon. Montmartre was still bombarded but once the armistice was ratified, and with Francis and Metternich still at Dijon, Alexander and Frederick William could embrace saying:[123] 'The cause of humanity has won.' At noon on 31 March 1814 the sovereigns with their suites and all the generals, including Schwarzenberg and Radetzky, entered Paris. Their procession lasted till 5pm. The campaign was over.

Napoleon had dominated Europe militarily from 1797. Until 1813 he had been defeated only once (by the Austrians at Aspern in 1809) but after holding Europe in thrall for a decade and a half, he had been dethroned after a campaign that lasted only seven and a half months. The brains behind that campaign had been Radetzky's.

In honour of this, the Emperor bestowed on Radetzky the Great Cross of the Leopold Order. Prince Schwarzenberg as supreme commander was awarded the Great Cross of the more prestigious Maria Theresa Order. Francis I, who half apologised to Radetzky for this, consoled him with the thought that he expected him to acquire it later.[124] And so, of course, he would.

It had certainly taken a great deal of effort on the part of both Schwarzenberg and Radetzky to push home their objectives. Gneisenau wrote to Schwarzenberg in June 1814:[125]

> What Your Excellency achieved in the most violent of all wars in history, given the unmentionable, innumerable difficulties you had to struggle with, how very much Your Excellency through your most kind and gentle conduct, mollified, unified and disarmed jealousy, resentment, suspicion, unruly ambition, proud ignorance, and audacious arrogance and how you led the contesting elements towards a common goal, posterity will speak of with admiration and I will not be the last among contemporaries to take part in this deserved homage to Your Excellency.

The reputation of the Austrian commanders was soon effaced however. Alexander I managed to make one final mistake, when, acting in Paris as 'the Agamemnon of the new Illiad',[126] he agreed to allow Napoleon to become sovereign of Elba. Metternich, still in Dijon, would have preferred to send the dethroned French Emperor somewhere nearer the South Pole (St. Helena was eventually deemed far enough away). Yet, thanks to Alexander, he was placed on an island off the coast of France, to which he returned in 1815 to be finally defeated. Immediately, all the achievements of 1813–14 were overshadowed by the quick triumph of Wellington and Blücher at Waterloo. Austria, moreover, had never made much of a fuss over its armies or military leaders, hence, despite their brilliant war record, they returned home to relative indifference. Even at the Congress of Vienna, the pamphleteers were praising the exploits of the British, Russians and the Prussians.

With regard to Radetzky himself, the war had physically shattered him. He wrote:[127] 'When in the campaign of 1813 I arrived at Basel my health was so destroyed that I could scarcely supervise the exacting work any longer.' From December 1813 to March 1814 he scarcely ever had time even to undress and several doctors advised him to stay behind. The Emperor's physician, Dr. Stifft, recommended a daily lunchtime drink of boiled Bordeaux, which Alexander I demanded be delivered to him each day by a Cossack wherever Radetzky was to be found and under whatever conditions, even on the battlefield. When he stayed at St. Cloud in August 1815 in the stifling heat, his rooms had to be heated to keep him warm. It took him three full years to recover from the war.

Radetzky also returned home to family problems. His wife was Countess Franziska (Fanny) Romana Strassoldo-Graffemberg, who had been only 17 years of age when Radetzky, then a major of 21, married her in the Niklaus Church at Strassoldo, the home of her parents, on 22 April 1798.

Before his marriage all the military personnel records on Radetzky had nothing but praise for him. He was a good companion, no gambler, drinker or trouble-maker and was articulate, good with superiors, subordinates and civilians, a good writer and possessed of outstanding talents in all professional skills required by the army. He was industrious, enthusiastic and efficient – in short an excellent candidate for promotion and a happy, unworried young man.[128]

With his marriage things changed, although not seriously until after 1816. Radetzky had always had doubts about marrying but Fanny had begged him to marry her and her mother had also put on pressure. As Radetzky later explained in a letter to his daughter Fritzi:[129] 'She was inexperienced and I honourable. Your mother wanted our union, which I always opposed on account of my limited income, since I had a fortune of only 2,000 florins of my own, was a major and commander of the Pioneers...' On the other hand, with his fine reputation, Radetzky reckoned on a swift promotion and a secure income of 5,000 florins and so 'got married so that people would not accuse me of destroying your mother's peace of mind'.[130]

When war broke out again, Fanny was taken by her mother to her father's house in Görz, but some months later joined Radetzky in Turin and spent the winter with him there. Meanwhile, he had been promoted Colonel and Adjutant General, possessed the complete confidence of the commanding general in Italy and had saved 1,000 ducats. When war separated them again, Fanny went to Verona, where his salary was paid in. This time the war ended badly, and Radetzky was transferred to Germany, although he had saved another 2,500 ducats which he left with his wife in Verona. After 1805, now a general, Radetzky took his wife and five children to Görz, leaving her to look after household affairs and the family's money, arranging for her to have two-thirds of his salary (4,000 florins) while he survived on 2,000.

It proved a tragic mistake. The young Countess Radetzky had no mind for money, had a large family to look after, and relied on servants who deceived and stole from her. She fell very heavily into debt and told nothing of her troubles to her husband, who, as Chief of the General Staff, was on a salary of 16,000 florins a year. It was only in 1816 after Radetzky returned home ill from the wars that he first discovered the catastrophic extent of his wife's financial mismanagement. In his own words to Fritzi: 'The creditors complained and I was left only with the choice of quietly assuming my wife's debts as my own or seeing her locked up in a debtors' prison. I chose the former.' The results, according to Radetzky, were 'the loss of all my possessions and insults of all kinds, and the setting back of my career by seventeen years'.[131] Creditors at first took one third of his salary and then one fifth, but in time his problem was solved. Although Radetzky thought that he was held unsuitable for major promotions, he was given the top job in Italy in 1830 when revolution was feared there and Francis I took over his debts. The *Hofkriegsrat* even gave him an addition to his salary to enable him to entertain in the fashion expected of him as commanding general in Italy.[132]

Whatever misery he felt he had been caused by his wife, there is no evidence that he blamed anyone but himself:[133] 'It was my own lot and punishment that I, from the goodness of my heart, was weak enough to enter a union which my reason, on account of my insufficient fortune had disapproved of.' He had always saved money, but his wife had never known how to. He also blamed himself for being absent so long in the field that he had not been able to take full control of his sons' upbringing. His relations with his wife, however, appear to have remained tender and loving and they continued to have children. Indeed, he fathered eight children by his wife – five sons and three daughters – and survived all but two of them.

All his sons joined the army. Two died in 1828 in their late twenties and two died in 1847, one aged 30, one aged 43. One daughter died in 1825 aged 19, another in 1827, aged 24. It was not the case, therefore, as one writer has it, that 'as four of the sons died early their parents were spared the expense of making provision for them'.[134]

If, with the end of the Napoleonic Wars, therefore, Radetzky's professional life became more relaxed and mundane, his personal life, on the other hand, became more strained. The responsibilities of maintaining a family proved unexpectedly difficult.

# 3

# EDUCATOR OF ARMIES

Radetzky was to become famous not merely on account of his record during the Napoleonic Wars and his achievements in 1848–9, but also because as chief of staff of the Habsburg army and later, as commander in Italy, he endeavoured to seriously reform the Habsburg army and had manifold ideas about every aspect of military life. This brought him into regular conflict with the authorities in Vienna, who, like Francis I himself, resented Radetzky's continuous stream of plans and proposals and who would have liked to have pensioned him off much earlier than proved possible. Fortunately, the revolutions of 1830 forced the Emperor to send Radetzky to Italy to prepare the army for war there; and since war did not come until 1848, Radetzky secured a new base from which to experiment and innovate within the army.

His immediate predecessor as chief reformer in the army had been the Archduke Charles,[1] who had defeated Napoleon at Aspern in 1809 but whose career came to an end after Wagram that same year. In 1801 he had been appointed Field Marshal and head of the *Hofkriegsrat* by his brother, Francis I, and empowered to introduce military reforms. He was then made War Minister with responsibility for both army and navy, but tended to stray beyond his ministerial territory and clashed with Francis who was jealous of his intellect and popularity – as demonstrated by his successful 1796 campaign, after which Charles had become known as the 'Saviour of Germany' and the Diet of the Holy Roman Empire had proposed building a statue of him.

His actual reforms were rather cautious, if sensible. For a start, he reduced the term of enlistment in the army from life to between ten and 14 years, 'partly to rejuvenate the ranks and partly to increase the popularity of military service'.[2] In 1801 he also established the General (Quartermaster's) Staff on a permanent basis; previously it had only become active in wartime. However, it remained too small in size to be effective, something that would only come to pass under Radetzky, when he was Schwarzenberg's chief of staff. After the humiliations of Ulm and Austerlitz in 1805 Charles had been appointed Generalissimus, in charge of all armies in wartime and the military establishment while peace prevailed. Once again he brought in reforms, but they were never completely carried through. Besides, his thinking was basically conservative. He saw the army as a long-service institution dominated by the nobility, whose main task was to preserve the dynasty. He had severe doubts about establishing a *Landwehr*, not merely on account of doubts about the effectiveness of such an institution, but over the thought of arming the populace. He also believed that raising large numbers of (albeit mostly untrained) men in this way would lull the Austrians into a false sense of security. Still, on account of the French threat and the state's lack of money, he reluctantly agreed to raise one in 1808. Hungary refused to participate in the experiment, which for political reasons also omitted Galicia, but the Austrian and Bohemian lands were supposed to raise 180,000 men in 170 battalions. Only 70 units were actually mustered in 1809 and according to Gunther Rothenberg:[3] 'During the war they failed as a home defence, but when their best units were brigaded with the regulars or used as individual fillers for the line, they did good service.'

Charles himself claimed that along with the introduction of the *Landwehr* he had made two other important innovations before 1809 – the formation of army corps and the reorganisation of the artillery, although he added 'that there was insufficient time for these innovations to become firmly established and they had to be employed before they had been tested'.[4] In fact, the practice of dividing armies into corps, modelled on the French, was introduced as late as February 1809, not long before war broke out. Each corps had about 30,000 men (estimates vary) and 64–84 guns. Each was divided into three divisions, one of which was designated as the advanced guard. The others comprised two or three line brigades each. There was no divisional cavalry but each division had a six-pounder support battery. The two reserve corps were regarded as elites composed of grenadier battalions and heavy cavalry. Each corps had its own staff. However, to make the system work properly corps commanders were needed who were energetic and not afraid to use their initiative as well as properly trained staff officers. Both were lacking. Generals had never previously had the opportunity to practise large-scale manoeuvres, while staff officers were under-educated, despite Charles's initiative in founding the *Österreichisch-militärische Zeitschrift* in an attempt to boost their knowledge. They remained slow and inefficient, although they could draw decent maps.

The third innovation which Charles had pointed to was his reorganisation of the artillery. Austrian guns had a very good reputation and Napoleon used any which he captured. The new artillery aimed to use 742 pieces in 108 batteries to provide mass fire, something which in practice happened less often than it should have done. Corps commanders did not appreciate the use of artillery, while individual artillery officers still thought in terms of using individual pieces. Still, brigades now received eight-gun batteries (the regimental three-pounders were withdrawn); the few six-pounders were usually given to the corps artillery reserve and combined with seven-pound howitzers as support batteries: while others were combined with rare 12-pound batteries to form position batteries or sent to the army artillery reserve. Position and support batteries were usually commanded by the corps artillery commander and a new body of support crews, the *Artillerie-Handlager* corps, was established to manage them. Artillery transports were brought under military control and cadres assigned to the batteries. If never as good as the French, the Austrian artillery still managed on occasion to deliver mass fire power when needed. This reform was perhaps one of Charles's most effective.

The other branches of the army, the cavalry and infantry, Charles simply failed to reform. The Austrian cavalry was composed of 35 regiments. Heavy cavalry comprised dragoons and cuirassiers; the rest (chevaux legers, hussars and uhlans) were regarded as light cavalry. Heavy cavalry regiments had six squadrons of 135 men, light cavalry eight squadrons of 150 men. All carried cut-and-thrust weapons, but the heavy cavalry also had straight and heavy swords, while the hussars and uhlans carried curved sabres, and the uhlans, lances. Each trooper also carried two pistols and each squadron carried at least eight carbines and eight short rifles. During the Turkish wars, cavalrymen were expected to shoot from the saddle; against the French they were expected to use cold steel. The cavalry suffered from a number of problems which Charles failed to solve. For a start there was a severe shortage of horses making the cavalry's effective strength only 22,000 troops rather than the 36,000 which existed on paper. Due to the practice of the corps commanders perpetually seeking cavalry support, it came to be used more as a support arm, fighting in individual squadrons or in two-squadron divisions, rather than as a separate strike force. And even when it was used as such it tended to be used in a line only two-deep, which was too thin to take on its French counterpart organised in compact columns. It was further weakened when its horse artillery, only partly mounted and not trained to support charges, were increasingly used as field artillery in 1809. Overall there was little sign of improvement.

Again, with regard to the infantry, nothing much was done – certainly nothing to simplify its extremely complex drill. There were 46 'German' and 15 'Hungarian' regiments, the former conscripted in the hereditary provinces (including the Slav ones), the latter volunteers raised by the Hungarian diet (and often not Hungarians). The infantry regiments raised outside Hungary (which was an incessant problem for Habsburg military planners) were organised into three battalions and two grenadier companies, which on campaign were usually detached and formed into separate elite battalions and brigades. Companies in the German regiments numbered 220 men, although they rarely reached full strength. The light infantry comprised 17 *Grenzer* (military border) regiments, each formed of three battalions of six companies, while in 1808 nine *Jäger* (sharp-shooter) battalions of six companies were raised. Most infantrymen carried a 1798 model 17.5 calibre musket, the Jäger troops being equipped either with carbines or short rifles. Ammunition for muskets was 60 cartridges; those with rifles got 100 rounds.

New infantry regulations were issued in 1807. These brought some changes but retained the battalion as the main combat unit as well as the three-deep line as the standard formation, with columns used only for attacks and assaults on fortifications. The main innovation was the 'mass', a formation one company wide and six companies deep. This replaced the square and allowed the infantry to manoeuvre, albeit slowly, in closed or open order. In closed order with soldiers touching the packs of those in front, it could withstand cavalry charges, although it was vulnerable to artillery fire. It could also manoeuvre on flat ground more readily than the hollow square and proved effective in 1809 at both Aspern and Wagram. However, in skirmishing or in broken terrain, the infantry proved less effective. Radetzky, indeed, believed that it was fairly useless against French *tirailleurs*.[5]

Charles did, however, try to make life more humane for the ordinary soldier and thus boost morale and make military life more attractive. Capital punishment was abolished in 1809, although he reintroduced it during the 1809 campaign. He condemned brutality as unworthy of a soldier and appealed instead to virtue rather than discipline: 'Love of monarch and an honest life ... obedience, loyalty, determination: these are the soldierly virtues.'[6] His manual which he published in 1806 entitled *The Fundamentals of the Higher Art of War for the Generals of the Austrian Army*[7] opened with the statement that 'war is the greatest calamity that can befall a state', while in 1809 the peace-loving commander wrote to Napoleon himself:[8] 'I feel flattered, Sire, to fight the greatest captain of the century. I would be more fortunate if destiny had chosen me to obtain for my country the benefit of a durable peace.'

It was Charles's manual for his generals of 1806 that marked him out as a conservative thinker, however, rather than a true innovator. It stuck to the assertion that there were fixed mathematical rules, that armies should be preserved intact and that they should never endanger their lines of communications. As in Maria Theresa's *Generalsreglement* of 1769 generals were seen to have their prescribed place in battle and were to carry out prescribed orders. The German military theorist and historian, Lieutenant General von Caemmerer in his book *The Development of Strategical Science During the 19ᵗʰ Century*[9] dissected Charles's writings in his fourth chapter and was appalled at the caution and contradictions he found in them. Such circumspection and and apparent vacillation can be seen thus:[10] 'If in the strategic plan the safety of the base and lines of communication have been considered to their fullest extent, and if the general is thoroughly satisfied on that point, he must, when on the offensive advance with the utmost boldness, but on the defensive hold obstinately every position he occupies. *Both, however, will be impossible and the state will suffer most pernicious consequences if the first principle has been neglected*' (author's italics). And:[11] 'Only when the last object, which would decide the fate of the state, is on the point of falling into the hands of the enemy, only as a last resort may the general risk a battle even with inferior forces; then he may depart from every rule, and disregarding everything else, attack only that point where victory is most easily gained. *It is the battle of a desperate man, the loss of which he does not survive*' (author's italics).

Such extreme caution, such emphasis on the defensive, was never part of Radetzky's art of war. Nor was his thinking generally conservative. Still, it is the Archduke Charles who has been remembered as Austria's finest general. Not only was he offered the imperial crown by Napoleon in 1805 on the day the Peace of Pressburg was signed, but he would be offered those of Poland and Belgium in 1830. Indeed, Wellington (whose judgements on contemporaries, it has to be said, do not generally pass muster), said of him:[12] 'We are none of us worthy to fasten the latchets of his shoes, if I am to judge from his book and his plans of campaign.' Radetzky was a completely different military man. He always favoured the offensive, was always prepared to take risks, and, most importantly, always won his campaigns.

That is not to say that there were not similarities between his position and that of the Archduke. Francis and his cronies at the *Hofkriegsrat* were no happier to hear of his schemes than Charles's. Again, the army after 1815 was neglected. Radetzky's 1809 criticisms always remained valid and peace meant that the army became the Cinderella service of the Habsburg state.

By October 1815, Radetzky had become so troubled by his 'evil, sad existence' that he wanted to leave the general staff and take command of an army division (Langenau's 'perfidious vanity' after his return to active service at headquarters had become 'unbearable').[13] On 2 November 1816 Radetzky would reach 50; he had already been as highly decorated as seemed possible; and with the onset of a peace that everyone hoped would be eternal, he expected that his war record would soon be forgotten. He also had financial worries, he was physically exhausted by the war, but his 1815 request was not granted for a year and he could not leave Vienna until the summer of 1816, when he took up the command of a cavalry division in Ödenburg in Hungary. He had 'the best memories' of the town from his previous spell of duty there. After two and a half years in the town he became *Adlatus* to the commanding general in Hungary, the Archduke Ferdinand d'Este, who wrote to him that he was particularly pleased to have him by his side, ready to take over during his long absences. However, 'on account of various causes' (including presumably his forced accommodation to his financial situation after learning of his wife's chronic indebtedness) Radetzky found his decade or so there 'a thoroughly unpleasant period, the mere mention of which even at a much later time, produced a distinct ill humour in the old man'.[14]

After 20 years as an FML (*Feldmarschalleutnant,* a rank he was given for his services during the battle of Wels-Ebelsberg in 1809) he was eventually promoted GdK (*General der Kavallerie*) in 1829 and in November of that year was made fortress commander of Olmütz in Moravia. He assumed this meant the end of his career and so, too, did his friends. One military expert has suggested, however, that the real motive in sending him there was not to see his time out, but to allow him the chance to pay off his debts, since the post benefited from extra income derived from the estates on the fort's glacis.[15] His appointment, therefore, had been an act of compassion. But certainly Radetzky himself did not see things that way and he may well have been right.

Matters took a sudden change with the outbreak of the revolutions of 1830 and the threat of renewed war between Austria and France. It was the ailing commanding general in Italy, Count Frimont, who now suggested to Francis that Radetzky was the man to be sent to Lombardy-Venetia to sort things out, although perhaps Frimont meant as his deputy.[16] Certainly the tale of his appointment, given its significance, deserves retelling. According to Helfert,[17] Francis summoned Radetzky to court in February 1831 and requested he do him the favour of commanding the army in Italy. Radetzky replied: 'I am no longer young and have debts', to which the Emperor responded with a smile: 'I will assume your debts and as for your age, that will be no problem either.' The following day, Radetzky was sent to be briefed by Metternich after which he was asked by Francis if he now knew everything. He replied:[18] 'The Prince spoke for three hours and I know nothing.' Francis then walked up and down with him, filling in the gaps. When Radetzky asked him why he had not declared war on France in 1830, the emperor replied that his troops had performed so badly the previous years in exercises before the Prussians that the latter had refused to back him: 'Isolated I could not undertake war. Thus I am commissioning you to wake up the army in Italy and prepare it for war.' In his own words, 'This was enough to enthuse Radetzky for the job.'

However, things did not immediately go smoothly. He was at first named merely as *Adlatus* to Frimont, who Radetzky found 'in declining health and unfit for [his] job' when he arrived in Milan. He then had some unpleasant months to endure when it appeared that he was expected to carry out Frimont's rather than his own ideas. When Frimont fell ill and left for Vienna in November 1831, he had to hand over control to Radetzky in any case, although astonishingly, given Francis's original request, General Ignaz Freiherr von Lederer, rather than Radetzky, was appointed as his official successor. However, according to Radetzky, von Lederer, of his own accord, sought an audience with the Emperor and on 23 December 1831, Radetzky was officially appointed commanding general of Austria's army in Italy after all.[19]

It was an historic day – and yet not everyone was pleased. Radetzky's reputation for energetic inventiveness predictably upset the bureaucrats. Baron Kübeck, head of the Court Accounts Office, for example, wrote in his diary[20] in February 1832 that the Archduke Charles had been confidentially consulted over the choice of Radetzky as commanding general in Italy, recommending him only because he presupposed that Baron Frimont would retain the supreme command – otherwise he would have chosen Bianchi. Now, however, Radetzky would be left unsupervised and full of new conceptions, with Hess as his chief of staff, a man who knew just how to give shape to them. His final judgement was: '... through these two, the folly is complete.'

Kübeck, in fact, showed great perception about the partnership that would develop between Radetzky and Hess. Heinrich Hess came from a patrician Viennese family and was 22 years younger than Radetzky. He had entered the imperial army in 1805 after a very thorough education at home, and had worked in the general staff from 1809 to 1815 under Radetzky himself. He had distinguished himself during the War of Liberation, particularly at Leipzig, and in 1815 had been promoted major. He made colonel after service with the troops, the general staff and in several special posts, in 1829. He was a richly talented officer who had educated himself well beyond the needs of the army. 'Reliable, not to say a man of exemplary tact, diligent, tireless, lively, brave, devoted to Radetzky, he incorporated the ideal of a general staff chief.'[21] If sensitive and cerebral, he was shielded by Radetzky from the rougher elements in his camp and the two men hit it off entirely:[22] 'They had discovered that they mutually reinforced each other and their contemporaries seem to have recognised this model relationship between commander and chief of staff.'

Yet in 1834, Hess was promoted major general and transferred to Moravia to head an army brigade there. Radetzky never established the same type of rapport with his three subsequent staff chiefs (and in 1848 secretly and successfully requested Hess's return). There were also other blows. On taking up his command in Italy, Radetzky led an army of 104,000 men and 5,000 horses, divided into two mobile army corps with altogether 52 battalions, 30 squadrons, 12 batteries and several fortress garrisons. In 1836 it was cut back to 62,000 men at which level it remained almost until 1848. Radetzky himself believed that at least 120,000 men were needed to win a war in Italy although 150,000 would be a better estimate. Even that figure was predicated on Piedmont remaining a faithful ally. His promotion to Field Marshal in 1836 and the award in 1838 of the Order of the Iron Cross first class after the coronation of the Emperor Ferdinand I as king in Milan, was little compensation. His army was now being halved, and he was now regarded in Vienna as 'a prophet of doom with hallucinations' whose demands were 'hobby horses and military frivolities for the most part', while he himself was 'an ageing grumbler'.[23]

Nevertheless, throughout his career Radetzky managed, whatever the circumstances, to make his mark on the army. As chief of the general staff after 1809 and even beforehand, he had managed to force through small but necessary reforms.

As has been seen, his work with the Pioneers had turned a neglected army institution into an elite corps. He also ensured that horse training was adequately carried out, recognising that horses, whether under the saddle, in front of guns, or pulling batteries, were vital to military success. He himself would spend no less than 75 years of his life in the saddle and would be one of the last great commanders to supervise battles from horseback In 1806–9 as cavalry brigadier and whenever afterwards he was a cavalry commander – particularly in Hungary – he would experiment with the use of cavalry for the best results for the army. One particular opportunity for initiatives came, however, when the *Hofkreigsrat* on 19 March 1806 ordered him to take charge not only of the Veterinary Institute but also other branches of the cavalry to reform their regulations and supervision.[24]

Austria's Veterinary Institute, on which many more would be modelled around the world, had been founded in 1767 as a school for treating and operating on horses but under Radetzky's supervision was much extended and reformed, with new, better teaching staff and courses. The period of study there was two years and the Institute was attended each year by 30–40 students who studied not merely anatomy but veterinary science and blacksmithery. After the death of its director in 1808 Radetzky brought in new personnel and made sure teaching was not interrupted. He also introduced new regulations and had a book published 'on the external structure of a horse' with copper drawings based on works by the painter Hess to demonstrate what healthy horses should look like. Works on horseshoes and the ages of horses were also planned. Radetzky thought such books would be better than many lectures. However, his work was interrupted by war, although in 1816 he became a member of the board of the stud-farm at Mezőhegyes, a position that allowed him to foster his interest in everything to do with horses, horse-training and riding.

He also established the Military Riding School (*Equitationsinstitut*) at Wiener Neustadt, set up to nurture the art of riding and to teach artillery and infantry officers how to ride. His plan of 1807 argued that the School would help consolidate the unity of the army and once the building was erected in 1808 teaching began for 34 pupils. As Brigadier of the School in 1810 Radetzky successfully justified the extension of teaching there to the higher arts of riding, dressage, maintenance, anatomy, shoeing, feeding and curing illnesses. A permanent staff was also provided since 'nothing is more damaging to a successful institute than changes in teachers'. Clearly there were many echoes of his work at the Veterinary Institute. Soon they both provided a model for institutes around the world.

Radetzky's work now brought to his attention the area of military transportation. An 1807 *Report on the Transportation Corps* discovered considerable 'sloppiness' and 'moral failings' in this, an area 'on which not rarely the most essential operations rely'. Radetzky argued that a central focal point had to be created and the men who made up the corps better trained. He also insisted that immediate help was required, since the 6,647 transport vehicles overwhelmed the corps commander each year with 8,000 treasury bills. Hence Radetzky drew up his *Instructions for the Transportation- and Horse-Breeding-Corps* as the 'nursery for the training of transportation' and was praised by the authorities for formulating a plan which did not impose any further strain on financial resources. As a result, all those physically or mentally incapable of further training were removed from the corps and all artillery men at the Riding School were assigned to it. Since transportation was seen as vital to the total mobility of the army, Radetzky in 1810 warned against any cuts in expenditure on it, 'since the state would not only be spared the cost of hiring transport but would itself make a considerable profit and would be able at the start of any war to provide the artillery with excellent horses and lads'.

Radetzky would never lose his interest in horses or the cavalry. From Buda in 1829, for example, in a long memorandum *On the Value of the Austrian Cavalry and Some Means to Raise It*,[25] he argued that given Austria's central position in Europe and the role of the army in its defence, it could not lag behind other states, as was unfortunately happening, in its military arrangements. Many issues were involved but in this memorandum he limited himself to the 'greatly diminished value of our cavalry'. For a start, he argued, there was too much dependence on importing horses from abroad instead of breeding them inside the Empire. This meant that Austria was dependent on horse-traders who had no interest in the quality of the animals and would use any means to disguise poor quality ones. They were also often delivered at the wrong time of year. He demanded therefore that horses should only be bought from estates rearing them at home. Hungary had 161 and Transylvania 125 private stud farms with 10,942 breeding mares between them. If the army used them then soon the industry could be expanded to the stage where it would always have a surplus of young healthy horses available. The light cavalry would then always be ready to be placed on a complete war footing. Moreover, the country would be more independent and could save itself money. He also made the point that if horses were well fed and looked after, they gave longer and better service.

According to Radetzky the regulations for the cavalry were far too general and did not distinguish between the various branches involved. There was far too much arbitrary practice, so that its condition had become 'anarchic' with no appropriate training involved. Things had been much better when the Riding School and cavalry inspectors existed, but by that point the School had been dissolved and the inspectors abolished. Other countries, meanwhile, had copied Austria's own arrangements with the result that their cavalry was now superior to Austria's. It was 'of the greatest urgency' therefore to reform the cavalry. Troopers should be trained in the use of weapons, and instructions for manoeuvres revised since many were now superfluous and new ones necessary, but totally ignored. Moreover manoeuvres should be carried out by large bodies of cavalry, not merely provincial ones. Radetzky then set out how to train the different branches as well as individuals, how to train cavalry corps made out of several regiments and then explained why the army as a whole should be divided into army corps. Other recommendations included the establishment of a cavalry artillery, the combination of the cavalry reserves of Hungary, Bohemia and Galicia, uniform cavalry training and exercises, and the careful selection of officers for staff duties, with promotions not based on seniority alone. However, Radetzky was only able to implement these reforms once he took over command in Italy.

Clearly as chief of the general staff he had a vested interest in working with the highest quality of staff officers – their selection and training was a subject that always remained important to him. In three important memoranda of 1810 he laid down the role of general staff officers within the army along lines that would endure for over a century.[26] These memoranda were meant to clarify not only their duties in war and peace but also their relations with other army officers. For example, in his *Draft Instructions for Allocating General Staff Officers to General Commands* he was at pains to ensure that general staff officers would not work behind the backs of or go over the heads of the local commander:[27] 'A general staff officer cannot follow a command of the Chief of the General Staff which contradicts the orders of the commanding general, just as he cannot execute one without the approval of the commander.' And to drive home the point that local commanders should not be alienated by the work of the general staff, he stressed:[28] 'Neither a staff officer nor those officers assigned to him can be used independently by the Chief of the General Staff. If this becomes necessary, the relevant arrangements will be made by orders given through the *Hofkriegsrat*.' Finally, to provide even further reassurance:[29]

'The Commander will inform the *Hofkriegsrat* through administrative reports, of the use made of general staff officers. He will also append these reports to the personnel files of the staff officers involved. In a second memorandum of 1810 *On the Duties of Members of the General (Quartermaster's) Staff*, Radetzky divided these into peacetime duties and those in war.[30] Wartime duties were subsequently divided between duties in battle and those outside of battle. Peacetime duties included: topographical knowledge and map-making; military surveying and sketching of the most relevant positions and posts for future defence; suggestions for peacetime quartering arrangements and possible changes, suggestions for peacetime camps and the carrying out of exercises in them; the drawing up of marching schedules for troops to enable them to concentrate on the border with respect to various contingencies that might arise; plans for attack or defence in the case of war breaking out with one or more neighbouring powers, be they weaker or stronger or in combination, with suggestions whether to react defensively or offensively; the composition of 'impartial' military histories; the direction of the War Archives; the direction of purely military business at territorial general commands; and, finally, 'the upkeep of secret knowledge of plans, military arrangements, and changes with respect to our neighbours, through well selected attachés at our embassies and a well conducted espionage.'[31]

Wartime duties, outside of battle, included: drawing up plans for marching against the enemy; the destruction of obstacles to, and the provision of support to expedite the advance of troops; the encampment of troops on march and within sight of the enemy; the reconnoitring of enemy movements and positions; the visual inspection of the most advantageous marching routes, camp positions, battlefields, and fixed positions advantageous to a defence; the analysis of enemy intentions through the use of agents or various reports from outposts; the drawing up of battle plans and preparing battlefields according one's own intentions insofar as a variety of circumstances permit; the keeping of a diary of everything militarily important in war, everything that makes knowledge of the enemy easier for a successor including future theatres of war and future war leadership, and everything that will serve for a future true and useful military history.

In battle the duties of general staff officers included: the leading and linking up of troop movements and the repulse of any obstacles deflecting these aims; paying attention to one's own or enemy weaknesses; immediately remedying one's own while exploiting those of the enemy; and the quickest moving on from one plan to the next should intentions or circumstances change. After a battle general staff duties included: an immediate plan on how to exploit the advantages gained with respect to war aims; or the fastest arrangements to save those defeated parts of an army and to unite them quickly; the composition of faithful and impartial records; cooperation in the conclusion of a ceasefire or peace in order not to face disadvantageous restrictions.

It is very clear from all of this how remarkably talented Radetzky believed a general staff officer had to be. Diligence was not enough. Nor were the usual skills. Over and above these, a general staff officer had to be well-trained in writing clearly, drawing and mathematics, all subjects that were not obviously mainly military ones, and able, moreover, to strive above and beyond the call of duty and display an unusually acute attention to detail. Radetzky particularly stressed the need for topographical knowledge; an eye for terrain was vital for almost all tasks. Yet this was one reason why staff work was not popular and Radetzky admitted that it might be highly unpleasant even for a well-educated officer, one who possessed these extra skills, to spend most of his time in 'the mechanical service of the General (Quartermaster's) Staff... Still, it is most unpleasant for the Director of this business if he has to deal permanently with disgruntled and unwilling subordinates.'[32]

Topographical drawing clearly was an unpopular and physically demanding task. Thus Radetzky advanced the idea of assigning it only to officers of certain ranks. According to his plan, all younger captains and first lieutenants of the general staff would have to undertake this duty, but with the knowledge that, once promoted, they would never have to undertake it again. This would free older officers from being mocked by younger colleagues when sent out to fulfil such assignments. Radetzky thought the new arrangement would also work better than posting officers on map duties on a particular year. To the objection that his new system, on the outbreak of war, would leave the army full of new young staff officers who, if good at map-making were untrained in war duties generally, Radetzky replied that if they were not already trained in map duties they would not be fit for anything else. Camps, routes, fortifications, plans and so forth were all contingent on geographical knowledge. A year later Radetzky would propose that cartography should be taught to general staff officers. The Mapping Corps was created in 1811 which solved several problems, while Radetzky arranged that surveying for strategical purposes should be extended by giving the Pioneers the task of mapping rivers. As a member of the Commission for the Organisation of Ships and Bridges he also supervised the merger of the Pioneers and Tschaikists (boatmen). Nor would it come as any surprise that when Radetzky took over in Lombardy-Venetia, he retained under his command until 1839 the *I.R. Istituto Geografico Militare*, which produced a well-known map of Lombardy-Venetia, and oversaw the mapping of Parma, Modena and Lucca as well as the Adriatic coast.[33] In spite of his emphasis on map-making, surveying and topographical drawing, Radetzky did concede, however, that all sorts of other talents – languages and riding skills, for example – were needed too. Still, he had a very clear – and very extensive – idea of what a general staff should do.

Another memorandum of 11 February 1811 on *Improvements to the Institution of the General Staff* demonstrates that Radetzky had thought over the role of staff officers very carefully.[34] Aware, he wrote, that changes brought resentment, he still wanted his staff officers to possess some initiative. Hence:[35] 'Responsibility does not consist in the precise following of orders but in the best possible execution of the same; in war, what has been done is less often worthy of punishment than what has not been done; everything depends on calculating as far as possible what can be left out or omitted when executing an order when one has been given the discretion to do so.' Officers free to use their discretion would do all that they could to fulfil their tasks. Again, although general staff officers were not to be totally free from controls, they should not be tied to one overriding idea. Senior general staff officers for their part should be sent to all branches of the army to pick up the widest experience in peacetime. On-the-job training before the enemy was not recommended. The chief of the general staff himself was to get to know as many people as possible so that he could always find the right man for any job. His officers should get to know the troops they served with, so that in war, the respect that they had already gained would encourage these troops to look to them for leadership. For this reason Radetzky warned against allowing the general staff to become a 'fruitful ground for adventurers, men with a good tongue, riding ability and a store of fancy words. Perhaps it was the presence of such people there who made the general staff such a focus for rivalries:[36] 'This is the history of all headquarters and the source of so many anecdotes if one wants to learn the causes of disasters or great enterprises.'

Radetzky preferred well-trained and hard-working officers, dedicated to their tasks and troops, but with the ability to exercise their own judgement. On 7 November 1811, therefore, he introduced a 'teaching course on the main branches of general staff duties for captains and first lieutenants present in Vienna .... to advance the reputation of the corps'. Among its first students was the future Field Marshal Hess. However, the course was interrupted by war, and although it restarted occasionally in Vienna and Verona, a *Kriegsschule* (Military Academy) was only first established in 1852.[37]

During the 1813 campaign Radetzky proposed a better system of promoting general staff officers so as to get the best educated and trained ones into the highest posts at an age when they could best benefit the army. In Italy he later called for general staff members to be sent more frequently among the troops so as to raise their morale and create a better esprit de corps among the army as a whole. Without a close bond between the general staff and the troops there could, he wrote, be 'no common spirit, nor unity, nor energetic activity on the day of danger'.[38] Promoting the abilities, morale and reputation of the general staff was one of Radetzky's lifelong obsessions.

In his second memorandum of 1810 he had referred among the peacetime duties of the general staff to the role of military attachés and spies. In fact, the introduction of military attachés was another of Radetzky's many achievements. Military progress after all depended on knowing what was happening in foreign countries. So with Metternich's help, Radetzky could achieve what the Archduke Charles had suggested in 1801, namely that officers could be attached to embassies abroad. Thus in 1810 Captain Johann Weiss was sent to Stockholm and in 1811 Major von Tettenborn was sent to Paris.

The *Instructions for a General Staff Officer Assigned to a Foreign Embassy*, drafted by Radetzky in 1810, remained in force till after 1918.[39] Under these, a 'military confidential', 'mission officer', 'commis' or 'cavalier' – the term military attaché was not used till 1859 – was to give a strict account to his ambassador of what he had done and whatever political or other useful knowledge he had acquired. The officer might be involved in military discussions or border reports, but for general purposes he would be expected to report on the military forces maintained by the state he was assigned to, relate any statements or reports indicating the possibility of war in the immediate or longer term, report on any operations likely to be undertaken by the state he was assigned to should war break out between it and another state, to make an analysis of the military geography of the state he was assigned to, including its offensive and defensive aspects, points of defence, fortification or those of any other military significance, to describe all military, political, police, academic and other institutions that might be relevant to military affairs and to read the latest literature on military affairs being produced there and to send back copies of all useful plans, statistical tables, maps, military almanacs, army lists, training manuals, school books, published instructions or anything else that could be studied, copied, adopted or adapted in Austria. Meanwhile the officer was to go about this cleverly and unobtrusively, acting as if he were pursuing matters of his own interest and refraining from discussing Austrian policy. He was to make as many useful contacts as possible and to seek the ambassador's help in all this. He was also, of course, to report to the ambassador. Once again, there was no indication that Radetzky expected his officers to go behind the backs of anyone. Metternich viewed all this positively since he understood the importance of military information in conducting diplomacy. Indeed, in the course of time the Austrian military would produce about a hundred ambassadors, including, of course, in 1848, Radetzky's own *Felddiplomat* (military diplomat), Prince Felix zu Schwarzenberg.[40]

Until the system of military attachés was well established, special arrangements often had to be made to achieve results. For example, General Augustin, who for years was Austria's chief weapons expert, had the opportunity as a delegate to Bernadotte's headquarters in 1813 to use an English Congreve Rocket at the siege of Friedrichsort, after which he submitted a report on the device. Radetzky, on this basis, arranged at the Congress of Vienna with the King of Denmark, whose adjutant was the rocket expert, Captain Schumacher, to send Augustin to Denmark to study rockets and on the basis of his experience the new weapon was introduced in 1817 and a new Fireworks and Rocket Corps was founded that survived till 1867. Two rocket ranges were also established in Italy. Radetzky himself, however, never really became convinced of the usefulness of rockets and insisted that they be tested under battle conditions against guns. He wanted no mishaps to occur.[41]

Intelligence work, as opposed to diplomatic work, did not provide the general staff under Radetzky with any great advances. Radetzky was well aware that both France and Russia maintained very good military espionage bureaux in Austria. He complained that military men who had risen in the diplomatic service failed to send the general staff any decent information, even when they were well-informed on foreign armies. An Austrian espionage bureau was therefore established and Metternich agreed to pay agents well and to treat them honourably. Yet Radetzky always had his doubts about certain types of spies:[42] 'A spy always remains a rogue, and if he has been used, he must either be made harmless or very well looked after.' Still, steady progress was made in obtaining information while expenditure on espionage rose from 60,000 to 100,000 Gulden annually. Radetzky also tried to manipulate the press but this was really Metternich's job.[43] After 1848 he reflected:[44] 'We have learned very much about the power of the press and feel, with more or less full consciousness, that perhaps it was precisely the neglect of this almost irresistible force that cost us streams of blood and the welfare of thousands... I often feel that we lack the support of a well-meaning press and the publicists up to such a task.'

The general staff also had the job of running the War Archives and here, too, Radetzky made improvements.[45] For a start, new rules were introduced to separate historical from archival work; general staff officers were given the task of writing up impartial accounts of military campaigns. (This was to remain a general staff task till 1938.) The Director of the Archive also had to show how materials could best be used for teaching and training members of the military. The outcome was descriptions of the campaigns from 1716–18, 1792, 1796–7, 1800, 1809 and 1811–12. The Archive also received the sources for the 1739–89 campaigns, along with instructions to publish these in the newly founded *Österreichische Militärische Zeitschrift* (Austrian Military Gazette). Radetzky, meanwhile, kept his eye on the classification and organisation of documents. In 1811 the so-called 'Military Library' at the Archive was extended and reorganised, while foreign requests were now generally complied with – even Jomini was given access to abstracts from Austrian *Feldakten* (field records), while the Archive copied a variety of regulations for Britain's Prince Regent. Radetzky, therefore, was a very good friend to the historical profession, however ill served he himself has been by it since his death.

Another subject which fascinated him throughout his long career – perhaps on account of his experiences in Mantua – was that of fortifications. Given his experience as chief of the general staff, he maintained an interest in the general defensive problems of the Monarchy, not merely local issues. Hence even in Italy his mind often turned to Austria's military situation as a whole. It was in Buda in Hungary in 1827, however, that he penned his most comprehensive memorandum *On Forts*.[46] This was a wide-ranging document that warned the authorities of the need to upgrade present defences and build more.

Forts, according to Radetzky, played an important part in national defence by helping to deflect or reduce the threat from any enemy in wartime. Attention, naturally, had to be paid to the cost of them and to changing diplomatic, indeed even domestic, circumstances:[47] 'In civil wars the aim of fortresses is to protect the government and citizens still loyal to it from rebels and to save mobile property from robbery and plunder,' he wrote rather prophetically. If they were to be maintained, however, a host of questions had to be asked of all forts: why had they originally been built? Were they still necessary? Were changes needed? Could they be used for other purposes? Were their locations still appropriate? Radetzky then considered the situation of the imperial provinces bordering the Ottoman Empire, since, he wrote, 'It may be asserted with great confidence that Austria in future times will have to conduct a war against the Porte or on behalf of the Porte.' Turkey, he could see, was in decline and lay 'not geographically but politically outside the European state system',[48] thus making her strategic position very weak: she was not guaranteed by the Vienna Treaties; Britain's possession of Malta and Corfu meant that all her harbours could be blockaded and the Dardanelles closed; Russia, now in possession of Poland, no longer risked a two-front war if she attacked her; and Austria's own possession of territories in Dalmatia meant she outflanked her. Since Turkey had allowed all this to happen without awakening from her lethargy, her future existence depended on an agreement between Britain, Austria and Russia. Yet the latter power needed to export her produce through the Black Sea and could only completely secure that trade by possession of Constantinople. Had Peter the Great's 'Great Eastern Project' therefore really been abandoned? On her Asian frontier, Turkey bordered on Persia, but that power, too, was in decline and divided between Russia and Britain. If strong and independent, she would make a dangerous enemy for Turkey and a natural ally for Austria. Radetzky, it must be said, had an extremely good grasp of international affairs.

Turkey, he also noted, was continuously subject to domestic wars, the Sultan having to deal with rebels in his various provinces. Radetzky himself saw the main threat coming from Egypt. Would one of these rebels be able to take over or divide the Ottoman Empire? And if so, would the European great powers benefit or lose out from such a development? The greater threat would come, he thought, if a new conqueror arose and seized the Sultan's throne, thus entailing more wars for him to consolidate his position. A divided empire, on the other hand, would benefit all the great powers.

Turkey's main defence lay in her core territory of Asia Minor and her greatest guarantee in the clever use of her institutionalised religion, Islam, to combine her spiritual and material resources. Yet even Islam was facing intellectual challenges from progressives; Radetzky believed that 'the progress of Enlightenment in Asia [would] undermine and destroy the support that the religion of Mohommed still supplies there'.[49] But this was not certain. Islam might renew its strength and the European powers should be sensitive to any revival. For the moment, however, these powers were wedded to peace. Trade had replaced war. Yet 'a single change in ruler can put an end to the present European system which favours peace.....  In Europe fears of the huge Russian preponderance can scarcely be hidden.... Everywhere in the dark, defence and security plans are being drawn up against this threatening spectre..... with so much combustible material glimmering beneath the ashes'... would peace prevail?[50] It was therefore wise, Radetzky believed, to examine Austria's defence problems in case war arose over this matter. Radetzky was never dismissive of Islam but it was in this discussion of Turkey that he noted:[51] 'It is more intelligent to support intellectual progress than to fight it. For it is only this progress which from time to time provides men with better objectives and devises new means to achieve these objectives.' Radetzky's lively military mind was not a reactionary one.

His memorandum now considered what would happen if war did break out between the two powers, allowing him to flex his military intellectual muscles over the military defence of all six Habsburg provinces bordering Turkey – the Bukovina, Transylvania, the Banat, Slavonia, Croatia and Dalmatia. Of course, if Austria took the offensive, she would send armed columns into Serbia and Bosnia towards Constantinople, declare all Turkish provinces independent, arm their inhabitants and lead them against the Turks. If she was placed on the defensive, however, Radetzky had to consider what invasion routes a Turkish army might take and what could be done to stop it. His phenomenal military knowledge of all the relevant routes, passes, geography and history led him to conclude that the Turks would most likely invade via Transylvania or Croatia, which meant the restoration of Karlowitz (Karlstadt) as a proper fort. At that time its escarpments had collapsed, all its drawbridges had been replaced by embankments and everything had been remodelled, so that at best it could only be described as an entrenched town. Radetzky also saw the fortifications of Karlsburg in Transylvania would have to be completed. Altogether, however, a defensive strategy relying on forts would force the enemy to divide his army, keeping parts of it behind on observation duty, parts which could then be picked off and destroyed. Meanwhile his Main Army would be too weak to achieve its objective.

Radetzky's attention to the defence of the Monarchy also led him to consider Austria's links with the German Confederation and, most important of all, the defence of Lombardy-Venetia.

Austria's main defence problem was that an attack from revolutionary France could come from Strasbourg via South Germany or Italy. The Defence Committee of the German Confederation had laid down that a joint Austro-Prussian force should protect the Upper Rhine, but no effective arrangements had been made by the mid-1830s to do this. The situation seemed all the more urgent to Radetzky, since it would take six week for Austrian troops to link up with South German ones if France did attack, placing the German army immediately on the defensive:[52] 'The Defence Committee has taken this evil completely to heart, and offered to do everything to get on with any one of the many projects submitted to it. Yet these proposals remain in the Federal Archive in Frankfurt and the money devoted to them in the coffers of the various German states.' Meanwhile, if France invaded (and even Switzerland was now looking threatening) South Germany lay open to her. There was no secure concentration point for the German troops, although Rastatt, Offenburg and Freiburg were the most suitable points to fortify. But given that nothing had happened by 1834 and that the costs to fortify all three might be unreasonable, Radetzky thought that Rastatt at least must be fortified as a matter of extreme urgency. Without such a fortress the South German troops would be 'far too weak' to wait for Austria successfully taking the initiative. Perhaps his impatience was driven by the fact that in 1832 in Milan he had drawn up a very long and detailed plan for the invasion and defeat of France, not to mention the capture of Paris, by a German (Austro-Prussian) army.[53]

It was, he wrote, 'doubly important' to think of the security of the Upper Rhine. The Lower Rhine was already protected by a belt of forts from Mainz to Wesel. Luxembourg itself was being fortified. Fortifications were supposed to being started at Germesheim. As the security guarantee provided by internal developments in France, Belgium and Switzerland for the peace of Germany diminished, the more Austria should feel duty-bound to take measures for her own preservation. The great war scare with France in 1840 would prove him right. Fortunately, however, France chose not to go to war either then or during the revolutions of 1848.

Meanwhile, as commander in Italy, he had more immediate problems to face. His mantra was:[54] 'God protect us from a defensive war in Italy (against France). If we assume this we are surely lost,' explaining in the introduction to a memorandum *On the Need for a Fortified Camp at Milan* that:[55] 'The physical and political shape of Italy, particularly Lombardy, is so disadvantageous to the defender and offers so many advantages to an aggressor coming from the west ...' The suggestions that had already been proposed for improving Italy's defence, however, never completely cohered. The most important ones had included a plan to make Sesto Calendo and Boffaloro the central positions for the defence of Mantua along the line of the Ticino; a project for an entrenched camp at Lecco; and a proposal for the fortification of Piacenza. Radetzky dismissed all three. The Ticino, for a start, was far too long to offer a line of defence; troops could not be concentrated at the right point in time. The distance from Pallanza to Pavia stretched over 15 German miles. By the time an enemy was reported to be crossing the Ticino, it would have already done so and made preparations to defend itself on the opposite bank before an Austrian army could arrive from a central point to stop it. There might also be another hostile army positioned between the Ticino and Mincio, where the terrain favoured the enemy. If Austria were then defeated, the whole of Milan and Lombardy would be open to conquest. Nor would the availability of an entrenched position at Lecco be of great help. A large army could merely observe this difficult debouche, while taking over the Lombard plain. It would then have no difficulty in supplying itself, while the Austrians would have to rely on the few resources of the Valtellina. Fortifying Piacenza might indeed hinder the enemy from advancing to the right bank of the Po and would leave that river under Austrian control, but a larger enemy could not be prevented from pushing on to Milan or from using light troops to push along the left bank of the Po to Brescia and Cremona, stir up the countryside and prevent relief troops from reaching Piacenza, or even Austrian reinforcements from reaching Italy. Moreover, it was 'problematic if [Milan] once lost, could ever be quickly reconquered'.[56]

The original pivot and manoeuvring point in plans for the defence of Lombardy with respect to the Mincio Line had been Verona, seen by many as a secure support and entry point from which Austrian troops could stop an enemy advance from the west or even from South and Central Italy, especially if linked with Mantua. Yet, according to Radetzky,[57] 'Verona exercises no influence on the defence of Lombardy and it is illusory to hope that from here or behind the Mincio at all, the territory between this river and the Ticino can be defended. Milan will always fall into enemy hands and be completely taken. To avoid this irreplaceable loss, the only solution is to take the offensive, cost what it might.' His comments on both Verona and Milan should be remembered when the 1848 crisis is described. So, too, should his comments on Piedmont,[58] whose loyalty as an ally he very much doubted.

Radetzky also considered the possibility that France, while pretending to attack through Piedmont, might actually secure agreement to attack through Switzerland. In this case, Milan would be directly attacked first. Such a French plan was not totally unlikely. France had recently secured her right flank with fortifications at Lyon and Grenoble. Besançon and Belfort secured her left flank and base. The Swiss might well back such a plan. The Austrians therefore had to be prepared. But how?

Radetzky's conclusion was to build an entrenched camp at Milan.[59] In or from Milan the army could either await reinforcements from the interior, or respond after an initially unsuccessful campaign, or link up with garrisons previously cut off, or, circumstances permitting, even attack and defeat the enemy, especially if he had split his forces. The fortification of the city would of course cost money, but Radetzky argued that deteriorating security would soon force the government to spend so much money and use so many troops on essentially police work, that only about 10,000–12,000 out of the 40,000 troops then stationed in Lombardy-Venetia would be available in emergencies.

The military situation was truly appalling. If war broke out, 20,000 men would be needed immediately. Another 30,000 reinforcements were probably available from the Tyrol, but under current conditions, they might take anything up to three months to reach Milan and would be full of the sick and the weak. In this light, only the fortification of Milan would be of any help. The French would need 40,000–50,000 men to observe such a fort and if Austrian garrisons still remained on the Po at Piacenza, Brescello and Borgoforte, French lines of communication would be insecure. There would thus be time for Austria to devise a winning strategy once reinforcements had been organised. The details of the fortification of the city therefore required 'closer examination'.[60]

Radetzky left these details to a famous military engineer, Captain Birago of the General Staff, with whom he conducted a lengthy correspondence. Birago reported that at least four Maximilian-type towers[61] with ten cannon each could be constructed around the city at relatively little expense – less expense indeed than that of 'the smallest fort in the Monarchy'.[62] These towers, however, would have to be supported by batteries of 68 cannon placed in between them, but they would solve Radetzky's problem. Otherwise, he repeated all of Radetzky's own arguments concerning the strategic significance of Milan and approved them. Predictably, however, nothing happened.

Not content with pushing for more fortifications, Radetzky also had time to think about the way the army was organised. His thinking at this time traced different paths. Much of the time he was concerned with the professionalism of his troops. Once in Italy and in supreme command there, he was determined to put into practice all the schemes he had been considering since 1815. Hence the army in Italy was run along very different lines to those elsewhere in the Monarchy. It was divided into two corps, one stationed in Lombardy, one in Venetia (under FML Baron d'Aspre); it held annual manoeuvres to improve its procedures and coordination; and all of its branches were trained in accordance with up-to-date regulations drawn up by Radetzky himself. All this activity caused a great deal of interest not merely in Vienna but also abroad. Representatives from foreign states and armies regularly visited Radetzky's camp or headquarters, while Vienna established a commission to examine 'whether Radetzky's innovations were at all necessary'. However, 37 out of 40 generals consulted approved of them.[63]

Radetzky did not have to draw up his Italian plans from scratch. In Buda, as Radetzky stated, 'he busied himself a great deal with the manoeuvrability of large formations of cavalry' which suffered from the lack of exercises caused by the lack of funds available.[64] However, Radetzky was able to conduct experiments as commander of his hussar regiment, which he used as the cadre of a brigade, and put down his conclusions on paper. He also had the opportunity to experiment with infantry and artillery units and so could draw up a draft plan in five parts on manoeuvrability. Nothing came of it, so it 'wandered unappreciated and unused to Olmütz' along with Radetzky. But there he 'discovered General Fleischer in the garrison who took a lively interest in this work and used it in practice in leading his brigade'.[65]

With the Italian appointment, however, Radetzky's time had come. He still needed to refine all his ideas by trial and error and commit them to paper in a way his troops could understand. Fortunately for a couple of years he had Hess by his side and the first *Instructions* for active service in the field (*Felddienst*) and on manoeuvre were issued when he was still Radetzky's chief of staff. Then came instructions for training in specific branches of the army. The whole training system was designed systematically, beginning with the smallest units and proceeding step by step to greater formations and combinations of branches, until finally all were working together. Meanwhile, all exercises had to be conducted against an enemy which was marked. Otherwise, exercises used opposing parties. Radetzky stressed the need for the troops to get as much practice as possible. They would leave their garrisons in May, therefore, and not return until the autumn. In preparations for manoeuvres and during the winter, school tables were used upon which an exercise ground displaying all features of the terrain was formed out of plastercine, with wooden pieces serving as army units. This way of learning soon became standard practice everywhere.

Radetzky's manoeuvres and instructions became famous. According to *Coburn's United Services Magazine and Naval and Military Journal* of London:[66] 'in 1833 he published a work upon the organisation of armies and kept the troops in the most efficient state by continued reviews, sham fights and other evolutions.' Officers, nay royalty, attended them from every part of Europe.

Another motive for the manoeuvres was that he wanted his troops to experience comradeship, the feeling of mutual dependency, a sense of 'being instructed by one another' (*Aufeinander-angewiesen sein*). This was a higher virtue than friendship. He taught them to value the communion that came with sharing privation, joy, glory, victory and death. Glory, he said, belonged to the army as a whole, not to any individual soldier. This ethic of comradeship became widely diffused and may have been the origin of the practice that Austrian officers developed of addressing one another as *du* rather than *Sie*. Indeed, the idea of the 'unknown soldier', it has been argued, can be traced to Radetzky's ideas. Certainly, according to Wolf-Schneider von Arno, 'the idea of comradeship was not so widely suffused in any army in the world as in Radetzky's', although one would need to look very far and very wide before accepting such a grand assertion.[67]

In turn, the troops clearly loved their Field Marshal, who made it clear that he would stand for no ill-treatment of them by superiors or anyone else. Any officer found guilty of beating a soldier was immediately banished from his army. Officers, instead, were told to communicate with their troops and answer their questions. The use of the cane was considered 'dishonourable' and permitted only under extreme circumstances. It filled men with contempt for their officers. Radetzky desired a just system of discipline with appeals possible all the way up to the Emperor, who was fortunately quoted as saying that the army was no institution of correction, far less a depot for criminals. That said, anyone who had served their time for committing a crime was welcome in the army, although Radetzky resisted the attempts by legal authorities to send all hardened criminals there; he predicted it would have 'the gravest results'. One authority concludes:[68] 'The army in Italy saw a person not as an instrument but as a soul bestowed with worth, a colleague and a comrade.' Radetzky himself campaigned to abolish the rank of 'common soldier', something that was achieved in 1857.[69]

Whether matters were really quite as *gemütlich* as this, one may doubt. Certainly, conditions seem to have been very different elsewhere in the Austrian army. Enlistment was considered a 'disaster' by peasants, the poorest of whom took to the hills and had to be hunted down when the recruitment commissioner arrived. Once caught the men would be chained, abused and sent, without any opportunity to say goodbye to their families, to some regimental garrison situated in any part of the Monarchy.[70] Inside the army, they were poorly paid and fed. In towns an infantryman might be able to take part-time work to boost his pay, but a cavalry trooper in a village had no such opportunity.[71] About one third of the men were sent home 'on leave' each year to save paying their wages and to allow the harvest to be collected.[72] As for the rest, they had to put up with strict punishments and officers who despised them. A Captain Basil Hall, a military visitor from England wrote:[73] 'I confess I was rather surprised when I learned that the punishments in the Austrian army are almost entirely corporal and very severe, and almost without nominal, and certainly without efficient control.' A hazel cane which just fitted into the bore of a musket was used by officers to administer punishments. A colonel could order 50, a major 40 and a captain 25 blows across the breeches on his own authority. And according to the English witness, it was 'right to state that the corporal punishments [were] intensively employed in every branch of the army and in many corps were almost the only method of discipline ever thought of'.[74]

The worst punishment was 'to run the gauntlet'. This involved a soldier, stripped to the waist, walking four to ten times between two rows of 150 troops on each side, armed with birch switches, who would then flog his naked back. A doctor had to be present and if the man could not complete the punishment, it was resumed later. 5,508 men were forced to endure the gauntlet in 1847 alone.[75]

It is unsurprising that the men therefore grew to hate their officers, who clearly despised them. According to one critic, the Austrian soldier was treated by his officers as helots were by Spartans. Officers avoided their men off duty and on duty they had no rights. Few enjoyed any popularity among their subordinates:[76] 'the majority of them lack the capacity to adjust themselves to the way of thought of the common man,' whom they addressed in the insulting third person singular as *er*. Many troops were left to fend by themselves or lost on exercises and had to be hospitalised, a horrific experience in itself. The end result by 1848 was repeated cases of common soldiers murdering their superiors (NCOs or subalterns) and then shooting themselves. When analysing why such usually apathetic and sluggish peasants would take such a step, the critic concluded:[77] 'such a deed is the result of a long-nourished, deeply-concealed resentment created by prejudiced, hard-hearted, inhuman treatment.' *If* Radetzky's army in Italy was organised so differently, as the above-quoted authority suggests, then the Field Marshal certainly deserved the affection of his troops and the name of 'father Radetzky'. But there is no reason to believe that the critic quoted here actually thought so, since his references to troops being neglected on exercise brings Radetzky's army specifically to mind.

Be that as it may, Radetzky himself in his utterances and writings spoke only of the need for compassion.[78] In October 1835, for example, he drafted a memorandum *On the Development of Conduct regarding the Troops in Italy which has Proved Necessary regarding Dislocation, Accommodation and Health*. In 1837 he introduced improvements in diet and accommodation, involving better food, beds, tents and hospitals. In 1836 compared to 1833 there were 16,078 fewer sick and 2,021 fewer fatalities. In 1853, Radetzky told the visiting Prussian military attaché: 'Take note if you ever become a commander to look after the stomachs of your men first, for a brave soldier who has nothing to eat can have no courage.' In 1848 he sent 400 Gulden to Austrian prisoners of war being held in a Genoese camp and received an affectionate reply from the troops:[79]

> To the most worthy Field Marshal our beneficient father: this 3rd of July has been a joyful day for 1,200 prisoners of war here in Genoa. An officer arrived with a kind message and with a present from Your Excellency of twenty kreuzers for each of us; and the assurance that Your Excellency would exert himself to effect our exchange. As the smoke rises from our pipes, which have so long been empty, with it ascend our prayers and wishes for our father.

'Father Radetzky' must have been moved.

The other side of this coin, of course, was the position of the officers. Radetzky was unusual in that he believed in promotion on merit – not by birth or seniority – and did not interest himself in uniforms.[80] 'I don't belong to that number of generals', he proclaimed, 'who spend a lot of time on the question of uniforms.' In 1848 officers and men were made to wear the same colour of uniforms and camp caps for comfort, with ranks distinguished by stars; officers were also allowed to have gold sword handles.

The issue which really obsessed Radetzky was officer education and training.[81] He believed that the more educated an army was, the less likely it was to start a war. But to conduct oneself successfully *in* war also necessitated instruction and intelligence. Officers should educate themselves when not on duty. Military honour without training was nothing. 'If you want a part in the play, you have to know what it is all about,' he would say, quoting Valentini. But he also confessed: 'I cannot force anyone to read good books or even sanctioned instructions.' That was why practical training – manoeuvres and exercises – was so important. Even generals could learn from them. The last thing Radetzky wanted was a parade army: 'The days are over when people can take their pride from external military splendour. The hour and the tone of the parade ground has disappeared along with the manoeuvre as a puffed-up spectacle.' He preferred to give his regiments reading rooms and libraries. There were 96 by 1847. In 1810 he had resurrected the *Österreichische Militärische Zeitschrift* to aid officer education. In 1810, too, he had drafted a teaching plan for cadet schools focusing on mathematics using the synthetic method. History was to be more patriotic and connected with geography, for which globes of the world were to be used. Pupils were to learn to express themselves but in a precise rather than a long-winded way. French was to be the main foreign language taught and fencing the main sport. Officer training was then to continue through general command courses, regimental educational departments, and a cavalry training institute for teaching personnel. In Verona he established a bilingual cadet company, schools for officers and schools for NCOs. Even the common soldier was to be taught how to read, write and count. In Hungary, he arranged a new training course for regimental training houses and had a Lieutenant Schlögl write new teaching manuals, which he praised to the Archduke Ferdinand, telling him: 'physical force alone does not achieve victory for an army; it loses if it lacks intellectual and moral resources … a host of failures derive from the neglected education of officers, which constitutes the soul of a military force.' His *Nachlaß* includes a proposal to establish a 'chair of military sciences' at Vienna University plus notes on an artillery academy, an 'officers' university' and a 'Polytechnic chair for war studies'. But entrance to any one of these institutions would have been by merit alone.

Radetzky's reforming zeal also led him – at least at first – to support the use of a *Landwehr* as a prelude to general conscription. There is some dispute whether a *Landwehr* still existed after 1815. According to Hall, the military observer quoted earlier, it certainly did, but another distinguished English visitor turnball reported:[82]

> The *Landwehr* unless embodied, which it never is in ordinary times of peace, receives no pay and exists only on paper, but this paper existence is with very little trouble or delay convertible at any time into corporeal reality; as the registers are excellently kept and each battalion has its full establishment of officers marked out, who from the retired or supernumerary list, are held ready to join at a day's notice.

Gunther E. Rothenberg, on the other hand, wrote that 'although the *Landwehr* had acquitted itself rather well in 1809, it was not an institution which recommended itself to the authorities, and it was progressively dismantled and completely shelved [he later refers to its "abolition"] in 1831.'[83]

Turnball's version is almost certainly the correct one as Rothenberg's view seems to be predicated on a misreading of a standard Austrian source where he confuses 'abolition' with 'activation'.[84] The 'activation' of the *Landwehr* in 1831 lends credence to Turnball's view and makes Radetzky's comments more interesting, since they now refer to a real institution. Certainly Radetzky himself wrote of a *Landwehr* in 1834 that really existed, even if he used the most disparaging terms:[85]

> The word *Landwehr* has no significance for us. We have no *Landwehr*. For the dragoons, cuirassiers, sappers, artillerymen etc who have served for ten or twenty years before they are stuck in a so-called *Landwehr* battalion, composed of completely newly-levied young people, that is to say, recruits, have nothing to offer to make a good impression on these young soldiers. On marches, moreover, they simply fill up the hospitals.

In 1828 Radetzky had written a fascinating memorandum setting down his *military observations on the position of Austria* which had painted a very different position of the *Landwehr* as a military institution.[86] He then saw Austria as threatened from all sides:[87] 'The Monarchy is isolated, hemmed in by a power seeking to aggrandise herself, shorn of all defensive barriers and military borders, without reliable confederal allies, and must seek the means to maintain herself from her own resources.' He considered what might happen if she were forced to go to war with Russia, France or Prussia. He liked nothing better than to play intellectual games of this sort. Besides, that was what he had been trained to do as chief of the general staff. Planning for all and any sorts of wars was his real business. Fortunately he could also win them when

called on. Towards the end of this essay, however, he approached another subject, one which again revealed how radical he could be in his thinking.

'The wise and great principle', he wrote,[88] 'of granting all states appropriate constitutions will probably within a short time be carried out in
all the other states in Europe and the aim towards which all peoples have
striven so long in vain, will thereby be fulfilled. But the peoples will not
be satisfied through constitutions alone.' In Radetzky's view they would
demand the abolition of the debts and the lowering of interest payments
caused by the long years of war. This would necessitate budget cuts, leading to cuts in the size of armies. But would not this endanger the security
of states, and, if so, what could be done about it? Radetzky's view was that
'the system of standing armies is suited to certain times and certain circumstances but not for all time and everywhere.'[89] In Radetzky's view, standing
armies had completely overshadowed *Landwehrs* in recent times: 'And yet,
the reliable strength of a state rests on an appropriately formed *Landwehr*.
This institution is the most natural and therefore the best.'[90] It delivered
proportionately the largest number of fighters to the state; it retained a
lively consciousness among the people that they were defending themselves,
and thereby created a fighting spirit, which did not easily degenerate, since
those it inspired never ceased to be citizens. Such a spirit, at such a level
made a people unconquerable. They would never be subjugated much less
destroyed. Ancient and medieval history proved this; indeed 'most recent
history leads us to the conclusion that, landwehrs, well led and of fairly
long existence have almost always become masters of standing armies.'[91]
The Swiss and Dutch provided recent examples, as did the French during
the revolution and the Americans in their War of Independence. So, too,
did the Spanish and Portuguese in the Peninsular War. There were lessons
to be learned which could not be overlooked. These included the fact that,
although *Landwehrs* were usually initially defeated they won out in the
end through learning and battle-practice. They did so on account of the
advantages they held: they were sleek and natural and lacked artifice; they
could be used anywhere; they could be assembled more easily and more
quickly; and finally, they fought for themselves. Thus Radetzky thought
they should be introduced everywhere since they would bolster external
defence, allow the standing army to be reduced and provoke no internal
problems. Austria should consider this carefully:[92]

A state which is only surrounded by other states which immediately seek
their security in landwehrs and therefore cut their standing armies, does not

need fortresses, because it does not need to fear a war. The paradox in this assertion disappears when, following the lesson of history, we recall that a nation standing completely under arms has never yet been fully subjugated. Yet where all hope disappears of making conquests through a war, war no longer has a purpose and so will very likely completely disappear.

This is a familiar argument as to why democracies today never make war on one another.

Unfortunately, Radetzky had to confess that Austria bordered Russia which was unlikely to have a constitution or military cutbacks in the next hundred years. This was a power which could quickly assemble an army of 150,000 men, cross Austria's open frontiers and prevent any *Landwehrs* from assembling. It would therefore soon be master of Upper Hungary and probably also of Vienna. Once again there was a need for fortresses. If the *Landwehrs* could use them and then attack the Russians, they would in time defeat them.[93]

After the 1830 revolutions, however, Radetzky's views on popular defence changed. In another memorandum, dated 1834, entitled *How can great and good armies be maintained with few costs?*[94] he wrote that Austria faced political and defence problems but lacked the financial resources to tackle them. After stating that the army as a whole must have a clear and consistent organising principle, he argued that it would be found not in a *Landwehr* system but in a cadre system, that is to say a system which kept a full complement of officers while reducing the number of troops. As for a *Landwehr*, his views had clearly changed on account of the revolutions in Germany and Italy:[95] 'The system of national defence is very enticing and is totally feasible in countries where there exists complete agreement between rulers and ruled. Yet such is not generally the case at present, not even in Prussia.' Prussia under 'the incomparable Scharnhorst' had created a *Landwehr* system to defeat Napoleon and had enjoyed disproportionate power so long as it existed. But everything had gone wrong since 1815 and there now existed not a true military spirit but political propaganda and swindling, just as religious fanaticism had earlier held sway. 'God knows when the political stupidity of men will reach an end,' Radetzky complained,[96] adding, 'I fear that it will happen only once a new conqueror has arisen who will make the people shudder for their independence, once again stirs up their national spirit, and so gives their thinking another twist or direction.'

It was these thoughts that convinced him that Austria must rely on the existence of a good and battle-ready army as its main priority. Theoretically, however, Radetzky always believed that the best army would be one raised by general conscription, covering all classes of the population and all areas of the Monarchy equally. He had no time for partial institutions like the *Insurrectio* of the Hungarian nobles or the various national guards of 1848. He wanted all citizens to play their part in defending the Monarchy:[97] 'If in a state military service is not regarded as the first basis of security, it weighs as an oppressive burden on a few ... in this case not only is justice not served, but permanent zeal is not distinguished from temporary nor excellent service from ordinary.' At root he was always a constitutionalist; yet political conditions made it impossible for him to demonstrate this before or after 1848.

Radetzky involved himself in carrying out a whole host of reforms and never stopped thinking about others. He was obsessed with educating and training the Austrian army to the highest possible level and wanted to treat his troops humanely although how much he was able to achieve even in this respect remains ambiguous. He was certainly prepared to contemplate political and military change along radical lines, but in the end despaired of this ever happening, partly on account of the growth of radical nationalism, partly on account of the miserliness of his paymasters in Vienna, and partly on account of the imperial bureaucracy.

In his memorandum of 1834 on squaring military reform with financial restrictions, he listed no less than 14 areas where reforms were needed. These included the need for equal length of service throughout the Monarchy; unlike Italian troops, German and Hungarian troops served for 14 years, not eight, which Radetzky thought was far too long and complained that it only produced invalids who cost the state a fortune.[98] Austria needed a better central administration. Radetzky himself recognised that the current one 'waste[d] a large part of the military budget' at the very time that the army itself had to make reductions in areas which were not purely military. The administration behaved as if the army existed for it and not vice versa: 'I have seen not merely whole regiments, but more than this, almost the whole army disbanded without the slightest reduction ever in the army of bureaucrats. On the contrary! Departments are always enlarged and daily more civilian posts are created.'[99] The army should have better clothing ('The Austrian soldier is the worst clothed in Europe and yet the clothing and arming of our troops costs the Treasury immeasurable sums')[100] and a better supply system. The present one 'paralyse[d] the army's mobility' and also led to corruption and to such interference from the *Hofkriegsrat* as to render general commands 'superfluous'; the state, Radetzky clamoured, should no longer tolerate the laughable way in which flour was supplied.[101] He called for better pay for officers, particularly subalterns, using cuts in administration costs to fund decent salaries for officers. The present ones 'must make people blush...... How can the military spirit or a feeling of honour flourish if officers are reduced to beggars?'[102] Higher administrative bodies were totally defective: 'What in Heaven's name has a collegiate system to do with a defence ministry whose administration cannot be concentrated enough? ... The *Hofkreigsrat*, as it now exists, is the most disconnected military organisation that was ever created.'[103]

Radetzky lamented the lack of training, particularly in the highest ranks. A general needed to be appropriately educated and have the proper military virtues such as natural intelligence, energy and insight. He did not have to be an academic but without all these qualities 'he will never be the general he ought to be'. Radetzky therefore opposed any strict system of seniority.[104] He thought that the complete reform of the general staff had now been subverted by 'theoretical pedantry' and 'engineering geography', not to mention the deliberate failure to fill vacancies.[105] He wanted to see improved grenadier regiments (the main need was for energetic officers)[106] and better artillery troops, who had more training than spirit. Their officers were promoted from the bottom up but this took too long and left them too narrow-minded and difficult to develop after their training courses. Why could not more graduates from the military academies join this corps? Again, magazine depots were too often full of defective materials. He thought that a few changes to the corps could pay really big dividends.[107] So too improvements should be made to the transport corps leading to great savings and helping the artillery corps[108] and reorganisation of the auxiliary troops, again saving expenditure.[109] Appropriate horse breeding and horse transport required a special report.[110] But Radetzky felt that outward appearance was overrated. Take the hussars for example: 'They are beautiful cavalry line regiments. This is true. But due to their pretensions in this respect they have sacrificed their real dedication to being vanguard troops. They are no longer hussars.'[111]

After listing all these areas for reform and improvement, Radetzky called for a commission of experienced military men to bring about at least some reforms:[112]

> Our army is old and has always been patched up and improved according
> to the needs felt at the time. There was never any regular plan worked out

*Plate 1*  Radetzky by Josef Kriehuber, 1849

*Plate 2*  Schloss Trebnitz, Radetzky's birthplace

Plate 3 Fanny, Radetzky's wife, Countess Franziska Romana Radetzky, born Countess Strassoldo-Graffemberg

Plate 4 Radetzky as a young man, c.1801

*Plate 5* Fritzi, Radetzky's daughter, Countess Friederike von Wenckheim

*Plate 6* Radetzky's military colleagues during the revolutionary wars. From top left clockwise: Field Marshal Wurmser; General Melas; General Hiller; and General Zach

*Plate 7*   Archduke Charles

*Plate 8*   The Battle of Wagram 1809

*Plate 9*  The Aftermath of the Battle of Leipzig 1813, with Blücher, Alexander I, Francis I, Frederick William III and Schwarzenberg. Courtesy of The Anne S.K. Brown Military Collection.

*Plate 10*  Field Marshal Blücher

*Plate 11*   General Gneisenau

*Plate 12*   Metternich

*Plate 13*    Francis I as Emperor of Austria

*Plate 14*    Alexander I, Emperor of Russia

*Plate 15*   Prince Charles Schwarzenberg, allied supreme commander, 1813–15

*Plate 16*   King Frederick William III of Prussia

*Plate 17*   Count Charles Clam-Martinitz

*Plate 18*    General Hess, Radetzky's Chief of Staff in 1848–49

*Plate 19*    General Schönhals, Radetzky's Adjutant in 1848–49

*Plate 20*  Battle of Custoza

*Plate 21* Battle of Novara

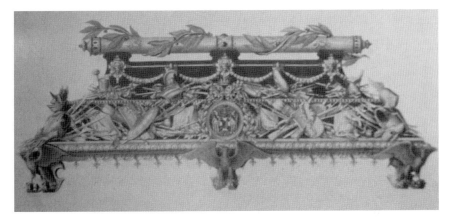

*Plate 22*  The ceremonial marshal's baton presented to Radetzky by the Austrian army

*Plate 23*  Radetzky in old age with victory moustache

*Plate 24*   Radetzky in old age without victory moustache

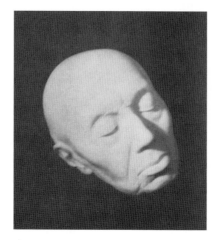

*Plate 25*   Radetzky's death mask

*Plate 26*    Radetzky lying in state in Milan Cathedral, 14–15 January 1858

*Plate 27*    The Obelisk with the entrance to Radetzky's mausoleum at Heldenberg bei Klein-Wetzdorf

*Plate 28*  Radetzky by G. Decker, c.1850

to form a basis according to some definite intention. This building therefore is now partly crumbling and needs great help. If that is to come about, then above all, these questions must be asked: What do we have? What do we want? What can we keep? What must we abolish? The answers to these will be the measure of what should be done.

Curiously, the state did seem ready to undertake some military reform at this time. A friend and supporter of Radetzky, General Count Carl Clam-Martinitz, undertook a whole series of army reforms between 1835 and 1840 as general adjutant to the Emperor and head of the military section of the Council of State (*Staatsrat*), these two positions between them making him *de facto* if not *de jure* war minister.[113] Clam, like Radetzky, was a Bohemian aristocrat, although his mother tongue was Czech. He also spoke German, French, Polish, and some English and had a knowledge of Latin and Greek. Unlike Radetzky, however, he was a supporter of the high aristocratic party and was admired by Kübeck, who called him 'the best and clearest mind, as well as the purest human being among the members of our regency'.[114] He was a close friend and admirer of Metternich and was widely expected to be his successor. When Metternich was gravely ill in the autumn of 1839, however, Clam made it clear he did not want the job but should be allowed to continue with his reform of the army; indeed, he drafted the Emperor's letter to Count Ficquelmont, then ambassador to Russia, to return to Vienna to deputise for Metternich, who, of course, recovered. It was Clam who died prematurely in 1840, leaving Princess Melanie Metternich to lament him in her diary as 'so necessary' and to fear the effect his death might have on her husband.[115] Still, today, like Radetzky or even Metternich himself, Clam-Martinitz is unknown to historians and their readers alike. The only work on him is an unpublished Austrian doctoral dissertation written in 1928. Even Gordon Craig's examination of 'command and staff problems in the Austrian army, 1740–1866' has nothing to say about him.[116]

His relevance to Radetzky's career and thought began in 1830 when Metternich, disgusted at the Archduke Charles's refusal to lead the army against France in 1830, turned to Clam who disliked the Archduke's 'denigration of the Austrian army and his overestimation of the French one'. Metternich in 1831 sent Clam to Italy to report on the situation there. Clam sent back word that it was 'very satisfactory', Frimont was up to the job, and that so long as Austria disposed of 'an imposing military force' things would be alright. He did not put much faith in the Italian people.

The actual military strength was only 40,000–45,000 men but could be raised in a crisis to 90,000. He advised against new recruiting in 1831 but suggested rather that regimental troops 'on leave' should be called in and regiments brought up to full strength.[117] In the countryside they formed 'an element of unrest' anyway. Interestingly, Clam warned against harbouring the 'illusion' that in war the Italians would stay loyal: 'all will desert us', was his prediction. Still, 'it is not a matter of numbers here but of appearances and not proving to them that we are sleeping as they allow themselves to say and hope.' In Clam's view even a small army could effectively control Northern Italy as long as it was seen to act with determination and authority. (Radetzky's manoeuvres were also designed to give this impression, although their propaganda value was hardly their main role.)

On 6 March 1835 Clam became general adjutant to the new, but mentally retarded, Emperor Ferdinand and was to protect him from misuse by others as well as from making 'unthoughtful expressions' before the troops. Clam had already been a member of the *Hofkriegsrat* and Francis I thought him sound. In 1835 he also became head of the military section of the *Staatsrat* (Council of State) and privy counsellor (*Geheimrat*) to the Emperor. Given his various positions, Clam could now implement the many changes he thought necessary in the army – all of them more or less those that Radetzky desired. The Vice-President of the *Hofkreigsrat*, who in fact was acting President and then President after 1834, Radetzky's old colleague from the campaigns in Italy, Count Hardegg, offered no resistance. Clam admired Radetzky and was close to Metternich, but did not like the Archduke Charles, although he often sought his advice, and he clashed regularly with Kolowrat who was in charge of financial affairs.

His views coincided with many of Radetzky's, although he opposed any reliance on a cadre system. He saw that the army 'had to progress with the times' and agreed that 'our army regulations have not been made deliberately in accordance with military laws and organic principles, but, more than any other in Europe, as a result of political, administrative-legislative and social circumstances.'

So what improvements did he propose? Among other things, the rights of regimental colonel-proprietors (*Inhaber*) were to be supervised to prevent abuse of promotions, which were to be based on talent and ability. 'Unity of morale' meant that officers who objected to regimental postings were told to go where ordered with their troops, whose morale they were instructed to raise. The sick were to be better treated and not allowed out of hospitals till they had properly recovered. Generals were to be forced to go on manoeuvres to get used to exercises and to gain practical knowledge, not just to conform carrying out service regulations, but to transform themselves into thinking, responsible and enthusiastic organs of the service in its mechanical and intellectual aspects, and to be active supervisors and promoters of the service regulations, and of the organisational and administrative rules and interests of the service. More troops were to get the chance to participate in exercises, although parade drill 'was not to become the characteristic quality of our army'.

One large area Clam tackled was reform of the *Hofkriegsrat*, (Court War Council) which by now had become dependent on the military section of the State Council. The War Council was run by its President and Vice-Presidents and its business divided into a number of military, political, economic and legal departments. All the economic, political and legal departments were headed by a Court Counsellor; the military departments were headed by a colonel or general. Joint affairs were considered by separate panels. Four generals were appointed as Counsellors who took part in these along with heads of the military departments when very important business came up. The Archduke Charles in 1803 had reduced the number of departments but had increased the number of panels (or boards) to three: military, political-economic, and legal. The general (i.e. territorial) commands were all directly responsible to the War Council. By 1835 they had lost what independence they once had and this was one reason why the Council was overloaded with business. Clam announced his intention of reforming the body so that people should take full responsibility for their duties and stop overloading others with business. The War Council would also get more money to pay off salary arrears, although in future 'appropriateness and capability' would be the criteria for those seeking new posts.

Clam also created a second Vice-President to help push through reforms. The first was now to oversee the military departments, and he (the second) the others, but both were to keep each other informed of their doings. Meanwhile a new Central Military Chancellery was established inside the Council under GM (*Generalmajor*) Peter Zanini. It was to deal with Italy and Germany, political and international affairs, promotions from GM upwards, the choice of staff officers for special assignments, the agenda for military departments, and individual communications with higher officers. The aim was to ensure that the War Council President could devote 'his undivided attention to the supervision of the energetic pursuit of business and the coordination of all parts of the whole, of the intellectual and moral as well as the material and purely service demands of military administration in all parts of my army', according to the Emperor's instructions. Hardegg was asked to prepare further reforms, but merely suggested increasing the number of departments, leading Clam to declare 'that one should not become depressed on account of the difficulties and relative ineffectiveness of the first steps'. He himself suggested that a military man be placed along-side a civilian at the head of each department, so that the military principle might prevail in all War Council discussions, although this was not adopted until after 1848. Inspectors – including the War Council President – were once again to be sent to inspect the troops. A new set of regulations was drawn up to define the administrative duties of the general commands rela-tive to the War Council. Other changes of regulations were prepared, but after Clam's death in 1840, almost all his work was neglected.

A second area for his attention, meanwhile, had been the general staff. Clam agreed with Radetzky that it now needed reforming. (Officially it was still called the General (Quartermaster's) Staff, a title derived from the time when its main role was really marking out encampments and preparing quarters in the field. The term *Grosser Generalstab* referred to the generality as a whole.) Clam laid down the aims of his reforms in two memorandums, one in 1835, the other in 1837. He proposed a more active link between the General Staff and the army and to fuse the General Staff with the General Adjutants, something that Radetzky had already proposed in 1811. But it was simply a proposal – he did not want to cost the War Council money (Staff officers were paid more). In any case, he thought that the War Council should henceforth select adjutants, who should receive better training, perhaps through a *Kriegsschule* (eventually set up, as previ-ously noted, only in 1852). In peacetime he proposed to divide the General Staff into three sections: one to act as teachers of the higher arts of war, one to fuse with the general adjutants, and one to be used by the chief of staff for special assignments. Talented officers should be attached to embassies and armies abroad; the chief of staff should be 'a charismatic personality' (*Führungspersönlichkeit*); from 1835 one sixth of general staff officers were to be allowed to marry, the best of them without putting down a 'caution' or deposit first.

With regard to the army generally, as well as the General Staff, per-sonnel files were to be better written and kept and outstanding officers made the subject of special reports. New regulations were drawn up to ensure that personnel reports on generals were also well organised. In par-ticular their qualifications in peace and war were to be noted as was their continued fitness for service. Any physical, moral or intellectual defects were to be reported and explained. Clam demanded an impartial assessment of all generals. Nor were the higher echelons of the army to become 'a welfare institution for old men'. Thus although the advantages of the seniority principle were recognised – it prevented arbitrary promotions and enforced equality of treatment – the opportunity to advance had to be given to talented younger men. His intentions were frustrated, however, by the Archduke Louis who argued that in peacetime an officer's qualities in war could not be determined, while passing over an officer who was due promotion on grounds of seniority would be to mortally insult him. Clam could not agree with the first point, so a compromise was reached whereby bad generals could be sent to command forts or inspect uniforms and poor major generals might be allowed to become interim division commanders.

As for captains and cavalry captains (*Rittmeister*), the same ambition to retain and promote good men was evident. Anyone who wanted to leave the army had to report to a commission to be evaluated. A talented officer might be offered more money or a promotion to major to remain. He worried, however, that officers whose failings got them into debt, but who could not be cashiered, got themselves pensioned off anyway. But military lawyers were happy to allow those guilty of moral failings to be declared invalids and pensioned off, although they would be discharged without honour and receive the pension only as an 'act of grace'. Regarding subalterns, Clam at long last negotiated them pay rises of between 25 and 33 per cent in 1838, overcoming Kolowrat's long-standing opposition. These were to be paid for by added expenditure (500,000 florins) and savings.

The question of pay increases then raised the issue of the military budget, which according to Eichorn at the Treasury had to be balanced. (His view was that in a Monarchy state expenditure had to be determined by income. His colleague Kübeck disagreed.) In fact, the War Council was always given an annual *Dotation* or fixed sum, but always over-extended itself under a number of different headings. Clam argued that compared with earlier years the army was now being run on the cheap and that compared with Prussia was providing extremely good value. For example, Austrian officers were much worse paid than Prussian or Russian ones. As a result it was agreed in future to divide the military budget into two categories: 'ordinary expenditure' and 'extraordinary expenditure', the latter being more flexible. This was regarded as a great victory for Clam, although in practice it changed little. Another victory came when in 1838 the length of military service in Austria and Hungary was reduced from 14 to ten years (*Landwehr* service was also reduced from six years to four). Clam had his doubts about this – he saw it as a possible step towards popular defence (*Volksbewaffnung*), but recognised that these reductions were a priority for agriculture and industry.

Changes in uniforms – from the abolition of tight trousers to the change in colours and the disuse of heavy cavalry boots – were brought in, but are of little historical importance. More important were the reforms of the army's educational establishments. Thus the military academies at Wiener Neustadt and Vienna had their courses shortened and their best graduates were allowed to enter the army as sub-lieutenants second class. School books were specially written for regimental training schools (Radetzky had already started doing this in Hungary), more money was invested in military medical training and the Riding School was re-established in Salzburg in 1835.

Since most of these reforms had already been proposed or were about to be proposed by Radetzky, it is fitting to end with Clam's part in judging Radetzky's reforms in 1833. A commission had been set up under Hardegg to examine what Radetzky was doing in Italy, since his innovations were being quickly copied by other generals, even though in certain points they contradicted service regulations. Radetzky's work, it will be remembered, fell into three categories: field instructions; manoeuvres with ever larger bodies of infantry; manoeuvres with ever larger bodies of cavalry. Clam found that the first were a good collection of all that was best in past practical ideas, enriched by new concepts, 'most of which are very respectable'. In fact they were issued as an appendix to infantry training and exercise regulations in 1836. Concerning Radetzky's instructions for cavalry manoeuvres, Clam had his doubts but since there were currently no relevant regulations, he maintained that 'without such instructions one could never escape the dilemma of either seeing formations for whose extension the exercise regulations have neither been thought up or written down literally exercised in an unsuitable place or, to avoid this, of allowing them to exercise arbitrarily anywhere or everywhere.' A commission was set up for further investigation, but Clam was still dissatisfied: 'all commissions, all small tests are always insufficient and precarious … [pitfalls included] the difference between theory and practice … the impossibility of avoiding any error of detail, still more the usefulness of continuous experience over small if important improvements.' Hence tests were undertaken which led in 1836 to the provisional issuing of *Instructions for tactical exercises of several regiments of the k.k. infantry*. They were issued again two years later after more trials brought approval and were later combined with the infantry drill regulations. In 1838 the equivalent cavalry instructions were published, again after trials in two general commands as an appendix to cavalry drill regulations. Later they were added to a new edition of the Archduke Charles's regulations of 1806.

Whether Clam's reform career amounted to a great deal may be doubted. Arguably his reforms of the *Hofkreigsrat* only increased the number of bureaucrats, although most of his other reforms, modest as they were, furthered or echoed the work of Radetzky himself. All the Field Marshal's complaints were recognised, his own reform of regulations officially incorporated, his views on promotion by merit and general staff reform taken up. Clam even managed to get more money out of the treasury, raise officers' salaries, cut the length of conscription and reform the military educational establishments. He, too, preferred educated officers, although he never shared Radetzky's more radical political leanings. The crucial point was Clam's unexpected death in 1840, meaning that Radetzky lost his greatest ally in Vienna. After 1840 any military reforming zeal in the *Hofkriegsrat* disappeared and Radetzky had to witness the growing political crisis in Lombardy-Venetia with increasing despair.

Radetzky's record as a reformer, whatever its shortcomings, stands out all the more since in the period 1815–48, there was very little military reform going on anywhere. In Prussia, the home of military reform, the movement ended in 1819 with the removal of Boyen as War Minister.[118] In Russia, the reformists had been associated with the Decembrist Revolt of 1825 and falsely with the mutiny of the Semenovsky Guards in 1820. Thereafter the man who dominated the Russian army was Field Marshal Prince Paskievich, who wanted to hear nothing at all of reform and took pride in breaking the men who favoured it.[119] In Britain the Duke of Wellington – Radetzky's British equivalent in the eyes of many contemporaries and the most influential figure by far in British military matters – simply used his official positions to stop any reforms.[120] A few did manage to slip through before the Crimean War but mainly in the early 1850s as a result of campaigns in the specialised military journals. Such journals were very active in France, too, but there, with the country's difficult reaction to Napoleon, and with the conquest of Algeria, more attention was devoted to 'little wars' than to the legacy of the Emperor. Once again, therefore, not much was done to modernise the French army, although its victories in Spain, Greece, the Crimea and Italy between 1823 and 1859 have been unfortunately overshadowed by its defeat by Prussia in 1870–1.[121] Jomini, of course, wrote his famous analyses of Napoleonic warfare in France, but they seem to have had more influence in the United States (where translations of his work were just about the only theoretical training that officers ever received before the Civil War) than in France itself.[122] Intellectually, then, Radetzky was a rare bird for his times.

His social life, although probably very conventional while commanding general in Italy, attracted all sorts of salacious rumours. One biographer suggests that if the records of the Austrian secret police regarding the armed forces had not been destroyed in 1927 when the Palace of Justice was burned down in Vienna, much material would survive to discredit him.[123] The same source accuses him and his wife of constant indebtedness and claims that Radetzky boasted of having fathered four illegitimate children after 1831 by Giuditta Meregalli, a washing-woman.[124] Another account suggests much the same: Radetzky lived the life of a spendthrift aristocrat of the old regime, regularly inviting 50 to 60 guests to join his table – a habit he continued all his life.[125] He was also an ardent gambler with no sense of money and each morning in Verona would throw handfuls of silver coins to crowds of beggars who gathered below his windows.[126]

No doubt Radetzky's private life, given his spectacular career, was bound to be the subject of gossip. It may well be, however, that much of the rumour was false. There is no proof of his affair with Meregalli or of his fathering children by her. Indeed, there is a good case to be made out that he himself always possessed a good sense of finance and that any debts he had were the result of the need to look after his young wife and large family, which, for example, had had to move house no less than 12 times in 33 years in the course of his career, in itself an expensive process.

For most of his life, too, Radetzky had little time to spend on leisure activities. He usually held more than one army post at any one time (Pioneer Commander *and* General Adjutant; Brigadier *and* in charge of horses for the army; Chief of the General Staff *and* section leader in the Hofkriegsrat; Divisionaire *and* Adlatus; Army Commander *and* Governor-General) and insofar as he had interests they were intellectual ones – collecting his library, reading history books – or looking after his horses. He did like a glass of wine or playing tarock, but insofar as sex was concerned his eight children do suggest a love for his wife, who lived with him in Italy. Indeed, after more than 50 years he would be thanking God that he had had her as a companion for life (she died in 1854).

Having five sons in the army also cost money: the boys needed several uniforms each plus spending money, not to mention deposits if they wished to get married. (The Austrian army only allowed one sixth of its officers to marry, in which case they had to deposit money – between 6,000 and

10,000 florins – a huge sum, to help provide for their families in case of death.[127]) Life as an army officer was not cheap in Austria, particularly if one's father was a general or Field Marshal and the family had a reputation to keep up. (Not that all Radetzky's sons managed to do this. Theodore, his eldest, had a bad reputation for being a drunk and a boor and had poor relations with his father.)

On the other hand, given his position, Radetzky felt socially obliged both to entertain all the dignitaries who came through Verona on the way to and from Venice or Milan (his table might host between 50 and 120 guests depending on the season) and to give to charities of all sorts as well as to soldiers, beggars and other poor people he met on the streets. He was still giving them money from his wheelchair at the age of 90. So he was a rare bird in more senses than one.

# 4

# PRELUDE TO REVOLUTION

In 1848 and 1849 Radetzky saved the Austrian Empire from dissolution by defeating the Italians. In so doing he gave the government in Vienna the courage not just to face down the Hungarians, who were moving towards complete independence, but also the Prussians who in 1850 began to plan for a united Germany which would have excluded Austria. Radetzky's success also gave heart to governments all over Europe which had been forced to make concessions to revolutionary nationalists and democrats. Perhaps now, they, too, could fight back and win. It was General Cavaignac, the French war minister and future prime minister, who said:[1] '...on events in Vienna depend not merely the fate of the Monarchy but the salvation of Europe'. The Baroness Blaze de Bury recorded in her reminiscences of 1848:[2] 'The proof of the importance of Radetzky's Italian campaign lay in the discouragement with which the revolutionists were seized upon the news of his successes. When the entrance into Milan of the Austrians was known in Paris, you would have thought the republicans had heard their death-knell. And perhaps they had! Custoza may have been to revolutionary rule what Leipsic was to the Empire, *le premier coup de cloche.*'

In fact, there was no 'may' about it. Radetzky's triumph encouraged the counter-revolution all over Europe. And had he *not* triumphed, the European balance of power would have been overthrown, the whole map of Europe altered, and European war between the powers made all but inevitable, since a dissolved Habsburg Monarchy would have led (most likely) to a united Germany under Prussia, which would have led (most likely) to war with France, which would have led (most likely) to Russian and perhaps even British intervention. As it was, the geopolitical map was left unaltered, although significant domestic political changes took place not merely in France and Sardinia but also in Vienna, where there was a change of monarch. The dynastic and military rulers of the Empire convinced themselves that the weak-minded Ferdinand, who, for example, had sacked the Croatian leader, Jelačić, on the request of the Hungarian premier, Batthyány, without consulting anyone, could no longer be trusted with the throne.[3] On Ferdinand's abdication, therefore, the young Franz Joseph succeeded as emperor, determined to unite his empire and run it from the centre through the army and the bureaucracy. Hence Radetzky's victory clearly had immense consequences not only for Austria but for the whole of Europe.

Traditionally, however, Radetzky's achievement has been treated simply as part of the history of the *Risorgimento*, the story of how Italy achieved unification. In this the Austrians have always been regarded as the villains. Yet, with the passage of time, and perhaps also as a result of the disappointing historical record of Italy after unification, the Austrian record has been revised. For example, one of the most recent accounts of Austrian rule in Lombardy-Venetia in the Metternich period has concluded:[4] 'Censorship, though irksome was less oppressive than in most Italian states and the bureaucracy...was neither marred by corruption nor unsympathetic to the conditions of the local population; the judicial system was characterised by remarkable even-handedness. Indeed the "black legend" of oppressive Austrian rule was the invention of patriotic propagandists who paid scant attention to reality.' The greatest historian of modern Italy, Denis Mack Smith, has written much the same[5] and to give him his due, Bolton King, one of the older, more distinguished historians of the *Risorgimento*, also wrote:[6]

> Though the emancipation of Lombardy and Venetia was the dream of every Italian patriot, Neapolitan and Roman and Piedmontese might well envy the institutions under which their inhabitants lived. The Austrian Empire was too strong, too much in evidence, to condescend to the indecent corruption of a petty tyranny...there was a regularity and robustness of administration, an equality before the law, a social freedom, which except in Tuscany and Parma, was without its parallel in Italy.

He even added that on the basis of her wealth, Lombardy-Venetia probably paid no more than her fair share of taxes.

It should also be remembered that after revolts in the Papal States, Metternich regularly came under pressure from the neighbouring population to annex Papal territory. In 1845, after one such revolt, even the anti-Austrian American consul in Turin had to report:[7] 'The Legations are reduced to such dreadful extremities that they would gladly seek refuge from priestly extortion in the more orderly and better regulated despotism of an Austrian Prince.' Metternich himself, however, was never interested in taking more Italian territory:[8] 'The same unquiet spirit which now led to the desire to join us would be turned against us as soon as Bologna came into our possession.' He believed that all Italian states, provinces and towns were mutually antagonistic and that this *Munizipalgeist* would allow Austria to divide and rule; Italians, given their mutual antipathies and jealousies, were incapable of self-government or unity. In fact, as the whole world knew, they had not been united since the Roman Empire. It would be better for them and everyone else, therefore, if they were ruled with a firm hand diplomatically from Vienna. All this should be kept in mind when considering Radetzky's role.

Austria in 1815 had accepted Lombardy and Venetia at the Congress of Vienna (they became the Kingdom of Lombardy-Venetia and Ferdinand, who became Austrian Emperor in 1835, was crowned in Milan in 1838 with the Iron Crown of Lombardy), not merely because they were rich provinces, one of which had access to the sea, but also because Metternich wanted to be able to crush the Italian Jacobins in what he saw as their centre in Milan. Yet, despite its good record in administration, justice and finance, despite the fact that one French visitor could even write that it was 'a veritable earthly paradise',[9] there was no disguising the fact that Lombardy-Venetia was run from Vienna. This did not matter too much because for a long time the Italian elites were prepared to cooperate with Vienna[10] but at some stage that cooperation began to wane. Radetzky's own adjutant general, von Schönhals, wrote:[11] 'Soon after the coronation [1838] a greater division was noticeable between the nationalities...' According to the same source, this disquiet now began to spread to the middle and lower classes, so that everyone knew it must lead to some kind of clash. He added:[12] '...how far, however, the poison had already contaminated the social organism, was naturally a secret and those contaminated could not themselves yet know.' The army soon became aware that it had become very unpopular; General von Stratimirovic recorded that 'the population hated us' in his memoirs of the period 1841–3, when he was stationed in Italy:[13] Many incidents took place – for example, despite wearing civilian clothes, off-duty Austrian officers were often set upon at night by vagabonds, stripped naked and tied to trees to await being freed by passing patrols. Still, nothing was done to change the way in which Austria administered her Italian kingdom.[14]

The Austrian army blamed all unrest on the selfish ambitions of the Lombard nobility in particular, although it basically could not see what the Italians had to complain about. The Archduke Maximilian d'Este, a leading general, wrote for example:[15] 'Austria ... can be called the common haven of all the surrounding nations, for she is their common refuge in every need, their protecting wall against every attack.' Italians would do well to consider how many of their countrymen had reached the highest military and civilian posts in Austria and had thus acquired a European reputation with which even the dream of a united Italy could not deceive them.[16] In short they should know their place.[17] Membership of the 'Austrian Confederation of Nations' was much better than silly dreams of a united Italy. Schönhals, for his part, was more measured in his judgements but still believed that Lombardy-Venetia enjoyed 'national and administrative independence as far as this was compatible with a centralised monarchy', a judgement which begged all the relevant questions.[18] He even blamed the Congregations (local diets) for neglecting their duty, but could not see that representative or democratic institutions would help. Bureaucracy could 'often be somewhat boring', but was rule by 'constitutional' ministers any better? Were they any less corrupt or nepotistic, any more moderate or responsible or efficient? The Austrian system at least had 'the advantage of stability'.[19]

On the other hand, he made no effort to defend the abuses of the police and censorship:[20] '... it is the duty of every state to make this necessary evil as little vexatious as possible, for nothing is more hateful than this constant interference in people's personal freedom .... Never yet has a police force prevented a revolution.' Radetzky no doubt endorsed these views, but he, too, believed that the best position for Italians was under the benevolent protection of Austria. He informed Count Hardegg, still President of the *Hofkriegsrat*, in January 1848:[21] 'I am and will remain master of Italy.' In February, he told the Viceroy, the Archduke Rainer:[22] 'I have sworn to the Emperor, my lord, to fight his enemies and defend his throne and rights; I will remain true to this oath till the last breath. I will weep over the blood that must flow, but I will spill it and let the Hereafter judge me.' In another letter of the same day he wrote of the 'naïve' Italians:[23] 'They ask in all seriousness, why, if they do not want us here, we do not go away?' adding, 'The thought that we would maintain Milan by force has just not occurred to them; the firm declaration that we would turn Milan into a battlefield makes no impression.' And yet, when it came to the crunch, Radetzky would take the highly calculated decision *not* to bombard Milan and turn it into a battlefield, since he loved the city too much. Indeed, the grateful citizens of Venice would present him with a glass table out of gratitude that Venice was not bombarded either.

By 1848, however, both the Austrian civil and military leadership in Lombardy-Venetia were expecting the worst. Matters had begun to get seriously out of hand when in June 1846 Pius IX was elected to the Holy See and through a series of liberal reforms, quickly made himself the first ever Italian national hero. Metternich was completely taken aback:[24] 'I had foreseen everything except a liberal Pope,' he declared. Radetzky was equally appalled and wrote to his daughter:[25] 'Things are quiet here but the fire is burning beneath the ashes. God alone knows how it will end. The Pope is flirting with the liberals and believes he is converting them.'

Other unforeseen events ratcheted up the tension. Gioberti's *Primato,* a bible of Italian nationalism, was republished in Rome; on 5 December 1846 the centenary celebrations of the expulsion of the Austrians from Genoa took place; and on 30 December the body of the Italian patriot Count Confalonieri, whom the Austrians had imprisoned in the Spielberg for high treason, was brought to Milan for burial amidst scenes of wild anti-Austrian feeling. At the end of 1846, too, the German Archbishop of Milan died, to be succeeded by a Milanese, who officially took up his post in September 1847, once again to unruly scenes of anti-Austrian sentiment. His appointment was seen everywhere as an Austrian surrender to Italian nationalism. Yet the political temperature had already risen to almost boiling point after Radetzky's 'occupation' of the Papal town of Ferrara on 17 July 1847 – the anniversary of the new Pope's inaugural amnesty, and less than two weeks after his announcement of the creation of a national guard.

According to the report of the British vice-consul who witnessed events in Ferrara, the Austrian forces (six companies of Hungarian infantry, two squadrons of cavalry and a small detachment of artillery with three field pieces) approached the town '.... in battle order. Orders were given to load their muskets and field pieces and march on Ferrara ... they paraded up and down several of our principal streets with artillery matches burning.'[26] Had Radetzky been stupid enough to declare war on the Pope? The whole of Europe certainly thought so, but the true explanation was much simpler. Under the 1815 treaties Austria had the right to station troops in Ferrara, although usually they simply occupied some barracks. Given recent turbulence in Rome, Radetzky had ordered his troops to occupy the citadel of the town as well, to show the radicals there that he was prepared to offer His Holiness protection. (It even turned out that Austrian reinforcements always entered towns with lighted tapers and in battle order.) Radetzky had simply convinced himself that the Pope, like all previous ones, was really a conservative and was being forced into reforms by radicals who were holding him prisoner. He also wanted to strengthen the resolve of other Italian governments against the nationalists, while the police authorities had been reporting that the public in Ferrara would support him. One report of January 1847 had read:[27] 'People believe that Radetzky will not tolerate a civil guard or patrols in Ferrara, since they say that, according to the treaties, with the exception of the carabinieri, which is only entrusted with police work, there can be no other armed force in that town apart from the Austrian garrison. If Radetzky should, therefore, oppose [what is happening in Ferrara] the news would be well received.'

Count Hartig, the former governor of Lombardy, who now sat on the Council of State and advised Metternich on Italian affairs, later wrote in his memoirs that Radetzky, although acting legally, had committed an 'anachronism' which the Austrian government was forced to support.[28] In fact, Metternich, who was sent a copy of Radetzky's orders, not merely approved them but initially went further in pressuring the Papal authorities than even Radetzky had intended.[29] Radetzky himself had been scrupulous in respecting Papal rights, as his correspondence with his commander in Ferrara, Count Auersperg, shows. Austria, in his view, had been strengthening or reducing its garrison in Ferrara for 33 years; his latest orders were no different or less legal. He told Auersperg:[30] 'I challenge the Roman government to show me where we have overstepped our rights ... Have we ever interfered even in the smallest way in the territorial sovereignty of the Holy See? ...' The same letter, however, ended with a typical Radetzkian flourish: he would defend Austria's Italian possessions 'to the last drop of blood'.

Metternich soon discovered, however, that all the precedents in the Ferrara affair were on the side of the Papacy. He instructed his presumed successor, Count Ficquelmont, former ambassador to Russia, on 22 August 1847 to go down to Milan to discover what could be done to make the government there more effective and to help clear up the Ferrara problem. He told Ficquelmont:[31] 'Marshal Radetzky has stretched his position to the limit and has adopted a very pronounced position .... There can be no question of military measures at the moment.' He told Radetzky:[32] '... Politics and warfare are indivisible strengths ... we, you and I, my dear Field Marshal have lived through difficult times ... may Heaven preserve you for a long time yet for the Emperor and the state.' Ficquelmont patronised him in a similar fashion, telling him,[33] 'Ferrara is the Citadel of our Rights' – a rather slimy phrase under the circumstances. Ficquelmont now made clear to all that Radetzky had overstepped the mark, while both he and Metternich culled the diplomatic documents to find a compromise solution. Count

Auersperg, meanwhile, wrote to his wife a letter denouncing Radetzky, a letter that was intercepted by the Austrian police.[34] The Field Marshal, he wrote, had blundered and should now take Ficquelmont's advice.

Radetzky may or may not have been shown this letter. We do not know. However, his tone to Auersperg did not alter, nor did his tone towards the Papacy. 'Show yourself responsive to any friendly approach', he instructed the fort commander,[35] 'so long as nothing is infringed. It is in our interest to prove that we have no hostile feelings toward the Roman government, but that we have acted as we have so far to preserve our rights and to maintain the law and order of our own states.' Metternich and Ficquelmont, however, unable to reach a compromise with Rome, agreed to withdraw the extra troops from Ferrara on 23 December 1847, to the army's disgust. Baron d'Aspre, head of the Venetian army corps, wrote to Captain Huyn of Radetzky's general staff:[36] 'In Ferrara our rights are trampled on. Our troops – I should say "we soldiers" – maintained our rights (perhaps because we had fought for them with our blood). The bureaucrats (die Feder) decided otherwise; we had to give up our rights – after we had clearly demonstrated them before all Europe. Scorn and derision were the result.'

The real result was that, outside of the army, Radetzky came to be regarded as a warmonger, someone who was itching to take on the Italian nationalists. Still, there were also a few glimmers of light. In December 1847 Metternich managed to arrange an increase of troops for Lombardy-Venetia, and the defensive treaties which he was negotiating with Parma and Modena also reached their final stages. The significance of Ferrara for defence needs was thereby diminished. Better still, from Radetzky's point of view, Metternich and Ficquelmont fell out, leaving Radetzky in a seemingly stronger position.

Ficquelmont had been entrusted among other things with the task of reforming the government of Lombardy-Venetia.[37] This was a subject he knew nothing about, yet he soon convinced himself that the root of the problem was that the initial powers granted in 1818 to the Viceroy, the Archduke Rainer, had been subverted by Vienna. He therefore proposed to strengthen the powers of the Viceroy's council. In fact, Rainer, who was none too bright, was never supposed to have had any real power, so that Vienna now hesitated to approve Ficquelmont's proposals. Metternich told him:[38] 'Only by centralising the action of the various branches of authority is it possible to establish its unity and hence its force. Power distributed is no longer power.' Again:[39] 'Here is what is needed: that what is ordered on this side of the Alps should be carried out on the other; that people there should not seek to weaken our directives but to put them into effect exactly as ordered.' And finally:[40] 'What would be dangerous would be to transfer what is known here as a *chancellery* beyond the Alps, since the same thing would be immediately claimed by other parts of the Empire.'

Ficquelmont was told not to make or promise any concessions, but the Viceroy, who had been led by Ficquelmont to believe that his reform plan would solve all problems, issued a proclamation – the very first of his viceroyalty – telling his subjects that he was awaiting decisions on reform from Vienna. Metternich exploded. He would not be seen to be forced into concessions and ruled out the possibility of any. He put his faith in the army and was relieved to hear that the Governor of Lombardy, Radetzky and the local Police Director, Count Torresani, were holding daily conferences. This was the only administrative reform, the concentrated executive authority, that Metternich wanted. The Viceroy was rebuked (and almost had a nervous breakdown); Ficquelmont resigned and ironically, as a former cavalry general, he was appointed President of the *Hofkriegsrat* – 'not the job he would have chosen' in the words of his wife.[41]

A couple of months previously, on 9 January, the Emperor had issued a declaration to his troops in the form of a *Handschreiben* (letter) to Count Hardegg stating his 'firm determination' to protect Lombardy-Venetia from internal and external enemies and placing his faith in the 'loyal devotion of [his] army'.[42] This in turn led to Radetzky's general order or proclamation of 15 January 1848 promising 'destruction to the enemy'. The key sentence read:[43] 'The machinery of fanaticism will break upon your loyalty and valour like glass upon a rock.' The Field Marshal would use his sword as he had done for 65 years already 'to protect the peace of a still recently happy land which a lunatic party now threatens to plunge into most inconceivable misery.'

Hardegg sent his most effusive congratulations on behalf of the Emperor.[44] But others were extremely frightened. The British minister to Turin, for example, had already written to Lord Minto, then *en mission* in Italy on behalf of the British cabinet, on 13 November 1847 that[45] 'Radetzky ... is pushing for war in Italy with all his influence'. He then wrote on 22 January 1848[46] that the proclamation had been published '... to push matters to extremity and go the whole hog ...'. But when Minto wrote to the British ambassador in Vienna that Radetzky's general order had 'raised a prodigious storm throughout Italy' and that he himself took it to mean 'the abandonment of the pacific Metternich policy', the ambassador, Lord Ponsonby, on 6 February wisely replied:[47] 'I am confident that Metternich's policy has not been abandoned.' Still, Radetzky was now seen everywhere as preparing for war. Ironically, within Lombardy-Venetia itself, his every move still seemed to be frustrated.

There was a whole list of issues on which the Field Marshal and Metternich seemed to be in disagreement. Mostly they concerned the internal and external security of Lombardy-Venetia. First there was the matter of policy, since Metternich, like so many others, feared Radetzky indeed wanted to take the offensive in Italy. A related issue was his request for reinforcements; the deteriorating political situation then brought a demand for martial law to be imposed; while in the meantime the military implications of a possible war with Switzerland had to be addressed. Finally there was the old chestnut of the fortification of Milan. In the period before the revolutions of 1848, Radetzky had his hands full of problems.

Metternich's policy in Italy in 1847–8 was 'not to intervene in either the Kingdom of Naples or the Papal States, but to erect the strongest barrier to disorder and to defend [Austrian] rights tenaciously wherever they [were] attacked'. It was also 'essential' to win back Piedmont 'from herself' into the conservative camp.[48] His strategy, therefore, was a defensive one, although there is reason to believe that Metternich retained doubts about it, for just before Radetzky 'occupied' Ferrara, he had toyed with the idea of a mobile task force which Radetzky could use to strike at external threats.

Confident in the loyalty of Austria's own provinces, Metternich in July 1847 thought that his real problem in Italy was one of exercising 'the greatest possible repressive influence on any revolution that [might] break out in Central Italy'. Hence his proposal for 'a special mobile task force', which would have to 'live off the land' it was sent against.[49] Metternich had even discussed the matter with Kübeck of the Treasury and Hardegg of the *Hofkriegsrat*.[50] He told them that he had no idea how many troops either Naples or the Papal States could use to resist revolution, or how many would desert, and reckoned, therefore, that Austria would have to bear the major burden of repressing revolution. In any case, he came up with a figure of 25,000 men with a reserve of 10,000 for his mobile task force. Hardegg said Radetzky's forces then stood at about 50,000 men and could be quickly raised to 64,000 by calling in the *Urlauber* (men on leave). He was sure that the men needed for the mobile task force could be found amongst those 64,000 and saw no difficulties arising for the defence of Lombardy-Venetia as a result. Kübeck's main concern was secrecy, in case public credit was affected, and costs, which would have to be kept as low as possible. Hardegg warned that secrecy would be impossible, but there would be no mention of interventions, merely 'security precautions'. The Ferrara episode, however, put an end to such speculation.

Radetzky's strategy had always been predicated on taking the offensive. This did not entail launching a war against Piedmont, but he was resolved, should war break out, that Austria would not wait to be attacked from the west. As has been discussed, Radetzky held that geography would favour the aggressor, be it either Piedmont or France. The River Ticino formed a political but not a strategic boundary, since both Lombardy and Piedmont geographically formed a single unit.

According to Radetzky, the fate of Milan, and indeed of Lombardy, depended on whoever won the decisive battle, which he reckoned would have to be fought within the first four days of hostilities breaking out. And to ensure that the victor was Austria, the latter needed sufficient troops and the military initiative. On 12 December 1847 he wrote that 'any other defence apart from a quick offensive is just not possible'[51] and a few days later that:[52] 'We must advance with the first cannon shots of the enemy.' Piedmont, he calculated, could raise an army of 120,000 with good artillery and would also receive support from other Italian states and from within Lombardy-Venetia itself. Austria, he added, could not 'temporise' or 'flinch': 'attack I will meet with attack'; 'forward lies our chance of victory'; 'in retreat lies weakness and destruction'. He needed 50,000 men to defeat Piedmont, 20,000 to guard the Po and 10,000 for garrison duty. If he had to, he would rely on reinforcements from the interior.

Radetzky felt he had to point this out as he had just heard the latest news from Vienna regarding reinforcements. On 8 December he had informed Hardegg that Vienna still did not take the threat facing its Italian kingdom seriously enough. He reminded him that the Italians hated the Austrians, saw the moment of their liberation approaching and that Italy, which had produced Napoleon, still contained both great intellectual forces and the strength to rise again. No statesman or politician could forecast the outcome of the present crisis. He ended with his usual flourish:[53] 'The loss of Italy would be a fatal blow for our monarchy. I will not live to see it. I will remain [here] to the end. Can destiny prepare a more enviable fate for me than to triumph or die on this soil which has been so bloodily contested?'

Radetzky was also convinced that Lombardy-Venetia would be attacked by Charles Albert of Sardinia, Austria's supposed ally. His support for Italian nationalism was well known and despite his reputation as a Hamlet, wavering between his alliance and the aggrandisement of his kingdom at Austria's expense, Radetzky saw that he had made up his mind against

Austria:[54] 'The King of Piedmont has removed the mask and I see myself compelled, therefore, to place myself in a state of war in order to fight before the gates of Milan at the beginning of next spring' – a remarkably accurate forecast.

In Vienna, however, the view was much more sanguine. According to Hartig, who was advising Metternich on Italy, even in January 1848 'an attack by the King of Sardinia was hardly credible':[55] 'An attack from King Charles Albert, without a previous declaration of war, and in direct opposition to his assurances of friendly alliance, could not but appear to men of justice and honour, such as were then in the Austrian cabinet, to be a moral and political impossibility.' Yet Radetzky knew Charles Albert personally and had often been his guest at court in Turin; he had even allowed the king to take over as *Inhaber* of his own regiment, the fifth hussars. He had no illusions about his politics or his morals.

In any case, Radetzky's views unsettled Metternich who told Ficquelmont in two separate letters of 6 December of his concerns. First:[56] 'If I am not mistaken, the Field Marshal is taking into consideration the possibility of an *offensive* operation in Italy from our side...' And again:[57] 'Today we have no intention of taking the offensive in Italy and if we judged the situation differently we would be making a great mistake.'

Radetzky had to defend himself, writing to Hardegg[58] that he had been 'entirely misunderstood'. He blamed the vague conceptions people had about the use of the term 'offensive' in military science. He had not been talking of 'a political solution' – 'that was not at all my intention'. In military matters the terms 'offensive' and 'defensive' were inseparable. Russia, for example, had acted defensively in drawing Napoleon into her wilderness, but her objective was still offensive. The main point, however, was: 'I will not fire the first shot, but if I am attacked – and my whole case rests on this assumption – then it seems to me that questions of policy must obviously give way to those of strategy.' He would act with courage and decisiveness but not 'foolhardiness... I intend no invasions.' He ended: '... we leave their development entirely to themselves.' Ficquelmont then wrote to Metternich that the confusion had been cleared up.[59] Both sides were now in agreement – only Radetzky's insufficiently clear use of the term 'offensive' had caused them to misinterpret his views.

This was not quite true, of course. Vienna still misinterpreted the policy of Charles Albert. There were also differences over the need for reinforcements, differences which had initially given rise to the confusion over the word 'offensive'. These had become clear after Radetzky in October 1847 had made a request for more troops. Metternich had prepared a report for the Emperor, with the support of the Archduke Louis, agreeing to an increase, but now wanted more information from Radetzky; if he provided sound answers then, according to Metternich, Vienna and Milan would then be 'in agreement'.[60] Ficquelmont and the Viceroy were sent copies of Radetzky's report and both endorsed it effusively.[61] Both claimed his views were 'absolutely correct', Ficquelmont adding in another letter a few days later:[62] 'We have no other attack to fear but one from the side of Sardinia.'

It became clear from Metternich's correspondence with Ficquelmont, however, that it had been precisely Radetzky's December reports which had given rise to doubts about whether he was planning an offensive war and Metternich, as a result, had judged Radetzky's increases too small for such an enterprise. In his view, 120,000 men would be needed for such an undertaking, with reserves of 30,000. However, he agreed with an estimation of 80,000 troops for domestic security but added that 'for economic reasons' reinforcements could only be sent 'as time and circumstances' required.[63] The State Conference had endorsed this policy.

Radetzky was furious:[64] 'It still appears that the situation in Italy is regarded in Vienna as not sufficiently urgent to justify more than the usual security precautions.' Still, he managed to arrange for 9,800 troops to be sent straight away with the promise of an extra 13,000 in case of an emergency. In the course of January 1848, Vienna then conceded another 9,000 men, raising Radetzky's army on paper at least to a potential 85,000. During February Vienna agreed to an extra two battalions of infantry, six squadrons of cavalry and two batteries. The cost of all this to the Austrian Treasury for 1848 was 5 million florins, according to Hartig,[65] yet these figures need to be put into perspective. These troops were to be sent by the cheapest means possible – on foot. This meant that when war broke out, despite the apparent increases, Radetzky had only 75,000 men at his disposal.[66] In January he had asked for troop strength to be raised to 100,000 men, while Ficquelmont quoted Metternich's own figures back to him and now demanded the 120,000 men which he, Metternich, had argued in the State Conference would be necessary in a war with Piedmont.[67]

In February Radetzky called for even more troops – 30,000–40,000 more in fact. When his request was passed on to the Treasury, it raised his permitted total to 90,000 and ordered enough reinforcements immediately to provide for 86,000. But then it laid down a hard treasury line:[68] 'disadvantageous consequences' would ensue from 'ever-continuing' troop reinforcements, which were already having a bad effect on 'public credit and the financial position of the Monarchy', so that no more reinforcements would be made until a 'close look' was taken at the whole Italian situation. The 'evil mood' and 'spirit of discontent' which Radetzky complained of, 'appeared to the representatives of the Treasury as no sufficient motive for sending further troops to Italy'. A different view might only be taken when 'events' took a different turn that 'really' necessitated a troop increase. 'Such an event might well only be recognised in the outbreak of a significant rebellion inside the Kingdom of Lombardy-Venetia or in a malicious, hostile attack from any one of the neighbouring states, whereas mere worries and fears, admittedly arising from full cause, but from causes which are already accounted for in the forces already standing at Count Radetzky's disposal, might not offer proper cause for further reinforcements.'

So Radetzky had to be content with what he had. He did not like it. 'What makes our isolated position so difficult,' he wrote,[69] 'is the impossibility of reacting to the danger which threatens, the sad necessity of having to sit back peacefully until we are attacked from within or without.' He added: 'This enforced and unnatural defensive position .... forces us to think at least about the means with which we can play this enforced role without injury to honour.'

The struggle over reinforcements coincided with another battle Radetzky had to fight with Metternich, this time over the issue of martial law. With the disturbances in Milan in September 1848 over the enthronement of the new archbishop, the deterioration in public order led to the demand for the introduction of martial law. On 23 September 1847 Metternich proposed to the Emperor that he should be prepared to introduce the same decree in Lombardy-Venetia that had been introduced in Galicia in 1846.[70] Both the Viceroy and Ficquelmont originally approved this measure, but both were under the illusion that the decision had already been taken, whereas the decree did not in fact take effect till 24 November 1848. In the meantime, Ficquelmont changed his mind, preferring to concentrate on his reform of the Vice-regal Council as a means of pacifying the population. 'The intelligent use of the ordinary means available' to the government and police would suffice at present, he wrote,[71] since many of the malcontents were not 'decidedly hostile' to the government.

The Viceroy's advisers, needless to say, fell into line behind him. He told the Viceroy that martial law should only be introduced when opposition became 'serious and active' or when the threat from outside began to have a serious affect on malcontents inside Lombardy-Venetia. Otherwise, the government might be seen to be overreacting, especially when the trouble-makers might be few in number.[72] The result was that the Viceroy and both governors accepted his arguments and Rainer chose not to publish the decree in November, 'Count Radetzky notwithstanding'.[73]

The Field Marshal, of course, had been urging the implementation of the decree as quickly as possible:[74] 'The whole social order is about to collapse ... the Revolution will only be kept in check by fear ... we have no time to lose .... (otherwise) streams of blood will flow.' Yet his views were completely disregarded. 'In Vienna', wrote Count Hübner,[75] Ficquelmont's designated successor in Italy in 1848, at the start of that year, 'people seem to have forgotten that Lombardy-Venetia exists.' According to the Archduke Maximilian d'Este the prevailing opinion was that the lands south of the Alps were inhabited by uncivilised barbarians who were hardly worth ruling.[76]

Radetzky's fears for the social situation had been stoked by violent outbursts in Milan. On 29 December 1847 Metternich concluded his new defence treaties with Modena and Parma, causing Ficquelmont to hope for a 'change in direction'.[77] But the opponents of Austria in Milan were planning further actions. The younger members of the Jockey Club came up with the idea of starting the new year with a tobacco boycott. Tobacco was a state monopoly in Austria and one which netted 4,386,000 lire per annum. Tobacco boycotts had already taken place in 1751 and 1756 and were almost part, therefore, of the city's political tradition. The boycott started on 2 January 1848 (it was raining on the 1st) and Italians were urged neither to smoke nor use snuff. Needless to say, the Austrians kept smoking and Austrian troops in particular enjoyed walking around town with their cigars in their mouths. Inevitably trouble broke out – either an Austrian blew smoke in the face of an Italian or an Italian knocked a cigar out of the mouth of an Austrian. In any case, riots ensued as early as 2 and 3 January, six people died, and many more were injured. Both sides blamed each other but Radetzky reported to Hardegg:[78] '... nowhere were our troops the attackers but were involved only though necessity and self-defence.'

While the Italians closed ranks, however, the Austrians broke asunder. Ficquelmont and the Governor of Lombardy, Count Spaur, blamed the troops. Radetzky denounced Ficquelmont. The latter demanded that Metternich sack the Field Marshal and even offered to replace him:[79] 'Although out of service in the army for many years, my rank, my experiences and the present difficulties could make me think of taking up military service again. I do not want to believe it but it could come to that eventuality.' This was a rather generous offer: although Wellington, never a good judge, had marked him out as one of the finest cavalry generals of the

Napoleonic Wars, Fiquelmont was 71 years old, suffered from lumbago, and could no longer ride a horse. In any case, Radetzky cooled down, ordered his troops back to barracks and let the streets be patrolled after receiving a note from Spaur that more or less accused him of turning a blind eye to the troops' behaviour.[80] Radetzky exploded and sent the governor an icy rebuke:[81] '...am I supposed to forbid our soldiers from smoking openly because the Jockey Club has so decided? ... So long as His Majesty has faith in me and leaves me at the head of the army in Italy, neither the mayor of Milan nor the Jockey Club will usurp the legal authorities.' Nevertheless, in his correspondence with Metternich, Ficquelmont[82] also blamed the troops; he even asked Radetzky to stop them smoking in public, to consign them to barracks on Sundays and public holidays and to order them to keep away from large population centres such as the Cathedral Square, the Corso and the Street de la Scala.

Soon the army began to see their beloved commander as a scapegoat. One unknown soldier wrote:[83] 'Does Austria exist only to be duped from every side?' One high-ranking officer wrote of Radetzky:[84] 'This man, so given to his duty and to his Emperor is, so to speak, proscribed. The popularity which he enjoyed among the people has now turned to the blackest hatred... Woe betide anyone who lays a finger on him. Then there really would be a bloodbath.' Radetzky was supposed to head an assassination list. He himself wrote:[85] '...A few days ago I was still a popular man; now I stand in the way.'

Metternich came under pressure from both sides. Radetzky warned him that the troops were being put under a severe strain.[86] Everyone in Milan knew who was behind the trouble and yet the civil authorities were doing nothing to restrain them. Mobs followed the patrols around the streets whistling at them and mocking them, but no one was ever arrested. No proclamations forbade unlawful assemblies. At some point 'military defiance and excitement' would confront popular 'frenzy and hatred' and he would not like to contemplate the results. Reports now also began to emerge of Austrian officers describing Austria's position in Italy as untenable. As a result Metternich backed Radetzky.[87] Was the central government in Vienna, he asked Ficquelmont, 'to undertake to run the police force in a town across the Alps?' Why were not the local authorities doing their job and imposing law and order?: 'The whole position is a tissue of faults, the greatest of which are to be found in the local administration.'

On the ground, however, there were still problems. The Viceroy sent instructions to the governors of Lombardy and Venetia on 14 January, telling them that[88] '...it is a decision for the political authorities whether to

in the army and how to supervise it'. His main point was that mili-
ry intervention should be limited and supervised by the civil authorities.
Ficquelmont then pushed his luck by writing to Metternich demanding
that similar instructions be sent by the *Hofkriegsrat* to Radetzky.[89] When
Hardegg refused – 'Where would it lead us if the military ... were to be
undermined?'[90] – Metternich again rebuked Ficquelmont:[91] 'If I had been
in charge of the public services in Milan I would not have hesitated in hand-
ing over the authors of the ban to the police immediately, irrespective of
their class, either after a confession or the disgrace of legal proceedings.'

The introduction of martial law, however, was to arise, not out of
events in Milan, but as a result of developments in Pavia. Students in the
town had been terrorising anyone found smoking, but Colonel Benedek –
the garrison commander in Pavia and another army hero in the Radetzky
tradition – had rebuffed the local delegate (the Austrian civil servant in
charge of the town) when he was asked to stop his troops smoking. He
told him that Radetzky had given orders to pay no attention to the 'street
committee' which had ordered the ban.[92] Radetzky, in fact, had already
secretly banned troops from smoking to prevent attacks on isolated soldiers
and had instructed Benedek to avoid clashes, but now the Field Marshal
decided that in Pavia the only solution was to introduce martial law.[93]
Ficquelmont, however, advised the Viceroy to set up a commission first to
see whose account of events in Pavia was correct.[94]

Radetzky as a result issued a proclamation to his troops, clearly attempting to reconcile them to civilian rule:[95] '... insult nobody; give no cause for
trouble; provoke nobody by unusual treatment.' Metternich, for his part,
was clearly very reluctant to see martial law imposed in Lombardy-Venetia.
On 8 February he wrote to Ficquelmont telling him:[96] '... with respect to
military measures *they have all been taken* ... The Marshal dreams of political war but there is no question of that ... At the moment the Italian provinces have all the military forces they require. What they lack is strong civil
government and I am the first to despair that it might ever be provided by
the Viceroy ...' On 17 February he wrote:[97] 'People cry "*if only there were
military rule*"; to govern is to govern; it does not matter what colour the
uniforms are, whether the costumes are military or civil. By getting rid of
the civil government, you make a vanguard out of your reserve; where then
is your reserve?' The civil government had to rely on the army 'but *not hide
behind it*.' The army, on the other hand, should remain a disciplined force
and hit hard, but only when ordered to by the civil authorities. Almost
immediately after he had written this letter, however, Metternich agreed to

impose martial law in Lombardy-Venetia. The Viceroy received his instructions to publish the decrees on 19 February and they went up in Milan on 22 February and in Venice on 25 February.

Why then had Metternich changed his mind? There have been various explanations offered – including a supposed threat by Radetzky and his highest officers to resign – but the archives provide no supporting evidence. What they do provide is a stream of complaints from high officials – including the Governor of Venetia and the deputy President of the *Hofkriegsrat*, Prince Hohenlohe – that if nothing were done, revolution would break out.[98] Presumably, as a result of these, Metternich's breaking point was reached and he simply conceded. The two sides, however, continued to quarrel and Hohenlohe even received a curious letter from the Emperor encouraging soldiers to do their duty.[99] Ficquelmont returned to Vienna and told Hartig that Radetzky was 'only a name'.[100] The army gave whatever thanks it thought was due for the introduction of martial law to Metternich. When he returned to Vienna from exile, Radetzky assured him that his name 'enjoyed the finest reputation in the army'.[101]

Metternich, indeed, deserved some praise. He had after all managed to squeeze some reinforcements out of the Treasury and during the squabbles with the civil authorities had, on the whole, backed the army. He never quite lost his distrust of Radetzky's instinctual support of the offensive in military operations, but on a couple of other issues he also took decisions which were designed to keep Radetzky happy. One of these was a plan drawn up sometime in January 1848 to invade the Canton Ticino in Switzerland to clear out the radicals there, who were selling guns and ammunition to Lombard revolutionaries and conspiring with Piedmont to invade Lombardy and stir up a nationalist revolt.[102] Once occupied, the canton was to be given a military administration under an 'appropriate general'. Eight battalions, three squadrons and one battery would provide sufficient troops for the job. Radetzky was to organise the military preparations in top secret. The Swiss would pay the costs of the expedition and there would be no further reinforcements sent to Italy to make up the troops sent to Switzerland. The plan, however, was never implemented, presumably because the diplomatic environment made this impossible. The Swiss civil war had been won by the revolutionaries, France having proved unable to help Austria intervene.[103]

Metternich's second cost-effective initiative to keep the army happy was to encourage Radetzky's scheme for the defence of Milan, a topic he had returned to in January 1848.[104] As has been seen, he had come to the conclusion in the 1830s that the Ticino offered no line of defence for Austria – among other things, its Piedmontese bank overlooked the Austrian one – and that only by holding Milan could he remain 'master of Italy'. Milan's importance, though, was not merely strategical. The city was 'the crowning point of Northern Italy' which 'set the tone for the whole of Italy'. The Austrians, he conceded, now ran it only through fear: 'No matter what we do to win the love of her inhabitants, to bind them to us with bonds of loyalty, it is useless.' Thus on no account could Milan 'be left unguarded in our rear'. Austria's military position, in short, lay in holding Milan as its centre of defence, whatever the views of its citizens, and advancing from there to attack Piedmont.

Milan, unfortunately, was in Schönhals's phrase, 'really an open city'.[105] Radetzky agreed: an enemy who marched on it would come 'not before its gates but into its very centre'. In many respects it was a monument to Austrian military neglect. Its city wall was broad but not very tall and could be scaled with ladders. The doors in this wall were little more than barricades. Its citadel had been destroyed by the French and now only contained barracks for the troops. As Schönhals put it:[106] 'We did nothing for the defence of our western borders; we traditionally relied on the cooperation of Piedmont.' Still, Radetzky made clear he was absolutely committed to the city's defence; he would never retreat from it. Indeed, he told the Emperor:[107] 'Everybody knows that such a retreat could take place only over my dead body.' His remarks would be remembered.

How then was Milan to be defended? Radetzky had an engineering colonel called von Tayber draw up a plan. Like Birago's in the 1830s it was cheap enough and involved constructing detached forts (seven this time) around the city in fixed positions.[108] Von Tayber also suggested constructing tower-type redoubts on the five greatest bastions of the citadel. These could protect not merely the city but the spaces in between the forts as well. Radetzky was impressed: '... if we are not involved in any foreign war in the spring, I shall have enough to do for one and a half years to get Milan into such a condition that we can watch unruffled the work of the innovators who are now shaking Italy at its foundations from the extreme tip of Sicily to the Alps.' But when imperial approval came through on 1 March 1848, only the fortification of the citadel had been approved and only 9,300 Gulden were made available for it.[109] If more money proved necessary, it would have to come out of the budgets of other military construction projects. Yet none of this mattered. Two weeks later revolution broke out and Milan fell to the enemy.

# 5

# SAVING AUSTRIA AND EUROPE AGAIN

Radetzky faced the greatest challenge of his life with the outbreak of revolution in Lombardy-Venetia in March 1848. He was now in charge and alone. He was not subject to the oversight of a supreme allied commander and a trio of absolute monarchs as had been the case in 1813–14. He had no allies to rely on at all. Success or failure depended entirely on himself and the outcome would determine not only whether the Habsburg Monarchy would continue to exist, but whether Europe's state system would undergo wars, convulsions and change.

He himself had warned often enough that revolution was approaching. He wrote to his daughter, for example, on 30 November:[1] '... I look forward to troop movements and *prepare myself for March – if it takes till then* (author's emphasis)...' On 4 December he told her:[2] '... Switzerland has been conquered by the radicals.... Now we have radicals to the right, Piedmont in front of us, whose king still wiggles, but who sooner or later will be carried away, and to the left, the Revolution in Central Italy. We must, therefore, create fronts on three sides...' On 11 January:[3] '... serious measures should have been taken but the contemptible weakness of the authorities have postponed them and made them almost impossible now... meanwhile the evil spirit [of revolution] is manifesting itself in the provincial cities so that I cannot pull out any garrisons.' Vienna had let him down. Martial law was not decreed till the end of February and even then the Viceroy insisted that troops remain in local garrisons. Metternich and the Treasury in Vienna had made sure that by the time revolution broke out he had only 75,000 troops under his command rather than the 120,000 he wanted. He was viewed as a warmonger. Milan had not been fortified. He himself complained:[4] 'One consolation remains for me – Vienna not Milan has beaten me. Until the last moment, at all points, I was the victor – had I only a few days' supplies enabling me to hold out, Milan would have been in my hands and with it the whole revolution would have collapsed.'

News from Vienna of Metternich's fall had reached Milan on the evening of 17 March and the revolution really got under way the next morning. That very day the deputy governor of Lombardy, Count O'Donnel, had given him an official note instructing him to keep the military out of any disturbances without first obtaining the permission of the civil authorities.[5] Ironically, on that same day: 'The troops were consigned to their barracks. The outbreak of a general uprising seemed improbable to me too. I found myself in my office when the storm broke, so that I had to flee to the Citadel in order not to be caught up in a mob.'

In retrospect some of Radetzky's views may appear rather self-serving. He still had 15,000 troops in the city as part of the 40,000 in Lombardy as a whole. The trouble was that in the confusion of revolution, with the erecting of barricades in the city, his troops were isolated and cut off, not merely in provincial garrisons but in the Citadel itself, particularly after the city gates were closed on the 19th. It proved impossible to supply them. He held his bakery only with difficulty, while he could not secure supplies of fresh meat that were not poisoned.[6] Initially the advantage may have lain with Radetzky, but things soon changed.

Still, the countryside remained relatively peaceful and the scattered Piedmontese army only in a state of mobilisation, with only three regiments in the vicinity of the border. Radetzky's plan, at least on 19 March was to retain the Citadel and other military buildings, to use mobile troops to quell the insurgents and to maintain a defensive posture on the bastions from which to repulse any external threat. Indeed, more troops were summoned to reinforce the city. However, on 20 March Radetzky's situation deteriorated: the insurgents gained ground, while his own troops began to run short of food and ammunition. Some were cut off in no less than 52 different locations and the Italian troops began to desert. Morale among others began to sink: they had to keep awake all the time and continuously try to rescue others. An attempt by foreign consuls to arrange a ceasefire was refused by the insurgents. Radetzky tried to win new ground in the centre, but the rebels pushed back his troops and then seized the Tosa and Ticino gates. They were better organised and coordinated by now and had put up some 1,651 barricades which proved enormously effective. Some of these barricades were mobile and sheltered mobile columns of insurgents.

After 20 March, Radetzky began to receive reports of losses and defeats suffered by his garrisons at Como, Bergamo, Cremona and Brescia.

There were reports of up to 10,000 armed peasants crossing into Lombardy from Switzerland, from the Canton Ticino.[7] There were also reports of Piedmontese activity near the frontier. On the night of 21–22 March Radetzky therefore took the decision to abandon the city. The Piedmontese factor was probably the least important for him; Charles Albert did not declare war till 23 March or reach Milan till 25 and 26 March, some two days after Radetzky had left the city. He had not needed to conquer it over Radetzky's dead body after all.[8]

Meanwhile Venice had fallen without a shot being fired in its defence. There had not even been a request for help made to D'Aspre's second army corps in Venetia. Schönhals explained its capitulation:[9] 'It was remarkable that shortly before the outbreak of the revolution, no reports reached the Field Marshal from Venetia. In particular no report whatsoever was confirmed from either the General Command or the two Corps Commands concerning the position of things there. One consoled oneself with the hunch that the authorities had nothing to report and that order had been in no way disturbed.'

Apart from the stunning complacency of this statement – 'one consoled oneself with the hunch' indeed! – the archives in fact contain the frankly desperate reports from Count Zichy, the garrison commander in Venice, as well as those of Admiral Martini, the commander of the Arsenal there. These reports were not only received by Radetzky but passed on by him to Vienna with reassurances that all was well. This was one reason why Zichy in mid-February turned directly to Vienna, along with Martini, who described how the government had lost all authority, how the Arsenal workers (who would soon tear his predecessor to pieces when he got lost in the building) were seething with discontent, and how an extra 15,000 troops at least would be needed to restore order. Zichy's 28 February report to the *Hofkriegsrat* asked:[10] '... how can people believe that the greater part of the navy [almost all Italians] is not evilly disposed towards the House of Austria and will not seize weapons to use against us at the first opportunity?' Yet the answer was on account of reassurances received from Radetzky such as:[11] '... however bad the spirit of things in Venice reveals itself to be, I harbour no fears on that account, because, on the one hand it is so easy to reinforce Venice that I myself would have no difficulties in putting down any attempt at an uprising.' Martini must surely have been astonished therefore at the replies he got to his pitiable reports from Vienna. One read:[12] 'You do not fail to recognise the difficulties of your present situation, but, on the other hand, one expects complete pacification from the steps now being taken by the high command which entitle people to hope for the best.' What steps? Martini's predecessor was murdered.[13] Zichy did not even ask d'Aspre for military support. He merely surrendered – and was later court-martialled.

The loss of Milan and Venice, of course, left huge supplies of munitions, weapons, money, and stores of all sorts in the hands of the Italians. It left Radetzky with a huge credibility problem in Vienna. Had he not turned out to be just another failed Austrian general? Was he not long past his prime at the age of 82? Was he to be admired simply for his bluster and those splendid flourishes and proclamations that his adjutant General Schönhals rather than he himself composed? In short was he not a figure out of *opéra bouffe*? Radetzky immediately proved the answer to be a resounding no.

It soon became clear to Radetzky that his garrison of perhaps 15,000 loyal troops could not hold out against a hostile population of 170,000, given the rebels' success in cutting off so many of his soldiers in isolated pockets and their skilful use of barricades. There was also the bad news coming in from provincial garrisons and the Piedmontese border. Thus before Charles Albert could arrive, Radetzky had taken the cool decision not to bombard the city – which would have been both desperate and destructive and would have left Austria for ever accused of barbarism[14] – but to evacuate it and allow his army to retreat in a disciplined fashion. There was perhaps no precedent in military history for a commander, who had not been previously defeated in battle, to undertake such a move. Yet Radetzky – as always – had a plan. He would withdraw until he had received reinforcements from the Austrian interior and then take the offensive – the only strategy he ever believed in – and smash the Italians once and for all.

In the judgement of one historian, his decision to retreat constituted not merely a decision but 'a wide-ranging programme'.[15] The great Quadrilateral of forts at the centre of Lombardy-Venetia, namely Verona, Mantua, Legnano and Peschiera, would become the base for his counter-attack. Verona, not Milan, would serve as the pivot of his plan, although before he heard of the fall of Venice, he did consider (astonishingly) a lightning counter-attack: 'My plan was was to position myself behind the Adda, to gather all my disposable troops, to open communications with all the fortresses in my rear, to (re)organise my army and then to attack Milan again.'[16] News of events in Venice, Brescia, Cremona and even Vienna meant that this was not feasible, but his ruthless determination is the point to note. Radetzky's own words to Ficquelmont at 5pm on 22 March were:[17] 'It is the most frightening decision of my life but I can no longer hold Milan.' The next day he was reporting from Melegnano:[18] 'My retreat is completely successful. *It is one of these sad masterstrokes of the art of war.* [author's emphasis]' The rest of his campaign would see many more. The Field Marshal would soon show Vienna and Europe his true worth.

Radetzky and his troops left Milan with only the clothes they stood up in. Families of officers and officials managed to rescue more belongings. Radetzky had four silver pieces in his pocket. A dragoon corporal managed to save his decorations. Munitions were left behind – it was more important to take what stores of money had been rescued by the troops. Some resistance was encountered in Melegnano, where the local city council had the 'cheek' to demand of Radetzky that he lay down his arms. The council even imprisoned a colonel Radetzky had sent to negotiate with it in the local castle. However, Radetzky bombarded the building, stormed the town and freed the man concerned. His retreating army met no more resistance.

In Lodi Radetzky received news of the fall of Venice. It was a hard blow, but rumours about Mantua proved false. It was held by the resourceful General Ritter von Gorczkowski, with Radetzky sending troops on a quick march to reinforce him. Having arrived at the Quadrilateral, on 3 April the Field Marshal issued a general order to his troops:[19] '... From higher considerations of the art of war, I have yielded as a general, not you! You were not defeated, you know that at all points where you appeared you remained victors. Soldiers, trust me, as I trust you! I will soon lead you forward to revenge the treason and breach of faith committed against you!' The old soldier had spent almost ten days in the same clothes and ten hours a day in the saddle; he had received all sorts of bad news, but had masterminded the retreat his army had to make. And already he was not only shouldering full responsibility but promising revenge!

Once the 2nd Army Corps with its 15,000 men had joined him, Radetzky had about 50,000 men and 136 guns.[20] He needed 12,000 men to protect the crossing points on the Mincio and a further 12,000 men to garrison the forts of the Quadrilateral. A corps of 5,000 was formed at Pastrengo to secure communication with the Tyrol, so that he was left with only 20,000 men to use as a mobile force.[21] He urgently required reinforcements from Austria. The period of real anxiety now began: all food, weapons, munitions and medical supplies in Lombardy had been lost. After ten days in bad weather his army had arrived at the Quadrilateral poorly clothed and many without boots. Nor was there much room for them in and between the four forts, and, as the Piedmontese advanced, that space became smaller, the army retreating to the space around Verona. All supplies had to come from Inner Austria, but the links were poor and in Vienna itself political conditions were hardly stable.

Charles Albert, on the other hand, whose arrival was expected any day, commanded an army of between 75,000–100,000 men. The main army heading towards the Mincio consisted of 50,000 Piedmontese plus 15,000–18,000 Papal troops under General Durando in Venetia. The other allies (Tuscany, the smaller Duchies plus Lombard volunteers) provided 10,000–12,000 men for the main army, while 15,000 Neapolitans should have been heading for the Quadrilateral from the south.[22] Thus Radetzky had imminently to face c.70,000–80,000 men aided by almost 20,000 men from Venice. He clearly had to fight on the defensive, given that he had only around 20,000 mobile troops, even if this went against all his instincts and experience. He could not even meet the enemy on the Mincio; he was restricted to an area around Verona. Yet Verona was an antiquated fort, relatively small in size, its bastions leading almost around the outskirts of the town, thus leaving his army with little room in which to manoeuvre. Nor could a battle be fought on the ramparts of the fort – this would lead to encirclement, while the approaches to the south and west were clear only for about 4,000 yards before the bastions of the fort rose sharply up to form a very steep slope (the so-called Curtain) with both sides adjoining the Etsch. Still, this area did offer a good, if tight, defensive position.

Of the other forts of the Quadrilateral, Legnano, the smallest, was the best armed. Mantua had 'hydraulic engines' and was considered strong both on that account and because of its commander, General Ritter von Gorczkowski, who would later, famously, respond in broken Italian to a nationalist citizens' committee which had asked him to remove the cannon threatening the town:[23] '*Mantovani buoni, Gorczkowski bono; Mantovani cattivi, Gorczkowski, boom, boom!* (Citizens of Mantua good, Gorczkowski good; citizens of Mantua bad, Gorczkowski boom boom!)' Peschiera was small, had been completely neglected, and was situated in an unlucky geographical position at the exit of the Mincio from Lake Guarda, both overlooked and accessible from the Lake itself. Given its proximity to the single line of communication with the Etsch Valley, it was bound to attract Piedmontese attention. Yet there was no time to rearm or strengthen it. There were also fears for the Tyrol at this time, but local volunteers (organised with the help of the Archduke John) plus General Welden's troops managed to keep control of the province.[24]

On 7 April Charles Albert's advance guard reached the Mincio and Radetzky withdrew his to the area around Verona. Charles Albert took up his main position opposite Radetzky's on the high ground around Sona and Sommacampagna.[25] He attempted a probe against Mantua, which failed, and it took him till 2 June to even capture Peschiera. Yet he did manage, after three days of fighting, to remove the Austrians from Pastrengo and Rivoli where they had been defending the link with the Tyrol. Yet nothing much happened for a month. In the meantime, Radetzky received some reinforcements, little by little, and strengthened his fortifications at Verona. Several hundred guns were prepared and placed on the bastions, not merely to defend the fort but to be ready, if needed, to put down any rebellion inside the city.

On 6 May Charles Albert with the whole Piedmontese army moved against Verona. His supporters inside the town had promised to start an uprising at the same time, so he had high hopes of victory. The battle began early in the morning. The Piedmontese attacked with vigour and were led with intelligence, directing their main thrust against Crocebianca and Santa Lucia. At Santa Lucia three Austrian battalions stood up to three Piedmontese divisions for three hours before retreating, but Radetzky did not give up. He found reserves from somewhere, recaptured Santa Lucia and organised a counter-offensive that drove the enemy back. After an honourable struggle, Charles Albert withdrew in the late afternoon.

The Piedmontese wrote off the encounter as insignificant and returned to their original positions, to put their faith in diplomatic developments. However, for the Austrians, Santa Lucia was crucial. In the view of one historian:[26] 'Radetzky's victory was more than a battle won – it was a successful campaign. Santa Lucia is the great, decisive turning-point in the events of 1848. The Austrian army, hardly half as strong as the attacker, had passed the test, its old self-confidence had been restored.' Even the young Franz Joseph was there to witness the victory. No uprising in Verona took place either and Radetzky's success was hailed in Vienna and Europe. The muse even inspired Grillparzer to write his famous lines to Radetzky:

*"Glück auf mein Feldherr, führe den Streich – In Deinem Lager ist Österreich!"*
(Good Luck my commander! Lead the attack! In thy camp is Austria!)

The battle also gave rise to other famous bits of poetry, particularly the song composed in memory of the famous exploits of the 10th Jäger Battalion, but victory had been made possible 'by the unbending will of the Field Marshal',[27] who in spite of his inferior numbers, his weak strategic position, his early loss of Santa Lucia, and the fear of an uprising inside Verona itself, stood coolly on the bastion of San Spirito directing his troops, and found the two extra battalions of reinforcements from the city's garrison at the key point in the battle to achieve the urgent victory.

Radetzky's luck then changed. One week after Santa Lucia, Hess, whose return Radetzky had requested secretly from Vienna, arrived at Verona to become his chief of staff. Two weeks later, the first reserve corps arrived from Austria bringing much-needed manpower, food and supplies. When revolution had broken out in Milan, Radetzky had sent Captain Huyn of his general staff to Verona to get reserves for the ensuing battle. Achieving nothing there, Huyn had gone on to Inner Austria with the famous instruction from Radetzky:[28] 'See what you can pull together.' ('*Schau, was Du zusammenbringen kannst.*') In Graz FML Count Nugent had then relinquished his post as head of the general command to organise all the troops in the region into a reserve corps at the Isonzo, with the blessing of the War Minister, Count Latour. By mid-April he had collected about 15,000 men. Yet between them and Radetzky stood General Durando's Papal troops, who had converted many towns into fortresses, supported by volunteers under the command of General Ferrari.

Nugent started his advance on 17 April and under normal circumstances – good weather, no enemy – his march should have taken three weeks. At the start of May he met Durando at Conegliano and, while his main force took shelter in the mountains, he sent a flanking unit to force the Italians back to Pederobba. Soon after that Nugent fell ill and was replaced by General Count Thurn, who soon faced the decision, once again, whether to attack Durando head on at Vicenza or bypass him. He decided on the latter course and on 22 May arrived at San Bonifacio, scarcely a day's march from Verona. Radetzky, however, had not agreed with his decision and he was ordered back to expel Durando from Vicenza – if this did not take too much blood or time, otherwise he could break off the attack. Thurn obeyed orders on the 23 May but did abandon the offensive when he saw the casualties likely to be involved, entering Verona on 25 May. Radetzky's decision was open to criticism – he badly needed the supplies and manpower of the Reserve Corps – but he was already thinking of taking the next step and did not want Durando compromising its chances of success.

Radetzky's confidence was now steadily growing: he had won at Santa Lucia, had been reunited with Hess, had received reinforcements and had consolidated his fortifications. Even God seemed to be on his side – on 29 April the Pope had publicly declared himself against the revolution and against war with Austria. Radetzky, in any case, now wanted to do something to relieve Peschiera. It had limited power of resistance and its fall would signify no decisive blow; still, it would furnish propaganda for the enemy.

Radetzky gave the Reserve Corps no more than two days to rest. He then reformed his army and having decided not to attack Charles Albert directly, led a flanking move by night on 27 May around his troops to fight a battle and relieve Peschiera. Ignoring cannon shots along the Piedmontese lines, Radetzky led his army towards Mantua, apparently to engage the southern Piedmontese front at Curtatone and Goito. There the first attack on 29 May was a resounding success, but heavy Piedmontese reinforcements, very heavy rain which turned the ground into swamp, and then the news that Peschiera had fallen after all on 2 June, brought the well-planned operation to an end. Radetzky's forces returned to Verona and the Piedmontese celebrated their supposedly 'decisive' victory.

Radetzky, on the other hand, who was quite unworried by this, and still determined to take the offensive, now decided to expel Durando from Vicenza and open up communications with the Isonzo. Hence he led his army out of the south western corner of the Quadrilateral against the north eastern enemy force. One part of his forces was ordered to move slowly and demonstratively towards Verona, as if returning there in defeat after Goito, while the main force under the Field Marshal himself, sped, despite difficulties with high waters, via Legnano to Vicenza, which was stormed on 10 June. Durando capitulated and promised to quit the theatre of war within days. Meanwhile, part of Radetzky's army returned quickly to Verona, where on 11 June part of Charles Albert's army had approached the Curtain from the west, having discovered that the Field Marshal had not retreated from Mantua to Verona after all. However, this tentative advance by the Piedmontese was abandoned on 12 June. The Piedmontese leadership, increasingly afraid that the war in Italy was becoming too revolutionary in character, was relying now perhaps on diplomacy to win the day; it was certainly prepared to abandon Manin's new Republic of Venice to the enemy.[29]

Certainly, there was a very good chance that Vienna would negotiate a peace behind Radetzky's back. For a start, it had sent down the former Governor of Lombardy, Count Hartig, as Peace Commissioner with Nugent's relief army, while pursuing diplomatic negotiations both directly with the Lombard Provisional Government established in Milan after Radetzky's retreat and indirectly with the Sardinians through London.

Count Hartig failed to mention his pacification mission to Lombardy-Venetia in the spring and summer of 1848, when he came to write his famous account of the 'genesis' of the revolutions in Austria. Given Radetzky's eventual triumph, this is not difficult to explain. Initially though Radetzky's reputation had sunk very low in Vienna; Milan had fallen, Venice had capitulated without a shot and Radetzky had chosen to lead his army in retreat into the Quadrilateral. Ficquelmont, therefore, who after the revolution briefly became first foreign and then prime minister of Austria, wrote to him on 20 April 1848 instructing him to be prepared for a negotiated peace.[30] In a rather patronising letter, he explained that an uprising 'as general and decisive' as the one that had just taken place could 'be put down only by an equally decisive war or by way of negotiations'. Yet 'even if Austria had the means to wage such a war of repression', it was not at all clear whether she could do so in the light of world and Italian opinion. The decision had been taken, therefore, to pursue peace negotiations even while the war was being continued. 'With luck', according to Ficquelmont, 'the struggle might be contained to the Venetian provinces', but (even) 'advantages in war' could 'only contribute to the restoration of peace through negotiations'. He therefore expected 'the closest identification of the military leadership with attempts to reach a peace'.

Radetzky was not informed of the details of any negotiations that might take place, although he might well have guessed that the Austrian plan was to surrender Lombardy in the hope of retaining Venetia. He was informed, however, that Count Hartig would be sent to Lombardy with instructions to take control of any territory won back by the Field Marshal. If in theory his job was to 'pacify' the Italians, in practice, as might have been predicted, it would be to 'pacify' Radetzky.

Peace negotiations were conducted on three levels after the outbreak of revolution in March 1848: through Hartig, once he had joined up with Nugent's relief army, which proved able, fairly quickly, as has been seen, to reinforce Radetzky; through Hummelauer, an Austrian diplomat who was sent to London in order to secure British mediation between Austria and the Italians; and through various emissaries who were sent to Milan in an attempt to split the Lombards from the Sardinians.

Hummelauer's mission was clearly a rather desperate one. Before he left he was told:[31]

> We find it impossible to give you any precise instructions. It is absolutely necessary for us to bring the Italian problem to a speedy end. See what support can be got from the English government. The essential thing for us is that a part of the state debt should be taken over. We lack the means to

wage a war in a sufficiently effective manner and even a battle won would not solve the problem. Let us know how you find things.

Fortunately for Radetzky, it proved impossible to win the British government over to a suitable compromise. When Hummelauer asked Palmerston to mediate on the basis of home-rule for Lombardy-Venetia, his offer was rejected on 23 May. The next day he suggested mediation on the basis of surrendering Lombardy and offering home-rule to Venetia. Palmerston accepted this proposal, but it was then turned down by the British cabinet on 3 June. Hummelauer returned to Vienna empty-handed.

Meanwhile, attempts were undertaken to split the Lombard provisional government in Milan from its Piedmontese ally. These, too, however, got nowhere. Another Austrian diplomat, von Phillipsberg, was sent to Milan with the offer of a separate Lombard kingdom under a Habsburg prince to be governed by an elected parliament. The mission, however, had an unexpected outcome. Von Phillipsberg was arrested and imprisoned on the grounds that his credentials were not in order. Undeterred, the imperial government then sent another agent, Schnitzer-Meerau by name, this time with an offer to grant Lombardy complete independence. The 'equitable conditions' attached were 'to comprise principally of the transfer of a proportionate part of the state debt of the Austrian Empire to Lombardy'.[32] The Lombards declined this proposal and by 25 June Schnitzer-Meerau was reporting that they were demanding independence not merely for Lombardy but for all Habsburg Italian territories as a prelude to negotiations.

The Field Marshal, meanwhile, had been complaining bitterly about Hartig's efforts at pacification, which struck him as ridiculous. They would, he insisted, be taken merely for weakness. In any case, he had no intention of cooperating with Hartig, telling the War Minister, Count Latour:[33] 'I will negotiate with these people only with the sword in my hand.' He maintained that Hartig's instructions were incompatible with the last instructions he personally had received from the Emperor (to act, if necessary, in accordance with the laws of war). On other occasions, he said he did not understand them. In any case, he believed that Hartig was being manipulated by the Italians, who were receiving permission from him to publish newspapers, which in turn carried false information and anti-Austrian propaganda. He took careful steps, therefore, to avoid meeting the man, while not neglecting to inform him – and Latour – that if martial law were lifted in Lombardy-Venetia – especially in the Quadrilateral, which was in a state of siege – he would lay down his sword:[34] 'I as a loyal subject can do nothing but obey. But I would then be compelled to lay down my command.'

In the middle of this dispute, however, a more serious problem arose. On 11 June, Wessenberg, the new foreign minister, instructed Radetzky to negotiate a ceasefire with the Piedmontese. The war was 'costly' and the army deserved a 'well-earned rest'.[35] The Field Marshal was thunderstruck. He wrote to Hartig in contempt:[36] 'We have sunk low, but by God not yet so low.' His reaction was to send his *Felddiplomat* (military diplomat), Prince Felix zu Schwarzenberg, who had been Austrian ambassador to Naples before the outbreak of revolution in Italy in 1848, to Innsbruck to overturn the decision. In fact, the decisive clash between the two men took place in Vienna. The foreign minister was mainly worried by the financial costs of the war and the possibility of French intervention. Yet Schwarzenberg, following arguments drafted by Radetzky, countered that there was little hope of saving money by surrendering Lombardy – the Italians would merely threaten Venetia and attack at the first opportunity, while Austria, meanwhile, would have to pay to keep a large army there on a permanent war footing to defend her remaining province. Again, it was not in France's interest to intervene to create a strong Italian state on her southern frontier. Nor was Radetzky intending to provoke the French by invading Piedmont – that was a danger he was well aware of. Finally, a *de facto* ceasefire already existed, since neither army was in a position to take the initiative. What was really needed was more troops and a decisive battle. Once Wessenberg heard of the failure of the Schnitzer-Meerau mission and of Lombardy's union with Piedmont, he was prepared to agree.[37]

By now Radetzky had also won on the issue of domestic policy and pacification. Count Hartig had resigned as Court Commissioner on 3 July. Only a few days beforehand, Radetzky had written to him:[38]

> I, too, honestly regret that there had to be differences between us in many respects concerning our views on the present state of Italy. However, I have had such bitter experiences, partly on account of the neglect of all my warnings and forecasts about conditions here, that Your Excellency will not reproach me if I now consider that out of this general wreckage I have at least kept my military honour unblemished. I also harbour the hope that Your Excellency will retain those friendly feelings towards me which you so often displayed in earler and better times.

The tide now seemed to be turning in Radetzky's favour. In June, the reactionary Field Marshal Prince Windischgraetz bombarded Prague and strengthened the counter-revolution; inside Italy, the Pope agreed after Vicenza that no more Papal troops would trouble Austria; events in Naples brought about the recall of Neapolitan forces. Renewed links with Austria and Venetia, plus the continued inaction of the Piedmontese, meant that Radetzky's position in Verona was transformed. Padua surrendered without a shot to Austrian forces on 14 June, Treviso on 16 June and Palmanuova on 25 June. With the exception of Venice itself, the whole of Venetia returned to Austrian rule. Meanwhile, reinforcements continued to arrive at Verona.

The Piedmontese also received reinforcements, about 30,000 in all, yet almost half were made up of deserting Lombards, whom Charles Albert deeply mistrusted.[39] He was also wary of revolution breaking out within his own kingdom, forcing him to leave behind the national guard and strong reserves in case they were needed. By the end of July, therefore, Charles Albert had 70,000–80,000 troops with which to challenge Radetzky's mobile force of perhaps 60,000 (out of an Austrian army total perhaps of 96,000 men and 261 guns). Radetzky, however, reckoned that his troops were much better trained and led – many of the new Piedmontese units lacked experienced officers – and was itching to resume the offensive. However, he was only able to do so once Schwarzenberg had killed off all government desires to conclude a ceasefire and a compromise peace.

Charles Albert, just as much as Radetzky, needed a military victory. He faced charges of military inaction and counter-revolutionary politics. His strategy, however, proved defective. Part of his army took up a strong position at Rivoli and cut off the road to the Tyrol to prevent support for Radetzky getting through. His main army, meanwhile, continued to take its stand on the heights of Sona and Sommacampagna in positions that would be difficult to overpower, with its left wing facing Verona and its right, extensively secured against any movement from Mantua, also ready to meet any movement from Verona, along a broad front from Villafranca to Roverbella. Yet the king decided to besiege Mantua, which had seven months' worth of supplies and had recently received two extra brigades for offensive occupation. Besieging Mantua not only employed part of the new reserves, but removed troops from other parts of the Piedmontese front line. These developments would soon prove fatal.

Radetzky's army meanwhile had been thoroughly reorganised into four corps and one reserve corps. The main force, including the first, second and the reserve corps, was stationed at Verona; the third, under General Count Thurn, was stationed in the Etsch Valley, south of Trent in the Tyrol; from the newly formed fourth corps two brigades were sent to Mantua; a third was initially entrusted with a special expedition to Ferrara, but was then also ordered to go to Mantua and was on its way there, when its commander, General Prince Liechtenstein, who had gone on ahead to talk to the fortress commander, was cut off there by the besieging Piedmontese; his brigade was then forced to return to Verona, where it came under the command of General Baron Simbschen. It would soon become famous. These movements seem to indicate that Radetzky's initial thinking was to begin his offensive from Mantua, but the Piedmontese siege of the fortress plus the failed Piedmontese probe against Verona persuaded him to attack Charles Albert directly.

Radetzky's new plan was that Thurn would clear the Piedmontese from Rivoli, thus weakening the Piedmontese front at Sona–Sommacampagna, which Radetzky's main force would attack from Verona. Its aim was then to break through to the Mincio and fight the Piedmontese on one or other bank. Thurn, in fact, had little success when he attacked on 22 July and broke off the fight that night, only to find that the Piedmontese had abandoned their positions anyway. Radetzky's frontal attack on Sona and Sommacampagna on 23 July, on the other hand, proved a complete success causing the Piedmontese to retreat behind the Mincio, leaving the most important crossing points in Austrian hands.

The Piedmontese forces around Villafranca, meanwhile, knew nothing of these events, so Charles Albert used them to launch a powerful attack on 24 July against Radetzky's left (southern) flank, hoping to break through and make contact with the rear of Radetzky's forces on the Mincio. The plan was ingenious and well planned. Four brigades were to regain the heights of Sona and Sommacampagna, which were defended only by a thin line of Austrian troops. These were reinforced by the Simbschen brigade who had been sent there on a hard march in blistering heat and some disorder. They fought extremely well for hours, but were eventually dispersed, leaving Charles Albert again in command of the heights in Radetzky's rear.

On 24 July Radetzky had still intended to fight on the Mincio, but with Charles Albert's breakthrough, it was clear a different, although decisive, battle would have to be fought the next day. The key was to be able to swing the whole Austrian army round to the south to face Sona and Sommacampagna again. This was a difficult manoeuvre, but Radetzky achieved it. Thus on 25 July General Baron d'Aspre's second corps threw back brigades of the Piedmontese right flank on the heights of Sommacampagna, aided by a brigade sent out from Verona. There, General Baron Haynau, Radetzky's most energetic commander who was now in charge of the fort, had been observing events through a telescope. Having witnessed the misfortune of the Simbschen brigade, entirely on his own authority, he had ordered a brigade under General Perin, already under orders to go to Castelnuovo, to replace it. Haynau was later awarded the commander cross of the Maria Theresa order for his quick thinking. Meanwhile, Custoza also fell forcing the Piedmontese to withdraw completely behind the Mincio. Radetzky reported:[40] 'A decisive victory has been the result of this hot day.'

After a retreating action at Volta (26 July) Charles Albert requested a ceasefire but terms could not be agreed. The Piedmontese, therefore, continued their retreat, albeit in a much more disorderly fashion than Radetzky four months earlier, although still in friendly territory. The new reserves almost all deserted. On 1 August, the British minister to Turin, Abercrombie, turned up at Radetzky's headquarters, again requesting a ceasefire. Radetzky, however, referred him to Schwarzenberg, his *Felddiplomat*, who told him that a ceasefire would only be negotiated in Milan once all Piedmontese troops had left Lombardy. On 4 and 5 August the Austrians stormed all the last Piedmontese positions before Milan and arranged the handover of the city.

At the last minute, however, Charles Albert was penned inside the Palazzo Creppi by unruly Milanese elements who accused him of betraying them. Shots were fired at his window and it looked as if the Piedmontese might even have to bombard the city to free their now humiliated king. However his troops managed to release him and a deputation from the city agreed with Radetzky that the Austrians would reoccupy it the next day. The mayor even asked Radetzky to hurry in case the populace plundered it beforehand. Could he have been given any greater satisfaction?

On 23 March Radetzky had called out to Milan, 'We shall return!'[41] Now on 6 August – 137 days later – he had kept his promise. A ceasefire was negotiated on 9 August which required eight days' notice to end. The state of war was over. Already on 30 July an emissary from the Emperor had tracked Radetzky down to give him both the personal congratulations of Ferdinand and the Great Cross of the Maria Theresa Order, which Francis I had prophesied after Leipzig that Radetzky would one day receive. His greatest ambition was now surely fulfilled. On 7 August he wrote to his daughter from Milan:[42]

> You see, my beloved Fritzi, that with God's help, on the fourteenth day of my offensive I have been fortunate to arrive here and set up my HQ in the Villa (which should be called Reale), to have defeated King Charles Albert in four hard-fought battles, latterly before the gates of Milan, and thus to have conquered Lombardy.... My possessions as well as the effects of others were sold for trinkets; I intend, where possible, to buy mine back... I will happily retire, since it is truly very difficult for me to endure the fatigue. I see, however, that I cannot let go of the machine which has not yet consolidated itself, so that I must patiently trust in God and keep a firm hold of the rudder.

He was still holding the rudder ten years later.

It was on a splendid evening in August 1848 at a concert at the *Wasserglacis* in Vienna that Johann Strauss the elder conducted his *Radetzky March* for the very first time. There was a storm of celebration. The march was demanded time and time again and soon, in one historian's singularly apt phrase, it became 'a national anthem without words'.[43]

Still, Radetzky's military career was not yet over. 1849 saw him win another great victory in an almost model campaign. If it had taken him 134 days in 1848 to defeat the Italians, Radetzky saw the March 1849 war out in just 100 hours.

The Piedmontese were attempting to take advantage of Austria's difficulties in Hungary by launching a war, both to aid their ally, Hungary's nationalist leader Kossuth, and to regain the honour, territory and prestige they had lost in 1848.

The Hungarians had been a complication for Radetzky right from the start of the 1848 campaign and were part of the nationality question he had to deal with inside his army. This concerned his South Slav as well as Hungarian troops but most seriously affected his Italian troops, who he was leading against fellow-Italians under the command of Charles Albert.

It used to be thought that the Habsburgs operated a very deliberate policy of divide and rule within their Empire and armed forces. One famous quote, attributed to Francis I, for example, ran (although no source was given):[44] 'My peoples are strange to each other and that is all right... I send the Hungarians into Italy and the Italians into Hungary. Every people watches its neighbour. The one does not understand the other.... From their antipathy will be born order and from mutual hatred, general peace.'

Yet this simply was not true. For example, in Hungary in 1848 the largest national contingent in the army was the Hungarians, who constituted 68 per cent of the infantry and 43 per cent of the army as a whole. Indeed, some regiments (the 38th and 45th for example) hardly ever left their recruiting areas. It might be argued, therefore, that the real Habsburg policy was to exaggerate the proportion of troops recruited locally in any province. And this was also the case in Italy. The largest national contingent in Radetzky's army was the Italians, constituting 39 per cent of the infantry and 33 per cent of the army as a whole.[45]

Radetzky had firm views on the nationality problem. In one of his previously-mentioned memoranda, in the context of the 'cadre system', he wrote:[46]

> In this context it would be necessary for regiments to remain continually in their home provinces... However, this system would very soon lead to *national* i.e. Bohemian, Austrian, Italian, Hungarian armies etc etc... Is this advisable and is it in the state's interest? I believe the answer would have to be No... the present moment would be a highly dangerous one for such a reform... Before this could happen... or would be advisable, the *Zeitgeist* would have to change considerably.

Radetzky in principle was fairly open minded on the question, but not politically innocent. There was a case for keeping all regiments in their own provinces, but not so long as nationalism was so strong. That did not mean, however, that he had any objections to the Italians being the largest contingent in the army in Lombardy-Venetia. Count Hartig, for example, on the eve of the revolutions, doubted the loyalty of these troops, but when he expressed these doubts to army leaders in Italy, he discovered that 'their loyalty had not only not been doubted, but every allusion to such doubts... was looked upon as a violation of their military honour'.[47]

In Italy in March 1848 of Radetzky's 61 infantry battalions, nine were Hungarian, six were Czech, ten were South Slav, 12 were Austrian and 24 were Italian. In a report of December 1847, he had written:[48] 'I do not mistrust these troops in the least; they will do their duty; but we must not expect more of them than is reasonable, particularly when they are being led into battle against their own compatriots.' Radetzky, therefore, was his usual cool, rational self, when analysing his situation.

Yet he was brought up against the reality of his own prophecy, for by the beginning of April, nearly 11,000 of his Italian troops had deserted – leaving the remaining 10,000 as an extra problem:[49] Where were they to be deployed? In the front line? There they could cross over, use their weapons against him and form a gap in the line of battle which had to be dangerous. In reserve they would threaten his rear; to keep them in the fortresses would be even more dangerous, since they could then deliver them to the enemy. The only solution remaining was to divide them up in such a way that only partial and gradual defections could result; in the worst circumstances he would 'disarm and dissolve them'. As it happened, more desertions did take place, although several regiments, particularly those which had been stationed in Italy for a long time, remained loyal.

The rising tensions between the Hungarians and South Slavs were also to create problems. The Hungarian government, guided by Kossuth and public opinion, refused to send extra troops to Italy and pressed for a political settlement there that would have meant surrendering at least Lombardy to the Italians. (The Hungarian master plan was to have the German provinces join a united Germany, the Italian ones join a united Italy, leaving Hungary to dominate the Monarchy.)

The Croats, on the other hand, remained loyal and sent Radetzky reinforcements. Yet from time to time, support from the South Slavs also looked precarious. The Serb Patriarch, Rajačić, for example, threatened to recall the *Grenzer* (troops from the Croatian military border) if he was not given more protection by the imperial army in southern Hungary against the Hungarians. Indeed, he even threatened to ally himself with the Piedmontese, a move which South Slav political radicals were actually advocating. Under these circumstances – made even more ominous by the fact that the Piedmontese in the theatre of war were refusing to recognise Hungarian troops as their 'real' enemies – Radetzky clearly needed to be seen to be neutral as far as the Hungarian Question was concerned.

In the end he managed to achieve this, although his personal sympathies lay with Jelačić and the Croats. To War Minister Latour he wrote:[50] 'I do not wish at present to examine the question whether the over-confidence of the Hungarians in their treatment of the nationalities existing beside them has given rise to the misfortunes which now threaten us from this side. It is enough that this misfortune has arisen.' His aim was to appear to be impartial and conciliatory; he also made arrangements for the mail and reading matter of the troops to be censored to spare them the news from Hungary and Croatia. Meanwhile he wrote to Rajačić:[51]

I do not intend to set myself in judgement over both parties which now threaten Hungary with unforeseeable misfortunes. But their leaders, whoever they are, will be harshly judged by world history. It cannot – it must not – come to a split in the Austrian army. The army is still loyal and is imbued with the noblest spirit. If it is forced to, it will take up arms to save the integrity of the Monarchy in the same way that it has triumphed over its external enemies.... I beg Your Excellency to mediate between the parties; employ the respect of your holy office to prevent the shedding of blood – is there no other way to reconcile the two parties apart from the most unfortunate way of all – civil war?

In other ways the Field Marshal also kept his distance from the Hungarian Question.

It was fortunate, perhaps, that he had no spare cash and could not, therefore, send funds to Jelačić. Likewise, if he allowed the Serb leader, Suplikač, to return home from Italy, he also granted the same privilege to the Hungarian War Minister, Colonel Mészáros. The future well-known military commander, Mollinary, recorded in his memoirs:[52] 'Thanks to the excellent spirit which Radetzky had inculcated into his troops, the actions of numerous emissaries of the Hungarian insurrection aimed at provoking desertions among our Hungarian soldiers by appealing to their national sentiment had only a very limited success.' Among the large number of Hungarian officers in the army, although their national feeling was very lively, very few quit Radetzky's army for the Hungarian one then being formed. Mészáros invited Mollinary, for example, to join the Hungarian army along with him, but Mollinary refused since his sentiments were for 'the imperial crown not merely the royal one'.[53]

If Radetzky could do nothing for Jelačić, the latter was able to do something for him. He agreed to a request from Schwarzenberg to issue a proclamation to the *Grenzer* serving in Italy. In part this ran:[54] 'Do not allow yourselves to be diverted by reports and fears for the safety of your homeland... be assured we feel strong enough to defend our nationality without assistance from you.' By November 1848, therefore, Radetzky could report to Vienna:[55] 'If so far I have had the great luck to see unity maintained among the nationalities of the army under my command, the greatest part of which consists of Hungarian and Croat regiments, it has been thanks only to the circumstances that the appearance of the government favouring one nationality at the cost of any other has been avoided.' A British report to Lord Palmerston, meanwhile, had reached the same conclusion:[56] 'With respect to the differences that existed between the Hungarians and the Croats, I understand that Field Marshal Radetzky, with his usual tact and talent, has managed to put an end to them.' It was a remarkable achievement.

In March 1849, however, Radetzky had a second war to fight with Sadinia-Piedmont and on 18 March he issued a proclamation to the Milanese:[57]

> Without hate or vengeance I returned to a city which I have loved and if I could not spare you all the burdens inseparable from war, I have neglected no effort to alleviate them; if, in spite of my warning rebellion should again raise its head, the punishment of the guilty will be quick and terrible, for I am strong enough to overthrow my enemy whether within or without the frontier.

To his troops he issued a general order in which he promised to lead them to a quick victory in Turin:[58] 'Follow your venerable leader into battle and victory. I shall bear witness to your brave deeds and the last act of a soldier's long life will be to be able in the capital of a faithless enemy to decorate the breasts of my valiant comrades with the insignia of courage won in blood and fame. So forwards. To Turin is the watchword. There we shall find peace.' But he had also mocked the Piedmontese. They had asked for a ceasefire in 1848, because they wanted peace. 'So they said. But instead of that they have armed for a new war. Well the peace we so generously offered them then we now intend to wrest from them in their capital.' The correspondent of the London *Times* found all this very regrettable:[59] 'although it is impossible to deny the force of the Marshal's logic or the truth of his sarcasms, we could have wished... that the pen had less of the keenness of his sword.' If Austrian rule were to last, it was not desirable to 'lash a hostile population into a fury or to torture a conquered people with taunts and gibes more incurable than the wounds of war.' Yet the journalist could not mask his respect for Radetzky:

> By a singular exception in this species of warfare, when a nation is supposed to be fighting for its independence, the enthusiasm is in this case on the side of the foreign enemy, the depression and division on the side of the troops of the champion of Italy. The whole Austrian army is as united as one man, filled with hatred and contempt for the enemy, galled by the insults so studiously offered to them during a long series of years by the Italian population in the great towns, and confident of victory under an experienced general. Their chief danger is an excess of presumption in their own strength, and of scorn for the forces opposed to them. But those forces are certainly not calculated to inspire any great respect...

Radetzky's inspiring leadership, on the other hand, was clear to all. His army was the smaller, yet the *Times* correspondent now expected it to win.

Piedmont's old, experienced generals were against the war. After all, victory had eluded them in 1848 under the most promising conditions imaginable. They had retreated almost in disarray. The huge amount of money poured into the army since and the speed of recruitment (including refugees from Lombardy and all over Italy) and rearmament had been impressive, yet the army lacked trained officers and NCOs, military discipline and confidence in its generals. According to two historians, its recruits were mere 'peasant lads with the ideas drummed into them by the Jesuits and other counter-revolutionary agents'.[60] For whatever reason, no general could be found inside Piedmont to command this army and four French generals turned down the job. The position eventually went to the Pole, General Chrzanowski, previously general staff chief, who could scarcely speak Italian, was very cold in his personal manner, who was hindered by envy and jealousy, and who never displayed any of the organisational talent he had shown in the Russo-Polish war of 1831. He demanded full military preparedness before war was declared, yet supposedly Radetzky in Milan heard that the ceasefire had been broken six hours before he did on 12 March 1849.

War would begin on 20 March after the eight days' notice had expired. Radetzky, who had been following events in the Turin Parliament, was not surprised by the news. Like his troops, he welcomed the fact that the limbo period of 'no war no peace' would finally reach an end.

Still, the Field Marshal faced several difficulties. He had had 30,000 sick and wounded at the end of the 1848 campaign and, given events in Hungary, reinforcements had been hard to come by. He had been given some, but nothing on the scale of Piedmont's rearmament. On the other hand, he could rely on the skill and confidence of his troops.

Both commanders were determined to take the offensive. Charles Albert was relying on a Lombard uprising in his support; Radetzky had to act quickly to prevent one. The Piedmontese war plan was based on the assumption that Radetzky could put no more than 40,000 men on the field and would therefore withdraw to the Mincio. Radetzky himself was aware of this false assumption and did everything, therefore, to exploit it. His movements until 19 March were designed to look as if his army was retreating to the Adda. Only on the morning of 19 March did his columns turn towards Pavia, where he planned to cross the Ticino under the protection of the fort, a movement which was kept secret till the very last minute. No general, not even the deputy chief of staff, knew till the evening of 18 March what was planned.

The Piedmontese main army, meanwhile, comprised five divisions accounting for 75,000–80,000 men. It stood on the Ticino under the king, distributed between Galliate, Trecate and Vigevano. Two divisions were stationed at Novara and a mountain brigade was detached to Oleggio. A support unit of two divisions, accounting for 30,000–35,000 men, was stationed south of the Po opposite Pavia at Sarzana under the well-known adventurer, General Ramorino. Altogether Charles Albert disposed of 100,000–110,000 men. Radetzky's whole army in Italy amounted to 119,000 men and 345 guns, of which initially only 59,000 men and 186 guns were available for fighting. His initial moves, however, misled the Piedmontese, who believed he was retreating and would have very few troops to use against them. Ramorino, for example, remained at Casteggio, instead of advancing on Pavia, convinced that Austrian movements around that fort were only demonstrations before an offensive was mounted against them south of the Po.

On 20 March, Charles Albert led one division across the Ticino into Magenta, but was not warmly received and found no Austrians. He only heard of Radetzky's own smooth, successful crossing of the Ticino when he returned to Trecate. Charles Albert's advance was already at an end. Instead, he ordered his divisions to concentrate at Mortara and Vigevano to prepare an attack on Radetzky. The next day Radetzky's first corps pushed the Piedmontese they encountered into Vigevano. His second corps arrived just before the onset of darkness at Mortara at 5pm. Despite this, D'Aspre ordered an attack and the Piedmontese retreated into the town. Colonel Ludwig Ritter von Benedek, the commander in Pavia in 1848, now offered pursuit but got lost in the dark and found himself surrounded. He then shouted to the Piedmontese in a loud, confident voice that *they* were surrounded and, in the darkness, they believed him. No less than 700–800 of them surrendered immediately. He then took prisoner six staff officers, 50 other officers, and another 1,500 men, while capturing five guns and a quantity of ammunition, a very large number of horses, 'and most dramatic of all the stables of the Crown-Prince Victor Emmanuel'.[61] So far, so good. Yet Radetzky did not know whether the main body of Piedmontese had retreated towards Vercelli or Novara – here darkness was a hindrance. Hence he had to plan his offensive for the 23 March with both objectives in mind. Chrzanowski, in fact, had ordered his troops to concentrate on the heights south of Novara.

D'Aspre for his part believed that Charles Albert would leave only his advanced guard at Novara, since otherwise the road to Turin would be left open. A defeat at Novara would therefore be catastrophic. He assumed, therefore, that the Piedmontese main force would have to be at Vercelli. On this advice Radetzky arranged to move his main force at 8am on 23 March against Vercelli – but *only* once D'Aspre's troops had taken and occupied Novara. However, D'Aspre encountered fierce resistance when he met the Piedmontese front at Olengo. Fighting then centred around a group of farm buildings at La Bicocca but the Austrians managed to hold on. Radetzky, who was with his third corps three hours south of Olengo when he heard the thunder of cannon, sent his troops marching towards the sound of gunfire. His whole army was now sent to Novara, since he knew no battle was possible at Vercelli, till Novara had been taken. In fact, thanks to his training, all his corps commanders had already set out for Novara before his orders had been received. From 4pm his own corps began to attack Olengo and train its guns on La Bicocca. The Austrians fought heroically and soon the troops were streaming into Novara and beyond.

That same evening Charles Albert abdicated his throne in favour of his son, Victor Emmanuel II. Charles Albert himself could neither accept a ceasefire nor acknowledge that all his dreams had been shattered. As Colonel de Bargé he passed the Austrian advance posts and FML Count Thurn's headquarters. He would later die in secret, self-imposed, exile in Oporto, Portugal.

At noon on 24 March, Radetzky met the new King of Sardinia-Piedmont to sign an armistice at the small village of Vignale, north of Novara. The Field Marshal was willing to make some concessions to uphold Victor Emmanuel's royal authority and seemed full of good will. Yet he insisted that Victor Emmanuel personally sign the armistice and guarantee it.

One week after the armistice, Haynau was forced to put down an uprising in Brescia by bombarding the town since the rebels would not agree terms. Despite an earlier record of disobeying commanders who had acted brutally, Haynau became known as 'the beast of Brescia' and 'General Hyena'.[62] D'Aspre got the job of suppressing the revolutions in the Papal States and elsewhere in Central Italy, while Venice, despite the fall of its main fort at Malghera on 28 May, held out till 24 August 1849. Exactly a year after Radetzky had re-entered Milan, on 6 August 1849, the Peace of Milan was signed. It lasted only a decade but outlasted Radetzky himself. Austria's territories and those of the junior Habsburgs in Italy were confirmed. Piedmont lost no territory but had to pay a hefty indemnity.

Once more, in the Novara campaign, Radetzky had displayed all his physical and mental powers, participated in all the exertions, and was as consumed as always with the offensive. Before the battle of Novara, in the preliminary celebrations of his name day on 18 March, he had promised the Grenadier Brigade to lead it personally in a charge against the enemy. The opportunity came when the Brigade began to form to attack La Biccoca. Radetzky was there and ready to charge, but, fortunately perhaps, the farm buildings were taken before the Grenadiers were ready. 'What a shame! The picture of the eighty-two year old charging would have been unique in world history,' wrote an Austrian historian before adding, 'If ever a commander could repeat Caesar's laconic report on his victory at Zela – veni, vidi, vici – with at least as much justification, it was Radetzky at Novara.'[63]

But was such a reputation deserved? Was Radetzky really the brains behind Austria's victories in 1848–9? A great dispute arose over this in the mid-1930s when newspaper articles gave the credit to Radetzky's chief of staff, General Hess, based on claims attributed to a later well-known army commander General Baron Mollinary. The latter had supposedly written in his diary: 'The first thing that, on my reporting to General Staff Headquarters, was impressed upon me by Staff Chief FML Baron Hess was: "Whatever questions you have, address them to me, *never* to the Field Marshal. The old man has absolutely no idea of what is going on (*Der alte Herr hat überhaupt keine Ahnung, worum es sich handelt.*)".'

This was quite an accusation, but did it have any basis in truth? Mollinary's memoirs are rather naïve about both Radetzky and Hess in many ways but more importantly they do not contain the damning quote. Nor is it contained in any manuscript of the memoirs or of any work by Mollinary contained in either Austria's war archives or its National Library.[64] Moreover, according to Mollinary's memoirs, Hess was not in Italy at the time of the battle of Santa Lucia and could not have greeted him when he arrived there since, according to Mollinary, they both travelled down from Vienna together.[65] Further evidence that the damning quote was indeed imaginary lies in Hess addressing Mollinary as *du*, the familiar form of 'you' in German (as in '*Daß du mir ja nie den Feldmarschall um was immer fragst*'). Yet according to Mollinary's memoirs, Hess never addressed his 32 years younger colleague as *du* even when in 1859 he was promoted major-general.[66]

Part of the problem was Radetzky himself. The Field Marshal was enormously generous in character. When he was asked to choose a verse to go under a selection of pictures to mark the day he was made a freeman of the city of Vienna (and on other occasions) he chose one from Zedlitz's *Little Book of Soldiers* (*Soldatenbüchlien*) that read:

> No individual won the prize,
> The last man in the army,
> Places the laurel leaves on his head,
> And shares in the honour of the fight.
> (*Kein Einzelner erfocht den Preis,*
> *Der letzte Mann in Heere,*
> *Steckt auf den Hut das Lorbeerreis,*
> *Und teilt des Kampfes Ehre.*)

In similar fashion he praised his closest colleagues to the authorities in Vienna. On Hess he reported:[67]

> To him – I testify it with all my heart – belongs by far the greatest part of the successes, which the armies of the Emperor achieved in the last campaign. Surveying all factors with a clear eye, quickly recognising the correct time to act, and quickly exploiting it, always having the highest aims in mind, he had my complete trust. I led the army with him at my side to certain victory. The army knew this and won.

On the day of Novara, Radetzky himself telegrammed Hess's wife as follows:[68] 'We defeated the enemy at Novara and while the glory of the day will be ascribed to me, the whole credit is due to him.' The Field Marshal had so much honour, he knew that none could be stolen from him. Perhaps posterity should learn from him.

It is quite clear from the best Austrian historians who studied him[69] that Radetzky was a true leader. Nothing of any importance failed to be submitted to him beforehand or to be approved or improved by him. Incoming reports were mostly read out to him but he himself carefully attended to outgoing matters. Orders to his generals or superior officers he executed often with his own hand. At every action he was present himself from start to finish, paying detailed attention, and at every critical juncture it was he, who, weighing up the momentary position with a critical eye, took decisions and gave orders. In this fashion Radetzky as leader was able to keep his cool at moments of greatest jeopardy and could infuse calm and confidence among those around him. He looked at situations as a whole and saw their essential features. His orders were often very simple: 'So give the orders for the cannon to thunder" captured Milan. 'See what you can pull together' was his instruction to Captain Huyn about reinforcements. 'He might also be permitted to make a bit of wind' was his order to the staff officer bringing Victor Emanuel to Vignale.[70]

Perhaps the most vital point was made by a leading military historian,[71] namely that all the military operations of 1848–9 had Radetzky's precise stamp. The three offensives – Verona–flanking-march–Mantua–Goito; then, Mantua–Legnano–Vicenza; and in 1849, Milan–mock retreat–Pavia–Novara – all shared a basic idea. One should also remember that the decisive offensive in July 1848 would also have been initiated at Mantua, had not the enemy opened a gap, which was observed 'with the eye of a falcon and pounced on with the force of an eagle'. This clarifies the similarity. The essential pattern ran thus: original application of force from two or more directions to attack a wing or a flank with maximum surprise and superiority. The moment of surprise itself had a special significance. In all of this one can see the Radetzky of Novi and Marengo, of Reichenbach and Leipzig.[72] Radetzky always demonstrated an ingenuity which the operations of 1848–9 displayed even more perhaps than his earlier ones. Yet Hess did play his part and Kübeck had been right. Radetzky teemed with ideas but Hess helped knock them into shape. In any final judgement, Hess's great talents should not be forgotten or underestimated – a mistake that of course Radetzky himself never made. Perhaps the verdict of another historian and former general staff officer should be remembered:[73] 'The victories, in any case, were not won by Radetzky or Hess – but by both, two men who appreciated, understood and mutually complemented each other.'

# 6

## RULING ITALY

Radetzky's last decade as a serving soldier was surely the least reward-
ing period of his career. He was a great international figure, recognised
at last as Europe's leading military commander, and commonly credited
with saving Europe in 1848–9 from revolutionary excess and international
warfare on the scale of 1793–1815, yet his task became one of constantly
suppressing revolution in a land where Austrian government grew increasingly unpopular, while neighbouring Piedmont under its great statesman
Cavour instituted better and more representative government (the parlia-
mentary constitution or *Statuto* introduced by Charles Albert in 1848 was
retained), gave succour to Lombard and Venetian refugees, reformed its
economy, and liberalised its relations with the Church. No longer, therefore, could Lombardy-Venetia offer an example of a freer, more liberal and
more prosperous society than that of her rival – as she had been able to do
during the Metternich period between 1815 and 1848.

In 1849 Radetzky appeared to have reached the pinnacle of his career.
With the end of the revolutions, the Field Marshal became Governor
General of Lombardy-Venetia, responsible for both civil and military
affairs. There was no longer a viceroy although governors were appointed
for Lombardy and Venetia and if the Central Congregations (Diets) disappeared (albeit, to be resurrected by Imperial Patent in July 1856), they
had never been of any significance in any case. More significantly, however, the supreme court of Lombardy-Venetia, the Senate, was abolished in
August 1850 and its functions transferred to Vienna's Supreme Court of
Justice. Meanwhile, the lower levels of administration remained the same
with delegates (the Austrian equivalents of prefects) and district commissioners relying on (appointed) wealthy and respectable Italians in provincial congregations and municipal councils to aid them collect taxes, run
schools, build roads and provide recruits. The situation after 1848–9, therefore, quickly came to resemble the situation before 1848–9, save that the
Monarchy under Schwarzenberg and Bach became even more centralised.

Franz Joseph at the very end of 1850 did away with cabinet government (the parliament promised by Schwarzenberg never having materialised), so that Francis I's system of absolute monarchy returned.

All major decisions once again had to be approved by the Emperor in Vienna, leaving the Field Marshal to complain about 'overgovernment by the bureaucracy' and to suggest that he and his officers could take care of things much more efficiently locally.[1] But power was never devolved. Indeed, after Radetzky's retirement in 1857 it was actually weakened locally when Radetzky's successor, the Archduke Maximilian, the Emperor's brother, was limited to a civilian role – leadership of the army being given to General Gyulai. The Archduke, in turn, therefore, was soon complaining about his lack of authority. He wanted to reform but found his brother, the Emperor, was no more prepared to listen to him than Francis, Ferdinand or Metternich had been prepared to listen to the viceroy before 1848, the Archduke Rainer. He complained:[2] 'We now live in a complete chaos and occasionally, I myself begin to ask if conscience permits blind obedience to Vienna's orders.' Nor did the unpopular and irascible Gyulai help him much as Austria's new military figurehead: in January 1859, when the 'guerra, guerra' chorus of Bellini's Norma was sung at La Scala and the audience took up the words, a furious Gyulai unsheathed his sabre and banged it on the floor in his box, inspiring the Austrian officers present to shout for war as well, before leaving the theatre. The following night after similar scenes, the performance was suspended.[3] By now Maximilian was complaining that he never knew whether the government in Vienna would approve of his actions or even whether he and his consort, the Princess Charlotte of Belgium, would return home alive from a promenade.[4] On 20 April 1859 he was finally relieved of his duties.

The decade after 1849, therefore, was hardly a successful one for the Austrians in Lombardy-Venetia, yet Radetzky, between 1849 and 1857 had tried to run the kingdom responsibly. Mazzini and Cavour between them, however, made his task impossible.

After peace had been signed in 1849, Azeglio, the Piedmontese prime minister, insisted that there was no desire on the part of his country to attack Austria:[5] 'If I had an army of 700,000 and Radetzky only four men and a corporal, I would not attack Lombardy,' he said. And again:[6] 'Even if Austria retired its last man from Italy and the Lombards begged us to occupy their land, we would not budge. And it is not just we untenured ministers who think so, the king shares these convictions and he will never swerve from them.' In 1851, after Piedmontese newspapers insulted Franz

Joseph, the Piedmontese government introduced a stricter press law making the government itself responsible for trying cases of insults to foreign sovereigns and abolishing jury trials in such cases. Still, no real rapprochement with Piedmont was achieved. As the Austrian minister to Turin put it:[7] 'Liberal ideas, inseparable in the king's mind from ideas of war and conquest, are too deeply rooted in that weak intelligence to allow one to hope for a complete and lasting return to saner doctrines.'

Italian nationalism was by now so widespread among the educated classes that the king would never have been allowed to oppose 'liberal ideas', even if he had wanted to. Moreover, if upper class and noble liberals would never be converted by Austrian reasonableness, Mazzini was working from London to frustrate any such policy by organising revolutionary conspiracies among the lower orders.

The Milanese, on the other hand, believed that Piedmont had failed them during the years of revolutionary struggle. In their view, Charles Albert had proved unable to exploit the victory that they themselves had won over Radetzky in March 1848 when the king had dallied uselessly outside Verona for months; he had then deserted them like a traitor in August 1848 after they had relinquished their republicanism to form a union with Piedmont; his son, Victor Emmanuel had put his own interests first in making peace; while the Venetians could think of little aid that they had received from Piedmont-Sardinia in 1848–9. Why had the Sardinian fleet done so little to help Venice, for example, during her siege? There was little sympathy, therefore, for Piedmont in Lombardy-Venetia immediately after her defeat in 1849.

Yet things still went wrong for Austria.[8] All measures taken by her, even the benevolent ones, were received with mistrust. The government, for example, wanted to attract Italian bureaucrats, to play a mediating role, yet the introduction of German into institutions of higher learning gave widespread offence. It also took ages to complete the railway line connecting Milan and Venice. Most of all, however, it was the fact that Austrian rule was seen not just as incorrigibly bureaucratic but oppressive that made reconciliation with the Italians impossible. The Austrians themselves, needless to say, believed they were merely meting out due punishment to traitors, subversives, terrorists and enemies, who had needlessly, yet bloodily, attempted in 1848–9 to end the benevolent rule of Austria in easily the best-run part of Italy.

Political developments can only be understood if the general economic background is explained. Economics and politics became inextricably entwined in the 1850s in Lombardy-Venetia under Radetzky and the general economic situation along with the ideological one, when taken together, explain Radetzky's actions after 1849.[9] Basically, the state faced bankruptcy as a result of the revolutions and the citizens of Lombardy-Venetia, whose actions were to a large degree responsible for this, would have to pay huge sums of money to make the Monarchy solvent again.

Austrian finance minister Krauss had informed the imperial Reichstag in May 1848 that Lombardy-Venetia at that time paid 110 million lire annually in taxes, of which 85 million covered local expenditure plus Lombardy-Venetia's share of interest on the state debt, the costs for the army, the government and the court. The surplus – some 25 million lire – therefore represented a profit to the state.[10] Now, despite the enormous costs which the inhabitants of the kingdom had borne supplying armies in 1848–9, not to mention the costs of destroyed buildings, the Austrians forced them – indeed, had to force them – to pay even more enormous sums to maintain the new administration.

One estimate suggests that the kingdom paid 170 million lire in taxes a year after 1849,[11] while another suggests that Lombardy from August 1848 to the end of 1851 paid 422 million lire, Venetia 240 million lire. These figures included huge increases in land tax, stamp duties and income tax, not to mention forced loans. Increases in land and business taxes alone accounted for 48 per cent of all tax increases after 1848. Italians believed  – perhaps not without justification, therefore, – that they were paying not merely for Austria's wars against Piedmont but also for her war against Hungary in 1848–9 and her mobilisation against Prussia in 1850.[12] And if this economic background was bad enough, there would be more bad news.

In the words of one historian, 'only a reasonably prosperous land could absorb the tribute Austria demanded of Lombardy in the 1850s',[13] yet real prosperity now eluded the kingdom, despite all the government's best efforts. Throughout the decade agriculture remained the main source of employment. Industry had begun to develop but Austria dragged out the pace of railway construction, relying instead on 'its much admired road system and the interlocking net of river, lake and canal'.[14] Traditionally the main industry of Lombardy had been silk-producing and the large surpluses the industry banked in London had oiled much of the import–export trade of Milan. Peasants looked after the silkworms and obtained mulberry leaves from landlords. The peasant families made up most of the labour force since steam power was still very rare. But in 1853 a dreadful disease known as pébrine appeared and killed off silkworms to the extent that silk production fell by two thirds in many places. The government immediately allowed the importation of raw silk and its consequent exportation as a finished product duty-free, but this did not succeed in maintaining the industry, which had always been a luxury one and subject to elastic demand. Como seemed to do better than most towns, but the prevalence of the disease added to the general air of depression in the 1850s.

If silk producers had it bad, wine producers were hit in 1855 by vine mildew that reduced crops seriously. Then cholera hit in 1855 and 1856, while a long-term dependence on corn, exacerbated by lack of money to buy meat or cheese, resulted in a substantial increase of pellagra. There was such a threat of famine that cereals had to be imported duty-free between 1852 and 1856. The silk trade usually paid for the import of wine, cheese, olive oil, cattle, fish, fresh fruit and vegetables, but with its relative decline, the whole economy suffered. Cotton production, like linen, was still small-scale in Lombardy. It lacked both capital and sources of energy – water-power had already been claimed by the silk industry for spinning mills. Lack of fuel and modern furnaces restricted the growth of metallurgical industries, while Brescia's armaments production was deliberately suppressed after its uprising in 1849.

In 1851 a system of protection was brought into the Monarchy to replace the previous one of prohibitions. Lombardy was favoured by a tariff which allowed the free entry of mulberry leaves, coal, rags (for the paper industry) and peat. High tariffs, however, were placed on colonial produce like coffee, tea, chocolate and cotton. (Cotton merchants found it easier to trade directly with New Orleans.) On average, there was a tariff of 10–30 per cent on agricultural items; 40–50 per cent on iron; and 20 per cent on manufactured and semi-manufactured goods. There were minimal export tariffs on raw silk and textiles. But the tax on raw silk was abolished and that on silk products reduced when in 1853 Austria signed its free-trade treaty with the *Zollverein* (the German Customs Union). In the 1850s silk still accounted for 77–94 per cent of all exports, which regularly exceeded imports. However, this trade surplus was more than offset by widespread smuggling.

It is difficult, therefore, to estimate the effects of Austrian trade policy on the Lombard economy, but no one seems to have suffered. The real setbacks were caused by natural disasters, not Austria. On the other hand, if her tariffs had been lower, the smuggling would not have been necessary. The peasants, particularly the landless ones, were not well-paid by the tenant farmers of the Po valley – nor by the many absentee landlords. But were they any better off elsewhere in Italy? Those peasant families who had contracts as spinners or weavers were probably the best off. This work could be done by women and children while the men could be employed in building work. But the general standard of living was low. Workers and artisans in Milan and the larger towns were probably better off.

Venice, after its siege, stagnated as a port for years. One English economist described it in 1850 as economically 'dead'.[15] Its very status as a free port was removed after 1849, its magistrates, teachers and lawyers purged, while most of the workers at the Arsenal were dismissed. Delegations to Vienna pleaded for the city and blamed its woes, unconvincingly, on foreign agents. The Emperor and his ministers were not impressed, although Radetzky in 1850 did what he could for the city, slashing the supplementary tax imposed on it from 25 to 5 per cent, allowing foreign goods to be stored on the island of San Giorgio, and restoring the dole for some of the workers dismissed from the Arsenal.

Still, 'Venice and Venetia were no utopias during the 1850s.'[16] Exports dropped by 15 per cent and imports rose by 18 per cent; wine and silk were afflicted by nature as in Lombardy; the terrain was more difficult for agriculture. Yet Verona exported large quantities of silk to Lombardy (without the figures entering the import–export statistics); tourists still wanted to see *La Serenissima*; and smuggling went on across the Lagoon. None the less, ships entering the waters of Venice grew neither in tonnage nor numbers throughout the decade. Was this stagnation, given the growth of the world economy at this time? Or did it matter, given that the value of goods coming in actually doubled across the decade? Venice was still producing about 2 million kilograms of glassware a year, but there was insufficient capital, skilled labour or power for industrial capitalism to put down firm roots in Venetia. Once again, Austria's neglect of railways was in evidence: Venetia had only 769 kilometres by 1859, Lombardy only 202 kilometres. All this was mitigated by the excellent system of roads, not to mention the Lloyd steamer service that carried goods and passengers from Trieste and Venice along the Po to Pavia and beyond to the Lake Maggiore and Ticino area. Still, Venice did not fully recover till the 1880s.[17]

Trieste, meanwhile, which had remained loyal in 1848–9, was rewarded by having martial law suspended in September 1849 and by becoming a city 'directly under the crown'.[18] In fact, it was joined with Gorizia and Istria and made into a new crownland. In April 1850 it was given a new municipal constitution, providing for its own mayor and elected council. (Workers, of course, like private employees, did not get to vote.) But that was as far as gratitude was extended. There was a reaction in Vienna when the new council voted to introduce Italian into the local gymnasia on an equal footing with German. Soon the city's national guard was dissolved, its tax privileges removed, conscription imposed and council elections came to an end.

Trieste was to remain happy with its main reward – the granting of its status as a free port. Like Venice, however, it, too, stagnated in terms of tonnage and came to serve, until the Suez Canal was opened, mainly as a port servicing the Austrian hinterland. The failure to complete the railroad to Vienna (no small engineering challenge, it should be noted), the greater reliance on steam, and lower manufacturing costs elsewhere leading to changes in traditional routes, were all contributing factors. Still, the Austrian Lloyd managed to double the number of its ships and almost triple their gross tonnage between 1850 and 1860, which provided economic stability.

There was no sign of disaffection with Austria – indeed, in 1854 the city's tycoons made a gift of a frigate to the Austrian navy to demonstrate their patriotism: it carried 30 cannon, disposed of 300 horsepower, and bore the name *Radetzky*. (In fact, the government had to take over the subscription and in 1855 the ship was launched in England. It took a prominent part in the fight against the Danes before Heligoland in 1864, although it took no part in the great Austrian naval victory at Lissa in 1866. However, it blew up in 1869 while on a cruise in the waters of Lissa and only one sailor escaped. According to the *Times* of London: 'the impression produced by the catastrophe is a very painful one.')[19]

It was not the general economic background, therefore, that made life difficult for Radetzky. The economy of Lombardy-Venetia was hardly flourishing, but it was basically all right, considering that the kingdom was recovering from invasion, rebellion and war. It was the manner in which Austria chose to see the revolution and chose to make those responsible pay for it, that brought difficulties for the Field Marshal, difficulties very much of his own creation. This and Mazzini's activities made any reconciliation between Austria and Piedmont impossible – even if Cavour had wanted one.

Radetzky, as has been seen, was no natural reactionary. He had written of his belief in progress, assumed that all western states would soon enjoy constitutions, and in April 1848 had written to Peter Zanini, Austria's first constitutional war minister, that he had received a copy of Austria's new constitution. He added:[20] 'It rests on so liberal a base that I take it to be the most liberal in Europe. That the press will find something in it to blame, we must of course expect, but I hope however, that the best part of the nation will find in it a guarantee of all the wishes and ideas with which they believe their happiness is bound.' Yet just as his views on creating national armies within the empire had changed as he had seen nationalism infect the *Zeitgeist*, so, too, did his political views in general. He had already seen how nationalism could divide the Magyars and Croats and had pleaded with both sides to avoid civil war in Hungary. Likewise he would plead with the deputies at Frankfurt not to divide Austria and Germany. In a heartfelt letter to a Dr. Egger, an Austrian deputy there, a letter whose contents are crucial for any understanding of the history of Central Europe, he wrote:[21]

> How was it possible that the thinking of those at Frankfurt could find favour through resolutions, such as your statement gave rise to, to force Austria to separate from Germany? For that would have to be the result if people intend to force through these principles. You should cast a glance over the map and ask yourself whether it is possible to rip the German provinces out of a state formation, in which they have found happiness and prosperity for centuries. Is it seriously believed in Frankfurt that this is possible through a vote? A true German heart beats in my breast but, truly, at this price, I would have to silence it. People in Germany talk a lot of drivel about the dangers of Panslavism, but in reality do everything to give life to this spectre, since rebellion has already become identified with being German. Austria with her non-German provinces contains 38 million people. May people in Frankfurt not forget that and not destroy such a federal partner with an inflexible Germanness. Austria will prefer to separate from Germany than from Austria. Time will tell whether my feelings are misguided... So ask the learned gentlemen of Frankfurt whether they can find a square mile in Germany on which Austria has not spilled its blood for the honour and salvation of Germany?.... [No, Austria will not allow itself be expelled] this same Austria which has supplied a long list of Emperors to the German throne.

Radetzky, therefore, had no time even for the new German nationalism. Instead he believed in a supranational Austria and a supranational army. No doubt he knew Grillparzer's lines:[22]

> *Die Gott als Slav' und Magyaren schuf,*
> *Sie streiten um Wörten nicht hämisch,*
> *Sie folgen, ob deutsch auch die Feldherrnruf,*
> *Denn: Vorwärts! Ist ungrisch und bömisch.*
> (When God created Slavs and Magyars,

They did not fight maliciously over words.
They followed their commander's call, even if it were German,
For 'Forwards!' is also Hungarian and Czech.)

He took such an outlook for granted and so, too, presumably did his
men. However, several more disappointments were in store for them, disappointments which must have ground down whatever liberalism they felt.

First, to their astonishment, the newly elected Reichstag in Vienna
as early as August 1848 refused to congratulate them on their victories
in Italy. One liberal deputy explained that the Left in the parliament
believed that the struggle in Italy was 'being waged only in the interest of
the dynasty but not in the interest of the people' and that it was clear that
the Italian provinces could only be retained through 'a colossal army, permanent martial law and permanent court martials'.[23] It believed that the
Empire's future lay in the Danubian lands. It was not impressed by arguments about the balance of power in Italy or about military honour either.
So when a deputy called Seelinger proposed a vote of thanks, the motion
was rejected. The Left suspected that it was a put-up job designed to win
approval for Austrian policy rather than simply to thank the troops for
their bravery and courage. It was also in dispute with the government over
conscription. The government had never informed the Reichstag of how
many troops it wanted to raise or how or for what purposes. Hence when
the Left decided to turn the motion into one on policy rather than one of
thanks, the government only managed to defeat the proposal by letting the
vote of thanks fail.

The Right, of course, exploited the outcome to stir up feeling against
the Left, the Reichstag and the constitution:[24] '... no effort was spared on
the part of the reactionaries to dream up the most incredible stuff for the
army, stuff which was supposed to have originated in the Reichstag...' As
a result 'a hatred mixed with contempt for the Vienna Reichstag' suffused
Radetzky's army as well as other parts of the armed forces.[25]

Radetzky's own patience exploded when Latour, the war minister, on
24 September 1848 circulated a letter to the army reminding commanders
that obedience to orders also meant 'upholding and respecting the constitutional institutions and arrangements in the state', which arrangements
'should in no wise give cause for complaint'. Radetzky replied that on
account of the hostile feeling expressed in the Reichstag, he feared that the
content of Latour's circular had been 'primarily directed against the troops
under my command'. He then wrote the most honest account of his own

political views as they were evolving under the pressure of revolution. It was typical Radetzky – measured, cool, rational but at the same time emotional and passionate. In short, it resonated, as so often, with suppressed fury.

'The army', he wrote,[26] 'has no reason to retain any prediliction for the system that has fallen. This system was, if it can be called a despotism, a civil – not a military despotism. The army was neglected, slighted; it, therefore, expressed no spirit of hostility at all towards the free institutions which His Majesty conferred upon his peoples.' The army had been far too occupied with its great and heavy duty to pay any special attention to political goings-on. Hence none of the addresses directed at the troops from many sides over the Hungarian-Croat question had been answered: 'I wanted no manifestos.' He then gave his view on freedom of the press, which had been abused to insult the army, adding bitterly: 'Rome did not reward her army in this way; nor did Greece; nor did the bloody French Republic; it was reserved for modern Liberty to present such an unworthy spectacle to the world.' Then he looked at the situation in Hungary and asked: '...where is the army supposed to derive its love for institutions that can bring forth into the world such moral and political abortions?', although his final paragraph made clear that the army would not oppose free institutions: 'I stand at the head of a great part of the army; I stand surety for this army; for its loyalty; for its devotion to the constitutional freedoms granted by His Majesty.' But he dreaded to think what might happen if the Emperor's rights or person were threatened.

Latour drafted a reply to inform Radetzky that it was Field Marshal Prince Windischgraetz's behaviour in Prague that had caused him to write the circular. But before the letter could be sent, Latour on 6 October 1848 was murdered by a mob which invaded the War Ministry in Vienna and hung his mutilated body from a lamp-post outside. Radetzky was appalled. Latour had been one of his greatest supporters. He could not believe that the Vienna garrison had been unable to save him. He, therefore, issued a famous proclamation to the troops, addressing the Vienna garrison as 'Field Marshal and the oldest soldier in the army', asking whether it had done its duty, but blaming only 'a small handful' of troops.[27] Its main point was that the army of Italy would not stretch out its hand in brotherhood unless the troops in Vienna realised what was happening to them: 'Soldiers! Open your eyes to the abyss that opens at your feet..... the mainstays of the social order have been destroyed; property, morality, religion are threatened with destruction. Everything that is holy and dear to man, everything on which the state is based and which it upholds, people are determined to destroy.

That, not liberty, is the aim of every rabblerouser who wants to drag you down to your ruin and shame.' Only when it could be said 'The army has saved Austria', would the shame of Latour's murder be atoned for. His army took a similar view. When asked to send representatives to the Reichstag, a petition signed by most of its leading officers was published in the *Milan Gazette* on 23 February 1849, rejecting the idea:[28] 'In every constitutional state there are two powers, the legislative and the executive, which can never be united. The army as an integral part of the executive power, can never, therefore, take any share in the legislative.' If it did so, army representatives might claim in parliament that they had a great army behind them, a claim that 'would soon put an end to freedom of discussion'. Taking part in such debates would also divide and split the army. So it preferred to stick to its main role of protecting the Emperor. 'It seeks to watch over the laws of the country, to protect the monarchy against domestic enemies as well as to preserve its integrity against foreign enemies; but it seeks to remain within the limits of the position which the legislatures of all nations assigns to the army.' So no representatives went to the Reichstag which had insulted it. Still, neither Radetzky nor his army had rejected constitutional institutions. The Field Marshal had stood surety for his army's devotion to constitutional freedoms; the army itself had argued its case against representation in the Reichstag from thoroughly constitutional premises.

How then did all this affect Radetzky's position in Italy? After Hartig's resignation, Count Montecuccoli had been sent to Italy to help the Field Marshal pacify the conquered kingdom. He agreed with Radetzky that law and order had to be established before any political initiatives could be undertaken. The trouble was that Wessenberg, Austria's prime minister in Vienna, wanted to push ahead with political reforms as soon as possible, the aim being to give Italians the new constitutional freedoms already conceded and enjoyed elsewhere in the Monarchy. Radetzky had no objections in principle. Astonishingly perhaps, as early as 10 August 1848, only a few days after he had defeated Charles Albert and re-entered Milan – he wrote to Wessenberg,[29] arguing that both provinces ought to be treated equally and represent one united state in roughly the same relationship to Austria as Hungary had been before her recent uprising. Foreign affairs, finance and military affairs should be administered from Vienna; internal administration, however, with some sort of gloss of independence, by an Italian Ministry in Milan. This, in his opinion, was the only possible way of reconciling Italian nationalism to the Monarchy and, most important of all, of retaining for Austria, as the greatest Italian state, the main voice in the affairs of Lombardy-Venetia. So Radetzky was willing to concede the Italians much more than Metternich, for example, could ever have envisaged.

But timing was all-important. Milan had just been reconquered. Other cities such as Como, Bergamo and Brescia, which had been in rebellion had not yet been occupied. If Vienna suddenly announced free elections and new institutions, it would be impossible for the army to maintain law and order. If all the exiles returned in a flood, not even an army of 150,000 men would be able to deal with the consequences. Radetzky again threatened to resign:[30] 'If I am to be responsible to the state then I intend to be master of the situation; if not, then those who believe out of misguided philanthropic views which do not apply to this country that they can govern it in some other way, will lose this land for the Emperor even more quickly than I have conquered it.' He himself would inform Vienna when conditions permitted new initiatives. Montecuccoli agreed:[31] For the time being the only guarantee of the security of the country and of future reforms resided in the army, which would have to remain concentrated in Lombardy-Venetia for some time to come, although he, too, wanted home rule for Lombardy-Venetia within the Empire. Radetzky, meanwhile, placed himself at the head of the civil administration of Lombardy and Venetia and Montecuccoli was happy to work with him in that capacity.

Wessenberg, however, on 20 September had got the Emperor to agree to a proclamation granting the Italians of Lombardy-Venetia full constitutional rights, respect for their nationality, and, worst of all from Radetzky's point of view, a full amnesty. When the Field Marshal sought to delay its publication, Wessenberg had it published in Vienna, forcing him to do the same in Milan 'in order not to compromise the imperial name'.[32] However, Wessenberg's agent in Milan, Metzburg, was forced to report back to Wessenberg that the proclamation had been a damp squib[33] and had been read in the entire city 'with great indifference'. The Milanese were still investing their hopes in Piedmont. So Radetzky, he added, was right after all: 'Until that time when peace is concluded the great aim of preserving law and order in the land can only be attained by the maintenance of a state of siege and military law.' The amnesty and the promise of new institutions were irrelevant.

Radetzky, for his part, was telling Wessenberg exactly what he thought:[34] his initiative would be seen as a series of cowardly concessions and ridiculed as an act of weakness; on the army it would make the same impression as a battle lost. He added: 'As for my personal position, I shall know within a few weeks what I shall have to do.'

Yet, as on previous occasions, the Field Marshal was not called upon to make good his threat. On 6 October 1848, Vienna had succumbed to revolution and was not rescued till the end of the month. The men who rescued it were hardly liberals, and though the government that was put into place under Schwarzenberg in November 1848 contained liberals of a sort, its policy became one of imperial unity. No home-rule for Lombardy-Venetia would henceforth be tolerated. And with the re-establishment of absolutism by Franz Joseph on 31 December 1850, even the hope of constitutional government came to an end. Radetzky, therefore, would no longer need to worry about political innovation. Instead he became Governor General of Lombardy-Venetia, head of both the civil and military power, but subject to the rule of Vienna. As has already been stated, the constitutional position reverted by and large to that which had existed before 1848. Radetzky's problems would now largely concern two areas: raising money and maintaining law and order; two areas, as will be seen, that would be very closely connected. Occasionally, however, he would be distracted by matters of foreign policy.

The issue of law and order – or Austrian brutality as far as Italians were concerned – was to trouble Radetzky as soon as he returned to Milan. For Novara did not bring an end to the fighting in 1849. An uprising in Brescia, which would not believe the news of Charles Albert's defeat, had to be suppressed. This task was given to one of Radetzky's best commanders, General Julius Freiherr von Haynau, who became known as the 'Beast of Brescia' or 'General Hyena' to his critics. He was already known as General *Einhau* ('Screw-loose' – from the German *einen Hau haben* – 'to have a screw loose') to his men. His suppression of the town would leave a huge stain on Austria's reputation and make Radetzky's task much more difficult, but was it deserved?

According to his Austrian defenders (including Mollinary and Schönhals) Haynau was in no way sanguinary. What happened in Brescia, according to them, was the fault of the Brescians themselves. In Schönhals's words:[35] 'How difficult it is to do justice to a man who is an enemy!' The charge of wanton blood-spilling at Brescia was completely irreconcilable with Haynau's character.

In Schönhals' account, Haynau, the son of the Elector of Hesse-Cassel, who had had a brilliant military career during the French revolutionary and Napoleonic wars, had been ordered during the Hundred Days by his brigadier, General Scheiter, to destroy a village near Besançon, whose inhabitants had massacred an Austrian patrol. The furious Scheiter had commanded

Haynau 'to surround the village, not allow a single soul to leave, so that the whole population would have to die in the flames'.[36] Haynau sought out Scheiter, who was still beside himself with anger, and pleaded with him only to punish the two guilty men, who the villagers admitted had carried out the massacre, but to leave the innocent alone. Scheiter had him arrested and told him he would be court-martialled if he did not obey orders. Haynau still refused, but the general eventually calmed down and revoked his instruction. The story did not end there. The Austrians were then attacked by guerrilla forces in the woods and 200 people were captured. It was not clear, however, whether these were the people who had attacked the troops or others who had merely been fleeing from the fighting. Haynau, however, was once again given the order to shoot them all and once again disobeyed, allowing them all to escape at night. This time his brigadier took the news better. But Haynau had risked his career once more to save 200 lives. Could he really be the 'Beast of Brescia'?

Haynau was certainly a truculent character. He himself demanded obedience, although he often gave it only reluctantly. Schönhals says that in these cases he was most often in the right. Frimont never liked or trusted him and kept back his promotion to colonel for four years. His command of his regiment in Venice was also subjected to an official investigation. Two men, however, saved his career: Francis I with whom he corresponded regularly, and Radetzky who admired his high spirits. It had been General Haynau, after all, who Radetzky left in charge of Verona, when he himself went off to lead his offensive in 1848. After Novara he was sent to command the troops blockading Venice, but was then sent to deal with Brescia, which would not surrender.

If Haynau was tough, so, too, were the Brescians, who had developed an armaments industry in their town and who had concealed a great number of weapons after the 1848 campaign in mountain valleys around the town. They were in receipt of funds from an 'insurrection committee' in Turin and had been drilling in the hills before the 1849 campaign got under way. The Austrians meanwhile had left only a few companies of troops behind in the small towns of the region, requiring as many troops as possible to face the larger army of Charles Albert. This was true of Brescia where the troops left behind were stationed in the citadel of the town. However, when war broke out the citizens had bloodily seized an Austrian weapons transport heading there and when the local commander then bombarded the town, barricades went up and 3,000 men with flintlocks prepared to hold out. They certainly defeated Count Nugent's attempts to take the town – he died of wounds trying to capture it, despite having 1,000 Romanian troops under his command. Then came news of Piedmont's defeat at Novara and a ceasefire, but the Brescians chose not to believe it. Priests encouraged the population to continue resisting.

Haynau now marched on the town with 3,000 men and stormed it, leading his men into the citadel. From here he issued a proclamation to the town authorities on the morning of 31 March demanding they surrender unconditionally. If at noon, he declared,[37] all the barricades had not been taken down, the town would be taken by storm, plundered and given over to all the cruelties of devastation. All exits were in the possession of his troops. A prolonged resistance would result in the ruin of the town. His proclamation ended: 'Brescians, you know that I keep my word!'

They knew it all right. The leaders of the town, however, at 11am asked him for another 48 hours in which to convince the fanatics that Piedmont had actually lost. Haynau gave them till 4pm that day. When the clock on the citadel tower struck four, the town was bombarded. Storming columns ran out from the citadel towards the east and south gates. Yet the insurgents still put a fight behind their barricades. Houses had to be searched one by one, although the Brescians maintained that the Austrians deliberately set them alight with turpentine. Veronese soldiers were said to have behaved worst, having been enraged by the previous treatment by the insurgents of sick and wounded Austrian soldiers. The next day the insurgents were still holding out and firing in the north-west part of the town, so Haynau now refused to issue a pardon. Two of his regiments had already lost twelve officers and over 200 soldiers. (One Italian account claimed 36 officers and 1,476 troops.[38]) A respected monk, however, acted as a mediator and the insurgents gave in. By the evening the whole city was in Austrian hands. According to Schönhals, Brescia had found a 'guardian angel' both in Haynau's moderation and the discipline of his troops. For his own part, he suggested:[39] 'Brescia had not merely well deserved its punishment, but had, through overconfidence and arrogance, demanded it.' Mollinary also considered that the town deserved its punishment, for having murdered sick and wounded Austrian solders.[40]

The day after their surrender Haynau ordered the inhabitants to surrender all their weapons on pain of death. The city and province were fined 6 million 'zwanzigers' (one fifth of a lire coins); over and above that, the  city had to pay 300,000 lire towards the upkeep of the wounded and the families of those killed. They had also to repay the state all its costs. The leaders of the insurgency had fled, but about 50 more or less compromised, among them a few priests, were shot and about the same number placed in Austrian regiments. To the complaints of Italians, the excuse was given that since the inhabitants had earlier voted to join Piedmont, they could not be treated as Austrian subjects. Sixteen members of a guerrilla group from Piedmont were then shot in the citadel. In July yet another 16 were hanged on the promenade.[41] Haynau was so admired by the army that he was eventually given command of the Hungarian campaign (which he, not the Russians, won[42]), but he was reviled by liberal Europe which called him the 'beast of Brescia'. Given the rules of war at the time, his own personal history, not to mention the behaviour of the Brescians, it was probably undeserved. He had little alternative but to act as he did – and he could have been much more severe.

The 'butchery' at Brescia, however, seriously damaged Radetzky's and Austria's reputation, particularly in Britain (where, in 1856, a visiting Haynau would be thrown in a vat of beer by British brewery workers). The trouble was that given the hatred between the two sides, Radetzky's policies always risked being undermined by incidents on both sides. The Brescia incident had taken place just as the war of 1849 ended. There was, however, to be no breathing space for the Field Marshal. For example, when Franz Joseph's birthday was celebrated in Milan on 18 August 1849, the inhabitants were warned by posters the previous evening not to join in the festivities. Austrian officers, however, who were excited by news of the final defeat of the Hungarians at Világos, gathered after their festive meal at the Café Mazza near the cathedral. Opposite was the balcony of a well-known lady glove-seller, who was pro-Austrian and who now hung her apron on her balcony bearing the Austrian coat of arms in black and gold. This gesture was greeted by the officers with applause but by the Milanese with whistling. The result was a confrontation, scuffles and the arrest of many Milanese. After five days an unsigned proclamation announced 20 people would be given 50 strokes of the cane, and 14 would be condemned to imprisonment with irons. The men were caned on the Citadel square, two women singers were caned inside the Citadel. The city council on 20 September was sent a bill for the canes as well as for ice, vinegar and bandages. When this was all written up in the Turin press, the military commander of Milan rebuked the city council for breach of confidentiality. That the authorities lacked any sense of humour was shown when a youth in Venice who sold potatoes as 'Viennese oranges' was condemned to 25 strokes of the cane.[43] So Radetzky was at the mercy of events; yet he could not police every municipality personally.

One factor which plagued him was the continuing number of bands of armed deserters which often attacked Austrian patrols. Anyone who reported a deserter received a reward of 72 lire; if a robbing deserter were reported, the reward went up to 600 lire. Communes which supported deserters were heavily fined; individuals were threatened with death. Several accounts suggest that about 960 deserters and others were executed between August 1848 and August 1849. (Priests, treachers and bureaucrats who had been supporters of the revolution were purged and replaced by loyalists.)[44]

The most ominous events were to take place in 1852 and 1853 thanks to Mazzini. In 1850 a Central European Committee of Democracy was established in London, with himself at its head but including other revolutionary luminaries such as Ledru-Rolin. It aimed, needless to say, to spread progress, nationality, liberty and humanity throughout Europe, albeit through the barrel of a gun:[45] 'Mazzini seems almost to have held that a raw peasant with a scythe in his hand and devotion to country was more than a match for French cuirassiers or the crack regiments of Francis Joseph.' But he needed funds and so bonds for a loan of £10 million were printed. Mazzini's representatives in Italy were to organise the sale of these through conspiratorial committees set up in Mantua, Venice, Padua, Vicenza, Treviso and other towns.[46] Possession of them in Lombardy-Venetia meant high treason and the death penalty. Still, conspirators all over Italy made brave efforts to sell them – mainly to wealthy people who supported Piedmont – even though Mazzini preached that monarchists had only interests, not principles. His disciples often seemed to believe they could achieve anything – from capturing fortresses to kidnapping Franz Joseph. And about 3,000 people seemed to be involved. Unfortunately, many were unmasked in 1852 leading to the execution of 11 respectable people in Mantua that winter with others being condemned to 15 years in irons.

The whole episode, which caused huge alarm for Radetzky's regime, eventually undermined any chance of reconciliation between the Austrians and Italians, especially as it was immediately followed by an armed uprising in the heart of Milan.

The conspirators were discovered by chance.[47] A silk-dealer named Pezzi was arrested near the Swiss border on suspicion of counterfeiting. But instead of false banknotes the police found him in possession of Mazzini bonds. Under interrogation he then named others and this led to the arrest of a respected Catholic priest and professor Don Erico Tazzoli. Unfortunately, Tazzoli, being a scrupulously honest man who feared accusations of stealing other people's money, as had been the case with so many other conspirators, had kept a register of all those who had bought bonds. But he had encrypted this information and under interrogation would not reveal his code. Even the Austrian police could not break it. (It was based on the Lord's Prayer in Latin and the first three lines of the fourth Canto of Dante's *Hell*. A numeral beginning with 1 and following in order was substituted for each letter, allowing the letter A for example to be substituted for one of 20 numbers in the Lord's Prayer.) But he was betrayed, allegedly under torture, by an assistant, Luigi Castellazzo, the son of a police official. Radetzky was sent the key at Verona on 24 May, but arrests did not follow till 17 June. Thereafter there were more confessions and more betrayals.

Since the charge against the prisoners was high treason, they were tried by a special military tribunal, whose chief inquisitor was a young blond Bohemian with piercing eyes, Lieutenant Kraus, who[48] 'pretends that the other prisoners have confessed, ... invents accusations and stirs up bad feeling between prisoners ... [and] promises immunity to those who confess'. What else was to be expected? Still, almost no one turned state's evidence, although out of 41, ten were condemned to death. Radetzky had to approve the sentences but the real decisions were left to Franz Joseph, who apparently wanted revenge. None the less, in the Austrian tradition, 31 were spared execution. And since it was also Austrian policy to halve the death list, only five in the end were hanged. They were all young and all died bravely. Then on 3 March 1853 another 27 were condemned, 23 of them receiving the death penalty. However, only three were executed. So out of 68 prisoners condemned to death as a result of the unmasking of the conspiracy, only eight actually died. And the charge was high treason. Radetzky's rule, therefore, was hardly as harsh as Italian propaganda painted it. But the trials ended in a tragedy. After Radetzky had published a proclamation announcing the end of the Mantua proceedings, a lawyer's clerk, Pietro Frattini, was allowed to hang. His pardon apparently arrived too late and citizens coming out of the cathedral in Mantua were shocked to find him hanging from a gallows. In the end, therefore, nine died, scores of others were imprisoned, and nearly 40 others fled the country.

Austria had every right, of course, to investigate treason. However, her traditions of dealing with prisoners did not help. The mothers of some of these young men were sent bills for the rope that hanged them. Money left by others was used to cover execution costs. The bodies of those hanged were flung, uncoffined, into unconsecrated earth near the gallows. In the minds of Austrian military men and traditionalists, traitors should have expected no more. But to the outside world this was bizarre behaviour from a Catholic state. The following verdict seems inescapable:[49]

Austria had overreached herself. She made the world shudder not at the proposed crimes of the conspirators but at her own brutality. Her examination simply served to show that her Italian subjects were irreconcilable. The conspirators were not criminals nor adventurers, but thoughtful, earnest men, including nobles, clergy and all grades of the bourgeoisie, inspired by the ideal of a free country, in whose behalf they gave their lives gladly.

On the other hand, Mazzini had also already overreached himself by launching an insane attack on the Milan garrison on 6 February 1853, that is to say, between the first batch of martyrs of Belfiore (the fort in Mantua where the executions took place) and the second. It was to be a huge political, not to mention conspiratorial, disaster, which would permanently undermine his influence in Italy among republicans and monarchists alike.

Mazzini's plot was quite simple.[50] His men would seize the Royal Palace, the headquarters of the Great Guard, and the Citadel in Milan, capture the Governor of Lombardy, set off a revolution in Milan which would be taken up all over Lombardy-Venetia and Italy, and the Austrians would be driven out. The Governor of Lombardy, Michael Strassoldo (Radetzky's son-in-law), would be dining as usual at 5pm with his generals and staff at the palace. Only a few sentries would be guarding the entrance. There would be only 25 soldiers at most to overpower and the task was entrusted to an old follower of Garibaldi named Fanfulla, who with a hundred men of the people would take the high officials prisoner. This would prevent the troops and police from being alerted to oppose the coup. The storming of the guards' headquarters, where 120 men and three howitzers were to be found, would be more difficult but the task was entrusted to a reliable plebian, 'whose name, I am sorry to say I forget,' explained Mazzini.[51] The taking of the Citadel was 'the vital thing', however, since it contained 12,000 muskets apart from those of its garrison. But 18 men with daggers were to overpower the 18 sentries in the forecourt of the Citadel and thereby allow 'two squadrons of plebeians numbering about 300' to take over the Citadel. Mazzini added:[52] 'While these surprises were being undertaken, 200 young men were to run amuck in twos and threes through the streets of the city and stab the soldiers and officers...It would have been the Sicilian Vespers all over again!...Everything had been thought of, and everything was provided for as far as possible.'

If need be, barricades were to be thrown up and the city's gas lighting shut down. Hungarian soldiers were expected to join the conspirators. Supporters from outside Milan, warned by lights from the Cathedral spire, would pour into the city from all directions. Mazzini and other revolutionaries were also ready to arrive:[53] 'If Milan had been able to fight for just two days, all of Lombardy would have been in flames.' So, too, it was hoped, would have been Sicily, Naples, Genoa and Piedmont. It would have been 1848 all over again!

If the movement at Milan had succeeded, the Austrian troops would have had either to evacuate the cities of Central Italy to concentrate on the Po, or, had they been willing to risk a fight, they could easily have been overcome by the popular movement – or so Mazzini thought! He had furnished 25,000 francs from the bond issue for the plot; he had sent a model for a primitive dagger, of which several hundred were made, and had even smuggled in a few bombs of the type that Orsini would later use in his attempt to kill Napoleon III of France. His enthusiasm infected the lower class leadership in Milan – the *Barabba* so feared by respectable citizens – while the latter held back. The plebs had already murdered a couple of 'traitors' and had even considered poisoning a great number of Austrians at a banquet; worse still, they had gone on strike for better pay, just before the plot was due to happen. Mazzini, therefore, was hardly in control.[54]

When five o'clock struck on 6 February, the thousands of supporters who were supposed to be on the streets were nowhere to be found. Neither was Fanfulla, who had fled. Another leader, Fronti, fled with 10,000 francs. The band which was to capture the Governor consisted of about 20, not 100, men, who quickly dissolved when Fanfulla failed to appear. A few barricades, however, were thrown up, while the most effective action was taken by small groups who went around the city stabbing unsuspecting Austrians in the throat with knives. Ten Austrians died and 54 were wounded, but the plot collapsed within an hour. The next day Strassoldo declared a state of siege and hanged seven of the prisoners who had been taken in droves. In the next few days nine more went to the gallows after a drum-head court martial. On 9 February Radetzky proclaimed martial law, ordered Milan to support the wounded soldiers and the families of those killed; vowed to remove all foreign suspects from the city; and levied a special contribution for the benefit of the garrison. He added:[55] 'I reserve to myself the infliction on the city of Milan, according to the result of the investigations, of the well-merited ulterior penalty and contributions.' Sentences were not passed till 18 July: 20 were condemned to death and 46 to imprisonment. But the death sentences were all commuted. Mazzini blamed the upper classes and the bourgeoisie, who had contributed neither a coin, a man nor a weapon, for the failure of the plot. (No Hungarian troops had joined in either.) The workers had been left to fend for themselves. Among the 16 hanged by Strassoldo were three porters, three carpenters, a teacher of gymnastics, a hatter, a butcher, a dramseller, a shoemaker, a combmaker, a café waiter, a printer and a milkman.[56]

Radetzky found the whole episode depressing. Hardegg had once written to him:[57] 'You have a very important position and a very delicate task in the fulfilment of which your genial personality can serve as a reassurance for the good cause.' Yet the Italians no longer found him genial. And he himself detested what he was now called upon to do. In a family letter of 19 March 1853, he wrote:[58] 'The endless sentencing oppresses me, yet there is nothing more to be done, save to keep watch and to be in an eternal state of readiness. Truly, a sad existence ... we humans are in a constant struggle – since we cannot change this, we will each have to bear our cross so long as God wills it.' He had always wanted to fight with magnanimity:[59]

> Basic human truths are the same everywhere...The wars which I have fought all my life ... were always fought within the boundaries of humanity! If you deprive the enemy of the latter, you drive him to despair and this despair creates great advantages for him: the right of the desperate to do anything; the courage of despair, which shrinks before nothing because it has nothing more to lose; and the peculiar, still unexplained, power of despair. In none of my wars have I allowed things to go so far. That would not just be against every human right, but against all military wisdom.

Hence the commutations. Hence, too, his policy towards deserters who he wanted to win back; hence his orders to officers not to shoot them. Indeed, his magnanimity towards the bands of deserters who now roamed the countryside was highly resented by the Italian peasants there. Still Radetzky insisted:[60] 'The rebels should realise that Austria knows how to fight not merely with weapons but also with magnanimity.' If his strategy was Napoleonic, his natural geniality was not. It was Napoleon after all who said:[61] 'Nothing is so remedial as setting fearful examples .... The peace of Italy can only be secured with streams of blood, by burning a couple of places down ... without the example of strength, the people of Italy will always revolt ... you do not win over a people with flattery ... their leaders must be killed.' Radetzky never believed this. His great attempt to win over the Italians was very different.

In an order of the day printed in the *Venice Gazette* on 18 February Radetzky described what had happened in Milan to the Venetians.[62] The radicals had surprised a few officers and men and had attempted to take over guardhouses. Blood had stained the streets of Milan, but he admired 'the firm attitude and the generous moderation of the garrison of Milan in that hour of treason.' He also praised its 'noble conduct' and 'its promptitude in responding to the call of its chiefs'. He ended by calling on his troops to remember what they were: 'in time of peace, the vigilant guardians of internal tranquillity and of the frontiers of the Empire; in time of war, the intrepid defenders of the Emperor and of the country, who both regard you with pride and affection.' Imperial sequins would be given to the injured. However, what was *significant* about the order was that the Field Marshal described the Mazzinians as 'a numerous band of *paid* assassins'. If in 1848 the leaders of the insurrection in Milan had been the richest nobles of the city, Radetzky now believed that in 1853 the *Barabba* were in the pay of these same Lombard nobles, albeit now in exile, and he was determined to have his revenge on them.

He used the conspiracy, therefore, to announce on 18 February the sequestration of the estates of the Lombard noble émigrés who had left Lombardy for Piedmont. They were blamed for financing and organising the plot and were now called upon to pay the consequences by losing the source of their wealth. The *Times* would later call 'this obnoxious decree' ... 'not only unwise but illegal'.[63] The Field Marshal's action, however, was scarcely impulsive; on the contrary, it represented the latest stage in a social, economic and political battle that more than anything else perhaps defined Radetzky's tenure as Governor-General of Lombardy-Venetia.

The Austrian government had become convinced before 1848 that opposition to it throughout the Empire was being generated by the local nobilities. This had been proved to be the case in Galicia (Austrian Poland) and was held to be true both in Hungary and Lombardy-Venetia. In Galicia in 1846, there had been a political revolt which had been led by the local nobles and gentry and which had been spontaneously suppressed by the local peasants in a sort of collective blood-lust. Austrian officials, although innocent, were accused by European liberals and Catholics (priests having been involved in the revolt and killed) of having paid for and organised the massacres.[64]

The whole episode turned out to be rather embarrassing as a result, but it provided Metternich and others with reason to believe that the Empire's peasantry – the majority of the population – was both loyal to its monarch and hostile to the nobility. Metternich, therefore, wrote to Radetzky, to spread the good news:[65] '... The real people are devoted to their monarch because he protects them .... The democrats have mistaken their base; a democracy without the prople is a chimera.' He told the Viceroy, the Archduke Rainer:[66] 'It is desired that the news of the result of this revolutionary undertaking is spread in Italy across the Po as quickly as possible.' The Governors of Lombardy and Venetia were instructed 'to spread the good news' and make sure it reached 'the desired audience'.[67] Ficquelmont, meanwhile, needed no convincing. In 1837 he had told the Tsar with regard to the Hungarian nobles:[68] 'It would need only a word from the court to wipe out this opposition by making the peasants think of an improvement to their lot, something which the nobles have no wish to grant them.' Before leaving Vienna for Milan he had spoken to the British ambassador, who had reported:[69]

> Count Ficquelmont said I was in error if I believed that all the Italian population was hostile to the Austrians, that, on the contrary, there were large numbers who disapproved greatly of what the Milanese agitators and others had done; that if Austria chose to avail itself of its actual power to raise the peasantry against their superiors, it would have perfect facility in procuring the ruin and destruction of those persons; 'but', added the Count, 'that is a policy I would rather die than adopt.'

The man who had confirmed to Metternich that the Galician massacres had been a contest between peasants and nobles, the man who Metternich had sent there to investigate personally and report back to him, had been Prince Schwarzenberg, Radetzky's own *Felddiplomat*.[70] The man who had put down the revolt in Galicia in 1846 and helped bring the local peasants back to sanity, was none other than Colonel Benedek, who by 1848 had become Radetzky's garrison commander in Pavia.[71] Hence even before the revolutions broke out, the army was convinced that any uprising would be the work of the nobility.

With the onset of the revolutionary crisis in 1848, views among the Austrian leadership hardened. Metternich asked Ficquelmont:[72] 'What do the Lombard nobility want? ... The driving force behind the unspeakable position of the country is coming without a shadow of a doubt from their side. Do they want to surrender their fortunes on the high altar of some incredible divinity and bring on the holocaust?' Ficquelmont agreed:[73] 'The most eminent families among the Lombard nobility are the promoters of it. The plot is already very old but it is only a year since the pact was made with Turin. It is the Italian movement which the Pope has extended to all the peninsula which has precipitated the enterprise.' The same diagnosis was believed by the army. One colonel wrote to a member of Radetzky's staff,[74] arguing that if Vienna should do anything it should start with the poor. As long as the court was open to the rich and the poor were left to starve, the emperor would have no party. The 'wanton, rich, *dolce far niente* living *Sciori* (aristocrats)' were the ones who should be trodden on, yet for 32 years Austria had opened her court to these people and neglected 'hard-working citizens and tradesmen'. Metternich agreed:[75] 'this most gangerous class of the population ... this bastard race of a fallen aristocracy' was how he described the Lombard nobility.

The Lombard aristocracy had indeed been alienated. Heraldic commissions set up after 1814 had queried their titles. Their sons believed that their rank alone entitled them to government jobs; they had no idea of going to university, passing exams or learning German to acquire them. One of their representatives complained to Metternich[76] of the 'work, profound study and long practice' required of patrician families and the wealthy even to acquire middling government posts. Gabrio Casati, the Mayor of Milan, stated the same thing to a future Austrian minister of 1848 in 1847.[77] Again, they did not like being summoned to court in the Austrian fashion rather than being personally invited – or having to wait in line while court officials checked the number of quarterings they possessed and those of their girlfriends. In Ficquelmont's own words:[78] 'To go to court and remain in one place until your name and rank are discovered is no longer a favour which it is impossible to resist.'

Many of these people, however, were also nobles of Piedmont, *sudditi misti*, whose families owned lands in both countries. And it was much more pleasant for them to visit Turin and go to court there – and easier to get jobs there or to send their sons to the military academy there – as Gabrio Casati, the mayor of Milan did. (Buol, the Austrian minister in Turin, accused him to his face of raising Sardinians.[79]) Schönhals, Radetzky's adjutant general, wrote:[80] 'The theatres and cafes are not the places where statesmen are produced and tiresome working up the ladder of service posts is not to the taste of rich Italians. We do not blame them for this. But at the same time they cannot accuse the state of violating nationality, partiality and neglect.' More and more, the army came round to a programme of aiding the peasantry and the poor.

The army on the eve of 1848 became increasingly interested in playing off the peasants against the nobles. The Archduke Rainer, the Viceroy,
responded, 'But, dear Radetzky, you are speaking like a revolutionary,' when
the Field Marshal suggested giving rights to the peasants in the tradition
of Joseph II. Yet Radetzky persisted:[81] 'Here in Italy, Austria has the bourgeoisie and the nobility against her. The counterweight is the peasant. The
peasant, although in the majority, is too light in weight. From the standpoint of *raison d'état*, what is more natural, more advisable, and more reasonable, than, so to say, giving him more weight through political rights?'
The Archduke Maximilian d'Este, another Austrian general and military
thinker, meanwhile, was thinking up a scheme whereby the country could
be policed by a militia of 50,000 'real peasants'.[82] The number of people
living in towns of over 7,000 people amounted to 1,190,449 persons. Those
living in the countryside numbered 3,674,158. The latter, he believed, supported the government, so that along with its feeble urban supporters, it
could rely on a large majority of the population. Out of these the Archduke
expected to raise his 50,000 real peasant volunteers by promising them that
each could free another 'real peasant, a farm labourer and to wit someone
from the same commune' from conscription into the Austrian army, if they
joined the militia. To make sure he got the right people – who were to be
given not merely uniforms but armour and a rifle which they could keep
at home along with three 'sharp bullets' – Maximilian laid down that they
should all be approved by the local mayor and priest. The Archduke, however, also expected that the social pressure from wives and mothers to have
their sons freed from conscription would really make the whole scheme
work. For officers, he expected to get retired army officers who would be
attracted by the extra pay. The main thing was that everyone would be
loyal. There would be companies of c.250 men in c.250 areas. Once called
out the militia would get their extra ammunition from the company NCO,
who would be a retired soldier with the key to the company depot. And
who would pay for the new body?: 'Everyone who utters an anti-govern-
ment opinion must immediately have such a tax levied on them and if a
register of all previous utterances were used to this effect, a fair amount of
money could be amassed, particularly from rich Milan. This money would
be more than enough to pay for the creation of a militia...' In short, the
nobles would pay for the country's new peasant defence force.

How widespread this view, that Austria should depend on the poor
and the peasants, actually was among army officers can be best understood
by a report received by the mayor of Milan himself. It concerned an officer

of the Paumgarten regiment, who had visited the dwelling house in Milan of a poor couple, Clemente and Elene Ziboldi, and began speaking to them with 'the most unexpected affability'.[83] Then, having made an argument of the misery of their abode, he tried to persuade them that it was the government's intention to improve the lot of the poor, that it wished to make the *signori* work them less and pay them more but that the *signori,* on the other hand, foreseeing how much would be demanded of them, were trying to arouse in the poor, old and silly grudges against the Germans. After the Tobacco Riots, Radetzky told Ficquelmont[84] that if he arrested a dozen of the most rich and distinguished good-for-nothings and had them exiled to some far off province for a couple of years, the rest of them would receive such a shock, that peace would soon return – as well as confidence in the government, which at that time was completely lacking among the pacific part of the population.

People's minds began to think more and more about Galicia. Already, in 1847, for example, when starving peasants marched with flags flying on Lecco and sacked the house and warehouses of a rich merchant there, 'the soldiers who were garrisoned in the city offered no resistance and allowed themselves to be disarmed and to be locked up in their barracks.'[85] Had they been deliberately helping the peasants? Metternich on 23 January 1848 was reflecting[86] how the government of the Kingdom of Lombardy-Venetia at the beginning of 1848 resembled Galicia in 1846. At the height of the Tobacco Riots, he lamented:[87] 'If the Lombards were Poles, we would have had the same scenes across the Alps at the beginning of 1848 that we had to deplore in Galicia at the beginning of 1846.' Then Austria's most popular newspaper, the *Augsburger Allgemeine Zeitung,* took up the theme:[88] The masses in Italy, as in Galicia, were not interested in political movements, but if revolution broke out, it would not be the farm labourers who would suffer as a class but the landowners and the rich. 'Since they alone are guilty, they alone should pay the price.'

Upper-class Italians soon realised what might happen and upper-class ladies increased their charity work. The Countess Maria Borromeo organised a committee for the relief of poverty which collected 108,600 lire to distribute to the poor. The house of Litta oversaw the distribution of bread and other commodities to the needy.[89] Investments were made in projects like the Treviglio–Brescia railway line to help provide work. The *Augsburger* noted all of this with great cynicism:[90] The *patrizi* and the reformers had now thought up the Machiavellian expedient of pretending to be benefactors to the paupers in order to win their devotion to make use of them in their schemes. But what if the poor saw through them? 'Ought the government to be blamed if, God forbid, the horrid scenes of Galicia, have to be re-enacted upon the fertile fields of Lombardy?' The hatred of the Austrian regime, and of the army in particular, for the North Italian aristocracy by 1848 was crystal clear. It was fully reciprocated of course. Radetzky and the military (to say nothing of Metternich and Ficquelmont), however, placed great faith in the peasant masses as supporters of the government. Radetzky's policies in 1848, therefore, should have come as no surprise to anyone.

It must be said that the outbreak of revolution in 1848 provided little evidence that the peasants or the poor favoured the Austrians. Those who died on the barricades in Milan were not the rich: rather, 61 carpenters, 53 shoemakers, 51 porters, 43 servants, 41 peasants, 39 blacksmiths, 36 bricklayers and 30 weavers.[91] Moreover, in the words of one Austrian officer:[92] 'The city was surrounded by armed and uproarious peasants who came running in their thousands, shooting at the soldiers standing on the bastions just as they were being shot at from the inside of the city.' Elsewhere in Lombardy it was much the same. On 20 March about 20,000 armed peasants took over Lecco;[93] 'columns of armed peasants' marched on Como and Bergamo and other towns had similar experiences.[94] Indeed, Charles Albert found the demonstrations in favour of him in the countryside 'even more remarkable than those in the towns'.[95] Moreover, these peasants persuaded thousands of their fellow peasants, serving in the army, to desert.[96] Peasant grievances and the priesthood seemed to be the two main motivating factors at work. Peasants wanted 'free possession of land' and the return of the *beni communali* (communal woods and pastures) which had been sold off. There was a refusal to pay taxes on food or tolls and a demand to extend share-cropping.[97] The priesthood had been hostile to Austria since the election of Pius IX and especially since the 'occupation of Ferrara'. About 100 priests fought at the barricades in Milan and the poet Tasca included in his *Lettera del Croata* the lines:[98]

> *Petri e fratri in mezzo a balle*
> *Sempre star con croce in mano*
> *Predegar cielo per Taliano*
> *E Tadesco maledir.*
> (Priests and monks in the midst of bullets
> Always stand cross in hand
> Praying to Heaven for the Italians
> And damning the Germans.)

Radetzky knew, as he put it, that 'the Italian clergy with few exceptions belong to our most open and dangerous enemies.'[99] He tried, therefore, to remove his troops from their influence and to have them confess only to army chaplains, since the regular priesthood had conferred on the Milan insurrection 'the character of a holy war'.[100] A minor official, echoing his views, wrote that:[101] 'Their priests are the promoters of these disorders, their priests are in touch with the first priest of Rome, who is the revolutionary number one.' There was even talk of organising battalions of fighting priests, while the Archbishop praised the work of the revolution and gave it his support:[102] '*Aurum Ecclesia habet, non ut servet, sed ut eroget et subveniat in necessitatibus.*'

Yet the poor were not exactly to inherit the earth. The priests had to tell them that 'equality did not equal communism', since the provisional government set up after Radetzky's retreat had no intention of undermining the land-owning classes on whom it depended.[103] Thus although the price of salt was lowered, the excise tax remained as did the capitation and the tithe. In short, 'the weight of the war was made to fall principally upon the poorer sections of the people and on the bourgeoisie employed in industry and commerce, protecting the landed bourgeoisie and aristocracy as much as possible.'[104] In fact, the war finances of the Lombard government were so contrived that industry and commerce, which accounted for less than one fifth of the country's wealth, contributed about one third the costs of the war.[105] And while some small attempt was made to tax industry and commerce progressively, there was never any attempt to produce a progressive tax on land.[106] As a result, landowners contributed no more to the war than the peasants. The latter, meanwhile, were frustrated with falling prices and Piedmontese requisitioning, so that when the authorities announced the conscription of those aged between 23 and 25 and due for call-up under the Austrian system on 25 June, plus those aged between 22 and 25 who had already served in it, the mood of the Lombard peasant turned from one of disappointment to one of rejection.[107] Cries of '*Viva Radetzky*' began to be heard in the countryside. Around Monza, indeed, the couplet could be heard:[108]

> *Viva Radetzky e viva Metternich*
> *La forca ai sciori e viva I povaritt!*
> (Long live Radetzky and long live Metternich,
> Give the lords the hayfork and long live the poor!)

Radetzky received the vivats of peasants all along his route to Milan.[109] By the time he arrived there – especially given the circumstances of Charles

Albert's departure – he now believed that he could fight a class war against the nobles and win it.

Radetzky, moreover, had a new score to settle. At the height of the insurrection he had had several Italian nobles arrested in Verona as trouble-makers and sent to Innsbruck to prevent them stirring up revolt.[110] Others (from Trent) had been sent back as hostages to Salzburg by a subordinate, only to be released by the Austrian authorities for lack of evidence.[111] Radetzky was furious. Failure to act in Milan and Venice, in his view, had already necessitated a war, so he wrote to the Archduke John:[112] 'Whether there is written evidence against these people to warrant a trial for state or high treason I know not.... It might be difficult to prove their guilt but there can be no doubt that they are guilty...' He did not want the authorities 'compromising' his position. His measures were 'extraordinary' and yes:[113]

> What has happened here is – I grant it – an attack on personal freedom, but what does this arbitrary action amount to in face of the means that are presently employed against us? An uprising is an uprising whether it is undertaken against a constitutional or an absolute monarchy. Every state has the right to take preventive measures against one.

Yet the men from Verona were also released on their word of honour to do no harm. Latour advised a very angry Field Marshal simply to lock up such people himself in future, rather than send them back to the authorities in Austria.[114] Radetzky would not forget this advice.

In the meantime, Montecuccoli was happy to be designated 'Imperial Commissioner Plenipotentiary under Field Marshal Radetzky'.[115] So the Field Marshal seemed to be in charge of civil as well as military affairs. This impression was aided by a proclamation from Count Pachta, General Intendant of the Army, dated 1 October 1848 which announced that the General Intendancy of the Army 'as the supreme military government' would henceforth be in charge of matters such as the police, the post, political events, gendarmerie etc. as well as feeding, accommodating and outfitting the army.[116] Given that the whole country remained under a state of siege, this did not, however, seem illogical. The British minister to Turin, on the other hand, told Palmerston:[117] '... the old Marshal has no idea of sharing power and he, therefore, distinctly states, that since they will send him no money from Vienna he must get some for himself in a summary and military manner and that for such an object he has no cause for the aid of a civil governor ... He therefore places Montecuccoli very gently on the shelf.'

According to another report Radetzky now 'assumed the tone and manner of a veritable sovereign'. He occupied royal palaces at Milan and Monza, held banquets and even invited the former Viceroy's sons to dinner, when they sat on his right.[118] Pachta served him well, but had an extremely bad reputation, leading Vienna to turn down Radetzky's request that it should decorate him.[119] And if the Marshal, meanwhile, managed to acquire money to run his regime, according to Montecuccoli in a report to Vienna, he did this 'by riotous requisitioning and the uncontrolled levying of taxes of all kinds on the municipalities'.[120] The army, however, had to get money somewhere and as Radetzky's chief of staff, General Hess, put it, replying to a question about a general amnesty:[121] 'Never. It would not accord with Austrian policy to pardon rebellious subjects. Their punishment must be, not death, but poverty. The people love us; the nobles, the rich landowners, hate us; we must, therefore, annihilate them.' Indeed, the army's campaign in favour of the poor and against the landowning classes had already begun.

On 7 August, the day after Radetzky re-entered Milan, the price of salt was reduced; it was announced that tax arrears would not be collected; and the poll tax was abolished. Tax reforms were introduced speedily: the stamp tax was changed and other taxes suspended.[122] On 15 August Catholic priests were instructed to carry out charity work in aid of the poor;[123] and on 27 August Montecuccoli announced an 'Extraordinary Commission for Public Relief', whose 'only task [would] be to provide the greatest possible relief of poverty, need and infirmity among the poor and unfortunate of the city of Milan and the Corpi Santi and to do so either by means of subventions of money, bread, firewood, etc., or through useful occupations as well as by shelter in charitable institutions in accordance with the respective statutes.'[124] Austrian proclamations of such inducements contained introductions like the following one:[125]

> Italians of the Kingdom of Lombardy-Venetia! See what Austria is doing for you! .... Already she has spontaneously released you from considerable debts and several million livres of rent, not only to the profit of the less well-off but to the advantage of all in order to soften as much as possible the evils created by a war which she certainly did not provoke.

The rich received a very different treatment.[126] Most of their homes, for a start, were converted into barracks: the army's headquarters were in the Litta Palace; the Borromeo Palace was made into a hospital. Precious archives were thrown into the courtyard of the house of the Marquis Trivulzio to make room for soldiers, who also took over the Institute for Young Noble Ladies. The homes of the Marchioness Buscha and the Duchess Serbelloni were turned into barracks. The house of the families of Belgiojoso and Uboldi were ransacked for arms (there was an arms museum there); while pillaging and looting took place everywhere. (Remember all the property of Austrian troops, officers and officials had been looted when they had been forced to leave Milan.) Radetzky did not seem to disapprove: he had already told Latour that he would threaten pillage and sequestration 'in order to prevent the exit in droves of the rich inhabitants from the cities'.[127] Now in Milan, he would carry out his threats while they were still there.

The British minister in Turin explained the situation, as he saw it, to Palmerston. Radetzky could get no money from Vienna and was forced to raise it from the Italians. The army between 6 August and the end of October, therefore, had collected a *rente foncière* of 19 centimes, whereas the usual annual rate had been 18. Thus the army had raised a whole year's land tax in three months. The minister continued:[128]

> There is this, however, to be said in defence of the measure, that it will relieve the peasants and rural inhabitants from paying contributions in kind for the supply of the army, the money now to be raised being applied to the payment of contracts entered into for the provisioning of the troops.

In other words, the money being squeezed out of the landowners and the rich to feed the army was going into the pockets of the peasants who Radetzky was seeking to win over. The British Vice-Consul in Milan estimated that landed property had been taxed 23.5 per cent by 24 November and this figure did not include 'the large contributions which have been raised on the many insurgent districts as a punishment'. But even this was not enough. Montecuccoli announced on 5 December that there would still be a deficit by 31 December in the Austrian accounts of 1.5 million livres. The land tax had brought in 44 million livres, but the army was costing 72 million. So the land tax was raised to 30 per cent, whereas previously it had been 3.5 per cent for the whole year.[129] As if to prove that he was not simply motivated by financial circumstances, but also by ideology, Radetzky had a proclamation issued,[130] stating that tax rises could not be passed on to lease-holders or tenants. Only the rich were meant to squirm. Altogether, between October 1848 and March 1849, Austria raised from Lombardy no less than 65 million livres in order to maintain her army there – and most of that came from the land-owning classes.[131]

Radetzky's most radical move, however, was his proclamation of 11 November 1848.[132] In it he declared it his duty to maintain public safety and to 'obtain an indemnification for the serious public and private injuries resulting from the revolution'. The emigration had been offered amnesty which they refused and instead of returning to claim it, they persisted in organising revolutionary acts, which were *'bringing the class of workmen and labourers of these provinces to (that) degree of distress and misery, against which it must be my care to provide'*. In the interest of justice, humanity and equity, therefore, he had reflected that *'the honest trader, the peaceful artisan, the peasant and the labourer, who, generally not of their own impulse but by a blind concession to the force of circumstances, bore a part in the political disturbances, should be treated with every possible consideration.'* He had decided, therefore, that extraordinary contributions should be demanded from members of ther late Provisional Government, prominent members of the so-called committees, and 'those who have placed themselves at the head of the Revolution, or have aided it by their acts or with their material or intellectual means'. The army, therefore, would assess their fortunes and determine an amount for indemnification purposes, which would have to be paid in full to 'the respective military chest' within six weeks. Otherwise, at the end of the six weeks, the property of the party concerned would be 'placed under sequestration and guardianship' in the readiest way possible in order from the profit of the sale of the produce of the same, payment of the sum assessed could be paid to the army. The land would be seized without any claim to alienation of it made after 18 March 1847. It ended: 'From these contributions, when paid, *succour shall be given to those in need*, in the mode and to the amount which shall hereafter be determined.' Clearly the army was to have its revenge on the noble revolutionaries.

The proclamation caused outrage everywhere. 'You will be shocked with the open way in which Radetzky endeavours to rouse the passions of the lowest orders against the rich and preaches the purest doctrines of Communism and Socialism,' the British minister wrote to Palmerston.[133] In a letter to the British prime minister, Lord John Russell, he added:[134] 'The decree contains ... the expression of such an odious principle, the stirring up of the passions of the poor against the rich, that, with example of the policy adopted by Austria of late in Galicia before their eyes, the unfortunate proprietors of Lombardy are naturally painfully alarmed.' In short, 'it was hardly possible to have devised a measure better calculated to enable the Marshal to work the ruin of the aristocracy of Lombardy, if such should be his will, than the one he has now published.'

The minister was right. And Palmerston was indeed shocked. The proclamation, he protested, expounded doctrines which belonged to 'the disciples of Communism' and which were 'subversive of the very foundations of social order'.[135] Nor was he misguided. Radetzky, along with the proclamation, had issued a list of 200 persons it applied to and the indemnities demanded from them. It was a roll-call of the entire Milanese aristocracy. Husbands, wives and children were all individually assessed and fined between 20,000 and 100,000 livres each. The *Consulta Lombarda*, the Lombard government in exile, protested that if the fines were paid, this would create such a lack of specie, that all commerce and trade in Lombardy would be ruined.[136] But the proclamation also encountered the opposition of Montecuccoli who had it analysed by a court lawyer, who declared it illegal, since it contradicted the forgotten amnesty proclaimed on 20 September.[137] So Radetzky had to back down and a few copies of another proclamation of 23 November signed by the military governor of Milan, Count Wimpffen, announced that the proposal would now apply only to those still in exile who opposed the government and those at home who continued to do so.[138] Those remaining abroad with official permission and who did not oppose the government; those at home who were behaving properly; and those who had returned in accordance with amnesty arrangements, would not be affected.

Montecuccoli now wrote to Wessenberg complaining about military rule and suggesting it should now be ended.[139] But on that very day Wessenberg was replaced as prime minister by Prince Schwarzenberg. He offered the Italians the opportunity to send representatives to the Austrian Reichstag – but sent the invitation on the anniversary of the Tobacco Riots, when the Milanese were wearing mourning and Radetzky was holding a magnificent ball in the Teatro alla Scala. Hence the invitation was refused, as it would have been anyway.[140] This rebuff, however, allowed Radetzky once again to seize the initiative.

Already on 30 December he had issued a proclamation instructing all immigrants 'whose complicity in the revolution' was not 'notorious' to return to Lombardy-Venetia by 31 January 1849.[141] Since no definition of 'notorious complicity' was given, nobody returned. Radetzky, already prepared for this, had instructed the local communes on 20 January to send him lists of citizens still living abroad without legal passports who possessed property worth more than 10,000 livres annually as well as the names of those guilty of high treason since 20 September or guilty of abetting such people with either material or intellectual means.[142] So Italians themselves were now given the task of drawing up lists of people whose properties would be sequestered. A Commission under Count Wohlgemuth, now military governor of Milan, supervised these arrangements and reported by 31 January that 31 individuals had been named whose fines amounted to 5,770,000 livres. If their agents would not pay up, government ones would be appointed to carry out the process. If personal property did not suffice to cover the fine, landed property would be sold.

The Italian members of Wohlgemuth's commission at first refused to serve but were told that if they did not they would face 'a council of war as in times of war'.[143] An appropriately-named Signor Ratti who did agree to serve found an effigy of himself hanging near his home bearing the words:[144] 'this time in effigy only, another time in reality'. Another commission was established for Venetia, but so much opposition developed to both that at the end of February Radetzky was forced to issue a proclamation insisting that all aid had to be given to commissioners by engineers, agents, etc. or anyone else asked to help on pain of severe punishment. Those who failed to pay fines would have their fines doubled.[145] Still, the non-cooperation of Italians made the work of the commissions very difficult, while it was interrupted altogether with the outbreak of Charles Albert's second war in March 1849.

In the negotiations after Novara, the British tried to get the army to change course in Italy. But the minister in Turin reported to Palmerston[146] that General Hess was imbued with the most hostile sentiments towards the upper class Lombards and those who had taken part in the late revolutionary movement in Lombardy and would have no part in any attempt to conciliate them. The General had also put forward 'the old and hackneyed argument' that severe measures were necessary to prove to the inferior classes of society that those in the upper grades were also subjected to punishment when guilty of any fault. Radetzky himself repeated the same view to Schwarzenberg on 13 April:[147] 'To humble the refractory rich, to protect the loyal citizen, but *in particular to exalt the poorer classes of the peasantry as in Galicia,* should be the principle on which from now on the government in Lombardy-Venetia should be based.' He therefore beseeched Schwarzenberg to set aside any futile clemency and let justice run its course completely, that is, even with regard to the rich aristocracy and the larger cities, who had sinned so severely against the imperial, royal government.

A few days later another of his proclamations demanded all fines should be paid by 1 May and on 3 May he refused to pass on to Franz Joseph an 'insufficiently respectful' petition for clemency from the city of Milan.[148]

His next big move came on 12 August when a new proclamation excluded from the amnesty 86 émigrés including all the big names – Borromeo, Casati, Litta, Rosales, Belgiojoso, Pallavicini – even that of Count Marco Greppi who had taken advantage of the amnesty to return and who now had to flee the country a second time.[149] The proclamation mentioned that some people had returned without consequence, but it warned that those who did not, if found to have involved themselves in treason, would pay the full penalty of the law. The fall of Venice and the punishments meted out there afterwards did nothing to suggest that the Field Marshal was not serious. Montecuccoli tried to stop all this by issuing a proclamation on 20 September 1849 increasing the land tax by 50 per cent over its 1848 value and promising that in return the military requisitioning and extra taxes would end.[150] The army simply ignored him. A few days later Mantua had an extraordinary tax of 400,000 livres levied on it and Brescia, which had already been milked of 6,500,000, one of 90,000.[151]

Between 8 September and 21 October Radetzky was in Vienna. Rumours began to spread that civil government was to be restored. They were reinforced when, on his return, Radetzky issued a proclamation heralding a reorganisation in government in line with 'the principles of the constitution and the needs of the country'. In fact, the country was being put under the care of a civil and military governor who would be responsible to the ministry in Vienna – Radetzky himself. Montecuccoli was given charge of the civil administration under Radetzky but Radetzky's son-in-law, General Michael Strassoldo, became his deputy. Pachta, on the other hand, was now pensioned off and the General Intendancy of the army dissolved.[152]

In the countryside, meanwhile, Radetzky had been attempting to win over the peasants by paying them properly for their grain and other crops and animals. The most delicate area for him was his policy towards deserters. As early as 3 September 1848 he promised them, and even those who had fought for the enemy, a pardon if they returned within three weeks – a period of grace which eventually was extended all the way to March 1851.[153] There was also an attempt to reward those who had remained loyal. Latour suggested that two years be subtracted from the service period of those who had fought in Italy and one year from that of those who had served elsewhere in the Monarchy; he predicted that this 'would have the most advantageous effect in the countryside...' He also suggested that former deserters who turned themselves in be sent home on leave.[154] Schwarzenberg, who served as Military Governor of Milan before returning to Vienna, meanwhile promised that there was no intention of calling anyone up.[155] Despite these moves, however, things went quickly wrong. By 27 September Radetzky was informing Latour that 'the granting of leave to soldiers who deserted has made a totally bad impression in the countryside'. People living there had welcomed the army getting rid of vagabond deserters who had become an army of thieves, but loyal troops had begun to threaten to desert, 'calculating that leave not punishment [would] follow treason'.[156] Radetzky, as a result, recommended the publication of a new series of measures, whereby loyal troops would get first preference for leave, followed by newly enlisting men from poor families; followed by those who had been disloyal but could not yet be usefully employed with the other troops. But his advice was rejected, Latour worrying lest the Italian regiments be in a process of reorganisation if another war broke out.[157] Yet he did not rule out the gradual granting of leave to the loyal Italian troops and their replacement by the enlistment of those who [had] registered under the general pardon. But the loyal were always to remain in the majority and no impression should be allowed that it was the faithless who were being rewarded.

Radetzky, however, for reasons that remain unclear, delayed publishing any plans until February 1849. Meanwhile, rumours began to increase that Austria would re-introduce conscription and thousands of peasant youths began to cross the Swiss and Piedmontese borders. Local military commanders, according to British reports, were making communal leaders responsible for preventing this under penalty of fines.[158] One reason for the unrest was the fact that between November 1848 and January 1849 the Austrians did undertake to list all those eligible for conscription who had been born between 1824 and 1828. The Military Governor of Milan informed the Lombards that this was 'only an administrative measure' but no one believed him. So Radetzky had the communes publish promises from him that no levy would be imposed in 1849.[159] Instead, in a proclamation published on 17 February 1849, he declared that company strength in Italian regiments would be 140 men but that 20 of each company would be sent home on leave. 'These twenty men shall be chosen from those who participated in the campaign and who have conducted themselves well. Special consideration shall be given to those solders who belong to poor families and can help them with their work. I repeat that these twenty men shall be entirely free from the obligations of military service.'[160] Meanwhile, deserters were again called to return, this time with the threat that if they did not, their families or the local commune would have to provide a substitute to serve out their time. The results were promising and after proclamations stating time and time again that there would be no conscription, 'the greater part of the deserters from the army gave themselves up and rejoined their regiments, while most of the emigrant peasants returned to their families.'[161] Radetzky, however, in order to discover how many men were still missing, ordered that between 29 April and 20 May 1849, the conscription lists for all those born between 1824 and 1828 should be compiled, where necessary procuring substitutes for the army. The countryside was furious.[162] Palmerston was told:[163] 'the indignation among the people, particularly the peasantry, at the gross breach of good faith on the part of the Austrian Government is such that I greatly fear there will be some serious outbreak shortly.' Resistance was manifested in every village, large or small, in Lombardy, forcing Radetzky on 10 May to annul all these arrangements and declare that his intentions had been misunderstood.[164] On 22 May he issued a proclamation saying that since almost all deserters had returned, all regulations concerning their families now ceased to have effect. Moreover, Italian regiments would be brought up to strength in the future only when it pleased His Majesty to order a new levy.[165] Radetzky, however, had probably forfeited the trust of the peasantry, despite his best intentions. The British certainly thought so. Abercrombie wrote to Palmerston:[166] 'It is the policy of the Austrians to declare openly that only one class of their Italian subjects, namely the nobles, are really disaffected towards them ... The information I have leads me to form a totally different conclusion ... that one feeling of deep-rooted hatred of the Austrians name pervades the minds of every man, woman and child throughout Lombardy.'

Proof that the Austrians themselves may have believed this may be provided by the attempt made by Piedmont in November 1849 to test the Austrian viewpoint. When General Dabormida was sent to Milan to negotiate the right of three notables, Raffi, Caulini and Caldirola to return to Piedmont, Schwarzenberg wrote to Radetzky, instructing him to make no concessions.[167] His view was[168] that the Sardinian government planned to get rid of the greatest number of the Lombard refugees who belonged to the poorer classes as quickly as possible, while at the same time offering the prospect of Sardinian citizenship to the rich. Schwarzenberg's sympathy for the poorer classes was non-existent. Austria was to do nothing for these refugees. Montecuccoli, who had got word of Dabormida's mission, on the other hand, decided to attempt to protect them. He told Radetzky:[169] 'A man must have a homeland. He cannot run around without a home.' If left to rot, these people would become Austria's most bitter enemies. Radetzky, whose sympathy for the poor seems to have been genuine, was convinced by the argument and had Montecuccoli write to Apponyi, the Austrian minister in Turin, in his name with instructions to reach an agreement. Groups of between 40 and 50 poor peasants would be allowed back into Lombardy under army supervision, so long as they had proper papers from Sardinia. But after more pressure from Schwarzenberg, Radetzky changed his mind, ordered Montecuccoli to write nothing and refused to meet Dabormida, insisting that the matter was a diplomatic one.[170] Schwarzenberg insisted with regard to the poor peasant refugees[171] that a vagabond's life would not turn them into peaceful, law-abiding citizens. His justice minister, Dr. Alexander Bach, agreed. Natural law gave Austria the right to protect herself from such people and hence she should not allow them in. He added[172] however, with regard to that part of the emigration which had wealth, that he could not remain indifferent to their fortunes being taken abroad: 'It appears necessary that these fortunes should be sequestrated and I think that the Civil and Military Governor should be instructed to introduce this measure where up till now it has not taken place.' It was only after Mazzini's abortive conspiracy of 6 February 1853, however, that Radetzky fully implemented this advice. And, as has already been seen, the irony was that the plot had been undertaken by the *Barabba* and had been boycotted by the rich. As the new British minister to Turin, Sir James Hudson duly noted this,[173] reporting that 'on the 6th instant it was the lower classes – exclusively (commonly called in Milan the Barabbas) who attacked knife in hand the Austrian outposts and the Chateau...' On the other hand, it has already been seen that thousands of ordinary workers refused to turn out to support Mazzini's plot. It is by no means clear that the poor as a whole were now united with their betters against the Austrians.

Less than two weeks after the uprising in Milan there was an assassination attempt on Franz Joseph himself who was lucky to escape a knife attack by a Hungarian journeyman-tailor, János Libény. A subscription organised by the Archduke Maximilian for a cathedral to be built to honour the Emperor's deliverance (the future *Votivkirche* in Vienna) then collected 73,000 livres in Milan.[174] Some émigrés returned under promises of good behaviour and the state of siege was relaxed from 1 October. The improvement increased gradually and in 1854 there were few arrests and no executions.[175] Franz Joseph's marriage to Elizabeth of Bavaria that same year afforded the Emperor the opportunity to pardon or reduce the sentences of 160 political prisoners in April that year, while on 1 May 1854 the state of siege was lifted. At about the same time Radetzky lifted the sequester on the patrimonies on 189 émigrés whose lands were too small to allow the rest of their families, who they had left behind, to survive. Yet the imperial finances were still precarious, so that Lombardy was asked to supply 40 million and Venetia 25 million florins. Lombardy managed 37,954,740 and Venetia 24,616,761.[176] Radetzky reported to his daughter that this 'semi-forced loan' had been collected without incident but he still feared for the future.[177] In fact, there was a further amnesty or reduced sentences in 1855 for those who had been found guilty of *lèse majesté* or disturbance of the peace. There were also changes in the criminal law, and on 15 July the government reactivated the Central Congregations, ignoring Radetzky's suggested alternatives.[178]

On 17 November the government heard a report from Count Friedrich Thun-Hohenstein, who the Emperor had commissioned to investigate affairs in Lombardy-Venetia. Thun apparently found little revolutionary threat, more a 'reticence' on the part of the upper classes to support the government (they feared what would be written in the Sardinian press if they did), but he blamed the army's attitudes and behaviour for much of the discord. His main recommendation was to bring the émigrés back home where they could be watched. Buol, the foreign minister, agreed and in the end the ministers agreed that sequestration should end. Bach wanted to ensure, however, that those who would not return should have to sell their properties. Bruck, the commerce minister, wanted a public announcement that sequestration would end, but found no support. In the end a compromise was reached for 1856: Radetzky would have the right to readmit those who applied to return on promise of good behaviour; those who were unwilling to return or feared they would not be allowed to do so could ask for a decision on their estates. Some would have to sell, but not all. If nothing happened, then the state could sell off property and deposit the proceeds of sale for the heir of the person concerned. Non-owners of property could either petition to return without penalty or seek the legal status of an emigrant. The Sardinian government could report the outcome to them confidentially. Bach convinced his colleagues that some forced sales would be necessary; revolution always involved some unpleasantness.[179]

The compromise worked for the most part, since by October 1856 most land under sequester had been freed. Yet 1,600 people had not bothered to contact the Austrian authorities. Hence the sequester was lifted totally on 28 October and those who had not requested permission to return by

1857 would be deemed to be emigrants. If they could prove 'naturalisation' by a foreign state, Austria would recognise their new citizenship. But they could always seek to renew their Austrian citizenship in the future.[180] Arrangements had to be made quickly since Franz Joseph and Elizabeth were visiting Lombardy-Venetia for an extended length of time from December to March, 1856–7 and on 2 December, while there, an imperial rescript publically ended sequestration and empowered Radetzky to receive petitions for repatriation. Seventy prisoners were also pardoned.

Franz Joseph, during his visit, according to one historian, also had to 'wrestle with "the Radetzky problem"' and 'face up to the old warrior's senility' in order to end the 'mess' in Verona.[181] Radetzky's usefulness seemed manifestly at an end. With his retirement, the emperor might send a new viceroy pledged to increasing concessions.

This hardly seems fair. True, Radetzky was now 90, but he was certainly not senile. On the other hand, even his own staff were divided over whether he should remain in office. The real question was what kind of regime did he symbolise? Was his presence a guarantee that Austria would always be willing to use military force to suppress any uprising that might take place and expect to win? – in which case, Radetzky was still a useful El Cid figure and the state of his health did not matter. Or was he a constant reminder of 1848–9, the living embodiment of unfortunate past conflict? In that case, might not a new civil and military governor be better placed to take the kingdom forward under the benevolent rule of Franz Joseph? The pessimists took one view, the optimists another. Radetzky in a sense was lucky: by the time the issue was put to the test, he had died. And without him, General Hess on his own proved unable to save Lombardy-Venetia against Piedmont in 1859 when she was supported by France. Maybe even Radetzky would have lost under these circumstances – but maybe not.

Certainly, Radetzky's position had always been insecure under Franz Joseph. The young emperor was always happy to load the old warrior with honours and attention – after all Radetzky's camp in 1848 had been a quasi-court and in Mollinary's words 'Austria then seemed truly only to exist' there, since it contained the Archdukes Franz Joseph, Albert, Charles Ferdinand, Leopold, William, Ernest, Sigismund, Rainer and Henry, not to mention three Prince Schwarzenbergs (Felix, Charles and Edmund), Prince Edward Liechtenstein as well as Counts Clam, Stadion and Paar.[182] Still, Franz Joseph was now concentrating military authority in the hands of his own adjutant Count Grünne, whose feelings for Radetzky were much less warm. For example in 1859 he wrote to Radetzky's successor as military commander in Italy, General Gyulai:[183] 'What is the matter with you? What an old ass like Radetzky could manage at eighty, you will surely be able to pull off.'

Worse still, Radetzky's closest advisers had been transferred after 1849. Hess, albeit at Radetzky's own insistent request, was made army chief of staff in Vienna. Schönhals, his long-serving adjutant, was appointed Federal Commissioner at the provisional German Federal Military Commission at Frankfurt. Benedek then replaced Hess as Radetzky's chief of staff and soon Colonel Eduard Staeger von Waldburg replaced Schönhals. Benedek remained in his post till Radetzky's retirement, Staeger in his until Radetzky's death. (For civil affairs, Radetzky's chief assistant at first was Ritter von Nadherny.)

Benedek, it will be remembered, was the army hero who had put down the revolt in Galicia in 1846 and who at Mortara in 1849 had caused the sensational surrender of thousands of Italian soldiers who had been surrounding him. Radetzky himself had known him since the start of his career when he had helped get him admitted to Wiener Neustadt as a pupil. (Benedek's father, a doctor, had cured Radetzky of a persistent illness, when he had been stationed in Hungary.) Many would later refer to Benedek as the 'second Radetzky', but although Benedek was brilliant leading a charge or in the heat of battle, he totally lacked the intellectual qualities demanded of a chief of staff.[184] In the words of his biographer:[185] 'Neither by temperament or by training was he fitted for staff work; he disliked it, perhaps even he a little despised it.' He certainly despised educated officers, had no interest in studying himself, and had little time for or interest in intellectual pursuits. Worse still, from the very start of his appointment he seems to have reached the conclusion that Radetzky should be pensioned off. For example, General von Kempen, the Police Minister, recorded in his diary[186] that Benedek, en route to Pest for troop exercises, had visited him and described Radetzky as 'decrepit', before discussing possible successors including General Nobili who had become Radetzky's military adlatus in 1851. To smooth over the hostility between Benedek and Count Rechberg, now civil adlatus, who Benedek could not bear, Staeger remained with Radetzky till his death as his general adjutant, which was fortunate, since he took the view that only Radetzky's physical presence was sufficient guarantee for Austria's security. Radetzky himself was aware of the tensions within his camp, since on 31 August he wrote to his daughter:[187] 'Rechberg comes at 3, I await Nobili hourly, because Benedek can no longer get on with the former. I am the Pantalon [the ever-swindled old man in the Italian *commedia dell'arte*] and must work hard to play the friend to all the idiots, while the confusion reigns above...'

At the very start of the 1850s he had other problems besides those of personnel. An army was assembled in Bohemia in 1850 in case war broke out with Prussia over the German Question, and had this happened, Radetzky would have been called upon to command it. Fortunately, the Prussians had surrendered to Austrian pressure at Olmütz at the end of November 1850, but at the start of the month, Radetzky had been summoned to Vienna, although it was not thought diplomatic to announce his nomination as army commander in Bohemia till later. In the meantime, his presence in Vienna, at parades, in discussions etc. was thought sufficient to deter Prussia from unwise acts. Radetzky, in short, was being used as El Cid already – and it seemed to work.[188]

Radetzky was not thrilled to be going to Vienna: he feared lest the German Problem would mean reductions in the army in Italy, which was already being deprived of his leadership. He wrote to Benedek:[189] 'I only request that the reconstruction of Venice should not be delayed, since dark clouds still hang over Italy.' He was also pessimistic about the chances of a peaceful German settlement, writing to his wife on 26 November 1850:[190] 'Although everyone still hopes and believes in a settlement, my view is very different and I believe that I will very soon be named and sent off. The dear old God lives, so I trust in Him that He will not abandon me.' And He did not, allowing Radetzky to return to Italy. Whether he admired the Prussians, who he was ready to fight, it is hard to say. According to the Prussian military attaché, he did:[191] 'He loves us Prussians...' According to Countess Thun, on the other hand:[192] 'He didn't like things Prussian – "Prussian wind". Even the fine Prussian manner of speaking was dreadful to such a simple man.' However, given his views on Austria's place in Germany, it would have been surprising if he had any sympathy with Prussia's position in 1850.

Certainly, he was happy to return to Italy, although foreign policy problems still dogged him. The advent of Napoleon III to power in France meant that he had to think continuously of war from that quarter. The outbreak of war between France and Russia over the Crimea (preceded by a crisis between Russia and Turkey over Montenegro), led to a crisis in relations with Switzerland, but this was mediated by the French. He made further trips to Vienna to meet the Tsar of Russia in 1851 and for Franz Joseph's wedding celebrations in 1854. As the only living Russian Field Marshal (an honour bestowed upon him by Nicholas I) he followed events in the Crimea with interest and wished he could be there commanding the Russian army, speeding up operations against the French: 'Heart and head both spoke to him of the unconditional need to maintain the Russian alliance,'[193] but by the summer of 1855 his health was failing.

His wife had died the previous year, although his correspondence with his daughter Fritzi and her husband and the occasional visit from his eldest son Theodor (who, despite strained relations, was with him when his wife died and would also be present at his father's deathbed) continued to sustain him.

The main family correspondence of Radetzky's which survives are the letters he wrote to his daughter and son-in-law between 1847 and 1857, both of whom he adored.[194] The letters are full of love, loyalty and support as well as the latest political and military news written clearly and concisely giving the most important details. Some letters to his wife have also been published from the years 1848–51 and these are written in exactly the same loving tone and with the same mix of devotion and political news.[195] Both collections reveal the Field Marshal as the warmest, most devoted and selfless husband and father and it is immediately obvious how much all these people loved, cared and worried about one another, about their health, their finances and their happiness. There was nothing they would not do for one another and their openness about their feelings leave the reader admiring the family's solidarity and warmth.

Could Radetzky really have betrayed his wife, even if she had once caused him so much pain? By 1847, of course, when the remaining family correspondence begins, he was in his 80s, but one suspects he had long ago forgiven her everything. Certainly on 4 November 1849 she penned a postscript to a letter from Radetzky to Fritzi, which read:[196] 'I can only tell you that I am very happy to be at the side of my dear and good husband; he is a true angel.' And writing to Fritzi on 5 November 1852, the Field Marshal declared:[197] 'Your mother has behaved wonderfully and I consider myself thankful that she is my companion.' She died on 12 January 1854, Radetzky telling Fritzi that she had 'passed to a better life'; also that Theodor had been there to help him.[198]

The few letters between the Field Marshal and Fanny that survive show how wonderfully close they really were. Most were written in the middle of war in 1848 and 1849 and he tells her that he has had no news of Theodor so that he is going to approach his regimental commander for some. He tells her how the war is going. He tells her that he has to go to

Vienna where he will be housed in the Burg but that he will call to see her on the way there and pick her up on the way back. He tells her not to be melancholic – 'you have been patient for so long, just try to be so for a short time longer'. He thanks her for the wonderful pillow she has made for him. He sends her 200 florins for a trip she has to make to Trieste. In the end though all depends on God: 'the dear God lives and I trust Him not to forsake me now.'

Radetzky not only wrote official reports every day but never failed to remember to write to his wife and daughter as well. They were always in his thoughts and news from them, when they were not at home with him, was the thing that gave him the greatest pleasure. Visits from his daughter and her family – especially after the death of his wife – helped keep him alive. He was the kindest and most humane of military leaders and perhaps the best loved of any commander by those who served under him.

The thread that joined his charity, his kindness to all, his good cheer and conviviality, his generosity and his personal modesty and sense of humour, was undoubtedly his religiosity. He was always a good Catholic and in all his letters expressed his hope that God would protect him and his troops, would not forsake them, but that in any case God's will was law.[199] On the death of his wife he told Fritzi that it had been a test. Later (16 November 1855), he would tell her:[200] 'God has given and taken and will take again .... think of your children and put your faith in God.' He claimed that God had led him to victory after victory and after each attributed his success to God's will. He faced death in much the same way. As a Christian 'I face the day of my death peacefully and without anxiety and face the last hour in gratitude to God.' In fact, of course, he had faced death in battle ever since he had been a teenager. In the middle of the last rites, when all thought him unconscious, he made the sign of the cross. He wrote his will as 'a good Catholic Christian in the name of God the Father, God the Son and God the Holy Ghost.' None the less, in his last general order, on his retirement, he ascribed his victories to his troops. God was usually given credit only in his private correspondence.

By 1855 Radetzky was becoming unsteady on his feet, his rides and walks were becoming shorter and walking upstairs was becoming more difficult. On 29 July 1855 he wrote to his daughter:[201] 'I was overcome by dizziness all of a sudden and was forced, therefore, to let go of the reins completely; I reported the matter to His Majesty, but was not pensioned off but forbidden to travel and have taken the appropriate measures.' His mind was still fresh and unbroken despite such incidents. On 2 November

1855 he celebrated his 89th birthday and for the very first time wrote his will. He was superstitious that this act would hasten his death, but it was about this time that Prince Kraft zu Hohenlohe-Ingelfingen, the Prussian military attaché, visited him and reported that, although the Field Marshal was 'all dried out and extremely small', his mind was fresh, he moved slowly and carefully, and still rode, having himself raised on to his horse, a very lively and active one. The day before the Prussian's arrival he had inspected a hussar regiment and had remained on his horse for three hours.[202] The small commander apparently looked rather mummified and a little repulsive – his lower eye-lids were paralysed and hung down, the inner red turning outwards. Yet his speech was so lively and attractive that people got over this first impression. He still rose at 5am, met his adjutants at 6am and then spent the whole day writing out his orders by himself.[203]

Why did he not seek to retire himself? After all, he had hinted to his daughter when he re-entered Milan in August 1848 that he would like to. And in 1852 in protest at the treatment meted out to his son – another army officer – he had threatened to retire, writing to his daughter:[204] 'What will result from this I know not, but as a man I owed it to myself not to appear as a dummy in front of my brave troops.' Colonel Theodore Radetzky was not a credit either to his family or the service; he was deeply in debt; he drank heavily and he had a conspicuous taste for low company. So notorious had he become that his position as a senior officer was an embarrassment, and the Emperor was anxious to get rid of him without scandal.[205] Benedek and Grünne were given the job of persuading him to retire, with the inducement of promotion to Major-General. The offer was accepted but Radetzky was furious at not being consulted. However, he later calmed down – he does not seem to have had much time for his son in any case. In the meantime he received a personal letter from Franz Joseph, dated 20 November 1852, which ran:[206]

> ...I beg you my dear Count, to further your truly irreplaceable service to me, since I happily grant you any favour or recuperation that your state of health perhaps may desire at the moment. You have already given me so many proofs of your devotion and self-sacrifice that I confidentially expect you to remain longer in my service, for which I express in advance my warmest gratitude.

And this wish would be expressed several times more – for example instead of a pension, the use of a carriage was prescribed in the summer of 1855, and in November 1856 Franz Joseph was quoted as saying 'a military government will exist in Verona till the final days of Field Marshal Radetzky.'[207] So Radetzky hardly experienced 'the thanks of the House of Habsburg' (an ironic phrase meaning Habsburg ingratitude). When Franz Joseph and Elizabeth came to Lombardy-Venetia at the very end of 1856 to announce that the Archduke Maximilian would be appointed Civil Governor, it is not even clear whether the emperor, who had last met Radetzky at his wedding in the spring of 1854, had already decided to retire the 90-year-old. However, in the words of his last assistant adjutant:[208] 'the whole appearance of the Field Marshal.... was that physically he had aged a great deal and made the saddest impression of decrepitude, so that it is highly possible, therefore, that exactly this feeling of the monarch was exploited by those closest to him, to finally bring about the retirement.'

Staeger was summoned to Venice in mid-December to see Count Grünne and given the task to persuade Radetzky to retire. Radetzky consented immediately and Franz Joseph rushed to Verona to see him for a heart-to-heart talk, in which he asked him to remain at his post till Maximilian could arrive in February 1858. Then, totally unexpectedly at the end of February Franz Joseph's farewell letter arrived offering him the use of several castles and asking his permission to seek his advice in the future. Unfortunately, however, it had been published in the *Mailander Zeitung* (Milan Gazette) before Radetzky could receive it. Why Grünne arranged this remains 'scarcely comprehensible'.[209] Still, Radetzky kept his adjutants, servants and doctors for his personal use. So he was well looked after. Yet when on 6 March the imperial couple took their final leave of the old warrior at Verona it was a sad occasion as no one expected them to meet again. Afterwards Radetzky had his long 'Novara moustache' shaved off – it had been his symbol of power as well as a sort of offering of thanks. He told Countess Thun:[210] 'I was discarded like a pressed lemon.' Clearly, even after 72 years of service, he had not really wanted to retire.

Radetzky would have loved to have remained at Verona, but the town was not big enough for both him and Gyulai. Hence he left for Milan, although a couple of hours before he was due to depart he slipped on a parquet floor and broke his left thigh bone. There was no hope at his age of it healing and he was confined to bed. The whole of Europe waited for news. But Radetzky's will was such that he recovered from the crisis and, done up in splints and a wheel chair, he was soon able to carry out his usual pursuits – receiving visitors, lunching with friends, and playing tarock. He even had a special carriage constructed which took him on his wheelchair to inspect parades and exercises. On one of these occasions on 10 November 1857, he contracted flu and pneumonia and on 31 December, still fully conscious, he received the last rites. Then he failed. Radetzky's last words to Staeger were:[211] 'Servants-Pay-Live well-Thank you-Leave me to die in peace.' And on 5 January at 8am he gave up the ghost:[212] 'The saviour of Austria, the Nestor of generals, the patriarch of statesmen had gone.' Both Austria and Russia entered official periods of military mourning for their dead Field Marshal. Much of Europe mourned with them.

In his will, Radetzky asked to be buried at the Heroes' Mountain at Wetzdorf near Stockerau in Lower Austria, about 50 kilometres from Vienna. It had been built by an army contractor, Parkfrieder, as a sort of Austrian Valhalla and Radetzky's old friend Field Marshal von Wimpffen already lay buried there. D'Aspre was buried there also and there were lots of busts of Austrian commanders and officers, many from 1848–9, as well. Franz Joseph had wanted Radetzky to be laid at the Kapuzinergruft in Vienna along with the Habsurgs, but in the end, he respected the Field Marshal's will. Popular opinion favoured burying him at Milan or Verona, but fortunately this did not happen. His remains lay in state in Milan on 14 January, when after being blessed in the Cathedral, they were transferred to Venice, where in a rare military act, they were taken down the Grand Canal to Malamocca. The Austrian fleet then took the body under the protection of two frigates to Trieste, where in a specially decorated locomotive, decked in flowers, it was taken to Vienna, where it arrived on 17 January to be taken to the church of the Arsenal. On a bright and cold day on 18 January, the body was taken by a cavalry brigade through the Herrengasse to the Kärtnertor. Here the Vienna garrison stood on the Glacis along with the Wiener Neustadt Military Academy. Franz Joseph rode up opposite the coffin and did the honours accompanied by a military salute from the bastions of old Vienna. Then he set himself at the head of the cortège, which processed via the Kärntnerstrasse to the Stephansdom. After the blessing, the Emperor led the procession to the Nordbanhof, from where the coffin left for Wetzdorf. Meanwhile the army took up its position on the Prater meadow as a last honour from the Emperor and with three funeral salutes and endless rifle fire, Radetzky's triumphal progress was over.

Curiously, Mollinary of all people was to record in his memoirs that soon after the death of Radetzky the army in Italy went into decline.

Returning there in 1858, Mollinary wrote:[213]

> However, after but a short period of time, I became aware to my great distress, that conditions in the army of Italy since I had left, had suffered a considerable turn for the worse. One saw that the intelligent hand of leadership was absent, that there was nothing to be seen of the great capability in manoeuvres that distinguished the troops under Radetzky. The change in morale which was apparent, manifested itself in a blasé, negative behaviour, which was embarrassing contrasted with what it once had been. Even the faith in the man who was once idolized was no longer preserved. In circles which passed judgement on everything, one heard the opinion delivered that the Field Marshal owed his great successes more to luck and the favour of accident, than to himself. Those who spoke in this way were dilettantes, incapable of displaying talents like Radetzky's, yet sought to console themselves in their own insufficient military knowledge and capabilities, while they dismissed the service of others. Certainly Radetzky had much great luck in his life, yet that consisted most of all in the fact that he lived at a time and under conditions, that favoured the use of his own talents. Any impartial judge recognises his great ability, his rich experience, his extraordinary energy, and the skill he possessed in handling people – qualities, when they were exceptionally united in one man, enabled him to achieve the extraordinary. Moreover, he did not simply pluck his successes from trees, but prepared them in long years of laborious work...

Perhaps Mollinary knew something of the truth about Radetzky after all.

One person, however, who still had nothing good to say about the Field Marshal was Mazzini, who wrote to the *Times* in exile in London, protesting about its obituary, which had begun:[214] 'Austria has lost her Wellington. Field-Marshal Count Radetzky is dead. Comparing Radetzky to Wellington and placing him on a similar national pedestal, we pay the highest tribute to the departed soldier that Englishmen can pay to a foreigner. To write the life of Radetzky would be no less than to write the history of Europe for the last 70 years.' It ended by saying that 'he possessed that peculiar attraction attributed to Frederick and to Napoleon.' The *Times* realised Radetzky's true significance.

Mazzini, however, not only objected to this but claimed (falsely) that the Austrian army in 1848 had been numerically superior to the Italians and that the Italians themselves had not been divided. These claims were easily rebuffed in a reply from the anonymous obituary writer. But the full bitterness of Mazzini was revealed by his claim that at the Great Exhibition

of 1851, men 'had gazed in disgust at the half-Tartar, half-apeish, igno-
ble physiognomy of Radetzky at the entrance to the Italian department.'
(*Coburn's United Services Magazine* had reported that 'the statue of him at
the Crystal Palace conveyed a very good idea of the Marshal'.)[215] Mazzini's
resentment, on the other hand, was very personal and clearly there were
many other Italians who would never admire the achievements of the old
soldier, as today we surely can.

# CONCLUSION

Radetzky's career was nothing short of astonishing. Has any other commander in history planned campaigns, won decisive battles, and supervised victories ten hours a day on the back of a horse at the age of 82? And for years after 1849 the same was still expected of him. When the old Field Marshal visited Vienna in 1854 for Franz Joseph's wedding, Police Minister von Kempen, a general in 1848, found him 'truly fresh in mind', proclaiming:[1] 'Piedmont cannot be trusted. There will have to be a serious clash. I'm ready to concentrate my forty-five battalions within eighteen days at Ficino; after a battle they will be in Turin on the sixth day.' He was in his 88th year but already had his next war all planned and was prepared to mount his horse and lead his troops all over again. And Vienna would have been only too happy to have given him the chance. He had been invincible. He seemed invincible still.

His life had been one of action since a teenager. He had won every honour that could have been awarded to a soldier. After Custoza he had been given the great cross of the Maria Theresa Order; after Novara, the Golden Fleece. Nicholas I of Russia had given him Russia's highest military order after Custoza, the military Order of St. George (first class) and after Novara he was made a Russian Field Marshal. Prussia gave him the Order of the Black Eagle (first class) and a host of other states followed suit, awarding him their highest decorations. His most prized gift, however, was the gold, silver and bejewelled marshal's baton presented to him by the Austrian army, whose officers had subscribed 14,000 Gulden to cover its costs.[2] There was an official reception for him in Vienna on 13 September 1849, which allowed him, on his way back to his now beloved Italy, to visit his daughter, his darling Fritzi, at Pressburg (Bratislava), and to meet his grandchildren. Franz Joseph had made him the gift of a castle in Laibach, which he also briefly visited on his return journey, but the cost of maintaining it was too much for him and the Emperor discreetly took it back.[3] (Rumour had it that he had rejected the title of Duke of Milan for the same reason.) In any case, once back in Italy, he resumed his routine of manoeuvres each year and resented being retired at the age of 90. Still, despite a broken thigh bone and the indignity of having to use a wheel-chair, he managed to inspect his troops and review parades as if nothing had happened. His troops adored him. What Haynau wrote to his former colleagues in Italy from Pressburg on 30 May 1849, when leading the campaign in Hungary, could have been written by any one of them or by any common soldier:[4] 'I prostrate myself at the feet of the Field Marshal. I love and revere him like a father. So long as there is breath in my body, I will never forget how kindly he treated me.' 'Father Radetzky' was no myth; some of his troops must have referred to him as 'Grandfather Radetzky'.

Today his career is forgotten, despite its singular significance. In 1813–14, after all, he helped defeat Napoleon. He did not do it single-handedly, but he was the brains behind the defeat.

Just think of what happened! Napoleon since 1796 had dominated Europe militarily. No power had been able to contain him. In 1805–7 in particular he had crushed the Austrians, Prussians and Russians, leaving both Austria and Prussia fearing for their very existence. Austria challenged him again in 1809, but was once more defeated. Then came Napoleon's invasion of Russia, which proved a huge disaster for the French. Yet Napoleon himself remained undefeated in battle, unconquered by any Russian army, even if his own had been brought low by the Russian winter, disease and maladministration. Once back in France he collected a new army, occupied Germany from the Rhine to the Elbe and again defeated the Russians and Prussians at Lützen and Bautzen. It was at this point that Austria again entered the picture.

Thanks to the diplomacy of Metternich, the brains of Radetzky, the military leadership of Schwarzenberg – not to forget, of course, the supreme courage of the Russian, Prussian and Austrian troops – Napoleon was now defeated at Leipzig, swept out of Germany and forced to abdicate after the allies had occupied Paris. And all this happened in less than eight months. Eight months! After 17 years of uninterrupted military success, Napoleon was confined to France, cornered outside Paris, and exiled to Elba. Yet historians, under the spell of *reichsdeutsche* historiography, still criticise the Austrians for supposedly having moved too slowly; instead, they praise Prussia, a state that fought Napoleon for only half as long as Austria, usually preferring to remain neutral and which in 1809 refused to come to her aid at all.

How fast was the coalition supposed to have moved in 1813–14 in any case? It had no railways, used bad roads, had to feed hundreds of thousands of men and had three armies to coordinate. And after 17 years of Napoleonic domination, would a month or so either way really have mattered? Moving from the Elbe via Leipzig to Paris, defeating Napoleon and his army en route, in only eight months and under these conditions surely seems fast enough. In short, it is high time for the myth of Austrian lethargy to give way to the realisation that Austrian participation was in fact the key to Napoleon's defeat. And that the brains behind that defeat were Radetzky's.

After 1815 Austria was still a leading power, again something that historians often fail to recognise, given their continuing pro-Prussian bias and their tendency to read history from Bismarck backwards. During the period itself, however, people were under no such illusion. Thiers for example in his speculations regarding war in 1840 rated Austria militarily more highly than Prussia.[5] And von Langenau, Saxony's former chief of staff, knew it too. Writing an introduction to a memorandum composed by Clam-Martinitz in 1836 on improving the Austrian army, he argued that all military dispositions since 1792 had been predicated on the division in Europe between the forces of revolution and counter-revolution. He then continued to make several points:[6] first, with regard to the revolutionary and Napoleonic wars, 'next to the French, it was Austria who was assigned the principal role', adding that 'even today the legitimist part of Europe can rely with confidence only on the Austrian army'. Since 1830 the threat of a new European revolutionary war had always been on the cards, so that Austria, Russia and Prussia must stick together – the forces of the German Confederation and the Italian princes in this context did not count for very much. Yet even Russia's forces were too far away to help if war broke out on the Rhine and Prussia's were undermined by her 'internal army structure'. In any future struggle, therefore, 'the Austrian army will more and more have to play the principal part'. The Russians could not put and maintain more than 100,000 men on the Rhine; the Prussians would make a greater effort, but might not be able to control revolutionary nationalist feeling in their army, 'which consists two-thirds of landwehr forces'. Nor was it clear how close relations between the Russian and Prussian armies would prove to be, so that 'Austria alone today can put 150,000 men on the Rhine, 100,000 men in Italy and thereby ensure the maintenance of that internal security required to bring the corps of troops needed to full strength.' His conclusion was that in the forthcoming 'war of opinion', the Austrian army would have to act for Europe where 'the existence of whole empires' would be at stake. The army, in short, would have to be in the highest state of readiness, both well-organised and well-trained.

All of this suited Clam and Radetzky, of course, who were both military reformers. Clam, as has been seen, had doubts about some of Radetzky's reforms, particularly those regarding the cavalry and large military formations. Indeed, he wrote to Radetzky suggesting that while his proposed regulations would produce excellent results when used by a general of his talents, lesser men would not understand them.[7] Still, the ambassador from Baden, a former Austrian soldier and colleague of Radetzky's, General von Tettenborn, wrote to Radetzky that all would be well:[8] 'I find them to be excellent, despite all the opposition ... The opposition has no strength and will be driven from the field.' And in the end he was proved right. Clam's opposition did not last.

Radetzky's new instructions, of course, had been the end result of years of detailed work on the mobility of military units and large formations. In Hungary he had worked on reforming cavalry tactics but had never stopped paying attention to all aspects of military and other sciences. In Ofen (Buda) he had studied not only horses but technology, economics and horticulture. According to his close collaborator:[9] 'All military innovations at home and abroad received his attention ... This thirst for knowledge never left him even in his oldest age. He took the best journals, read a great deal and collected everything with true industry at a time when his complete leisure was spent ordering and researching.' This meant that he collected a rich library of books and maps and even owned a collection of edited and unedited manuscripts and cartographical works from the period of the Turkish wars right up to the end of the French campaigns. Unfortunately, 'the greatest part of these was lost during the Milan uprising of 1848 and the loss hit him very hard.'[10]

Still, before then, in Italy, he could put into practice and onto paper the results of his thinking and experiments in Hungary in the 1820s. He was helped at first by Hess, his friend and chief of staff, till intrigue in Vienna (the probable cause) separated them in 1834. Radetzky referred to Hess as his 'right hand' and 'alter ego' ('*zweites Ich*'): '... Hess alone completely understood him, was completely devoted to him, and judged men and things from the same standpoint. Four years spent together, mutual discussion of opinions, drafts of proposals and events, which were disected from all sorts of angles for hours, satisfied a real need for Radetzky.'[11] Both men took their enforced separation very hard.

Hess was much closer to Radetzky than the latter had ever been to Schwarzenberg during the 1813–14 campaign. The Field Marshal would recall him to Italy in 1848, but 'in the fourteen years of separation they wrote to each other regularly and enthusiastically and saw each other on a variety of occasions. For Hess missed no opportunity to visit the man he loved and admired.'[12]

In the meantime Radetzky's annual manoeuvres attracted the attention of Europe. He was visited in Milan not only by officers of every state but by kings and emperors – Nicholas I of Russia in 1846 and Frederick William IV of Prussia beforehand. Nicholas greeted him wearing the uniform of a colonel of the Radetzky hussars. Frederick William left saying 'I have to go now, my wife is waiting below.'[13] Yet the list of visitors was a curious one. Metternich himself confessed surprise when in 1834 it included the commander and leading officers of the French force then occupying the Papal port of Ancona.[14] Since they were full of praise for Radetzky's work, Metternich wondered why they had risked coming – they did run the risk after all of having to issue a counter-invitation.

One visitor Radetzky looked forward to seeing was his old English comrade-in-arms from the Napoleonic Wars, General Sir Robert Wilson, who was due to visit him in 1840.[15] In a letter of 28 December 1839, the Field Marshal outlined what he had in store for him when they met. He would reunite all his cavalry in the plain of Pordenone and carry out large manoeuvres for five days in the Mincio area. There he would see that Radetzky's way of life had hardly changed: 'It is always my companions at arms who occupy me and to tell you the truth it is my unique work and pleasure to bring my little army to complete perfection (*donner à ma petite armée sa dernière perfection*) in order to render it resistant to any events. I have been very saitisfied with our manoeuvres and lack only your presence for my happiness...'

What Sir Robert Wilson would have seen was described in a detailed report of the 1833 manoeuvres in *Coburn's United Services Magazine and Naval and Military Journal*.[16] The Austrian manoeuvres of the last autumn had attracted great attention and officers of almost all nations had been present as spectators. The troops had been divided into two supposed contending armies drawn up on opposite banks of the Mincio, with one army led by Radetzky, the other by his close colleague, Count Wallmoden. The magazine then gave the most detailed account of everything that happened between 7 and 9 October.

It is unclear whether Wilson ever made his visit, but on 6 April 1841, Radetzky wrote to the general to congratulate him on receiving the Maria Theresa Order, which the Field Marshal believed he richly deserved. He added:[17] 'Despite our age, the two of us will still be able to withstand the fatigues of a campaign once more, although the troubles and mistakes of the cabinets seem to be abating and we are guaranteed if not a durable at least a momentary peace.' This was written in the aftermath of the 1840 war crisis with France. Radetzky then added that, thanks to a homeopathic cure, his health had recovered and he now felt himself 'once again in full fitness and ready for any eventualities'.

The manoeuvres were also attended by a variety of Sardinian officers who later became enemies. Indeed, perhaps inevitably, they took place on territory that would figure prominently in 1848 and 1849. As *Coburn's United Services Magazine* would put it in 1858 reviewing Radetzky's career:[18] 'It was now that Radetzky's long and intimate acquaintance with the country destined to form the scene of action stood him in good stead; the very ground on which the annual manoeuvres had been conducted was the theatre of war.' Indeed, Heller could write of Custoza:[19] 'The battle took place on the same heights that we used to criss-cross in all directions during the mock battles of earlier years. At that time, when the high-minded GdK, Count Wallmoden, occupied that castle of Custoza, situated on a steep mountain escarpment in the shade of dark cypress trees overlooking the plain, not one of us thought that the Sardinian officers then gathered around the commander and enjoying his hospitality, would be our enemies fourteen years later.' The manoeuvres, then, succeeded in rather unexpected ways.

Radetzky, of course, wanted to do more than hold manoeuvres and introduce new regulations for his troops. He also wanted troop reinforcements and the modern fortification of nearly all fortresses, but particularly of Milan. The military engineer, Birago, had recommended Maximilian towers as the means of doing this cheaply. The Archduke Maximilian himself backed the scheme, although he reckoned that 30 towers would be needed, so that the costs would be greater. His views were roughly the same as Radetzky's:[20] 'It would be impossible for an enemy army to cross the Ticino as soon as a striking force half as strong or slightly bigger than that of the enemy were positioned in a fortified Milan.' Yet nothing happened, and has been seen, Radetzky had to fight a continuous and wearying battle with Vienna's War Council and Treasury to get any more resources. He himself pressed particularly for better hospital and medical care for his troops, but was told by Count Hardegg, his old comrade-in-arms from his pioneer days, now president of the War Council (*Hofkriegsrat*):[21] 'I fear I have to state that in my opinion one has to try at present to request what is realistic. As to the hope that doctors will soon make such rapid progress in arts and sciences, I cannot accept .... we for our part can only supply what will keep poor sick soldiers clean and prevent them from going under from lack of sustenance, and ensure that order is kept in hospitals.' Nobody was more concerned than he, he insisted, to see the troops properly fed and clothed, but this aim had to be and could be met without overwhelming the state with debt. People had to see that 'two plus two equals four'. Radetzky, however, never gave up pursuing his aims, even if, occasionally, he and Hardegg fell out. Hardegg, for his part, never ceased protecting the army from the Treasury and other parts of the civil administration, including, as has been seen, pressure from Metternich and Ficquelmont. However, his strength gave out not long before the outbreak of revolution. On 10 February 1848 he wrote to the Treasury after its latest refusal to send reinforcements to Italy:[22] 'Under such circumstances there is nothing left for me but to lay down and die.' He fell ill with anger that same day and died a week later.

Radetzky, who had lost a close friend, simply went on protesting to Vienna anyway:[23] 'People seem forever unable to take the situation in Italy sufficiently seriously in order to allow things to follow the usual prescriptions. But it is thereby forgotten that we are not dealing with princes and ministers, but with a people who hate us and believe that the time has come for them to enter the ranks of great nations.'

He got nowhere. Vienna was horrified and surprised when its ally, Charles Albert, invaded its Italian territory without even declaring war – indeed, right up till the last moment Sardinia's diplomats were denying any hostile intentions.[24]

Vienna was even more horrified when Milan and Venice fell and Radetzky chose to retreat to the Quadrilateral. Yet what was he supposed to have done? Bombard Milan when the whole country was in uproar and there were no supplies available? Clearly the Field Marshal with his 15,000 soldiers, in a city in revolt with 170,000 inhabitants, could not allow himself to be surprised by a Sardinian army at least four times as large. Thus his retreat to Verona arose from a completely correct strategic calculation: he had coolly accepted that he should first retreat in order to counter-attack later. His retreat was executed brilliantly – 'one of those sad masterstrokes of the art of war', as he himself described it to Ficquelmont.

Naturally he was itching to resume his beloved offensive. He wrote to Latour:[25] 'Within a short space of time I will have collected 40,000 men and then there can be a battle between me and Charles Albert.' Defeat never seems to have occurred to him. When Charles Albert attacked him in Verona, he won the highly significant victory at Santa Lucia. This restored faith in the Austrian army and in Radetzky throughout Europe. The Emperor wrote to him praising his heroism and that of the army and taking consolation from his victory for the 'misfortunes' which had befallen his states. He added:[26] 'I retain the soothing confidence that your strength will not diminish and that the cause of Right and the free institutions granted by me will be deservedly and gloriously defended.' These free institutions, of course, were ones that the basically progressive Radetzky had never opposed. He had always believed in constitutions and had been happy to be sent a copy of the Austrian one. Still, his immediate task was to win battles and expel the enemy from Lombardy, something he achieved, astonishingly, within the next two weeks. Radetzky could certainly never be accused of acting slowly. By 6 August he was reporting to the Emperor:[27]

> The city of Milan is ours!... The army took the offensive from Verona two weeks ago. During this time it has fought successful battles at Sommacampagna, Custoza, Volta, Cremona, Pizzighetone and two days before Milan and is now, on the fourteenth day, master of the Lombard capital. The army and its leaders therefore believe that they have faithfully fulfilled their duty to their beloved Emperor and dear Fatherland, since no enemy remains on Lombard soil.

His stunningly successful offensive had taken only fourteen days!

Even when the Vienna Reichstag refused to register a vote of thanks to his army, Radetzky still undertook to defend the Emperor's new free institutions (one deputy had even asked the war minister 'whether he had already given thought to reducing the size of the army?'),[28] but the murder of Latour and events in Germany and Hungary certainly cooled any faith he had in liberalism or democracy. In the event, the advent to power of Prince Schwarzenberg in Vienna and the abdication of Ferdinand in favour of Franz Joseph, meant that these free institutions would not survive in any case.

Radetzky, meanwhile, had another campaign to fight. Charles Albert had rearmed and, eager to help the Hungarians and to restore his own battered reputation, declared war on Austria at the end of March 1849. Radetzky, who had been expecting war to be renewed, took the offensive immediately and defeated the Sardinians in four days or one hundred hours to be precise. The Sardinians had again greatly outnumbered him, but with Napoleonic speed and decisiveness he took them by surprise and destroyed them. Their king, disgraced beyond all measure, had little choice but to abdicate. There was no need even to pursue the Sardinians to Turin.

Their new king was only too happy to accept terms which left his own territory intact. Military history offers no second example of an enemy being completely defeated within four days.

As Civil and Military Governor of Lombardy-Venetia till 1858, Radetzky spent most of his time dealing with Mazzinian conspiracies and attempting to win over the Italian poor and peasantry against the nobles and rich landowners of the kingdom. Once again, his progressive side took control. He had to raise the money anyway, but chose to do so in a way that he believed would benefit the majority. The whole army supported him in this. Radetzky and the military believed that the Mazzinians and the Lombard nobles were connected:[29] 'A large part of the nobility that was richly endowed with landed estates was blind enough to identify the true intentions of this cowardly conspiracy with the glory and greatness of Italy.' Radetzky's plan backfired and, in retrospect, constituted his greatest defeat. The peasants misinterpreted his aims. The rich and educated classes, on the other hand, were never interested in anything the Austrians had to offer. As Daniel Manin, the defeated leader of the Venetian Republic, was to put it in a letter from Paris denouncing Franz Joseph's reorganisation of Lombardy-Venetia after Radetzky's retirement:[30] 'We do not ask for Austria to become more humane, we want her to go away altogether.'

Nationalists are seldom interested in partial independence, bargains, compromises, accommodations, home-rule or any other deals from imperial or colonial powers. Grant them concessions and they will merely up the ante, that is, ask for more. Metternich knew this and therefore was only ever willing to concede cultural freedoms. In the case of Lombardy-Venetia, the influence of Mazzini proved how right he was. The Mantua trials, and particularly the botched uprising in Milan in February 1853, showed just how intransigent the 'party of action' really was, despite its lack of popular support. Hence Radetzky's plan for a class war in Italy failed.

But this defeat was his only one. In purely military terms, he remained invincible. Did this matter? Did the later defeats and final disappearance of the Monarchy mean his career and its achievements had been in vain? Hardly. Radetzky, without doubt, twice saved Austria and Europe from revolutionary success and radical geopolitical change. His defeat of Napoleon meant not only had Europe been liberated from the scourge of French military rule but that America, the Caribbean, the Near East, and India had also escaped whatever fate Napoleon at the head of a united Europe would have had in store for them. Likewise in 1848, but for him, a united Italy, an enlarged and revisionist Hungary and a united Germany would have soon been locked in conflict with either France or Russia or both. It is far too simplistic to deny him real world-historical significance.

Was he a military genius? If one takes the term to mean a great commander who always won his battles and campaigns decisively, who, even more than that, challenged the military assumptions of his day, brought in military reforms, and thought deeply about war, then yes, indeed he was. Well before Napoleon's strategy and tactics had been analysed, rationalised and presented to the world by Jomini and Clausewitz, indeed even before Napoleon himself had fully developed them, Radetzky was already arriving at much the same concepts of warfare: employ the offensive; have a flexible plan; use your general staff to implement it; replace the line with the column; make use of artillery; attack the enemy with superior force at its weakest point, preferably by surprise. This was all Napoleonic, almost *avant la lettre*. Nor was Radetzky dogmatic. He insisted that his officers know the local terrain and adapt to it. Against Napoleon he drew up his famous *Ermattungsstrategie*, the Radetzky Plan, so often referred to inaccurately as the Trachenberg Plan, which, although based on the offensive, adapted it to the exigencies of fighting another military genius. In 1848, he took a calculated decision to abandon Milan temporarily so as to be able to take the offensive once he felt adequately reinforced. He was sufficiently confident in his own genius and in the ability of the army he had trained, to go over to the offensive without worrying about being greatly outnumbered.

Astonishingly, he was already 82. He spent ten hours a day on his horse and supervised every battle himself. Still, it took him 14 days on the offensive in 1848 before he could re-enter Milan. No doubt his initial setbacks rankled with him. In 1849, therefore, he was ready to lead his troops properly. This time his achievement was exemplary. Charles Albert's numerically superior army was smashed in a mere four days. Radetzky's military genius was now made obvious. With any luck, this book will have made it obvious all over again.

# NOTES

## 1 EARLY CAREER

1  Eduar Brabec, *Der junge Radetzky* (Vienna, 1915), pp.3, 6.
2  Alan Sked, *The Decline and Fall of the Habsburg Empire, 1815–1918*, 2nd edition (London and New York, 2001), pp.2–3.
3  Oscar Regele, *Radetzky. Leben, Leistung, Erbe* (Vienna and Munich, 1957), pp.18–22.
4  Radetzky, 'Erinnerungen aus dem Leben des Feldmarschall Grafen Radetzky. Eine Selbstbiographie', *Mitteilungen des k.k. Kriegsarchiv*, Neue Folge, Volume 1 (1887), pp.1–79, p.5.
5  *Der k.k. österreichische Feldmarschall Graf Radetzky. Eine biographische Skizze nach dem eigenen Dictaten und der Correspondenz des Feldmarschalls von einem österreichischen Veteranen*, (in fact, Heller von Hellwand, with whom Radetzky arranged for this assisted autobiography to be published immediately following his death), Stuttgart und Augsburg (1858), p.5.
6  For Radetzky's criticisms of intellectual life at the Theresianum and in the army, see his *Erinnerungen*, pp.5–6.
7  Oskar Freiherr Wolf-Schneider von Arno, *Der Feldherr Radetzky*, (Vienna, 1934), p.15. (This work was issued as a *Sonderdruck* from Heft 3 of the *Militärwissentschaftlichen Mitteilungen*.)
8  Quoted in Friedrich Walter, 'Feldmarschall Leopold Joseph Graf Daun (1705–1766) und Feldmarschall Gideon Ernst Freiherr von Laudon (1717–1790)', in Hugo Hantsch (ed.), *Gestalter der Geschicke Österreichs* (Innsbruck, Vienna and Munich, 1962), pp. 263–292, p.276.
9  Quoted in Charles W. Ingrao, *The Habsburg Monarchy 1618–1815*, 2nd edition (Cambridge, 2000), p.209.
10  Regele, *Radetzky*, pp.31–32. Radetzky's regiment in 1789 was 61 per cent noble although even the engineers in 1800 were 42 per cent noble, the figures changing considerably however if the high nobility is separated out.
11  Regele, *Radetzky*, p.38; Wolf-Schneider von Arno, *Der Feldherr Radetzky*, pp.15–16.
12  Radetzky, *Erinnerungen*, p.6.
13  Radetzky, *Erinnerungen*, p.6.
14  Radetzky, *Erinnerungen*, p.7.
15  Heller, *Graf Radetzky*, pp.6–7.

16  For the diplomatic and military background to the French Revolutionary and Napoleonic Wars, see *inter alia* the relevant volumes of the *Cambridge Modern History* and the *New Cambridge Modern History*, Morse Stephens, *Revolutionary Europe, 1789–1815* (London, 1911), and Derek McKay and H.M. Scott, *The Rise of the Great Powers, 1648–1815* (Harlow, 1983).

17  For Radetzky's criticisms of Austrian military strategy and tactics during the French revolutionary wars quoted here and in the next paragraph, see, Radetzky, *Erinnerungen*, pp.8–10.

18  Radetzky, *Erinnerungen*, pp.10–11.

19  Heller, *Graf Radetzky*, pp.8–9.

20  Heller, *Graf Radetzky*, p.12.

21  Radetzky, *Erinnerungen*, p.15.

22  Heller, *Graf Radetzky*, p.13.

23  Regele, *Radetzky*, p.45.

24  Vienna, Kriegsarchiv, Kriegsgeschichtliches Manuskript 114 von Major Baron von Bittner; Regele, *Radetzky*, p.49.

25  Wolf-Schneider von Arno, *Der Feldherr Radetzky*, pp.16–17.

26  Radetzky, *Erinnerungen*, p.27.

27  Vienna, Kriegsarchiv, Kriegsgeschichtliches Manuskript 113 von Major Baron Stitterheim; *Mitteilungen des k.k. Kriegsarchiv*, 1878, pp.181–2; Regele, *Radetzky*, p.49.

28  Radetzky, *Erinnerungen*, pp.27–8.

29  Radetzky, *Erinnerungen*, p.28.

30  Radetzky, *Erinnerungen*, p.30.

31  Radetzky, *Erinnerungen*, p.35, ft.1.

32  Radetzky, *Erinnerungen*, p.35, ft.2 and pp.36–7 on Austrian–Russian military relations.

33  Heller, *Graf Radetzky*, p.32. Regele, *Radetzky*, p.56, gives a slightly different wording of the report.

34  Regele, *Radetzky*, p.57.

35  Radetzky, *Erinnerungen*, p.45.

36  Wolf-Schneider von Arno, *Der Feldherr Radetzky*, p.19.

37  For Radetzky's account of the clash, see his *Erinnerungen*, pp.49–50.

38  Heller, *Der Graf Radetzky*, p.46.

39  Radetzky, *Erinnerungen*, p.56.

40  Regele, *Radetzky*, p.63.

41  Radetzky, *Erinnerungen*, p.57.

42  Volume for 1854, pt. I, *Radetzky*, pp.14–25 and 177–84, p.17.

43  Hermann Hüffer, *Quellen zur Geschichte der Kriege, 1799–1800*, Leipzig, 1900, p.452.

44  Radetzky, *Erinnerungen*, pp.59–60.

45  Heller, *Der Graf Radetzky*, p.58.

46  Hüffer, *Quellen etc.*, p.513.

47  Ingrao, p.229.

48  For the Prussian Reform Movement, see *inter alia* Guy Stanton Ford, *Stein and the Reform Era in Prussia, 1807–1815* (Gloucester Mass., 1965), James J. Sheehan, *German ,History, 1770–1866* (Oxford, 1989), Gordon A. Craig, *The Politics of the Prussian Army, 1640–1945* (Oxford, 1964) and Martin Kitchin, *A Military History of Germany from the eighteenth century to the present day* (London, 1975).

49  For details, see Chapter 2.

50  Heller, *Der Graf Radetzky*, p.63.

51  Radetzky, *Erinnerungen*, pp.60–1.

52  Heller, *Der Graf Radetzky*, p.68.

53  Radetzky, *Erinnerungen*, p.64.

54  It should also be pointed out that Metternich had sent the Archduke the French order of battle before the war started, allowing him to boast in a report of 23 March 1809 that Charles should know the French army as well as his own. See Alan Sked, *Metternich and Austria. An Evaluation* (London 2008), p.41.

55  Vienna, *Kriegsarchiv*, Milit. Maria Theresien Orden Archiv, 73–87, Promotion, 1809 bis1811; Regele, *Radetzky*, p.76.

56  Regele, *Radetzky*, p.78.

57  Regele, *Radetzky*, p.81.

58  Radetzky, *Erinnerungen*, p.64.

59  Heller, *Der Graf Radetzky*, p.84.

60  'The Archduke bears no responsibility for the outcome of the battle.' *Streffleurs Österreichische Militärische Zeitschrift* (1892), p. 158. Velzé in the *Mitteilungen des österreichischen Kriegsarchivs* (1909), p. 200, concludes the same. He was simply too far away.

61  Heller, *Der Graf Radetzky*, p.91. Radetzky allowed himself on two occasions to be demoted to second proprietor of the fifth hussars – first to allow George IV of Great Britain to become first proprietor and later to allow Charles Albert of Sardinia the same honour. This made his contempt for the latter in 1848 even greater.

62  Radetzky, *Erinnerungen*, p.69.

63  Quoted in Manfried Rauchensteiner, *Kaiser Franz und Herzog Carl. Dynastie und Heerwesen in Österreich 1796–1809* (Munich, 1972), p.6.

## 2  SAVING AUSTRIA AND EUROPE

1  The report itself was destroyed when the Palace of Justice (and the archives it contained) was burned down in 1927. See Edmond Glaise-Horstenau, 'Radetzky. Zur Wiederkehr seined Todestages', *Neues Wiener Tagblatt*, Nr.5, 5 January, 1933.

2  Radetzky, *Erinnerungen*, pp.69–70.

3  Heller, *Der Graf Radetzky*, pp.103–4.

4  Heller, *Der Graf Radetzky*, p.103, p.111. Regele's *Radetzky*, p.108, also stresses Metternich's great understanding of the military context of his policies.

5  Heller, *Der Graf Radetzky*, pp.106–9.

6  Wolf-Schneider von Arno, *Der Feldherr Radetzky*, pp.30–3.

7  For details, see Alan Sked, *Metternich and Austria. An Evaluation* (London, 2008), p.41.

8  Ibid, Chapter 2.

9  For Russia in 1812–1814, see the splendid new work by Dominic Lieven, *Russia against Napoleon. The Battle for Europe, 1807–1814* (London, 2009).

10  For the debate among historians, see Gordon A. Craig, *The Politics of the Prussian Army, 1640–1945* (Oxford, 1964), p.59.

11  Walther Heydendorff, *Österreich und Preußen im Spiegel der österreichischen Geschichtsauffassung* (Vienna, 1947), p.303. Compare Gunther E. Rothenberg, *The Napoleonic Wars* (London, 2004), p.174.

12  Rothenberg, *The Napoleonic Wars*, pp.176–7.

13  Viktor Bibl, *Radetzky. Soldat und Feldherr* (Vienna, 1955), p.130.

14  For Metternich's brilliant diplomacy, see Chapter 2 of Alan Sked, *Metternich and Austria. An Evaluation* (Basingstoke and New York, 2008). For the quote, see p.45.

15  Rudolph von Friederich, *Geschichte des Herbstfeldzuges 1813*, 3 Vols (Berlin, 1903–1906), Vol. 1, *Vom Abschluss der Waffenstillstand bis zur Schlacht von Kulm,* pp.146–7.

16  Heller, *Der Graf Radetzky*, p.130.

17  Radetzky, *Erinnerungen*, p.72.

18  Radetzky, *Notaten für die Feldzüge 1813 und 1814,* Radetzky, Nachlaß, Vienna, Kriegsarchiv.

19  Radetzky, *Erinnerungen*, p.73.

20  'Ein Memoire Radetzky's, das Heerwesen Österreichs beleuchtend, aus dem Jahre 1809', *Mitteilungen des k.k. Kriegsarchivs* (1884), pp.361–70.

21  Helmuth Rössler, *Oesterreichs Kampf um Deutschlands Befreiung*, 2 Vols (Hamburg, 1940), Vol. 2, pp.132–3, 221, which also discuss the obstacles Radetzky had to overcome.

22  Regele, *Radetzky*, p.118.

23  Regele, *Radetzky*, pp.115–16.

24  Regele, *Radetzky*, p.120.

25  Quoted in Heydendorff, *Österreich und Preussen*, p.289.

26  Rothenberg, *The Napoleonic Wars*, pp.178–9.

27  Tim Blanning, *The Pursuit of Glory, Europe 1648–1815* (London, 2007), p.641: 'A more concrete and to my mind more convincing explanation for the French victory in the west can be found in the number of soldiers mobilized by the two sides. The table of major battles during this period, together with the troop strengths of the two sides involved, printed as an appendix to Gunther Rothenberg's *The Art of Warfare in the Age of Napoleon*, reveals that whenever the allies were able to assemble even roughly the same number of troops as the French, they won. It seems difficult to avoid the conclusion of Gilbert Bodinier: "All the victories achieved by the republican armies were due to their numbers.... On every occasion that their numerical superiority

was slight ... or when they were numerically inferior to the enemy, the French were defeated." '

28  See for example Friederich's comments on the strengths of the various corps in the three allied armies in the first volume of his work, *Geschichte des Herbstfeldzuges* etc. See, too, the rejection of Austria's official figures for her armed forces in the summer of 1813 by the British commissioner to the Russian army, i.e. Colonel The Hon. George Cathcart, *Commentaries on the War in Russia and Germany in 1812 and 1813* (London, 1850), p.195, where he makes the preposterous claim regarding Austria's troop numbers that 'not more than 50,000 took the field with the allies at any time during the war in Germany or France'. Cathcart's prejudice was pro-Russian. He had been educated and brought up at St. Petersburg where his father had been British ambassador and spoke Russian fluently. His colleague, Stewart, commissioner to the Prussian forces complained: 'Cathcart will be more of a Russian than an Englishman soon, he is so bigoted to his Emperor...' Quoted in Sir Charles Webster, *The Foreign Policy of Castlereagh, 1812–1815. Britain and the Reconstruction of Europe* (London, 1950), p.140.

29  'My headquarters is now overrun by Russians and by all sorts of people attached to me by the king in great numbers. My table is daily 40 people strong. If I don't get additional food I'll be as thin as a dog.' Blücher to Hardenberg, Steigau, 16 August 1813. Quoted in Wilhelm Capelle (ed.), *Briefe des Feldmarschalls Blücher* (Leipzig, 1942), pp.56–7.

30  For the course of events during the campaign see the works already cited by Friederich and Lieven, but also a huge work by the greatest historian of the diplomacy of 1813–1814, Wilhelm Oncken, who eventually wrote down everything he knew in his *Das Zeitalter der Revolution, des Kaiserreiches und der Befreiungskriege*, 2 vols (Berlin, 1884–1886). Vol. 2, which covers the Napoleonic period, is, like the first almost 1,000 pages long. Radetzky's *Notaten* on 1813–14, 200 pages in German *Handschrift* give vital information on key points. There are also works in general for English readers, namely David G. Chandler's classic, *The Campaigns of Napoleon. The Mind and Methods of History's Greatest Soldier* (New York, 1966) and the smaller but still excellent account, Gunther E. Rothenberg, *The Napoleonic Wars* (London, 1999).

31  For Metternich, see Sked, *Metternich and Austria*. But also see below.

32  *Letters of Lady Burghersh (afterwards Countess of Westmorland) From Germany and France During The Campaign of 1813–1814* (London, 1893), pp.160–1.

33  For what is known, the best place to start is Karl Obermann, 'Diplomatie und Außenpolitik im Jahre 1813, unter besonderer Berücksichtigung der Rolle Metternichs', in Fritz Straube (ed.), *Das Jahr 1813. Studien zur Geschichte und Wirkung der Befreiungskriege* (East Berlin, 1963), pp.131–60.

34  Regele, p.119

35  Ibid.

36  They include Friederich, Lieven, and Gordon Craig.

37  Karl Griewank (ed.), *Gneisenau. Ein Leben in Briefen,* 3rd edition (Leipzig, 1939), Gneisenau to Radetzky, St. Arnold, 15 January 1814, pp.282–4.

38  Quoted in Regele, p.125.

39  Radetzky, *Notaten*.

40  Wilhelm Wlaschütz, *Gechichte der Kämpfe Österreichs. Kriege unter der Regierung des Kaisers Franz. Vol. 2, Österreichs entscheidendes Machtaufgebot* (Vienna, 1913), p.102.

41  For the background and debate over the Trachenberg Plan, see Friederich, Heller, and Criste plus two key articles: Karl Woynar, 'Österreichs Beziehungen zu Schweden und Dänemark vornehmlich seine Politik bei der Vereinigung Norwegens mit Schweden in den Jahren 1813 und 1814. Mit Benützung von Acten des kuk Haus-Hof- und Staatsarchiv in Wien', *Archiv für österreichische Geschichte*, Vol. 77 (1891), pp.379–537 and Gustav Roloff, *Die Entstehung des Operationsplan für den Herbstfeldzug von 1813, Militär-Wochenblatt* (1892), issues 58 and 60, pp.1564–72 and 1612–18. The footnotes in the multi-volume Soviet series on Russian diplomatic documents are simply based on out-of-date literature and of no use for research.

42  Carl von Plotho, *Der Krieg in Deutschland und Frankreich in den Jahren 1813 und 1814*, 3 vols (Berlin, 1817), Vol. 2, pp.5–6.

43  Friederich, p.99.

44  For Clausewitz's inability to understand the strategy, see the interesting essay by Gordon A. Craig, 'Hanns Delbrück; The Military Historian', in Gordon A. Craig, *War, Policy and Diplomacy. Selected Essays* (London, 1966), pp.22–45.

45  Friederich, p.99.

46  Wilhelm Capelle (ed.), *Briefe des Feldmarschalls Blücher* (Leipzig, 1942), pp.12–13.

47  Friederich, Vol. 1, p.237.

48  Vienna, Kriegsarchiv, Radetzky Nachlaß.

49  Radetzky, *Notaten*.

50  On 2 August a Michael Ambruster, a government official, wrote a report to the Police Minister making references to Radetzky's strong pro-German views. Radetzky, according to Ambuster, 'should always take care, so long as the Austrian army is not on German soil, to spread only Austrian patriotism, and to speak of Germany as rarely as possible, and especially, not to speak too much of German freedom as understood by the *Tügenbund*, whose members, if I only half understand them, will become the most dangerous enemies of the Monarchy.' See Viktor Bibl, *Radetzky. Soldat und Feldherr* (Vienna, 1955), p.145.

51  Radetzky, *Erinnerungen*, p.74.

52  Ibid.

53  Ibid.

54  Ibid.

55  Heller, p.149. 'As far as the Russian armies are concerned, it has become a habit always to claim that these are much stronger than they really are and no general, apart from their commander and their quartermaster general, knows their actual strength.'

56  Franz Joseph Adolph Schneidawind, *FM Graf Radetzky, sein kriegerisches Leben und seine Feldzüge vom Jahre 1784–1850* (Augsburg, 1851), p.272, ft.

57  Felix Markham, *Napoleon* (New York, 1966), p.206.

58  Schneidawind, p.280.

59  Ibid, p.284.

60  Radetzky, *Denkschriften militärisch-politischen Inhalts aus dem handschriftlichen Nachlaß des kk. Österreichischen Feldmarschalls Grafen Radetzky* (Stuttgart and Augsburg, 1858), pp.164–5. (*Entwurf für die künftigen Operationen*, Teplitz, 4 September, 1813.)

61  Radetzky, *Denkschriften*, pp.171–3.

62  Heller, p.234, ft.1.

63  Radetzky, *Notaten*.

64  Baron Karl von Müffling, *The Memoirs of Baron von Müffling. A Prussian Officer in the Napoleonic Wars*, Napoleonic Library (London, 1997), p.388.

65  Webster, p.168, ft.2.

66  *Letters of Lady Burghersh etc*, pp.66–7.

67  Radetzky, *Notaten*.

68  Müffling, p.439, ft.

69  Müffling, p.90.

70  Müffling, p.100.

71  Müffling, pp.101–2.

72  A. von Jansen, *König Friedrich Wilhelm III in der Schlacht* (Berlin, 1907), p.185. The date was 18 August 1813.

73  The Rev. Herbert Randolph MA (ed.), *Private Diary of Travels, Personal Services and Public Events during Mission and Employment With The European Armies in Campaigns of 1812, 1813, 1814. From the invasion of Russia to the Capture of Paris. By General Sir Robert Wilson CMT,* 2 Vols (London, 1861), Vol. 2, p.86.

74  Ibid, p.464.

75  Ibid, pp.183–4.

76  Quoted in H. Kerchnawe and Alois Veltzé, *Feldmarschall Karl Fürst zu Schwarzenberg, der Führer der Verbündeten in den Befreiungskriegen* (Vienna and Leipzig, 1913), p.166.

77  Johann Freidrich Novak (ed.), *Briefe des Feldmarschalls Fürsten Schwarzenberg an seine Frau, 1799–1816* (Vienna and Leipzig, 1913), pp.332–3.

78  Czech State Archives, Prague, *Acta Clementina*, Carton 26.

79  Griewank, pp.269–73, Gneisenau to Clausewitz, 16 November 1816.

80  Thomas Stamm-Kuhlmann, *König in Preußens großer Zeit. Friedrich Wilhelm III. der Melancholiker auf dem Thron* (no date or place of publication, merely Siedler Verlag), p.304.

81  Griewank, pp.266–7. Gneisenau first made the request on 31 October 1813.

82  Müffling, p.472.

83  Radetzky, *Notaten*.

84  Quotes in Roger Parkinson, *The Hussar General. The Life of Blücher. Man of Waterloo* (London, 1975), p.137.

85  Radetzky, *Notaten*.

86  Radetzky, *Notaten*. A longer version is to be found in his *Erinnerungen*.

87  Theodor von Bernhardi, *Denkwürdigkeiten aus dem Leben des kaiserl. russ. Generals von der Infanterie Carl Friedrich Grafen von Toll*, 5 Vols (Leipzig, 1858), Vol. 4, *Beilage* II, pp.814–16.

88  Oncken, Vol. 2, pp.720–1 for Radetzky's memorandum and the whole episode.

89  Schneidawind, p.305.

90  Radetzky, *Notaten*.

91  Ibid.

92  Schneidawind, p.308.

93  Griewank, pp.288–9, Gneisenau to Hardenberg, Brienne, 2 February 1814.

94  Radetzky, *Notaten*.

95  Ibid.

96  Ibid.

97  Griewank, pp.294–300, Gneisenau to Clausewitz, Paris, 28 April 1814.

98  Radetzky, *Notaten*.

99  Ibid.

100  Ibid.

101  Ibid.

102  Ibid.

103  Ibid.

104  Griewank, pp.286–288, Gneisenau to Stein, Dammartin le St. Père, 27 January 1814.

105  Griewank, Gneisenau to Hardenberg, Laon, 10 March 1814.

106  Radetzky, pp.290–293, *Notaten*.

107  Griewank, pp.294–300, Gneisenau to Clausewitz, Paris, 28 April 1814.

108  Radetzky, *Notaten*.

109  Karl Fürst Schwarzenberg, *Feldmarschall Fürst Schwarzenberg* (Vienna, 1964), p.277.

110  For the clash, see Webster, pp.212–13.

111  Ibid.

112  Bibl, pp.191–2.

113  Griewank, pp.290–3, Gneisenau to Hardenberg, Laon, 10 March 1814.

114  Müffling, pp.167–8.

115  Ibid, p.170.

116  Capelle, pp.54–5, Blücher to Bonin, Paris, 30 April 1814: '...I decisively defeated Napoleon at Laon...'

117  Schneidawind, p.313.

118  Parkinson, pp.195–6.

119  Ibid, p.196.

120  Radetzky, *Notaten*.

121  Lord Burghersh, *Memoir of the Operations of the Allied Armies under Prince Schwarzenberg and Marshal Blucher during The Latter End of 1813 and the Year 1814* (London, 1996), pp.180–4.

122  Schneidawind, pp.318–21.

123  Ibid, p.237.

124 Gräfin Leopoldine Thun, *Erinnerungen aus meinem Leben*, 3rd edition (Innsbruck, 1926).

125 Quoted in Karl Fürst Schwarzenberg, *Feldmarschall Fürst Schwarzenberg* (Vienna, 1964), p.355.

126 The biting phrase comes from A. Sorel, *L'Europe et la Révolution française* (Paris, 1904), Vol. VIII, pp.185–6.

127 Radetzky, *Erinnerungen*, pp.75–6.

128 Regele, p.481.

129 Bernhard Duhr S.J. (ed.), *Briefe des Feldmarschalls Radetzky an seine Tochter Friedericke, 1847–1857* (Vienna, 1892), p.18.

130 Ibid.

131 Ibid, p.19.

132 Regele, pp.483–4.

133 Duhr, p.19.

134 Ibid.

## 3  EDUCATOR OF ARMIES

1 On Charles, see the works by Rothenberg (cited above) and Andrew Uffindell, *Great Generals of the Napoleonic Wars and Their Battles, 1805–1815* (Staplehurst, Kent, 2003).

2 Uffindell, *Great Generals*, pp.162–3.

3 Rothenberg, *The Emperor's Last Victory, Napoleon and the Battle of Wagram* (London, 2004), p.47.

4 Archduke Charles, 'Denkschrift über die militärischen-politischen Verhältnisse in Oesterreich von 1801–1809', *Ausgewählte Schriften*, Vol. 6, pp.356–7.

5 Radetzky, *Erinnerungen*, p.8.

6 *Dienst-Reglement für die k.k. Infanterie* (2 Parts) (Vienna, 1807–8), I, pp.1–2 and II, para.5.

7 *Grundsätze der höheren Kriegs-Kunst für die Generäle der österreichischen Armee* (Vienna, 1806).

8 J. Pelet, *Mémoires sur la Guerre de 1809* (Paris, 1824), Vol. 2, p.179.

9 English translation (London, 1905).

10 Lt. Gen. von Caemmerer, *The Development of Strategic Science During the 19th Century* (London, 1905). p.58.

11 Von Caemmerer, *The Development of Strategical Science*, p.61.

12 J. Croker, *The Croker Papers* (London, 1885), Vol. I, p.338.

13 Radetzky, *Aus meinem Leben, 1814–1847*, *Österreichische Rundschau*, Vol. XIV, 1/3, 1908, pp.172–179, p.177.

14 Heller, *Der Graf Radetzky*, pp.285–6.

15 Edmund Glaise-Horstenau, 'Radetzky. Zur 75 Wiederkehr seines Todestagen', *Neues Wiener Tagblatt*, No.5, 5 January 1933.

16 Wolf-Schneider von Arno, *Der Feldherr Radetzky*, p.45.

17 Joseph Freiherr von Helfert, *Geschichte der österreichischen Revolution* (Freiburg, 1909), Vol. 2, p.84.

18  Radetzky, *Aus meinem Leben, 1814–1847*, p.178.
19  For the whole story and the quotes above, see Radetzky, *Aus meinem Leben, 1814–1847*, p.178.
20  Maximilian Freiherr von Kübeck (ed.), *Tagebücher des Carl Freiherrn von Kübeck*, 2 Vols (Vienna, 1909), Vol. 1, Pt. 2, p.550.
21  Wolf-Schneider von Arno, *Der Feldherr Radetzky*, p.50.
22  Wolf-Schneider von Arno, *Der Feldherr Radetzky*, p.50.
23  Wolf-Schneider von Arno, *Der Feldherr Radetzky*, p.47. The figures quoted can be found on p.54.
24  For his work on cavalry, horses and transportation, as well as quotes used here on these subjects, see Regele, *Radetzky*, pp.408–11.
25  Radetzky, *Denkschriften*, pp.452–78. ('*Ueber den Werth der österreichischen Kavallerie, und einige Mittel ihn zu heben.*')
26  Radetzky, *Denkschriften*, pp.23–6 ('*Entwurf zu einer Instruktion für die Generalkommanden, die Zutheilung der Offiziere des Generalstabes betreffend. Wien 1810*'); pp.32–9 ('*Ueber die Beschäftigungen der Offiziere des Generalquartiermeisterstabes. Wien den 24 Oktober 1810.*'); and pp.40–7 ('*Instruktion für einen bei einer auswärtigen Gesandschaft zugetheilten Offiziere des Generalquartiermeisterstabes. Wien im Jahre 1810.*')
27  Radetzky, *Entwurf etc.*, p.23.
28  Radetzky, *Entwurf etc.*, pp.23–4.
29  Radetzky, *Entwurf etc.*, pp.25–6.
30  Radetzky, *Ueber die Beschäftigung etc.*
31  Radetzky, *Ueber die Beschäftigung etc.*, p.33.
32  Radetzky, *Ueber die Beschäftigung etc.*, p.36.
33  For these developments, see Regele, *Radetzky*, pp.404.
34  This was not included in the very large number of his published *Denkschriften*. Regele summarises it (without giving any source reference), in *Radetzky*, p.399.
35  Regele, *Radetzky*, p.399.
36  Regele, *Radetzky*, p.400.
37  Regele, *Radetzky*, p.400.
38  Regele, *Radetzky*, p.401.
39  Radetzky, *Denkschriften*, pp.40–7, *Instruktion etc.* See note 24, Chapter 3.
40  The latest biography of whom is by Stefan Lippert, namely, *Felix Fürst zu Schwarzenberg. Eine politische Biographie* (Stuttgart, 1998). His military career is covered in pages 51–9 and pp.117–79.
41  Regele, *Radetzky*, pp.413–14.
42  Regele, *Radetzky*, p.403.
43  For Metternich's notorious role in spying and police work, see Alan Sked, *Metternich and Austria. An Evaluation* (London, 2008), Chapter 5.
44  Regele, *Radetzky*, p.403.
45  Regele, *Radetzky*, pp.404–5.
46  Radetzky, *Denkschriften*, pp.398–422. ('*Gedanken über Festungen. Ofen, 1827.*')
47  Radetzky, *Gedanken etc.*, p.401.

48  Radetzky, *Gedanken etc.*, pp.404–5.

49  Radetzky, *Gedanken etc.*, pp.408–9.

50  Radetzky, *Gedanken etc.*, pp.410–11.

51  Radetzky, *Gedanken etc.*, p.408.

52  Radetzky, *Denkschriften*, pp.543–52. ('*Wie kann man gute und grosse Heere mit wenig Kosten erhalten. End Dezember 1834.*'), p.551.

53  Radetzky, *Denkschriften*, pp.479–513. ('*Uber eine Operation der verbündeten Heer gegen Frankreich, mit besonderer Rücksicht auf die Armee des Oberrheins. Mailand im Jahre 1832.*')

54  Regele, *Radetzky*, p.407.

55  Radetzky, *Denkschriften*, pp.514–34. ('*Ueber die Nothwendigkeit eines festen Lagers bei Mailand. Mailand 1834.*'), p.514.

56  Radetzky, *Ueber die Nothwendigkeit etc.*, p.518.

57  Radetzky, *Ueber die Nothwendigkeit etc.*, p.519.

58  Radetzky, *Ueber die Nothwendigkeit etc.*, p.519.

59  Radetzky, *Ueber die Nothwendigkeit etc.*, p.520.

60  Radetzky, *Ueber die Nothwendigkeit etc.*, p.524.

61  These were defensive fortified towers, first constructed around Linz about ten years previously by the Austrian general and military thinker, the Archduke Maximilian d'Este, the brother of the Duke of Modena. Unfortunately they proved too easy to destroy and after a series of experiments were abandoned – although not before 1848.

62  See Radetzky, *Ueber die Nothwendigkeit etc.*, pp.525–34 for Birago's report.

63  Wolf-Schneider von Arno, *Der Feldherr Radetzky*, p.49.

64  Radetzky, *Aus meinem Leben, 1814–1847*, p.177.

65  Radetzky, *Aus meinem Leben, 1814–1847*, p.177.

66  Volume for 1854, *Radetzky*, pp.14–25 and 177–184, pp.19–20.

67  Wolf-Schneider von Arno, *Der Feldherr Radetzky*, p.52.

68  Regele, *Radetzky*, p.421.

69  Regele, *Radetzky*, p.421.

70  Maximilian Bach, *Geschichte der Wiener Revolution im Jahre 1848* (Vienna, 1894), pp.27–8.

71  Peter Evan Turnbull, *Austria*, 2 Vols (London, 1840), Vol. 2, p.297.

72  Johann Springer, *Statistik des österreichischen Kaiserstaates*, 2 Vols (Vienna, 1840), Vol. 2, p.254.

73  Capt. Basil Hall, 'Notes on the Austrian Army', *United Services Magazine* (September 1835), p.178.

74  Hall, *Notes*, p.179.

75  *Oesterreichs Innere Politik*, Count Schnirding (?) (Stuttgart, 1847), p.182, ft.

76  Fenner von Fenneberg, *Oesterreich und seine Armee* (Leipzig, 1847), pp.61–5, 71–3, 140–43.

77  Fenner, *Oesterreich etc.*, p.69.

78  For the quotes and evidence in the next paragraph, see Regele, *Radetzky*, pp.425–6.

79  Quoted in *Coburn's United services Magazine and Naval and Military Journal* (1854), Pt. I, 'Memoir of Marshal Radetzky', pp.242–56, p.248.

80  Regele, *Radetzky,* pp.429–30.

81  On education and training, see Regele, *Radetzky,* pp.416–20.

82  Turnball, *Austria*, Vol. 2, p.282.

83  Gunther E. Rothenberg, 'The Austrian Army in the Age of Metternich', *Journal of Modern History*, Vol. 40 (1968), pp.155–65, p.160.

84  The misreading is of a reference in Vol. I, p.48 of Alphonse von Wrede's *Geschichte der k. und k. Wehrmacht,* 5 Vols (Vienna, 1893–1900).

85  Radetzky, *Wie kann man etc.*, p.541.

86  Radetzky, *Denkschriften,* pp.423–51. ('Militärische Betrachtung der Lage Oesterreichs. Im Jahre 1828.')

87  Radetzky, *Militärische Betrachtung,* p.426.

88  Radetzky, *Militärische Betrachtung,* p.446. However, in a discussion of a possible war with Russia, he wrote (p.437): 'The general tendency of European states to grant themselves firm constitutions, brings no relief from such anxieties. The majority of Russia's population receives much too low a level of education to be able to hope that it could be raised even in a hundred years to the level where, through a constitution of the kind prevailing in other lands it could abstain from wars of conquest.'

89  Radetzky, *Militärische Betrachtung*, p.447.

90  Radetzky, *Militärische Betrachtung*, p.447.

91  Radetzky, *Militärische Betrachtung*, p.448.

92  Radetzky, *Militärische Betrachtung*, p.450.

93  Radetzky, *Militärische Betrachtung*, p.451.

94  See note 50, Chapter 3.

95  Radetzky, *Wie kann man*, pp.537–8.

96  Radetzky, *Wie kann man*, p.538.

97  Regele, *Radetzky*, p.394.

98  Radetzky, *Wie kann man*, p.541. (*Under '1. Ungleiche und allzulange Dienstzeit'.*)

99  Radetzky, *Wie kann man*, p.54 and p.542. (*Under '2. Komplicirte und dennoch fehlerhafte Kriegsverwaltung'.*)

100  Radetzky, *Wie kann man*, p.543. (*Under '3. Unglaublich fehlerhaftes Montursystem'.*)

101  Radetzky, *Wie kann man*, p.543. (*Under '4. Ein sehr schlechtes Verpflegsystem'.*)

102  Radetzky, *Wie kann man*, pp.543–4. (*Under '5. Eine Bezahlung ser Offiziere'.*)

103  Radetzky, *Wie kann man*, p.544. (*Under '6. Gänzlich fehlerhafte Einrichtung der obersten Kriegstelle'.*)

104  Radetzky, *Wie kann man*, p.545 (*Under '7. Im Allgemeinen fülbarer und dem Dienst höchst nachteiliger Mangel an Ausbildung, besonders in den höheren Graden'.*)

105  Radetzky, *Wie kann man*, p.545 (*Under '8. Gänzliche Umgestaltung des Generalquartiermeisterstabes'.*)

106 Radetzky, *Wie kann man*, pp.545–6. (*Under '9. Verbesserungen bei den Grenadiieren'*.)

107 Radetzky, *Wie kann man*, pp.546–7. (*Under '10. Die Artillerietruppe'*.)

108 Radetzky, *Wie kann man*, p.547. (*Under '11. 'Verbesserungen bei Fuhrwesen'*.)

109 Radetzky, *Wie kann man*, p.548. (*Under '12. Ein änlishes'*.)

110 Radetzky, *Wie kann man*, p.548 (*Under '13. Zweckmäßige Remontirung und Remontentransporte'*.)

111 Radetzky, *Wie kann man*, p.548. (*Under '14. Bei den meisten Regimentern'*.)

112 Radetzky, *Wie kann man*, pp.548–9.

113 Clam, a key figure in Austrian history in this period, has been absolutely neglected by historians. What follows is a summary of Fritz Pflegerl's unpublished Vienna University doctoral thesis of 1928, *Graf Carl Clam-Martinitz als Diplomat und Heeresreorganisator von 1830–1840*. Nothing else, as far as I know, exists on him.

114 Maximilian Von Kübeck (ed.), *Tagebücher*, Vol. 1, p.761.

115 Prince Richard von Metternich and A. von Klinkowström (eds), *Aus Metternichs nachgelassenen Papieren*, 8 Vols (Vienna, 1880–4), Vol. VI, pp.369–71.

116 Gordon A. Craig, 'Command and Staff Problems in the Austrian Army, 1740–1866', in *War, Politics and Diplomacy, Selected Essays* (London, 1966), pp.3–21.

117 It is important to realise that between one third and one half of the troops of the Austrian army might be on leave ('*auf Urlaub'*) at any time. Industrialists and estate-owners who needed cheap labour for factories or harvesting needed to have these people at hand. The army did not care in times of peace, since it was spared the expense of paying them. But if the *Urlauber* weren't employed they constituted a very large reserve of idle, potential trouble-makers in the countryside. Thus, for example, they got the blame for the 'horrors' committed by peasants in Galicia in 1846. On the other hand, the army could quickly call them in, if and when they were needed for military purposes. See Johann Springer, *Statistik des österreichischen Kaiserstaates*, 2 Vols (Vienna, 1840), Vol. II., p.254.

118 See note 7, Chapter 1.

119 See John Sheldon Curtiss, *The Russian Army under Nicholas I, 1825–1855* (Durham NC, 1965).

120 See Hew Strachan, *Wellington's Legacy. The Reform of the British Army, 1830–1854* (Manchester, 1984).

121 See Paddy Griffith, *Military Thought in the French Army, 1815–1851* (Manchester, 1989).

122 See Herman Hattaway, *Shades of Blue and Gray. An Introductory Military History of the Civil War* (Columbia and London, 1997).

123 Viktor Bibl, *Radetzky, Soldat und Feldherr* (Vienna, 1955), p.19.

124 Ibid.

125 John Presland, *Vae Victis. The Life of Ludwig von Benedek, 1804–1881* (London, 1935), p.62.
126 Ibid.
127 For details of this and of the financial problems of Austrian officers during this period, see Alan Sked, *The Survival of the Habsburg Empire. Radetzky, the Imperial Army and the Class War, 1848* (London and New York, 1979), pp.16–26.

## 4 PRELUDE TO REVOLUTION

1 Quoted in Hugo Kerchnawe, *Die Überwindung der ersten Weltrevolution* (Innsbruck, 1932), p.61.
2 The Baroness Blaze de Bury, *Germania: Its Courts, Camps and Peoples*, 2 Vols (London 1850), Vol. II, pp.144–5, ft.2.
3 Heinrich Friedjung, 'Entgegnung auf den Angriff eines hungarischen Historikers', *Historische Aufsätze* (Stuttgart and Berlin, 1919), pp.126–34, p.133: 'Batthyany's audience with the Emperor demonstrated the pressing necessity to persuade Ferdinand to abdicate and put a ruler on the throne who could see with his own eyes and make judgements and take decisions with his own mind.'
4 David Laven, 'The Age of Restoration', in John A. Davis (ed.), *Italy in the Nineteenth Century* (Oxford, 2000), pp.51–73, pp.58–9.
5 Denis Mack Smith, *Victor Emanuel, Cavour and the Risorgimento* (Oxford, 1971), pp.7–9.
6 Bolton King, *A History of Italian Unity*, 2 Vols (London, 1912), Vol. I, pp.51 and 53.
7 Howard A. Marraro, 'An American Diplomat Views the Dawn of Liberalism in Piedmont, 1834–48', *Journal of Central European Affairs*, Vol. 6 (1946–7), pp.75–6.
8 Prince Richard Metternich (ed,), *The Memoirs of Prince Metternich*, 5 Vols (London, 1880), Vol. III, p.93.
9 Quoted in E. L. Woodward, *Three Studies in European Conservatism: Metternich, Guizot and the Catholic Church in the Nineteenth Century* (London and Edinburgh, 1963), p.104, ft.1.
10 For further information, see David Laven, *Venice and Venetia under the Habsburgs, 1815–1835* (Oxford, 2002); Marco Meriggio, *Amministrazione e Classe Soziale nel Lombardo-Veneto (1815–1848)* (Bologna, 1983); and Eugenio Tonetti, *Governono austriaco e notabili sudditi: Congregazioni e municipi nel Veneto del Restaurazione (1815–1848)* (Venice, 1997).
11 General K. von Schönhals, *Erinnerungen eines österreichischen Veteranes aus dem italienischen Kriege der Jahre 1848 und 1849* (Stuttgart and Tübingen, 1853), p.31.
12 Schönhals, *Erinnerungen etc.*, p.31.
13 General von Stratimirovic, *Was Ich Erlebte* (Vienna and Leipzig, 1911), p.19.

14  For the story of why and how any reform was resisted see Alan Sked, 'Metternich and the Ficquelmont Mission of 1848: the Decision against Reform in Lombardy-Venetia', *Central Europe*, Vol. 2, No.1, pp.15–46.

15  From a manuscript entitled *Blick auf Italien im Herbst 1847*, Vienna, *Kriegsarchiv*, KA, *Feldakten, Krieg im Italien, Hauptarmee*, Fascicle 213.

16  Maximilian d'Este, *Blick auf Italien etc.*

17  Maximilian d'Este, *Blick auf Italien etc.*

18  Schönhals, *Erinnerungen etc.*, p.24.

19  Schönhals, *Erinnerungen etc.*, p.25.

20  Schönhals, *Erinnerungen etc.*, p.26.

21  Vienna, *Kriegsarchiv*, Radetzky to Hardegg, Milan, 4 January 1848, KA CK (Präs) 1848, No. 46.

22  Vienna, *Kriegsarchiv*, Radetzky to Rainer, Milan, 9 February 1848, KA CK (Präs) 1848, No.136.

23  Vienna, *Kriegsarchiv*, Radetzky to Rainer, Milan, 9 February 1848, KA CK (Präs) 1848, No. 475.

24  Letter from M. Dumon to the Comtesse de Boigne, London, 21 September 1848, in M. Charles Nicoullaud (ed.), *Recollections of a Great Lady, Being More Reminiscences of the Comtesse de Boigne* (London, 1912), p.339.

25  Bernhard Duhr (ed.), *Briefe des Feldmarshalls Radetzky an seine Tochter Friedericke, 1847–57* (Vienna, 1892), pp.45–6.

26  G. F-H and J. Berkeley, *Italy in the Making, 1846–1848*, Vol. II, *June 1846–I January 1848* (Cambridge, 1936) (reproduced 1968), p.217.

27  *Carte Secrete della Polizia Austriaca in Italia Estratta dell'Archivio di Venezia e publicate per commissione di D. Manin*, Vol. III (Capolago, 1851), doc. 555. The *timing* of Radetzky's decision to intervene seems to have been determined by the assassination in Ferrara of the suspicious but pro-Austrian figure, Baron Baratelli, on 14 June. See Friedrich Engel-Janosi, *Österreich und der Vatikan, 1846–1918*, Vol. I, *Die Pontificate Pius' IX und Leos XIII, 1846–1903* (Graz, 1958), pp.28–9.

28  Count Hartig, *Genesis or Details of the Late Austrian Revolution by an Officer of State*, appended to Archdeacon Coxe's *History of the House of Austria* (London, 1853), p.63.

29  For a full account of the episode which, according to the Berkeleys (see note 114, Chapter 3) led directly to war in 1848, see Alan Sked, 'Poor Intelligence, Flawed Results: Metternich, Radetzky and the Crisis-Management of Austria's "Occupation" of Ferrara in 1847', in P. Jackson and J. Siegel (eds), *Intelligence and Statecraft. The Use and Limits of Intelligence in International Society* (Westport Connecticut and London, 2005), pp.52–86.

30  Vienna, *Kriegsarchiv*, KA CK (Präs) 1847, 1371, Radetzky to Ausersperg, Milan, 21 August 1847.

31  Vienna, *Haus-Hof-und Staatsarchiv*, StaatskanzleiAkten, Provinzen, Lombardei-Venezien, Karton 23, Metternich to Ficquelmont, Vienna, 22 August 1847.

32  Joseph Alexander Freiherr von Helfert, 'Casati und Pillersdorff und die Anfänge der italienischen Einheitsbewegung', *Archiv für Österreichische Geschichte*, Vol. 91 (1903), p.331.

33 Helfert, *Casati etc.*, p.331.

34 Helfert, *Casati etc.*, pp.454–6. Auersperg did not like being separated from his wife while in Ferrara. While he thought the revolution must be resisted, he believed Radetzky to be 'confused in his ideas'.

35 Vienna, *Kriegsarchiv*, KA CK (Präs) 1847, 1443, Radetzky to Auersperg, Milan, 3 September 1847.

36 Helfert, *Casati etc.*, pp.484–6.

37 On Ficquelmont, see Alan Sked, 'Metternich, and the Ficquelmont Mission of 1847–48: the Decision against Reform in Lombardy-Venetia', *Central Europe,* Vol. 2, No. 1 (May, 2004), pp.15–46.

38 Vienna, *Haus-Hof-und Staatsarchiv*, SAPL-V, K 23, Metternich to Ficquelmont, Vienna, 23 January, 1848.

39 Vienna, *Haus-Hof-und Staatsarchiv,* SAPL-V K 23, Metternich to Ficquelmont, Vienna, 17 February 1847.

40 Vienna, *Haus-Hof und Staatsarchiv,* SAPL-V K 23, Metternich to Ficquelmont, Vienna, 23 January 1847.

41 Comte F. de Sonis (ed.), *Lettres du Comte et de la Comtesse Ficquelmont à la Comtesse Tiesenhausen* (Paris, 1911), p.149.

42 Vienna, *Kriegsarchiv,* KA CK (Präs) 1848, No. 65, Emperor to Hardegg, Vienna, 9 January, 1848.

43 Vienna, *Kriegsarchiv,* KA CK (Präs) 1848, No. 165. Correspondence between Emperor, Hardegg, Radetzky and Metternich, 21 January 1848.

44 Vienna, *Kriegsarchiv,* KA CK (Präs) 1848, No. 165.

45 Federico Curato (ed.), *Gran Bretagna e Italia nei documenti della Missione Minto,* 2 Vols (Rome, 1970), Vol. I, pp.188–9, Abercrombie to Minto, Turin, 13 November 1847.

46 Curato (ed.), *Gran Bretagna etc.*, Vol. I, pp.326–8, Abercrombie to Minto, Turin, 22 January 1848.

47 Curato (ed.), *Gran Bretagna etc.*, Vol. I, pp.326–8 and Vol. II, pp.5–6, Ponsonby to Minto, Vienna, 6 February 1848.

48 Vienna, *Haus-Hof-und Staatsarchiv*, SPL-V, K23, Metternich to Ficquelmont, Vienna, 22 August 1847.

49 Vienna, *Haus-Hof-und Staatsarchiv,* SPL-V, K38, Metternich to Emperor, Vienna, 17 July 1847.

50 Vienna, *Haus-Hof-und Staatsarchiv,* SPL-V, K38. *Protokoll* of the meeting with Hardegg and Kübeck, Vienna, 20 July 1847.

51 Vienna, *Haus-Hof-und Staatsarchiv,* SPL-V, K23, Radetzky to Hardegg, Milan 12 December 1847.

52 Vienna, *Haus-Hof-und Staatsarchiv,* SPL-V, K23, Radetzky to Ficquelmont, Milan, 16 December 1847.

53 Vienna, *Haus-Hof-und Staatsarchiv,* SPL-V, K23, Radetzky to Hardegg, Milan, 12 December 1847.

54 Duhr, *Briefe des Feldmarschalls etc.,* p.63.

55 Hartig, *Genesis,* p.65, ft. and p.101.

56  Vienna, *Haus-Hof-und Staatsarchiv*, SPL-V, K23, Metternich to Ficquelmont, Vienna, 6 December 1847.

57  Vienna, *Haus-Hof-und Staatsarchiv*, SPL-V, K23, Metternich to Ficquelmont, Vienna, 6 December 1847.

58  Vienna, *Haus-Hof-und Staatsarchiv*, SPL-V, K23, Radetzky to Hardegg, Milan, 12 December1847.

59  Vienna, *Haus-Hof-und Staatsarchiv*, SPL-V, K23, Ficquelmont to Metternich, Milan, 18 December 1847.

60  Vienna, *Haus-Hof-und Staatsarchiv*, SPL-V, K38, Metternich to Emperor, Vienna, 18 November 1847.

61  Vienna, *Haus-Hof-und Staatsarchiv*, SPL-V, K23, Ficquelmont to Metternich, Milan, 21 November 1847; K5, Archduke Rainer to Metternich, Milan, 22 November 1847.

62  Vienna, *Haus-Hof-und Staatsarchiv*, K23, Ficquelmont to Metternich, 24 November 1847.

63  Vienna, *Haus-Hof-und Staatsarchiv*, K23, Metternich to Ficquelmont, Vienna, 6 December 1847.

64  Vienna, *Haus-Hof-und Staatsarchiv*, K23, Radetzky to Hardegg, Milan, 12 December 1847.

65  Hartig, *Genesis etc.*, pp.64–5.

66  The figure given by Radetzky's adjutant, General Schönhals, in his *Erinnerungen etc.*

67  Vienna, *Haus-Hof-und Staatsarchiv*, KPL-V, K512, Radetzky to Emperor, Milan, 1 February 1847; K23, Ficquelmont to Metternich, Milan, 11 January, 1848.

68  Vienna, *Kriegsarchiv*, KA CK (Präs) 1848, Radetzky to Hardegg, Milan, 9 February 1848.  At the end of the month the Emperor wrote to Hardegg, telling him: 'In future, no proposition which entails additional financial expenditure is to be presented to me before a preliminary agreement has been reached with the treasury praesidium.' Treasury protocols and this letter are found in this same file.

69  Vienna, *Kriegsarchiv*, KA CK (Präs), Radetzky to Hardegg, Milan, 3 February 1848.

70  Vienna, *Haaus-Hof-und Staatsarchiv*, SPL-V, K23, Metternich to Ficquelmont, Vienna, 23 September 1847.

71  Vienna, *Haus-Hof-und Staatsarchiv*, SPL-V, K23, Ficquelmont to Metternich, Milan, 3 December 1847.

72  Vienna, *Haus-Hof-und Staatsarchiv*, SPL-V, K5, Ficquelmont to Rainer, Milan, 10 December 1847.

73  Vienna, *Haus-Hof-und Staatsarchiv*, SPL-V, K5, Rainer to Metternich, Milan, 21 December 1847.

74  Vienna, *Kriegsarchiv*, KA CK (Präs) 1847, No. 46, Radetzky to Rainer, Milan, 2 December 1847.

75  Comte de Hübner, *Une Année de ma Vie, 1848–9* (Paris, 1891), pp.33–4.

76  Archduke Maximilian d'Este, *Blick auf Italien etc.*

77 Vienna, *Hasu-Hof-und Staatsarchiv,* SPL-V K 23, Fiquelmont to Metternich, Milan, 29 December 1847.

78 Vienna, *Kriegsarchiv,* KA CK (Präs) 1848, No.78. For his reports on the riots, see Nos. 45, 46, 56, and 90.

79 Vienna, *Haus-Hof-und Staatsarchiv,* SPL-V, K23, Ficquelmont to Metternich, Milan, 7 January 1848.

80 Vienna, *Kriegsarchiv,* KA CK (Präs) 1848, Nos. 46 and 178, Radetzky to Hardegg, Milan, 4 January, 1848.

81 Vienna, *Haus-Hof-und Staatsarchiv,* SPL-V, K23, Ficquelmont to Metternich, Milan, 7 January 1848.

82 See ft. 365.

83 Helfert, *Casati etc.,* p.483.

84 Helfert, *Casati etc.,* pp.500–2. Count Wratislaw to Captain Huyn, 1 February 1848.

85 Vienna, *Kreigsarchiv,* KA CK (Präs) 1848, No. 54, Radetzky to Hardegg, Milan, 5 January 1848.

86 Vienna, *Kriegsarchiv,* KA CK (Präs) 1848, No. 45, Radetzky to Hardegg, Milan, 3 January 1848.

87 Vienna, *Haus-Hof-Und Staatsarchiv,* SPL-V, K23, Metternich to Ficquelmont, Vienna, 8 January 1848. But cf. R. v. Metternich and R. v. Klinkenstrom (eds), *Aus Metternichs Nachgelassenen Papieren etc.,* Vol. VII, p.529, 'from the diary of Princess Melanie': '...It almost seems as if Radetzky has been reproached for allowing his men to smoke cigars.'

88 Vienna, *Kriegsarchiv,* KA CK (Präs) 1848, No. 1051, Archduke Rainer to Ficquelmont, Milan, 14 January 1848.

89 See note 47, Chapter 4.

90 See note 47, Chapter 4.

91 Vienna, *Haus-Hof-und Staatsarchiv,* SPL-V, K23, Metternich to Ficquelmont, Vienna, 23 January 1848.

92 Vienna, *Haus-Hof-und Staatsarchiv,* SPL-V, K23, Benedek to Lugani, Pavia, 11 February 1848.

93 Vienna, *Haus-Hof-und Staatsarchiv,* SPL-V, K23, Radetzky to Rainer, Milan, 12 February 1848.

94 Vienna, *Haus-Hof-und Staatsarchiv,* SPL-V, K23, Ficquelmont to Rainer, Milan, 15 February 1848.

95 Vienna, *Haus-Hof-und Staatsarchiv,* SPL-V, K23, Ficquelmont to Metternich, Milan, 17 February 1848.

96 Vienna, *Haus-Hof-und Staatsarchiv,* SPL-V, K23, Metternich to Ficquelmont, Vienna, 8 February 1848.

97 Vienna, Haus-Hof-und Staatsarchiv, SPL-V, K23, Metternich to Ficquelmont, Vienna, 17 February 1848.

98 Vienna, *Kriegsarchiv,* KA CK (Präs) 1848, No. 475, Hohenlohe to Radetzky, Vienna, 27 February 1848 and *Haus-Hof-und Staatsarchiv,* SPL-V, K19, Palffy (Governor of Venetia) to Metternich, Venice, 12 February 1848.

99  Vienna, *Kriegsarchiv,* KA CK (Präs) 1848, No.584, Emperor to Hohenlohe, 7 March 1848.

100  Franz Hartig (ed.), *Metternich-Hartig. Ein Briefwechsel des Staatskanzlers aus dem Exil, 1848–1851* (Vienna, 1923), p.33.

101  Érzsebet Andics, *Metternich und die Frage Ungarns* (Budapest, 1973), p.320.

102  Vienna, *Kriegsarchiv,* KA CK (Präs) 1848, No. 267 for correspondence between Metternich, the Emperor, Hardegg and Radetzky of 1 February on the subject.

103  R. Bullen, 'Guizot and the Sonderbund Crisis', *English Historical Review,* Vol. LXXXVI (July 1971), pp. 497–526. But see also, Jacob Baxa, 'Radetzky und der Sonderbundskrieg', *Schweizerische Zeitschrift für Geschichte,* Vol. 23 (1973), pp.510–26.

104  Vienna, *Kriegsarchiv,* KA CK (Präs) 1848, No. 256, Radetzky to Hardegg, Milan, 24 January 1848. Attached was a report drawn up by his general staff.

105  Schönhals, *Erinnerungen,* p.67.

106  Schönhals, *Erinnerungen,* p.67.

107  Vienna, *Kriegsarchiv,* KA CK (Präs) 1848, No. 165, Radetzky to Hardegg, Milan, 15 January 1848.

108  See note 63, Chapter 4.

109  Vienna, *Kriegsarchiv,* KA CK (Präs) 1848, No. 256 for correspondence between the Emperor and Hohenlohe of 1 March 1848. Hohenlohe had placed no importance on the second part of the plan. Perhaps he had been informed that Maximilian-type towers did not work. This apparently had been the experience of the towers around Linz. See the report in the *United Services Journal* for January 1837, p.100 for British readers.

## 5  SAVING AUSTRIA AND EUROPE AGAIN

1  Duhr, *Briefe,* p.65.

2  Duhr, *Briefe,* pp.65–6.

3  Duhr, *Briefe,* p.68.

4  Josph Alexander Freiherr von Helfert, 'Radetzky in den Tagen seiner ärgsten Bedrägnis', *Archiv für Österreichische Geschichte* (Vienna, 1906), Vol. 95, pp.145–62, Radetzky to Ficquelmont, Montechiari, 30 March 1848, p.161.

5  Helfert, *Radetzky etc.,* Radetzky to Ficquelmont, Milan, 18–19 March 1848, p.150.

6  Helfert, *Radetzky etc.,* Radetzky to Ficquelmont, Milan, 19 March 1848, p.153.

7  Helfert, *Radetzky etc.,* Radetzky to Ficquelmont, Milan, 21 March 1848, p.158. See also, Jacob Baxa, 'Radetzky und der Kanton Tessin, 1848–49', *Schweizerische Zeitschrift für Geschichte,* Vol. 27 (1977), pp.132–81.

8  For the best discussion of the 'Five Glorious Days of Milan' as the Italians see them, see Varo Varanini, 'I veri Motivi della Ritrata di Radetzky da

Milano', in *Atti e Memorie del XXVII Congresso Nazionale, 19-20-21 Marzo 1948*, Istituto per la Storia del Risorgimento; Cimitato di Milano (Milan, 1948), pp.725–30.

9  Schönhals, *Erinnerungen,* p.57. For his full account of the fall of Venice, see pp.101–9. It should be pointed out that Schönhals must himself have felt humiliated by the fall of Milan, for he had assured Count Hübner, who had just arrived there: 'The imperial army in Italy, 75–80,000 men, is more than sufficient to destroy Charles Albert's in the space of four days.' (See Hübner, *Une Année* etc., pp.33–4.) On the other hand, the 1849 campaign achieved precisely that.

10  Vienna, *Kriegsarchiv,* KA CK (Präs) 1848, Nos. 531–9, Zichy to *Hofkriegsrat,* Venice, 28 February 1848.

11  Vienna, *Kriegsarchiv,* KA CK (Präs) 1848, No. 471, Radetzky to Hardegg, Milan, 20 February 1848.

12  Vienna, *Kriegsarchiv,* KA CK (Präs) 1848, Nos. 531–9, Hohenlohe to Zichy, Vienna, 4 March 1848.

13  Vienna, *Kriegsarchiv,* KA CK (Präs) 1848, No. 539, Martini to Radetzky,Venice, 21–22 March 1848. He described how Colonel Marinovich, the former commander of the Arsenal, had been hacked to bits there: 'It proved impossible to save him ... In times of great excitement one must expect everything.' Indeed.

14  Schönhals, *Erinnerungen* (and Wolf-Schneider von Arno afterwards) laid great stress on the assertion that Radetzky deliberately refrained from bombarding Milan, i.e. that he made a clear decision not to. Acccording to his adjutant (pp.80–1): 'Milan does not know what it owes to the mildness of the Field Marshal during these days of treason and murder. Had he submitted to the natural vexation which the treason had caused to grip him and his soldiers, he could have repeated Barbarossa's historic tragedy.... The Field Marshal ... had no projectiles to employ – a real bombardment was not possible – but he had 12 howitzers and not a few rockets among his batteries. In any case the Field Marshal had the idea to bring these howitzers together in one battery and have them bomb the city. He gave up the idea because any thought of devastation was far from the human kindness of his heart. In any case, it did not solve the problem. He did not want to destroy Milan because he wanted to save for the Emperor and the Empire a city which he hoped one day to see give up its delusions and recognise it was only the victim and plaything of reckless demagogues and deluded ambition.' The situation was perhaps more complex than that and has become rather confused in the secondary literature. For example, Benedek's biographer, Presland, *Vae Victis,* p.65, writes that after initially refusing to bombard the town, Radetzky did bombard it, adding: 'A bombardment in 1848, though serious enough was not comparable with such a punishment in modern times; there was a great deal of noise and a good many caualties among people who were in the open streets, but not a wholesale destruction of buildings. There were scenes of comedy in the midst of the fighting.' The account is apparently based on Hübner's diaries in *Une Année de Ma Vie.* However, the account is false. Radetzky did use heavy guns to signal

to the troops on 18 March to take up their emergency positions and a heavy gun was used to shoot down the doors of the city hall and a few barricades thereafter. However, there was no general bombardment of the city, although Radetzky certainly threatened it and the foreign consuls in Milan certainly feared it. The story can be accurately traced through two primary sources, Radetzky's own account of what happened, published years later (Radetzky, 'Die Märztage des Jahres 1848 in Mailand' in *Österreichische Rundschau*, Vol XIV, 1908, pp. 339–48) and his letters to Ficquelmont written at the time (Helfert, *Radetzky etc.*). From Helfert, we can trace his thoughts at the time. On early 19 March he wrote: 'I am determined at all costs to remain master of Milan. If people do not desist from fighting, I will have the city bombarded.' Later that day he wrote: 'I still hope to return the city to obedience without a bombardment and thus have not resorted to this extreme measure yet today but only used the guns against barricades and some dangerous points; but I always fear that no other method will remain for me.' On 21 March he reported that the foreign consuls on the day before had beseeched him not to resort to a bombardment and that his reply was that everything depended on whether the city stopped attacking him. But by now he was reporting that 'as things stand I recognise the impossibility of holding my position in Milan'. He then organised an orderly retreat in five columns without thinking of a bombardment. Most likely he had never wanted to resort to this 'extreme measure' in any case. (Helfert, *Radetzky etc.*, p.152, p.153, p.155 and p.158.)

15  Wolf-Schneider von Arno, *Der Feldherr Radetzky*, p.61.

16  Helfert, *Radetzky etc.*, Radetzky to Ficquelmont, 24 March 1848, pp.159–60 for his original plan.

17  Helfert, *Radetzky etc.*, p.158. Radetzky's letter is dated 5pm, 22 March 1848.

18  Helfert, *Radetzky etc.*, p.159.

19  Wolf-Schneider von Arno, *Der Feldherr Radetzky*, pp.65–6.

20  For the general military narrative see, Heinz Helmert and Hans Jürgen Usczek, *Bewaffnete Volkskämpfe in Europa, 1848–1849* (East Berlin, 1973); Karl Edler von Prybila, *Geschichte der Kriege der k.u.k. Wehrmacht von 1848 bis 1898* (Graz, 1899); and G.F-H and J. Berkeley, *Italy in the Making, January 1ˢᵗ 1848 to November 16ᵗʰ 1848* (Cambridge, 1940).

21  I take the figures in this account from the very useful book by Heinz Helmert and Hans Jürgen Usceck, *Bewaffnete Volkskämpfe in Europa, 1848–1849* (East Berlin, 1973), pp.73–4.

22  Helmert and Uscek, *Bewaffnete Volkskämpfe etc.*, p.73.

23  Eduard Staeger von Waldburg, *Ereignisse in der Festung Mantua 1848* (Vienna, 1853), pp.2–21.

24  On the state of the Quadrilateral forts, see Wolf-Schneider von Arno, *Der Feldherr Radetzky*, p.68.

25  For the battles themselves, I have followed the account in von Arno, which is the best for describing them from Radetzly's own viewpoint.

26  Wolf-Schneider von Arno, *Der Feldherr Radetzky*, p.70.

27  Wolf-Schneider von Arno, *Der Feldherr Radetzky*, p.72.

28  Wolf-Schneider von Arno, *Der Feldherr Radetzky*, p.73.

29  See the Marxist criticisms of Helmert and Usceck, *Bewaffnete Volkskämpfe etc.*, p.75.

30  Angelo Filipuzzi, *Le Relazione Diplomatiche fra L'Austria e il Regno di Sardegna e la Guerra del 1848–49*, 2 Vols, Vol. 53 in the series of documents published as Fonti per la Storia del Risorgimento (Rome, 1961), Vol. 1, pp.53–4, Ficquelmont to Radetzky, Vienna, 20 April 1848.

31  Filipuzzi, *Le Relazione Diplomatiche etc.*, Vol. 1, pp.108–11, Lebzeltern to Hartig, Vienna, 20 May 1848.

32  Filipuzzi, *Le Relazione Diplomatiche etc.*, Vol. 1, pp.151–2, Wessenberg to Radetzky, Innsbruck, 13 June 1848.

33  Vienna, *Kriegsarchiv*, KA MK (1848), No. 1370, Radetzky to Latour, Verona, 9 May 1848.

34  Vienna, *Kriegsarchiv*, KA MK (1848), No. 2777, Radetzky to Hartig, Verona, 18 June 1848.

35  Filipuzzi, *Le Relazione Diplomatiche etc.*, Vol. 1, pp.151–2, Wessenberg to Radetzky, Innsbruck, 13 june, 1848.

36  Filipuzzi, *Le Relazione Diplomatiche etc.*, Vol. 1, pp.170–3 (Addendum A), Radetzky to Hartig, Verona, 19 June 1848.

37  Filipuzzi, *Le Relazione Diplomatiche etc.*, Vol. 1, pp.168–70, Wessenberg to Radetzky, Innsbruck, 19 June 1848.

38  Filipuzzi, *Le Relazione Diplomatiche etc.*, Vol. 1, pp.189–94 (Addendum), Radetzky to Hartig, Verona, 30 June 1848.

39  Helmert and Uscek, *Bewaffnete Volkskämpfe*, pp.79–80.

40  Vienna, *Kriegsarchiv*, KA MK (1848), No. 3908g, Radetzky to Latour, Headquarters Alzarea, 25 July 1848.

41  Wolf-Schneider von Arno, *Der Feldherr Radetzky*, p.65.

42  Duhr, *Briefe*, p.84.

43  Wolf-Schneider von Arno, *Der Feldherr Radetzky*, p.84.

44  Oscar Jászi, *The Dissolution of the Habsburg Monarchy* (Chicago and London, 1966), p.82.

45  Alan Sked, *The Survival of the Habsburg Empire. Radetzky, the Imperial Artmy and the Class War, 1848* (London and New York, 1979), pp.49–51.

46  Radetzky, *Wie kann man etc.*, p.537.

47  Count Hartig, *Genesis etc.*, p.65, ft.

48  Vienna, *Kriegsarchiv*, KA CK (Präs) 1847, No.?, Radetzky to Hardegg, Milan, 12 December 1847.

49  Vienna, *Kriegsarchiv*, KA MK (1848), No. 302, Radetzky to Zanini, Verona, 4 April 1848.

50  Vienna, *Kriegsarchiv*, KA MK (1848), No. 2863, Radetzky to Latour, Verona, 23 June 1848.

51  Vienna, *Kriegsarchiv*, KA MK (1848), No. 4844, Radetzky to Latour, Milan, 3 September 1848.

52  Baron Antoine de Mollinary de Monte Pastello, *Quarante-Six Ans dans l'Armée Austro-Hongroise, 1833–1879* (Paris, 1913), 2 Vols, Vol. 1, p.111.

53  Mollinary, *Quarante-Six Ans*, Vol. 1, pp.111–12.

54  Vienna, *Kriegsarchiv*, KA MK (1848), No. 2863, Radetzky to Latour, Verona, 23 June 1848.

55  Vienna, *Kriegsarchiv*, KA MK (1848), No. 6070g, Radetzky to war Ministry, Milan, 21 November 1848.

56  *British Foreign and State Papers* (London, 1865), Vol. 44, p.725, Vice-Consul Campbell to Palmerston, Milan, 22 October 1848.

57  Quoted in *Coburn's United Services Magazine and Naval and Military Journal* (1858), Pt.I, 'Memoir of Marshal Radetzky', pp.242–56, pp.249–50.

58  Heller, *Der Graf Radetzky*, pp.381–2.

59  The *Times*, 27 March 1849.

60  Helmert and Uscek, *Bewaffnete Volkskämpfe etc.*, p.211.

61  John Presland, *Vae Victis, The Life of Ludwig von Benedek, 1804–1881* (London, 1934), p.89.

62  For the main defence of Haynau, see Karl von Schönhals, *Biografie des kk. Feldzeugmeisters Julius Freiherr von Haynau* (Vienna, 1875).

63  Wolf-Schneider von Arno, *Der Feldherr Radetzky*, p.95.

64  The best account of this dispute is to be found in the chapter of Wolf-Schneider von Arno's *Der Feldherr Radetzky*, pp.96–106, entitled: *Radetzky **und** Hess – Nicht – Radetzky oder Hess.*

65  Baron Antoine de Mollinary de Monte Pastello, *Quarante-Six Ans dans l'Armée Austro-Hongroise, 1833–1879* (Paris, 1913), 2 Vols, Vol. 1, p.103.

66  Mollinary, *Quarante-Six Ans*, Vol. 1, p.128.

67  *Der Feldzug der österreichischen Armee in Italien 1849* (Vienna, 1852), p.39.

68  From the article entitled 'Feldmarschall Baron Hess' in the *Neue Freie Presse* of 14 April 1870.

69  Joseph Alexander Freiherr von Helfert, *Geschichte der österreichischen Revolution*, 2 Vols (Freiburg, 1909), Vol. 2, p.93.

70  Wolf-Schneider von Arno, *Der Feldherr Radetzky*, p.105 for these examples.

71  Wolf-Schneider von Arno, *Der Feldherr Radetzky*, pp.96–7.

72  Wolf-Schneider von Arno, *Der Feldherr Radetzky*, p.97.

73  Edmund Glaise-Horstenau, 'Radetzky' in the *Neues Wiener Tagblatt*, 5 January 1933.

## 6  RULING ITALY

1  Quoted in Friedrich Walter, *Die österreichische Zentralverwaltung*, Pt. III, Vol. I, Die Geschichte der Ministerien Kolowrat, Ficquelmont, Pillersdorff, Wessenberg-Doblhoff und Schwarzenberg (Vienna, 1964), p.374.

2  Heinrich Benedikt, *Kaiseradler über dem Appenin: Die Österreicher in Italien, 1700 bis 1866.*

3  Raffaello Barbiera, *Il salotto della Contessa Maffei* (Milan, 1940), pp.208–9.

4  Lina Gasparini, 'Massimiliano d'Austria: Ultimo governatore del Lombardo-Veneto nei suoi ricordi', *Nuova Antologia*, 377 and 378 (1935), pp.249–68, 353–87, 550–79 and 105–31, p.572.

5   William A. Jenks, *Francis Joseph and the Italians, 1849–1859* (Charlottesville, 1978), p.29.

6   Jenks, *Francis Joseph etc.,* p.32.

7   Jenks, *Francis Joseph etc.,* p.35.

8   Hermann Reuchling, *Geschichte Italiens,* 3 Vols (Leipzig, 1870), Vol. 3, p.149.

9   On the economy of Lombardy-Venetia in the 1850s, see B. Caizzi, 'La crisi economical nel Lombardo-Veneto nel decennio 1850–59', *Nuova Revista Storica,* Vol. 42 (1958), pp.205–22; Ira A. Glazier, 'Il commercio estero del Regno Lombardo-Veneto dal 1815 al 1865', *Archivio Economico dell'Unificazione Italiana,* Vol. 15, 1st series (Rome, 1961); G. Luzzatto, 'L'Economia Venezia dal 1796 al 1866', in *La Civiltà Venezia nell' Eta Romantica* (Venice, 1961). Jenks also gives a good survey in Chapter 4 of his book.

10  Reuchling, *Geschichte Italiens,* Vol. 3, pp. 139–40.

11  Leopold Marchetti, 'Il decennio di resistenza', in *Storia di Milano,* Vol. 14 (Milan, 1960), pp.501–2.

12  Reuchlin, *Geschichte Italiens,* Vol. 3, p.140.

13  Jenks, *Francis Joseph,* p.56.

14  Jenks, *Francis Joseph,* p.56.

15  Luzzatto, *L'Economia Venezia,* pp.105–8.

16  Jenks, *Francis Joseph,* p.63.

17  Luzzatto, *L'Economia Venezia,* pp.105–8.

18  On Trieste, see Jenks, *Francis Joseph,* pp.66–70.

19  London *Times,* 1 March 1869.

20  Vienna, *Kriegsarchiv,* KA MK (1848), No. 958/966.

21  Ludwig Jedlika, 'Feldmarschall Josef Radetzky (1766–1858)'. in Hugo Hantsch (ed.), *Gestalter der Geschichte Österreichs* (Innsbruck, Vienna and Munich, 1962), pp.371–7, p.376 and Edmund Glaise von Horstenau, 'Österreichs Wehrmacht im deutschen Schicksal', in J. Nadler und H. von Srbik (eds), *Österreichs Erbe und Sendung im deutschen Raum* (Salzburg and Leipzig, 1937), pp.207–22, p.214.

22  Quoted in Glaise von Horstenau, *Österreichs Wehrmacht etc.,* p.215.

23  See *Enthüllungen aus Österreichs jüngster Vergangenheit. Von eimen Mitglied der linken der aufgelösten österreichischen Reichstages* (Hamburg 1849), p.64.

24  *Enthüllungen etc.,* pp.66–8.

25  Joseph Alexander Freiherr von Helfert, *Im Wiener konstituierenden Reichstag. Juli bis Oktober 1848* (Vienna, 1904), p.103.

26  For the whole correpondence see Vienna, *Kriegsarchiv,* KA MK (1848), No. 6598. This includes Latour's circular of 24 September, Radetzky's reply of 30 September from Milan and Latour's draft reply from Vienna of October 1848.

27  Filipuzzi, *Le Relazione Diplomatiche,* Vol.1, pp.280–4. Metzburg to Wessenberg, Milan, 18 October 1848.

28  *British Foreign and State Papers,* Vol. 44, pp.393–4.

29  Vienna, *Kriegsarchiv,* KA MK (1848), No. 4294, Radetzky to Wessenberg, Milan, 10 August 1848.

30  Vienna, *Kriegsarchiv,* KA MK (1848), Nos. 5172 and 4252, Radetzky to Latour, Milan, 7 and 12 August.

31  Filipuzzi, *Le Relazione Diplomatiche,* Vol. 1, pp.210–13, Montecuccoli to Wessenberg, 10 August 1848.

32  Filipuzzi, *Le Relazione Diplomatiche,* Vol. 1, pp.264–5, Montecuccoli to Wessenberg, Milan, 8 October 1848.

33  Filipuzzi, *Le Relazione Diplomatiche,* Vol. 1, pp.265–9, Metzburg to Wessenberg, Milan, 10 October 1848.

34  Filipuzzi, *Le Relazione Diplomatiche,* Vol. 1, p.271, Radetzky to Wessenberg, Milan, 9 October 1848.

35  Karl von Schönhals, *Biografie des k .k .Feldzeugmeister Julius Freiherrn von Haynau* (Vienna, 1875), p.5.

36  Schönhals, *Haynau,* pp.17–19 for the story.

37  Reuchling, *Geschichte Italiens,* Vol. 3, pp.136–7.

38  The alternative figures come from Coppi. Reuchling dismisses them and uses figures given by Schönhals. See Reuchling, *Geschichte Italiens,* Vol. 3, p.137 ft.

39  Schönhals, *Haynau,* p.47.

40  Mollinary, *Quarante-Six Ans,* Vol. 1, p.165.

41  Reuchlin, *Geschichte Italiens,* Vol. 3, pp.137–8.

42  Istvan Deak, *The Lawful Revolution. Louis Kossuth and the Hungarians 1848–49* (New York, 1979), p.305.

43  For both stories, see Reuchlin, *Geschichte Italiens,* Vol. 3, pp.138–9.

44  Reuchlin, *Geschichte Italiens,* Vol. 3, pp.139–40.

45  William Roscoe Thayer, *The Life and Times of Cavour,* 2 Vols (London, Boston and New York, 1911), Vol. 1, p.249.

46  A facsimile can be found in G. Luzio, *I Martiri di Belfiore* (Milan, 1905), Vol 1, p.27.

47  The whole affair is covered in great detail from original sources in Thayer, *Cavour,* Vol.1, pp.252–63.

48  Thayer, *Cavour,* Vol. 1, p.255. Jenks, *Francis Joseph,* p.45 writes: ' "Auditor" Alfred Kraus inaugurated an outstanding career "for the emperor" with his brilliant tactics as an inquisitor.'

49  Thayer, *Cavour,* Vol. 1, p.262.

50  The standard treatment of 1853 is Leo Pollini, *La rivolta di Milano del 6 febbraio 1853* (reprinted Milan, 1953). See also Franco Catalano, *I Barabba* (Milan, 1953). A more recent account is Brigitte Mazohl-Wallnig, ' "Hochverräter" und österreichische Regierung in Lombardo-Venetien. Das Beispiel des Mailänder Aufstandes im Jahre 1853', *Mitteilungen des Österreichischen Staatsarchivs,* Vol. 31 (1978), pp.219–31. Some historians blame the fiasco not on Mazzini but on his local agents who lost control of the situation, but this seems slightly casuistical.

51  Mazzini's own account of *Il Moto del 6 Febbraio* is to be found in A. Saffi (ed.), *Scritti Editi e Inediti di Giuseppe Mazzini,* Rome, 18 Vols (Milan and Rome, 1861–1891), Vol. VIII, pp.209–28.

52  See note 59, Chapter 3.

53  See note 59, Chapter 3.

54  Thayer, *Cavour,* pp.264–5.

55  Quoted in Thayer, *Cavour,* Vol. 1, p.266.

56  See note 59, Chapter 3.

57  Heller, *Der Graf Radetzky,* p.325.

58  Regele, *Radetzky,* p.345.

59  Franz Ferdinand Hoettinger, *Radetzky. Ein Stück Österreich* (Leipzig and Vienna, 1934), p.256.

60  Regele, *Radetzky,* p.345.

61  Quoted in Regele, *Radetzky,* p.348.

62  The order was printed in the London *Times* on 28 February 1853.

63  The *Times* 7 January 1858. This was Radetzky's obituary.

64  For the most recent overall account of 1846 in Galicia, see Anton Gill, *Die polnische Revolution, 1846. Zwischen nationalen Befreiungskampf des Landadels und antifeudaler Bauernerhebung* (Munich and Vienna, 1974); for a contemporary attack on Austria's role, see the anonymous French work, *La Vérété sur les Événemens de la Galicie* (Paris, 1846). For the most recent investigation of the Austrian role, see Alan Sked, 'Benedek and Breinl and the "Galician Horrors" of 1846', in L. Péter and M. Rady (eds), *Resistance, Rebellion and Revolution in Central Europe: Commemorating 1956* (London 2008), pp.87–98 and Alan Sked, 'Austria and the "Galician Massacres" of 1846. Schwarzenberg and the Propaganda War. An Unknown but Key Episode in the Career of the Austrian Statesman', in L. Höbelt and T.G. Otte (eds), *A Living Anachronism? European Diplomacy and the Habsburg Monarchy. Festschrift für Francis Roy Bridge zum 70. Geburtstag* (Vienna, Cologne and Weimar, 2010), pp.56–118.

65  Vienna, *Haus-Hof-und Staatsarchiv,* SAPL-V, K38, Metternich to Radetzky, Vienna, 16 March 1846.

66  Vienna, *Haus-Hof-und Staatsarchiv,* SAPL-V, K5, Metternich to Rainer, Vienna, 5 March 1846.

67  Vienna, *Haus-Hof-und Staatsarchiv,* SAPL-V, K6, Palffy to Metternich, Venice, 10 March 1846.

68  Quoted in Erzsébet Andics, 'Metternich és az 1830-as évek Magyar reform-mozgalma', *Századok* (1972), pp.272–309, p.304.

69  *British Foreign and State Papers,* Vol. 37, p.968, No. 214, Viscount Ponsonby to Viscount Palmerston, Vienna, 2 April 1848.

70  His latest, and most thorough, biographer, Stefan Lippert, like all previous ones, seems to know nothing about it. See Stefan Lippert, *Felix Fürst zu Schwarzenberg* (Stuttgart, 1998). See note 64, Chapter 6.

71  On Benedek's role, see Sked, *Benedek and Breinl,* but also Heinrich Friedjung (ed.) *Aus Benedek's Nachgelassenen Papieren* (Leipzig, 1901).

72  Vienna, *Haus-Hof-und Staatsarchiv,* SAPL-V, K23, Metternich to Ficquelmont, Vienna, 23 January 1848.

73  Vienna, *Haus-Hof-und-Staatsarchiv,* SAPL-V, K23, Ficquelmont to Metternich, Milan, 3 December 1847.

74  Joseph Alexander Freiherr von Helfert, 'Casati und Pillersdorf und die Anfänge der italienischen Einheitsbewegung', *Archiv für Österreichische Geschichte*, Vol. 91 (1902), pp.500–2, Lt.Col. Count Wratislaw to Captain Huyn.

75  Vienna, *Haus-Hof-und Staatsarchiv*, SAPL-V, K23, Metternich to Ficquelmont, Vienna, 8 January 1848.

76  Franco Arese, 'La Lombardia e la Politica dell'Austria: un collioquio inedito del Metternich nel 1832', *Archivio Storico Lombardo*, Vol. LXVII (1950), pp.5–57, p.24.

77  Helfert, *Casati und Pillersdorf etc.*, pp.18–19.

78  Vienna, *Haus-Hof-und Staatsarchiv*, SAPL-V, K23, Ficquelmont to Metternich, Milan, 3 December 1847.

79  Carlo Casati, *Nuove Revelazioni su I Fatti di Milano nel 1847–48*, 2 Vols (Milan, 1885), Vol. 1, p.147.

80  General K. von Schönhals, *Erinnerungen eines österreichischen Veteranes aus dem italienischen Kriege der Jahre 1848 und 1849* (Stuttgart and Tubingen, 1853), pp.23–4.

81  Ferdinand Franz Hoettinger, *Radetzky, Ein Stück Österreichs* (Leipzig and Vienna, 1934), pp.87–9.

82  Vienna, *Kriegsarchiv, Feldakten*, F(ascicles) 213 and 214, a series of manuscripts by the Archduke which, among other things, outline this scheme. The manuscripts are entitled: *Blick auf Italien im Herbst 1847; Blick auf die Lage des Lombardo-venezianischen Königreiches, Anfangs 1848; Blick auf die Lage Italiens, Anfangs 1848 (Nicht Unwendbar); Über die Nothwendigkeit dass Österreich die Lombardie behalte;* and *Ein Wort für die Gegenwort*. The main arguments are found in the two first articles but the scheme comes up in all of them.

83  Casati, *Nuove Revelazioni etc.*, Vol. II, pp.21–3.

84  Vienna, *Kriegsarchiv*, KA CK (Präs) 1848, No. 44, Radetzky to Hardegg, Milan, 3 January 1848.

85  Franco della Peruta, 'I contadini nella rivoluzione lombarda del 1848', *Movimento Operaio* (1953), pp.525–75, p.543.

86  Vienna, *Haus-Ho- und Staatsarchiv*, SAPL-V, K23, Metternich to Ficquelmont, Vienna, 25 January 1848 (second letter of that day).

87  Vienna, *Haus-Hof-und Staatsarchiv*, SAPL-V, K23, Metternich to Ficquelmont, Vienna, 8 January 1848.

88  N. Bianchi Giovini, *L'Autriche en Italie*, 2 Vols (Paris, 1854), Vol. 2, p.21.

89  Della Peruta, *I contadini etc.*, pp.539–40.

90  Della Peruta, *I contadini etc.*, pp.542–3.

91  Pio Pecchiari, 'Caduti e feriti nelle Cinque Giornate di Milano: ceti e professioni cui apparterano', *Atti e Memorie del XXVII Congresso Nazionale* (Milan, 19-20-21 Marzo 1948), pp.533–7, p.535.

92  *Archivio Triennale delle Case d'Italia dall'Avvimento di Pio IX al Abbandono di Venezia*, 3 Vols (Capolago-Chieri, 1850–55), Vol. 2, p.247.

93  Della Peruta, *I contadini etc.*, p.550.

94  *Archivio Triennale,* Vol. 2, p.469. For the role of the Begamaschi, see Tullia Franzi, 'I volantari bergamaschi nel Quatantotto', in *Atti e Memorie,* pp.227–32 and Ippolito Negrisoli, 'Bergamo al riscosa', *Atti e Memorie,* pp.495–504.

95  Della Peruta, *I contadini etc.,* p.551.

96  Della Peruta, *I contadini etc.,* p.552.

97  Della Peruta, *I contadini etc.,* p.559.

98  Achille Marazza, *Il Clero Lombardo nella Rivoluzione de'48* (Florence, 1852), 2 Vols, Vol. 2, p.15.

99  Marazza, *Il Clero Lombardo etc.,* Vol. 2, pp.278–9.

100  Marazza, *Il Clero Lombardo etc.,* Vol. 2, pp.10–13.

101  Marazza, *Il Clero Lombardo etc.,* Vol. 2, pp.278–9.

102  Marazza, *Il Clero Lombardo etc.,* Vol. 2, pp.14–15, p.19. p.25 and pp.113–4.

103  Della Peruta, *I contadini etc.,* pp.562–5.

104  Della Peruta, *I contadini etc.,* pp.562–5.

105  Della Peruta, *I contadini etc.,* pp.562–5.

106  Della Peruta, *I contadini etc.,* pp.562–5.

107  Della Peruta, *I contadini etc.,* pp.562–5.

108  Ausano Labadini, *Milano ed alcuni Momenti del Risorgimento Italiano* (Milan, 1909), p.32.

109  And he saw this for himself. Vienna, *Kriegsarchiv,* KA MK (1848), No. 3913, Radetzky to Latour, Fresto, 31 July 1848.

110  For the relevant correspondence, see Vienna, *Kriegsarchiv,* KAMK (1848), No. 1059 and three Addenda from 24–30 April 1848.

111  Vienna, *Kriegsarchiv,* KAMK (1848), No. 1059, Radetzky to Zanini, Verona, 30 April 1848 in which he describes the arrested Counts Thun, Manci, Lizzo and Festi as 'the leaders of the Italian party'.

112  Vienna, *Kriegsarchiv,* KAMK (1848), No. 1059, Radetzky to Archduke John, Verona, 28 April 1848 (Addendum II).

113  See note 74, Chapter 6.

114  Vienna, *Kriegsarchiv,* KA MK (1848), No. 1059 (Addendum II), Latour to Radetzky, Vienna, 14 May 1848.

115  *Raccolta degli Atti ufficiali dei Proclami ecc. Emananti e pubblicati in Milano dalle diverse Autorità durante L'I.R. Governo Militare,* Vol. 1 (6 August 1848–31 March 1849) (Milan, 1849?), pp.139–40.

116  *Raccolta* etc., Vol. 1, p.156.

117  Federico Curato (ed.), 'Le Relazioni Diplomatiche fra L'Austria e il Regno di Sardegna e la Guerra del 1848–49', 2 Vols, Vols 53 and 54 in the series *Fonti per la Storia d'Italia,* 3rd Series, 1848–1860 (Rome, 1961), Vol. 1, pp.385–6, Abercromby to Palmerston, Turin, 30 September 1848.

118  Bianchi Giovini, *L'Auitriche en Italie,* Vol. 2, p.65.

119  On Pachta, see Vienna, *Kriegsarchiv,* KA MK (1848), No. 5674, Doblhoff to Latour, Vienna, 2 October 1848. Doblhoff concluded that Pachta was scarcely fit to wear a decoration, the test being whether the public would applaud the Emperor's decision.

120  See note 81, Chapter 6.

121  Bianchi Giovini, *L'Autriche en Italie*, Vol. 2, p.102.

122  Bianchi Giovini, *L'Autriche en Italie*, Vol. 2, p.59. See also *Raccolta*, Vol. 1, pp.45–7.

123  *Raccolta*, Vol. 1, p.232.

124  *Raccolta*, Vol. 1, p.33 and pp.218–9.

125  Bianchi Giovini, *L'Autriche en Italie*, Vol. 2, pp.69–70.

126  Bianchi Giovini, *L'Autriche en Italie*, Vol. 2, pp.66–7.

127  Vienna, *Kriegsarchiv*, KA MK (1848), No. 2861, Radetzky to Latour, Verona, 23 June 1848.

128  Curato, *Le Relazioni Diplomatiche etc.*, Vol. 1, pp.385–6, Abercrombie to Palmerston, Turin, 30 September 1848; but see also, *British and Foreign State Papers*, Vol. 44, pp.823–4, Vice-consul Campbell to Palmerston, Milan, 24 November 1848.

129  *British Foreign and State Papers*, Vol. 44, pp.842–3, Campbell to Palmerston, Milan, 5 December 1848.

130  *Raccolta*, Vol. 1, p.359. It went on to say that this did not apply to taxes not concerned with the upkeep of the army.

131  Antonio Monti, 'Il Contributo dei Lombardi alla prima Guerra dell'Independenza', *Nuova Rivista Storica*, Vol X (1926), pp.241–6, p.245.

132  Filipuzzi, *Le Relazioni Diplomatiche*, Vol. 1, pp.324–6 (author's italics).

133  Curato, *Le Relazioni Diplomatiche*, Vol. 1, pp.442–3, Abercrombie to Palmerston, Turin, 13 November 1848.

134  Curato, *Le Relazioni Diplomariche*, Vol. 1, pp.450–3, Abercrombie to Lord John Russell, Turin, 19 November 1848.

135  *British Foreign and State Papers*, Vol. 44, pp.770–1, Palmerston to Ponsonby, Foreign Office, London, 20 November 1848.

136  *British Foreign and State Papers*, Vol. 44, pp.812–4. For the reactions of the *Consulta Lombarda* at this time, see Federico Curato, *1848–49. La Consulta Straordinaria della Lombardia (2 August 1848–20 March 1849)* (Milan, 1950).

137  Filipuzzi, *Le Relazioni Diplomatiche*, Vol. 1, pp.332–6. Metzburg to Wessenberg, Milan, 20 November 1848.

138  Filipuzzi, *Le Relazioni Diplomatiche*, Vol. 1, pp.332–6, pp.336–7. Also *British Foreign and State Papers*, Vol. 45, pp.308–9.

139  Filipuzzi, *Le Relazioni Diplomatiche*, Vol. 1, pp.339–40, Montecuccoli to Wessenberg, Milan, 21 November 1848.

140  *British Foreign and State Papers*, Vol. 45, pp.255–7 and 308–9. Bianchi Giovini, *L'Autriche en Italie*, Vol. 2, p.89.

141  Bianchi Giovini, *L'Autriche en Italie*, Vol. 2, p.92.

142  Bianchi Giovini, *L'Autriche en Italie*, Vol. 2, p.95.

143  *British Foreign and State Papers*, Vol. 45, pp.310. Also p.362, Campbell to Palmerston, Milan, 16 February 1849.

144  *British Foreign and State Papers*, Vol. 45, pp.389–90, Campbell to Palmerston, Milan, 25 February 1849.

145  See note 106, Chapter 6.

146  Curato, *Le Relazioni Diplomatiche*, Vol. 2, pp.169–72, Abercrombie to Palmerston, Turin, 2 April 1849.

147  *Filipuzzi, Le Relazioni Diplomatiche*, Vol. 2, pp.34–5, Radetzky to Schwarzenberg, Milan, 13 April 1849.

148  London, *National Archives*, PRO, Foreign Office, 7/371, Campbell to Palmerston, 21 April 1849.

149  *Raccolta*, Vol. 2, pp.328–32. Also London, *National Archives*, PRO, Foreign Office, 7/371, Campbell to Palmerston, Milan, 13 August 1849.

150  Bianchi Giovini, *L'Autriche en Italie*, Vol. 2, pp.111–12.

151  Bianchi Giovini, *L'Autriche en Italie*, Vol. 2, p.112.

152  Bianchi Giovini, *L'Autriche en Italie*, Vol. 2, pp.115–16.

153  *Raccolta*, Vol. 1, p.100 and pp.607–8; Vol. 5, pp.78–9 shows that periodic extension continued till at least 31 March 1851.

154  *Raccolta*, Vol. 1, pp.66–7. Vienna, *Kriegsarchiv*, KAMK (1848), No. 4478, Latour to Emperor, Vienna, 9 September 1848. Also Latour to Radetzky, the same day.

155  *Raccolta*, Vol. 1, pp.18–19.

156  Vienna, *Kriegsarchiv*, KAMK (1848), No. 5563g, Radetzky to Latour, Milan, 27 September 1848.

157  Vienna, *Kriegsarchiv*, KAMK (1848), No. 5563g, Latour to Radetzky, Vienna, 4 October 1848.

158  *British Foreign and State Papers*, Vol. 45, p.309, Campbell to Palmerston, Milan, 26 January 1849. See also *Raccolta*, Vol. 1, pp.326–7.

159  *Raccolta*, Vol. 1, pp.400–1 and pp.476–80.

160  *Raccolta*, Vol. 1, pp.476–80.

161  London, *National Archives*, PRP, Foreign Office, 7/371, Campbell to Palmerston, Milan, 7 May 1849.

162  *Raccolta*, Vol. 2, pp.29–33 and pp.108–10. (cf. pp.53–4.)

163  London, *National Archives*, Foreign Office, 7/371, Campbell to Palmerston, Milan, 7 May 1849.

164  *Raccolta*, Vol. 2, p.154 and pp.167–70.

165  *Raccolta*, Vol. 2, p.186.

166  *British Foreign and State Papers*, Vol. 45, pp.301–13, Abercrombie to Palmerston, Turin, 26 January 1849.

167  The correspondence between Schwarzenberg and Radetzky for 1849 is considerable but contains little on the internal affairs of Lombardy-Venetia. The reason is probably that since both men agreed on almost everything, Radetzky had a free hand.

168  Franco Valsecchi (ed.), 'Le Relazioni Diplomatiche fra l'Austria e il Regno di Sardegna', 2 Vols (Vols 66 and 67 in the series *Fonti per la Storia d'Italia*, Vols 3 and 4 in Series III, 1848–1860) (Rome, 1963), pp.36–7, Schwarzenberg to Radetzky, Vienna, 13 December 1849.

169  Valsecchi, *Le Relazioni Diplomatiche*, Vol. 1, pp.42–5, Apponyi to Schwarzenberg, Turin, 18 December 1848.

170  See note 131, Chapter 6.

171  Valsecchi, *Le Relazioni Diplomatiche*, Vol. 1, pp.61–3, Schwarzenberg to Apponyi, Vienna, 14 January 1849.

172  See note 133, Chapter 6. Schwarzenberg's letter to Bach of 29 December and Bach's undated reply are both appended to Schwarzenberg's letter to Apponyi of 14 January 1849.

173  London, *National Artchives*, PRO, Foreign Office, 67/192, Sir James Hudson to Lord John Russell, Turin, 9 February 1853.

174  Jenks, *Franz Joseph etc.*, p.47.

175  Leopoldo Marchetti, 'Il decennio di resistenza', in Pt 5 of Vol. XIV ('Sotto l'Austria') of *Storia di Milano* (Milan, 1960), pp.502–65, 563.

176  Marchetti, *Il decennio etc.*, p.565.

177  Duhr, *Briefe*, pp.136–7.

178  Jenks, *Franz Joseph etc.*, p.49.

179  Jenks, *Franz Joseph etc.*, pp.49–50.

180  Jenks, *Franz Joseph etc.*, p.50.

181  Jenks, *Franz Joseph etc.*, p.138 and p.51.

182  Mollinary, *Quarante-Six Ans*, Vol. 1, p.110.

183  Joseph Redlich, *Emperor Franz Joseph of Austria. A Biography* (reprint) (Hamden, Connecticut, 1965), p.261.

184  On Benedek, see John Presland, *Vae Victis, The Life of Ludwig von Benedek, 1804–1881* (London, 1934).

185  Presland, *Vae Victis*, p.143.

186  Karl Joseph Mayr (ed.), *Das Tagebuch des Polizeiministers FML Kempen von 1848–1859* (Vienna, 1931), p.261.

187  Duhr, *Briefe*, Radetzky to his daughter, Milan, 31 August 1851, p.119.

188  Wolf-Schneider von Arno, *Der Feldherr Radetzky*, p.113.

189  Friedjung, *Aus Benedeks Nachgelassenen Papieren*, p.188.

190  'Briefe des Feldmarschalls Grafen Radetzky an seine Gattin, 1848–1851', *Österreichische Rundschau*, Vol. XVIII, 1 (1909), pp.48–53, p.53.

191  Prince Kraft zu Hohenlohe-Ingelfingen, *Aus meinem Leben*, Vol. 1, p.350.

192  Thun, *Erinnerungen*, p.122.

193  Wolf-Schneider von Arno, *Der Feldherr Radetzky*, p.119.

194  Bernhard Duhr, S.J. (ed.), *Briefe des Feldmarschalls Radetzky an seine Tochter Friedericke, 1847–1857* (Vienna, 1892).

195  H. Hinnenberg (ed.), 'Briefe des Feldmarschalls Grafen Radetzky an seine Gattin, 1848–1851', *Österreichische Rundschau*, XVIII, 1/3 (1909), pp. 48–53.

196  Ibid, p.97.

197  Ibid, p.107.

198  Ibid, p.127.

199  Duhr, pp.25–7.

200  Ibid., pp. 2–7

201  Duhr, *Briefe,* p.144.

202  Hohenlohe-Ingelfingen, *Aus meinem Leben*, Vol. 1, pp.384–6.

203  See note 156, Chapter 6.

204 Duhr, *Briefe*, p.106.
205 Presland, *Vae Victis*, p.147.
206 Duhr, *Briefe*, p.107.
207 Mayr, *Das Tagebuch des Polizeiministers FML Kempen*, 17 November 1855, p.379.
208 Major Baron Beaulieu-Marconnay, 'Radetzkys Lebensabend', *Österreichische Wehrzeitung*, Issue 47, November 1927.
209 Wolf-Schneider von Arno, *Der Feldherr Radetzky*, p.124.
210 Wolf-Schneider von Arno, *Der Feldherr Radetzky*, p.124, ft.68.
211 Wolf-Schneider von Arno, *Der Feldherr Radetzky*, p.125.
212 Wolf-Schneider von Arno, *Der Feldherr Radetzky*, p.126.
213 Mollinary, *Quarante-Six Ans*, Vol. 2, pp.7–8.
214 The *Times*, 7, 12 and 13 January, 1858.
215 Volume for 1854, Pt. I, *Radetzky*, pp.14–25 and 177–84, p.178.

## CONCLUSION

1 Bibl, *Radetzky*, p.334.
2 Regele, *Radetzky*, pp.445–69 gives an exhaustive list of all Radetzky's honours, awards, memorials etc.
3 Heller, *Der Graf Radetzky*, pp.394–5.
4 Heller, *Der Graf Radetzky*, p.370, ft.1.
5 Sked, *Metternich and Austria*, p.96.
6 The whole of Langenau's essay is reproduced as a footnote covering pages 182–8 of Heller, *Der Graf Radetzky*.
7 Heller, *Der Graf Radetzky*, pp.302–8 prints Clam's very long letter.
8 Heller, *Der Graf Radetzky*, p.309.
9 Heller, *Der Graf Radetzky*, pp.286–7.
10 Heller, *Der Graf Radetzky*, p.287.
11 Heller, *Der Graf Radetzky*, p.328.
12 Heller, *Der Graf Radetzky*, p.329.
13 Heller, *Der Graf Radetzky*, p.338 for Nicholas's visit, p.339 ft. for Frederick William's, p.337 for a visit from the future Alexander II of Russia.
14 Heller, *Der Graf Radetzky*, p.327.
15 London, *British Library*, Sir Robert Wilson Papers, Add. 30.122, folios 369–70.
16 Volume for 1834, Pt. I, *Austrian Review on the Mincio*, pp.183–90, p.184.
17 London, *British Library*, Sir Robert Wilson Papers, Add. 30.122, folios 386–7.
18 Volume for 1858, Pt. I, *Memoir of Field Marshal Radetzky*, pp.242–56, pp.247–8.
19 Heller, *Der Graf Radetzky*, pp.370–1.
20 Heller, *Der Graf Radetzky*, p.333.
21 Heller, *Der Graf Radetzky*, pp.319–20.
22 Heller, *Der Graf Radetzky*, p.350.

23  Heller, *Der Graf Radetzky,* p.344.
24  Heller, *Der Feldherr Radetzky,* p.352.
25  Heller, *Der Graf Radetzky,* p.356.
26  Heller, *Der Graf Radetzky,* pp.361–2.
27  Heller, *Der Graf Radetzky,* pp.374–5.
28  Heller, *Der Graf Radetzky,* p.376.
29  Heller, *Der Graf Radetzky,* p.343.
30  Pietro Orsi, *Modern Italy, 1748–1898* (New York, 1899), p.241.

# CONCISE BIBLIOGRAPHY

## PRIMARY SOURCES

### AUSTRIAN ARCHIVES

Vienna, *Kriegsarchiv.*
Centralkanzleiakten (Präsidialreihe 1847/48).
Ministerium des Kriegswesensakten (Präsidialreihe) 1848/9.
Feldakten, 1847/8, Kartons 213 and 214.
Radetzky Nachlaß, especially his *Notaten für die Feldzügen 1813 und 1814.*
Archduke Maximilian d'Este Nachlaß.
Vienna, *Haus-Hof-und Staatsarchiv.*
Staatskanzleiakten, Provinzen, Lombardei-Venezien.
Staatskanzleiakten, Kriegsakten, Karton 512.

### LONDON, NATIONAL ARCHIVES

Foreign Office: 7/371 and 67/192.
British and Foreign State Papers, Vols. 37, 44 and 45.

### PUBLISHED DOCUMENTS

Radetzky's own writings are the most valuable of these and include:

'Erinnerungen aus dem Leben des Feldmarschalls Grafen Radetzky. Eine Selbstbiographie', *Mitteilungen des k.k. Kriegsarchiv,* Neue Folge, Vol. 1 (1887), pp.1–79; and 'Aus meinem Leben, 1814–1847', *Österreichisches Rundschau,* Vol. XIV, 1/3, 1908, pp. 172–179.

Then there is *Der k.k.österreichische Feldmarschall Graf Radetzky. Eine biographische Skizze nach dem eigenen Dictaten und der Correspondenz des Feldmarschalls von einem österreichischen Veteranen* (Stuttgart and Augsburg, 1858). The 'veteran' concerned was Heller von Hellwand, with whom Radetzky had arranged for this 'ghosted' autobiography to be published immediately following his death.

Heller also arranged for Radetzky's many memoranda that fill his *Nachlaß* to be published. These are contained in *Denkschriften militärisch-politischen Inhalts aus dem handschriftlichen Nachlaß des k.k. österreichischen Feldmarschalls Grafen Radetzky* (Stuttgart and Augsburg, 1858).

For Radetzky's personal life, the key source is Bernhard Duhr SJ. (ed.), *Briefe des Feldmarschalls Radetzky and seine Tochter Friedericke, 1847–57* (Vienna, 1892). But see, too: A. Hinnenburg (ed.), 'Briefe des F.M. Gf. Radetzky an seine Gattin, 1848 bis 1851', in *Österreichische Rundschau*, Vol. XVIII (1908).

Other important published sources include the collections of diplomatic documents published by the *Istituto Storico per L'Età Moderna e Contemporanea* in the series *Fonti per la Storia d'Italia*. These include:

(a) Frederico Curato (ed.), *Le Relazioni Diplomatiche fra La Grande Bretagne e il Regno di Sardegna*, 2 Vols (Rome, 1961);

(b) Frederico Curato (ed.), *Gran Bretagna e Italia nei Documenti della Missione Minto*, 2 Vols (Rome, 1970);

(c) Angelo Filipuzzi (ed.), *Le Relazioni Diplomatiche fra l'Austria e il Regno di Sardegna e la Guerra del 1848–49*, 2 Vols (Rome, 1961);

(d) Franco Valsecchi (ed.), *Le Relazioni Diplomatiche fra L'Austria e il Regno di Sardegna*, 2 vols (Rome, 1963).

## PUBLISHED ACCOUNTS, DIARIES ETC.

The key memoirs for 1848–9 are those of Radetzky's long-serving Adjutant, General Schönhals, who also wrote Radetzky's famous war-time proclamations and conducted his correspondence. His memoirs are:

*Erinnerungen eines österreichischen Veteranen aus dem italienischen Kriege der Jahre 1848 and 1849* (Stuttgart and Tubingen, 1853). They are infamous for not mentioning Radetzky's chief-of-staff, Hess, since Schönhals detested Hess, whose close relationship with Radetzky he resented. Some key letters from Radetzky in 1848 are printed by Joseph Alexander Freiherr von Helfert in his article 'Radetzky in den Tagen seiner ärgsten Bedrängnis', *Archiv für österreichische Geschichte*, Vol. 95 (1906).

Regarding the 1813–14 campaign, there are a number of sources which are invaluable, particularly the letters of Gneisenau, but also those of Blücher. See, therefore, Karl Griewank (ed.), *Gneisenau. Ein Leben in Briefen*, 3rd edition (Leipzig, 1939) and Wilhelm Capelle (ed.), *Briefe des Feldmarschalls Blücher* (Leipzig, 1942). The memoirs of Blücher's quartermaster general, Baron Müffling, are equally invaluable, namely *The Memoirs of Baron von Müffling. A Prussian Officer in the Napoleonic Wars*, Napoleonic Library (London, 1997).

There are also the diaries of Sir Robert Wilson, who accompanied the allies through the campaigns from 1812 to 1814 and himself played a distinguished part in them not merely by becoming the British commissioner to the Austrian army, but by participating in the fighting, sometimes even playing a key role in battle. His papers are in the British Library but those concerning the campaigns against Napoleon have been published in the Rev. Herbert Randolph (ed.), *Private Diary of Travels, Personal Services and Public Events, During Mission and Employment*

*With The European Armies in Campaigns of 1812, 1813, 1814. From The Invasion of Russia To The Capture of Paris, by Sir Robert Wilson CMT,* 2 Vols (London, 1861).

The British representatives to allied headquarters also published accounts of the campaign, namely G. Cathcart, *Commentaries on the War in Russia and Germany in 1812 and 1813* (London, 1850), the Marquess of Londonderry, *Narrative of the War in Germany and France in 1813 and 1814* (London, 1830), and Lord Burghersh, *The Operations of the Allied Armies in 1813 and 1814, under Prince Schwarzenberg and Marshal Blücher* (London 1822). Cathcart, however, is blatantly pro-Russian and anti-Austrian, Burghersh unsympathetic to Austria, while Londonderry is more neutral. There are also the published letters of Burghersh's young wife, who met him in Germany in October 1813 and travelled to Paris with the allied sovereigns, namely, *The Letters of Lady Burghersh (afterwards Countess of Westmorland) From Germany and France During the Campaign of 1813–1814* (London, 1893).

On the Russian side, the key work is T. von Bernhardi, *Denkwürdigkeiten aus dem Leben des kaiserlichen russischen Generals der Infanterie Carl Friederich Grafen von Toll,* 5 Vols (Leipzig, 1858). Bernhardi tries to give Toll credit for the Trachenberg Plan; however, later research has made this claim irrelevant.

## KEY BOOKS

There is nothing in English on Radetzky save my own work, namely, one book, *The Survival of the Habsburg Empire. Radetzky, the Imperial Army and the Class War, 1848* (Longman, London and New York, 1979) and one long article, 'Poor Intelligence, Flawed Results: Metternich, Radetzky and the Crisis-Management of Austria's "Occupation" of Ferrara in 1847', in P. Jackson and J. Siegel (eds), *Intelligence and Statecraft. The Use and Limits of Intelligence in International Society* (Westport Ct., 2005), pp.53–86. There are not even many works in German.

The key ones are Oskar Regele, *Radetzky. Leben, Leistung, Erbe* (Vienna and Munich, 1957) and Oskar Freiherr Wolff-Schneider von Arno, *Der Feldherr Radetzky* (Vienna, 1934). There are also Viktor Bibl's *Radetzky. Soldat und Feldherr* (Vienna, 1955) and Franz Joseph Adolph Schneidawind, *FM.Gf. Radetzky, sein kriegerisches Leben und seine Feldzüge vom Jahre 1784–1850* (Augsburg, 1851).

However, some other works are worth mentioning.

On the campaign of 1813–14, there are the works of the Austrian general staff, particularly, Otto Criste, *Österreichs Beitritt zur Koalition* (Vienna, 1913) and Walter Wlaschütz, *Österreichs entscheidendes Machaufgebot* (Vienna, 1913) plus those of the head of the historical section of the Prussian General Staff, Rudolf von Friederich, namely *Die Befreiungskriege,* 3 Vols (Berlin, 1911–13). Today, they have been joined by the excellent work of Dominic Lieven, *Russia against Napoleon. The Battle for Europe, 1807–1814.* Two works in English on the Napoleonic Wars, however, need mentioning: David G. Chandler, *The Campaigns of Napoleon* (New York, 1966) and Gunther E. Rothenberg, *The Napoleonic Wars* (London, 2001). Not to be omitted are the essays in Gordon A. Craig, *War, Policy and Diplomacy. Selected Essays* (London, 1966), particularly the one on 'Problems of Coalition Warfare: The Military Alliance Against Napoleon, 1813–1814'.

On the diplomatic background for 1813–14, see A. Fournier, *Der Congress von Chatillon: Die Politik im Kriege von 1814* (Vienna, 1914); Henry Kissinger, *A World Restored* (London, 1957) and Alan Sked, *Metternich and Austria. An Evaluation* (London, 2008).

For 1848, see my book on Radetzky mentioned at the start of this section; also, G.F-H and J. Berkeley, *Italy in the Making. January 1st 1848 to November 16th. 1848* (Cambridge, 1940).

For the period after 1848, see William A. Jenks, *Francis Joseph and the Italians, 1848–1859* (Charlottesville, 1978) and the third volume of Hermann Reuchling, *Geschichte Italiens,* 3 Vols (Leipzig, 1870).

For other works, see the Endnotes.

# INDEX